OECD Environmental Performance Reviews: Brazil 2015

OECD
BETTER POLICIES FOR BETTER LIVES

This work is published on the responsibility of the Secretary-General of the OECD. The opinions expressed and arguments employed herein do not necessarily reflect the official views of the Organisation or of the governments of its member countries.

This document and any map included herein are without prejudice to the status of or sovereignty over any territory, to the delimitation of international frontiers and boundaries and to the name of any territory, city or area.

Please cite this publication as:
OECD (2015), *OECD Environmental Performance Reviews: Brazil 2015*, OECD Publishing, Paris.
http://dx.doi.org/10.1787/9789264240094-en

ISBN 978-92-64-24006-3 (print)
ISBN 978-92-64-24009-4 (PDF)

Series: OECD Environmental Performance Reviews
ISSN 1990-0104 (print)
ISSN 1990-0090 (online)

The statistical data for Israel are supplied by and under the responsibility of the relevant Israeli authorities. The use of such data by the OECD is without prejudice to the status of the Golan Heights, East Jerusalem and Israeli settlements in the West Bank under the terms of international law.

Revised version, November 2015
Details of revision available at: *http://www.oecd.org/about/publishing/Corrigendum-EnvPerfReviewsBrazil2015.pdf*.

Photo credits: © iStockphoto/filipefrazao, © iStockphoto/Alatom.

Corrigenda to OECD publications may be found on line at: *www.oecd.org/publishing/corrigenda*.

Preface

Brazil has made considerable progress in aligning its economic growth and poverty reduction efforts with the advancement of environmental sustainability. Natural resources are essential to the country's development: Brazil is the world's fourth-largest agricultural producer and a major global player in mining and oil production, and hydropower generates most of its electricity. However, economic growth, urbanisation, agricultural expansion and infrastructure development have also meant increased energy consumption and environmental pressures. Brazil now needs to recover growth while continuing to eradicate poverty, reduce inequality and social exclusion, and ensure a sustainable use of environmental assets.

This is the first *OECD Environmental Performance Review* of Brazil. It assesses the country's progress in achieving its environmental policy objectives, focusing on the period since 2000. The *Review* provides 53 recommendations to help Brazil green its economy and improve its environmental governance and management, with a strong emphasis on fostering biodiversity policy and managing protected areas.

A megadiverse country, Brazil hosts the largest rainforest in the world. Progress in reducing deforestation in the Amazon has been impressive, as a result of resolute government efforts and the expansion of protected areas over thousands of square kilometres. Indeed, Brazil's comprehensive strategy for deforestation control can serve as a model for other countries. The new Forest Code and its innovative implementation and enforcement instruments are expected to greatly help further reduce illegal forest clearing and reconcile the objectives of agricultural development and biodiversity conservation. Still, Brazil needs to remain vigilant and thoroughly implement all the environmental programmes that it has put in place. It is a matter of securing sufficient financial and human resources, improving co-ordination across levels of government and ensuring effective policy implementation at the subnational level.

This *Review* is the result of a constructive policy dialogue between Brazil and the countries participating in the OECD Working Party on Environmental Performance. We stand ready to support Brazil in the implementation of the recommendations outlined in this study. I am confident that this collaborative effort will be useful to improve our understanding of how to tackle our many shared environmental challenges.

Angel Gurría

OECD Secretary-General

Foreword

The principal aim of the OECD Environmental Performance Review programme is to help member and selected partner countries improve their individual and collective performance in environmental management by:

- *helping individual governments assess progress in achieving their environmental goals;*
- *promoting continuous policy dialogue and peer learning;*
- *stimulating greater accountability from governments towards each other and public opinion.*

This report is the first OECD review of Brazil's environmental performance. It assesses the country's progress in achieving its domestic objectives and international commitments. Such objectives and commitments may be broad aims, qualitative goals or quantitative targets. A distinction is made between intentions, actions and results. Assessment of environmental performance is also placed within the context of Brazil's historical environmental record, present state of the environment, physical endowment in natural resources, economic conditions and demographic trends.

The OECD is indebted to the government of Brazil for its co-operation in providing information, for the organisation of the review mission to Brasília, Anavilhanas National Park and Chapada dos Veadeiros National Park (17-27 August 2014) and of the policy mission to Brasília, Rio de Janeiro and São Paulo (23-27 March 2015), and its facilitation of contacts both inside and outside government institutions.

Thanks are also due to the representatives of the three examining countries: Catherine Dumouchel (Canada), Øyvind Lone (Norway) and Pedro Liberato (Portugal). The review also benefitted from the co-operation of Carlos Mussi and Kristina Taboulchanas from the United Nations Commission for Latin America and the Caribbean and input from Aaron Bruner and Susan Edda Seehusen from Conservation Strategy Fund.

The authors of this report were Ivana Capozza, Britta Labuhn, Eugene Mazur and Sara Moarif from the OECD Environment Directorate. Brendan Gillespie and Nathalie Girouard provided oversight and guidance. Carla Bertuzzi provided statistical support. Rebecca Brite copy-edited the report. Annette Hardcastle and Clara Tomasini assisted with the production and publication of the report and Jennifer Calder provided administrative support.

The OECD Working Party on Environmental Performance discussed the Environmental Performance Review of Brazil at its meeting on 17 June 2015 in Paris, and approved the Assessment and Recommendations.

Table of contents

Boxes

Tables

Figures

Reader's guide

General notes

Signs

The following signs are used in figures and tables:

. . : not available

– : nil or negligible

. : decimal point

Country aggregates

OECD Europe: This zone includes all European member countries of the OECD, i.e. Austria, Belgium, the Czech Republic, Denmark, Estonia, Finland, France, Germany, Greece, Hungary, Iceland, Ireland, Italy, Luxembourg, the Netherlands, Norway, Poland, Portugal, the Slovak Republic, Slovenia, Spain, Sweden, Switzerland, Turkey and the United Kingdom.

OECD: This zone includes all member countries of the OECD, i.e. the countries of OECD Europe plus Australia, Canada, Chile, Israel, Japan, Korea, Mexico, New Zealand and the United States.

BRIICS: Brazil, Russia, India, Indonesia, China (People's Republic of) and South Africa.

Country aggregates may include Secretariat estimates.

Currency

Monetary unit: Brazilian real (BRL).

In 2014, USD 1.00 = BRL 2.35

In 2012, USD 1.00 = BRL 1.95

In 2010, USD 1.00 = BRL 1.76

Cut-off date

This report is based on information and data available up to May 2015.

Abbreviations and acronyms

ABEMA	Brazilian Association of State Environment Authorities
ANA	National Water Agency
ANAMMA	National Association of Municipal Environment Agencies
APP	Permanent Preservation Area
ARPA	Amazon Region Protected Areas programme
BNDES	Brazilian Development Bank
CAR	Rural Environmental Cadastre
CBD	UN Convention on Biological Diversity
CDM	Clean Development Mechanism
CETESB	Environmental Sanitation Technology Company of São Paulo state
CIDE	Federal fuel tax
CNRH	National Water Resources Council
CO_2	Carbon dioxide
CONABIO	National Biodiversity Commission
CONAMA	National Environmental Council
CRA	Environmental Reserve Quota
CSR	Corporate social responsibility
CTE	State Tripartite Technical Commission
CTN	Tripartite Technical Commission
DMC	Domestic material consumption
EGS	Environmental goods and services
EIA	Environmental impact assessment
EMS	Environmental management system
FAO	Food and Agriculture Organization of the United Nations
GDP	Gross domestic product
GEF	Global Environment Facility
GHG	Greenhouse gas
IBAMA	Brazilian Institute of Environment and Renewable Natural Resources
IBGE	Brazilian Institute of Geography and Statistics
ICMBio	Chico Mendes Institute for Biodiversity Conservation
ICMS	State-level value added tax
INPE	National Institute for Space Research
IPEA	Institute for Applied Economic Research
IPI	Federal tax on manufactured products
IPVA	Motor vehicle ownership tax
ITR	Rural land tax
LCR	Local content requirement
LULUCF	Land use, land-use change and forestry
MCid	Ministry of Cities
MCTI	Ministry of Science, Technology and Innovation
MMA	Ministry of the Environment
MSW	Municipal solid waste
NGO	Non-government organisation
NO_x	Nitrogen oxides
ODA	Official development assistance
PAC	Growth Acceleration Programme

PDE	Energy Expansion Plan
PES	Payments for ecosystem services
PET	Polyethylene terephthalate
PM	Particulate matter
PNIA	National Panel of Environmental Indicators
PNMA	National Environmental Policy
PNMC	National Climate Change Policy
PNRS	National Solid Waste Policy
PPCDAm	Action Plan for Prevention and Control of Deforestation in Amazônia Legal
PSE	OECD Producer Support Estimate
R&D	Research and development
REDD	Reducing Emissions from Deforestation and Forest Degradation
RL	Legal Reserve
SEA	Strategic environmental assessment
SFB	Brazilian Forest Service
SINIMA	National Environmental Information System
SISNAMA	National Environmental System
SNCR	National System of Rural Credit
SNIS	National Sanitation Information System
SNUC	National System of Protected Areas
SO_x	Sulphur oxides
tCO_2eq	Tonnes of CO_2 equivalent
TCU	Federal Court of Accounts
TPES	Total primary energy supply
UN-ECLAC/CEPAL	United Nations Economic Commission for Latin America and the Caribbean
UNEP	United Nations Environment Programme
WHO	World Health Organization
ZEE	Ecological-economic zoning

BASIC STATISTICS OF BRAZIL (2013 or latest available year)

(Number in parentheses refer to the OECD averages)*

PEOPLE AND SOCIETY

Population (million)	198.0		Population growth (%, latest 5-year yearly average growth)	0.9	(0.6)
Share of population by type of region: (Brazil 2010)			Population density per km^2	23.3	(34.8)
Predominantly urban (%)	26.0	(48.0)	Income inequality (Gini coefficient, 2012)	52.7	(31.4)
Intermediate (%)	24.0	(26.2)	Poverty rate (% of population with less than USD 2 a day, PPP)	6.8	
Predominantly rural (%)	50.0	(25.1)	Life expectancy	75.0	(80.4)

ECONOMY AND EXTERNAL ACCOUNTS

Total GDP (BRL billion)	4 845		Imports of goods and services (% of GDP)	15.3	(28.9)
Total GDP (USD billion)	2 247		Main exports (% of total merchandise exports)		
GDP, latest 5-year average real growth (%)	2.8	(0.8)	Vegetables, animals, food products	35.1	
GDP per capita (1 000 USD PPP)	15.2	(37.9)	Fuels, minerals	22.2	
Value added shares (%, 2012 Brazil and 2011 OECD)			Machinery, transport	18.3	
Primary sector	5.7	(1.4)	Main imports (% of total merchandise imports)		
Industry including construction	25.0	(23.8)	Machinery, transport	33.8	
Services	69.3	(74.7)	Fuels, minerals	20.0	
Exports of goods and services (% of GDP)	13.1	(28.6)	Chemicals	15.9	

GENERAL GOVERNMENT

Percentage of GDP

Expenditure	38.6	(41.9)	Fiscal balance	-3.1	(-4.2)
Revenue	35.6	(37.7)	Environmental taxes: (% of GDP)	0.7	(1.6)
Gross financial debt	62.2	(109.3)	(% of total tax revenue)	1.9	(5.1)

LABOUR MARKET, SKILLS AND INNOVATION

Unemployment rate, (% civilian labour force)	5.4	(7.9)	Patent applications in environment-related technologies (% of all technologies, average 2009-11)[a]	9.2	(11.3)
Tertiary educational attainment of 25- 64 years-olds (%, 2012)	13.0	(32.2)	Gross domestic expenditure on R&D (% of GDP)	1.2	(2.4)

ENVIRONMENT

Energy intensity (Brazil 2012): TPES per capita (toe/cap.)	1.4	(4.2)	Water stress (Brazil 2012) (abstraction as % of available resources)	1.0	(9.5)
TPES per GDP (toe/1 000 USD, 2005 PPP)	0.11	(0.13)	Water abstraction per capita (Brazil 2012) (m^3/cap./year)	420	(830)
Renewables (Brazil 2012) (% of TPES)	40.7	(8.8)	Municipal waste per capita (Brazil 2012) (kg/cap.)	290	(520)
Carbon intensity (energy-related CO_2, 2012): per capita (t/cap.)	2.2	(9.7)	Material productivity (2011) (USD, 2005 PPP/kg)	0.4	(1.8)
per GDP (t/1 000 USD, 2005 PPP)	0.2	(0.3)	Terrestrial and inland water protected areas (% of total area)[b]	17.2	
GHG intensity (2012):[c] per capita (t/1 000 USD, 2005 PPP)	5.3	(12.5)	Land area (1 000 km^2, 2012)	8 358	
per GDP (t/1 000 USD, 2005 PPP)	0.40	(0.40)	% of arable and cropland	10	(12)
Exposure to air pollution ($PM_{2.5}$) (2012, µg/m^3)	5.7		% of meadows and pastures	23	(23)
Road vehicle stock (veh./100 inhab.)	35	(57)	% of forest land	62	(30)
			% of other land (built-up and other land)	5	(34)

* Where the OECD aggregate is not provided in the source database, a simple OECD average of latest available data is calculated where data exist for at least 29 member countries.

a) Higher-value inventions that have sought patent protection in at least two jurisdictions.

b) Official protected areas according to Brazil's National System of Protected Areas (SNUC).

c) Excluding emissions/removals from land use, land-use change and forestry.

Source: Calculations based on data extracted from databases of the following organisations: OECD, IEA, IMF, UN, World Bank.

Executive summary

Brazil's continued development depends on the sustainable use of environmental resources

Brazil is the world's fifth largest country and the most biodiverse. The world's largest tropical rainforest, the Amazon, and 12% of global freshwater resources are in Brazil, together with vast reserves of fossil fuels and minerals. An energy mix that is largely based on the use of hydropower and biofuels helps keep the economy's carbon intensity low. Vibrant growth and effective social policies lifted millions of people out of poverty over the 2000s. However, growth has decelerated since 2012 and income inequality remains high.

More people now have access to electricity, clean water, sanitation and waste management services, although regional disparities are large. Fast urbanisation, agricultural expansion and infrastructure development have increased the pressure on the environment. Severe water shortages have hit the South-east region in recent years, and inadequate wastewater treatment has caused water and soil contamination, particularly in densely populated areas. Air pollution is of concern in major cities. Waste generation has grown with rising living standards and landfilling is the primary disposal method. Total greenhouse gas emissions have dropped by more than 40% since 2000 with the decline in deforestation, but emissions from energy use in industry and transport have grown. Brazil needs to continue to ensure sustainable use of its environmental resources and reduce poverty and inequality, while tackling slow growth and rising unemployment. With lower commodity prices and subdued export demand, improving domestic policies is all the more important.

Progress in reducing Amazon deforestation has been impressive

In 2004 Brazil launched a whole-of-government deforestation control action plan combining advanced monitoring systems, strengthened enforcement, credit restrictions, expansion of protected areas and promotion of sustainable natural resource use. Resolute plan implementation and international support, notably via the innovative Amazon Fund, resulted in a 75% decline in the annual deforestation rate of the Amazon. However, progress has been uneven across states in the region; about 4 800 km^2 of Amazonian forests are still lost every year and pressures remain high in the tropical savannah. Brazil needs to further promote sustainable livelihood options in forest areas to make them more attractive than illegal land clearing, while continuing to strengthen monitoring and enforcement. Thorough implementation of the new Forest Code and its Rural Environmental Cadastre will be crucial to reconcile the objectives of biodiversity conservation and agriculture development, thereby contributing to controlling deforestation in the Amazon and other biomes.

Nearly 2 000 protected areas provide large socio-economic opportunities

The number and surface of official protected areas has more than doubled since 2000, when Brazil established its National System of Protected Areas (SNUC). The Amazon Region Protected Areas programme has largely contributed to this achievement. Protected areas within the SNUC now cover more than 17% of Brazil's terrestrial areas and inland waters, but less than 2% of marine areas. Additional areas are protected within indigenous lands and private lands that are set aside in compliance with the Forest Code. Management of protected areas has improved, but human and financial resources are not yet adequate to ensure that all protected areas meet their environmental objectives and unleash their socio-economic development potential. Tourism and sustainable forestry could be scaled up with more engagement from the private sector. This would also help reduce dependence on the public budget and international finance.

Brazil has ambitious biodiversity targets but policy coherence needs to be improved

Brazil's 20 national biodiversity targets to 2020 are aligned with its international commitments. In 2015 the parliament approved comprehensive legislation to facilitate the commercial and scientific use of genetic resources and traditional knowledge, while ensuring the fair treatment of indigenous and traditional communities. Brazil has increasingly used programmes of payments for ecosystem services (PES) and income support for rural communities. However, state PES regulations are highly heterogeneous; many such programmes are not systematically monitored and their environmental effectiveness is not clear. A federal PES law would improve consistency and effectiveness. More efforts are needed to mainstream biodiversity considerations into sectoral policies, including agriculture and energy policies.

Environmental laws are stringent but implementation gaps persist

Brazil has developed a comprehensive and advanced environmental legislation framework. The financial resources and institutional capacity of federal environmental institutions have grown markedly, and interagency collaboration has improved. Progress has been made in clarifying the boundaries of environmental responsibilities across levels of government and in streamlining environmental licensing. However, licensing procedures are still reported to be excessively cumbersome, delaying important infrastructure projects. Institutional capacity varies widely across regions and is often limited, which makes effective implementation and enforcement of environmental policies challenging.

Brazil should make a wider use of green taxes and remove harmful tax exemptions

Environmentally-related taxes accounted for 0.7% of GDP in 2013, below the level observed in most OECD countries. Most revenue stems from taxes on vehicle ownership, but tax rates are not linked to vehicles' environmental performance. In a welcome move, in early 2015, the government raised the federal fuel tax rate on petrol and diesel, which had been zero since mid-2012. However, tax rates are low in international comparison and are not linked to fuels' carbon content. Fuels used in sectors other than road transport (e.g. agriculture and industry) go largely untaxed. Charges on water abstraction and pollution, implemented in a few states, are the only form of levies on natural resource use and pollution. Overall, Brazil would benefit from extending the use of green taxes and charges and removing harmful tax exemptions as part of a comprehensive tax reform. This would help encourage a more efficient use of energy and natural resources.

Brazil needs to further improve its infrastructure and remove barriers to eco-innovation

Brazil has stepped up public investment in environment-relevant infrastructure. In 2014, 15% of lending by the Brazilian Development Bank, the biggest provider of long-term finance, was environment-related. Various forms of support helped Brazil become the world's seventh largest investor in renewable energy in 2014. Yet the coverage and quality of infrastructure need to be expanded and improved, particularly for wastewater treatment, sanitary landfills and public transport systems. Inadequate pricing of water and waste services, red tape and weaknesses in project planning delay infrastructure delivery and discourage private-sector engagement. Brazil is more specialised in green technologies than other BRIICS economies, although weak science-industry links, skills gaps and a complex incentive system hamper eco-innovation and the diffusion of environmental technology, goods and services. Various forms of trade protection, including local content rules, limit competition and raise technology costs. Brazil would benefit from more systematically integrating environmental objectives into public investment programmes and economic policies more generally.

Assessment and recommendations

The Assessment and Recommendations present the main findings of the Environmental Performance Review of Brazil and identify 53 recommendations to help Brazil make further progress towards its environmental policy objectives and international commitments. The OECD Working Party on Environmental Performance reviewed and approved the Assessment and Recommendations at its meeting on 17 June 2015.

1. Brazil's environmental performance: An overview

The world's fifth largest country, Brazil is hugely diverse with respect to climate, vegetation, land use, population, social patterns and economic activity. It is endowed with large areas of fertile soil, huge water and forest resources, and mineral, oil and natural gas reserves. Natural assets have always been a mainstay of its economic development and have a strong social component. Brazilians are proud of their country's natural wealth, and their environmental awareness has increased. As in other emerging economies, economic expansion, urbanisation and rising income levels have also meant increased environmental pressures from growing demand for land, water, materials, energy and transport, as well as increased pollution and waste generation. Managing the natural asset base sustainably and equitably and decoupling economic growth from environmental pressures is paramount if Brazil is to achieve resilient and inclusive economic development.

Climate change

Brazil has a clean, low-carbon energy mix, largely based on the use of renewable energy sources. Renewables, mainly hydropower and biofuels, accounted for more than 40% of total primary energy supply in 2012, one of the highest shares in the world (Figure 1). As a result, greenhouse gas (GHG) emissions from energy generation and use are relatively low compared to many OECD countries. Strong economic growth in the 2000s and the rise of a middle class triggered a rapid increase in energy use, mainly in industry and transport. Nevertheless, the energy intensity of the economy (energy supply per unit of gross domestic product, GDP) remained fairly stable at levels below the OECD average.

The policy framework for climate change mitigation is a positive example of integration of environment-related concerns into sectoral policies. The 2010 National Climate Change Policy established an economy-wide target of limiting projected GHG emissions by between 36.1% and 38.9% by 2020. Brazil launched climate change programmes in sectors such as energy, iron and steel production and agriculture, as well as deforestation control. It is also developing a system, known as SMMARE, to monitor implementation and GHG reduction outcomes of these programmes. Nineteen states have adopted climate change laws and targets, but co-ordination between national and subnational climate policies is fragile.

Brazil has made great progress in reducing its carbon footprint. GHG emissions have declined by more than 40% since 2000; in 2012, they were below the 2020 target (Figure 1). The dramatic decrease in deforestation levels and associated GHG emissions has more than offset the rapid growth in emissions from energy and agriculture, the sectors that today account for the bulk of emissions. Rising demand for mobility has led to a doubling of the vehicle fleet, increased energy use and GHG emissions from transport and higher environmental pressures in many urban areas (Figure 1).

Brazil is developing a climate change adaptation plan. There is consensus that climate change may have considerable negative impact on some economic sectors, notably agriculture and infrastructure, and exacerbate existing pressures, such as water shortages.

Figure 1. **Selected environmental performance indicators**

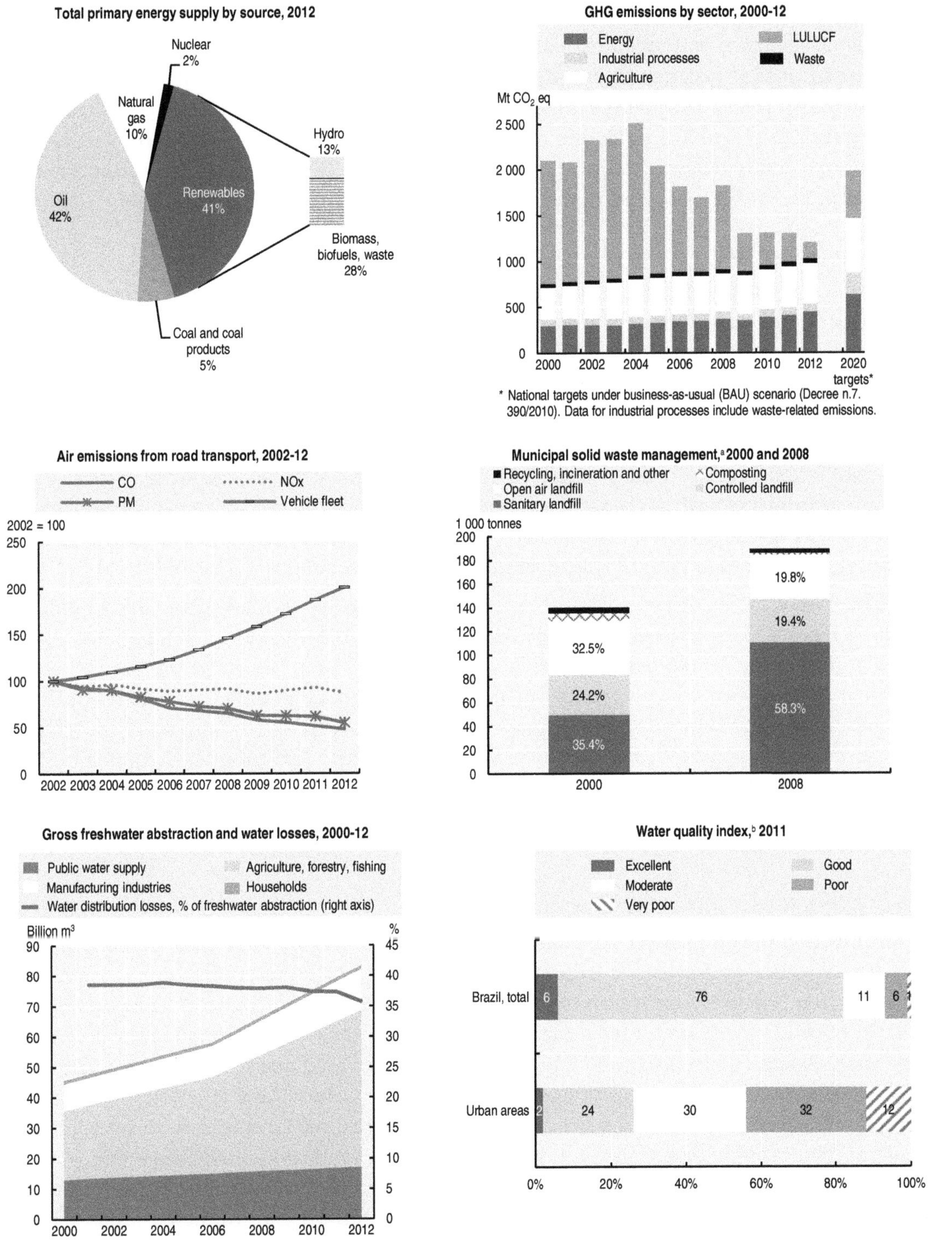

a) Includes waste originated from households, offices, institutions, commerce and waste from selected municipal services. Controlled landfill: site operating in compliance with technical control procedures, but not requiring environmental mitigation measures. Sanitary landfill: site operating in compliance with technical control procedures and environmental mitigation measures.

b) Water quality index (IQA) calculated as weighted average of nine parameters. The index varies from 0 to 100. Water classes: "excellent" (≤79); "good" (51-79); "moderate" (36-51); "poor"(19-36); "very poor" (≤19). The last two categories refer to unsafe drinking water.

Source: ANA (2013), *Conjuntura dos Recursos Hídricos no Brasil*; IEA (2014), *IEA World Energy Statistics and Balances* (database); MCTI (2014), *Estimativas anuais de emissões de gases de efeito estufa no Brasil*; MMA (2014), *Inventário Nacional de Emissões Atmosféricas por Veículos Automotores Rodoviários, 2013*; MMA (2012), *National Plan for Solid Waste*; UNSD (n.d.), UNSD Environmental Indicators.

StatLink http://dx.doi.org/10.1787/888933279326

Air quality

Air pollution has been reduced in all major cities, but peak concentrations of small particles have grown and regularly exceed national air quality standards (IBGE, 2013). Air pollution causes high economic, social and health costs in major metropolitan areas. Brazil is revising its national air quality standards in accordance with World Health Organization guidelines. The states are in charge of air quality regulation and monitoring, but only 12 states had some type of monitoring system installed in 2012, and few of them provide consistent, accessible data. Less than 2% of municipalities monitor air quality.

Waste management

Municipal waste generation has grown with rising living standards and urbanisation. The share of the population with access to waste collection services has increased, but only about half the population has access to such services in rural areas. As in many emerging economies, landfilling is the primary waste disposal method (Figure 1). The 2010 National Solid Waste Policy (PNRS) established key principles and directives for sound waste management that are compatible with OECD standards. However, the PNRS implementation is challenged by a lack of consistent waste data and capacity gaps at the municipal level (Section 2). Federal government support for landfill construction has helped reducing the amount of waste disposed of in non-sanitary landfills, although Brazil fell short of its national target to close all uncontrolled landfills by 2014.

The PNRS also introduced a "reverse logistics system", an approach similar to the extended producer responsibility systems operating in most OECD countries. It requires all manufacturers, distributors and retailers of pesticides, batteries, tyres, lubricating oils, fluorescent lamps and electronic devices, and their components, to recover these products at the end of their useful life. Insufficient recycling infrastructure and limited municipal capacity for separate waste collection are the main bottlenecks in implementation of these extended producer responsibility programmes. The federal government has encouraged the formation of co-operatives of waste pickers, who are key players in the waste recovery business, thereby linking environmental and social objectives. However, composting and recycling remain very limited.

Biodiversity conservation and sustainable use*

Brazil is the world's most biodiverse country. It remarkably expanded the land area under environmental protection in the 2000s, which has been crucial in combatting deforestation. The deforestation rate drastically declined in the Amazon from its latest peak in 2004, although pressures remain high in some other regions, notably the tropical savannah (Section 4). In 2014, official protected areas covered about 17% of the territory. Additional terrestrial areas are protected within indigenous lands and in private lands that comply with the Forest Code requirements. The code requires landholders to set aside a share of their land for forest and soil conservation and restoration, including along water bodies and sensitive areas (Section 4). Overall, these areas cover more than 40% of the national territory, or more than twice the surface within official protected areas. This makes Brazil's protected area system one of the world's largest. The share of total area and the degree of protection vary across regions and ecosystems, however. Work is ongoing to extend the marine areas under protection from the current 1.5% of territorial waters and exclusive economic zone to 5% by 2020 (Section 5).

* See Sections 4 and 5 for details.

Water resources

Brazil is endowed with 12% of the world's freshwater resources, about 70% of which are located in the Amazon basin. It has introduced modern instruments of integrated water resource management. Water resource plans, prepared at the national, state and river basin levels with broad stakeholder participation, lay out priorities, programmes and projects. However, such plans cover only half the territory and, where they exist, are poorly implemented and fail to guide water resource allocation (OECD, 2015a).

Water use permits (for abstraction and other uses) are issued by national or state water agencies, depending on the jurisdiction of the water body. Federal and state water permit systems could be better integrated to improve water management in shared river basins. Water abstractions, especially for agriculture, have dramatically increased since 2000 (Figure 1). Water scarcity has become an economic and social constraint in the more populated and economically developed areas in the South-east region due to climatic factors and inefficient water use (ANA, 2013). Obsolete and undersized infrastructure is a major cause of high losses in water distribution (Section 3).

In an approach that is fully consistent with best practices in OECD countries, Brazil has introduced a system of quality classification of surface water bodies that is based on their main uses and establishes quality standards corresponding to each use class. Water quality is low in many densely populated urban areas, a fact that is often related to insufficient infrastructure for sewage collection and treatment (Figure 1). While access to potable water in urban areas is now almost universal, 56% of the urban population had access to sewage collection systems in 2011, with large regional variations. In some areas, environmental and health impacts resulting from insufficient sanitation and high levels of fertiliser and pesticide use are significant (MMA, 2010; 2015).

Recommendations on climate change policy and air, water and waste management

Climate change policy

- Rapidly implement the sectoral programmes to mitigate GHG emissions and speed up the development of the SMMARE system to monitor results; ensure that effective measures are replicated and scaled up.
- Further advance the development and implementation of the climate change adaptation plan with the involvement of all sectors, levels of government and stakeholders; ensure that the strategy adequately reflects economic, social and environmental impacts, including on biodiversity and water availability and quality.

Air pollution, water and waste management

- Develop an effective nationwide air quality monitoring system, with consistent methodologies and data collection across states.
- Establish consistent and compatible criteria for water allocation and ensure that wastewater discharge limits are set in accordance with use-based water quality standards.
- Strengthen solid waste management by:
  - better enforcing hazardous waste management regulations to eliminate the disposal of hazardous waste in municipal landfills without prior treatment;
  - establishing the National Solid Waste Management Information System, as required by law, and using it to facilitate implementation of "reverse logistics" programmes for key product waste streams.

2. Environmental governance and management

Multilevel environmental governance framework

Since the 1980s, Brazil has developed a comprehensive environmental policy and institutional framework. The main nationwide policy-making body is the National Environmental Council (CONAMA), established in 1981, a high-level advisory and deliberative committee that brings together representatives of all government levels and principal stakeholders. The institutional capacity and staff of the federal Ministry of the Environment (MMA) have grown remarkably over the last ten years. The MMA has gradually come out from its long-standing isolation from sectoral policy making and has increasingly engaged in constructive dialogue with other line ministries. This has led to recent progress in integrating environmental issues into the economic and social agendas. Nevertheless, as in many other countries, an institutional culture of multiple silo-type ministries still prevails. Ensuring high-profile leadership or co-ordination would help improve policy coherence and enable a whole-of-government approach to sustainable development.

All states and nearly all municipalities with populations over 100 000 have established functioning environmental institutions, although their level of development varies considerably. For instance, about a quarter of municipal environmental councils were inactive in 2013 (IBGE, 2014). Many state agencies face a significant challenge to attract and retain qualified technical staff. The Brazilian Institute of Environment and Renewable Natural Resources (IBAMA) has tended to play a supplemental role to the state agencies, especially where institutional capacity is limited, such as in the North and North-east.

The federal and state governments have invested in capacity building, but there still is a need for better information on state and local environmental policy implementation. The associations of state (ABEMA) and local (ANAMMA) environmental agencies have undertaken activities to promote co-operation and information exchange among member institutions. The National Water Management Pact is a good example of a co-operation strategy involving authorities at all administrative levels, one that could help improve dialogue and capacity across government levels and serve as a model for other environmental policy areas.

The combination of Brazil's high economic and social heterogeneity and its decentralised federal governance system creates significant multilevel governance challenges. Progress was made with Complementary Law 140/2011 and Presidential Decree 8437/2015, which clarified the boundaries of federal, state and local jurisdiction over environmental issues. However, implementation and co-ordination challenges remain. Co-ordination bodies are abundant but often lack the decision-making tools, capacity and resources to get to grips with vested institutional interests. Addressing their weakness and the low capacity of most subnational authorities would help establish a nationwide level playing field in setting and enforcing environmental requirements.

Financing of environmental institutions

In the Treasury's budget classification by government function, allocations for environmental management grew by 48% over 2010-14 to about 0.4% of the federal budget (Senado Federal, 2015). In 2014 the Ministry of Planning, Budget and Management launched a project to track environment-related spending across the government, in co-operation with the Institute for Applied Economic Research. This is of particular importance because the MMA budget is relatively small and other ministries and agencies contribute a large part of public environmental expenditure. This initiative will help improve understanding of the effectiveness and efficiency of public resource allocation; it should be continued with rigour and, over time, extended to state and municipal spending.

The two largest federal environment-related funds (the National Climate Change Fund and the Amazon Fund) have sound monitoring systems and have been effective in securing resources for environmental projects, including international finance. Most states and large municipalities operate environmental funds, partly fed by revenue from environmental fines; by comparison, in most OECD countries revenue from fines goes to the government budget, as the incentive to collect revenue may hamper actions to prevent non-compliance. Brazil also uses part of its oil and gas revenue to fund environmental and climate mitigation objectives. Earmarking resources to funds for environmental purposes may be necessary to secure reliable, sufficient resources, but can reduce the flexibility and efficiency of revenue allocation.

Environmental legislation

The Brazilian Constitution recognises the people's right to an ecologically balanced environment. Since the adoption of the 1981 National Environmental Policy Law, Brazil has developed a comprehensive and advanced environmental legislation framework at the national level and in most states. There are, however, implementation gaps to be addressed. The stringency of environmental requirements varies substantially across jurisdictions, reflecting local priorities and capacity constraints. This raises concerns about potential "environmental dumping", in which highly polluting industries would establish facilities in states that lack the capacity to set and enforce environmental regulations.

Environmental licensing, compliance and enforcement

Brazil does not have an integrated system of land administration across the three levels of government. Unclear definition of property rights for both public and private holders has historically exacerbated problems of unplanned and unauthorised land use, including forest clearing. The recently established Rural Environmental Cadastre (CAR) system is an important step towards addressing environmental aspects of regularisation of rural holdings (Section 4). There is no federal legal requirement for strategic environmental assessment of territorial plans and other development programmes, although some states have made it mandatory and ecological-economic zoning covers more than 70% of the territory. In urban areas, municipal master plans have been required since 2005. They combine but do not integrate individual components on sanitation, transport, housing, etc., and are still rarely implemented.

Environmental licensing (which incorporates environmental impact assessment, EIA) is a crucial regulatory instrument at all government levels. In practice, however, it has become a bureaucratic administrative process without adequate consideration of location, technological alternatives, potential environmental impact and mitigation measures (ABEMA, 2013). While technical and institutional capacity for environmental licensing has improved at federal level, weak institutional capacity of subnational environmental authorities, inadequate project planning and design, and occasional interference of local economic and political interests hinder the effectiveness, timeliness and transparency of the process. The licensing process has increasingly become an arena for wide-ranging discussions on development options and their consequences – environmental, social and others.

Complementary Law 140/2011 and a subsequent presidential decree made the division of licensing responsibility across the three government levels more objective, depending on a given project's scale, location and extent of potential environmental impact. However, a clearer regulation of measures and mechanisms to compensate the environmental impact is needed.

As in other policy areas, various factors contribute to weak law enforcement in many states and municipalities: insufficient human resources limit inspections to responding to incidents; administrative fines are often ineffective due to very low collection rates; and environmental liability is sporadically applied. At the same time, the role of federal and state prosecutors in civil and criminal environmental enforcement has increased, which has helped ensure compliance. Socio-environmental responsibility initiatives in the financial sector are important factors in promoting compliance and good practices. Since 2008 the Central Bank has issued resolutions incorporating socio-environmental concerns in financial activities, including credit restrictions for non-compliers (Section 4). However, businesses often lack enough information and incentives to adopt sustainable practices voluntarily.

Environmental democracy

Public participation is an eminent feature of Brazil's environmental governance, including membership of non-government organisations (NGOs) in multistakeholder decision-making bodies – e.g. government councils and protected areas management committees (Section 5) – mandatory public consultation as part of environmental licensing, and guaranteed citizen access to environmental information and justice. However, the mechanisms for taking account of civil society views in environmental decision making should be strengthened further.

Federal laws provide important guarantees of citizens' access to environmental information. The National Environmental Information System (SINIMA) is responsible for developing a consistent policy directed at the production, collection, systematisation and dissemination of environmental information. Brazil's statistics institute, IBGE, publishes sustainable development indicator reports every two years and the MMA has been working to develop a set of key environmental indicators (the National Panel of Environmental Indicators, PNIA) consolidating available environmental data. Despite these efforts, environmental information remains fragmented, which undermines policy analysis and the public's ability to influence environmental policy development and implementation.

3. Greening the economy in the context of sustainable development

The sustainable development framework

Brazil has moved up the ranks of the world's largest economies and made considerable progress towards sustainable and inclusive growth. It enjoyed robust economic growth over most of the 2000s, which helped narrow the income gap with OECD countries. Growth has slowed since 2012, however (OECD, 2015b). The large conditional cash-transfer programme Bolsa Família, which is recognised as an international best practice, has helped halve the number of people living in extreme poverty (*bolsa* means grant or stipend). Health service coverage and educational outcome have also improved, but income inequality and territorial disparities are large. Brazil needs to restore strong growth while continuing to address social challenges and enhance conservation and sustainable use of its environmental assets.

Recommendations on environmental governance and management

Environmental governance

- Streamline the multitude of horizontal and vertical co-ordination bodies, with a view to eliminating overlaps and gaps of responsibilities and, ultimately, improving policy coherence and effectiveness; consider establishing a national system for quality control and accountability.
- Build on the associations of state (ABEMA) and local (ANAMMA) environmental agencies to create a network of regulators at all administrative levels and enhance their capacity through exchange of experiences and good practices; consider implementing a programme for strengthening capacity at subnational level.
- Consider replicating multilevel governance mechanisms such as the National Water Management Pact to other environmental policy areas to promote integration and dialogue across levels of government and reduce regional disparities in environmental performance.
- Streamline funds dedicated to environmental management and projects; systematically monitor the use of environmental funds to ensure that it is in line with policy priorities, transparent and cost-effective.
- Develop a uniform system for the collection and management of environmental data, including on environmental law implementation (input, output and outcome indicators) and economic aspects of environmental policies (expenditure and revenue accounts; environment-related goods, services and employment).

Environmental licensing, enforcement and compliance

- Introduce and enforce a legal requirement of strategic environmental assessment of municipal territorial plans and sectoral development programmes, which should be used to integrate the economic, social and environmental aspects of land use.
- Streamline the environmental impact assessment and environmental licensing requirements across and within administrative levels; clarify the boundaries of compensation actions that have socio-environmental objectives and those that pursue social objectives; develop procedural guidance for each stage of the licensing process and build capacity of licensing authorities.
- Strengthen the capacity of environmental inspectors at all government levels, emphasise proactive (planned) compliance monitoring, improve collaboration with federal and state prosecutors and develop broader opportunities for "citizen enforcement" by engaging local communities in compliance monitoring.

Since the early 2000s, Brazil has launched several initiatives to address the economic, social and environmental strands of growth and sustainable development in an integrated manner. These included the 2002 Agenda 21, which has long been considered the national sustainable development strategy, although it lacked implementation mechanisms. Some cash transfer programmes have targeted environmental and social objectives simultaneously, as a significant part of the population, especially in rural areas, depends on the sustainable use of natural resources (Section 4). Some programmes for agriculture, industry, energy and infrastructure development have started to include an environmental dimension. These positive initiatives could be consolidated into a coherent strategic framework for a green economy and sustainable development.

Greening the system of taxes and charges

In the context of a broader tax reform, there is scope to extend and improve the use of environmentally related taxes and remove potential environmentally perverse tax exemptions and subsidies so as to promote more efficient and sustainable resource use. In 2013, revenue from environmentally related taxes in Brazil accounted for about 2% of total tax revenue and 0.7% of GDP, below the levels observed in most OECD countries.

While fuel prices were deregulated in the early 2000s, between 2006 and 2012 the government kept prices below the world market level. In addition, the rate of the federal fuel tax (CIDE) gradually declined. These implicit subsidies kept petrol prices artificially low and provided no incentive to moderate private car use, while harming the ethanol industry. When petrol and diesel prices were raised in 2012, the CIDE rate was set to zero as a compensating measure.

In a welcome move, the government reintroduced positive CIDE rates in early 2015, but rates are not linked to fuels' energy or carbon content. As in most countries, diesel is taxed at a lower rate than petrol despite its higher carbon content and emissions of local air pollutants. Consumption of fuels in sectors such as agriculture and industry remains largely untaxed. The economy-wide effective tax rate on CO_2 emissions is, therefore, one of the lowest among OECD countries and the BRIICS group of emerging economies (Brazil, Russia, India, Indonesia, China, South Africa) (OECD, 2015c). The finance ministry has undertaken a comprehensive assessment of carbon pricing options, including a carbon tax and a cap-and-trade system, with a view to providing policy recommendations in 2017. This is a step in the right direction and could build on previous attempts to introduce subnational GHG emission trading systems.

Revenue from vehicle taxes has grown with the increase in vehicle ownership, but tax rates do not consider vehicles' environmental attributes. Reduced purchase tax rates for flex-fuel cars have stimulated sales of these cars, which account for the majority of all passenger cars. Only a few states have implemented water abstraction and pollution charges, but unit prices are low and have had limited effect on decisions about water allocation and use (OECD, 2015a). There are no other charges on natural resource use and pollution.

Environment-related investment and financing

Public investment in infrastructure increased with the 2007 Growth Acceleration Programme and its 2011 successor. This will help sustain growth and improve service delivery. The 2011 programme also included a stronger environmental dimension with increased resources for sanitation, transport and energy. Some investment programmes have considered sustainability criteria and potential climate impacts, although not in a systematic manner.

The Brazilian Development Bank (BNDES), the biggest provider of long-term finance, has stepped up its environment-related lending activities, which accounted for 15% of its total lending in 2014 (Figure 2). The BNDES has also introduced environmental screening for its major lending projects and some sectors with potentially high environmental impact (e.g. soya, sugar and ethanol, meat processing, fossil energy). However, weaknesses in project planning, design, implementation and monitoring have delayed infrastructure delivery, discouraged private-sector engagement and resulted in federal money remaining unspent. This is especially true for environment-related infrastructure such as for sanitation and urban transport, which is the responsibility of local governments, as well as for large infrastructure projects in sensitive areas, such as the Amazon.

Figure 2. **BNDES environment-related disbursements have increased significantly**

Disbursements by sector, 2002-14

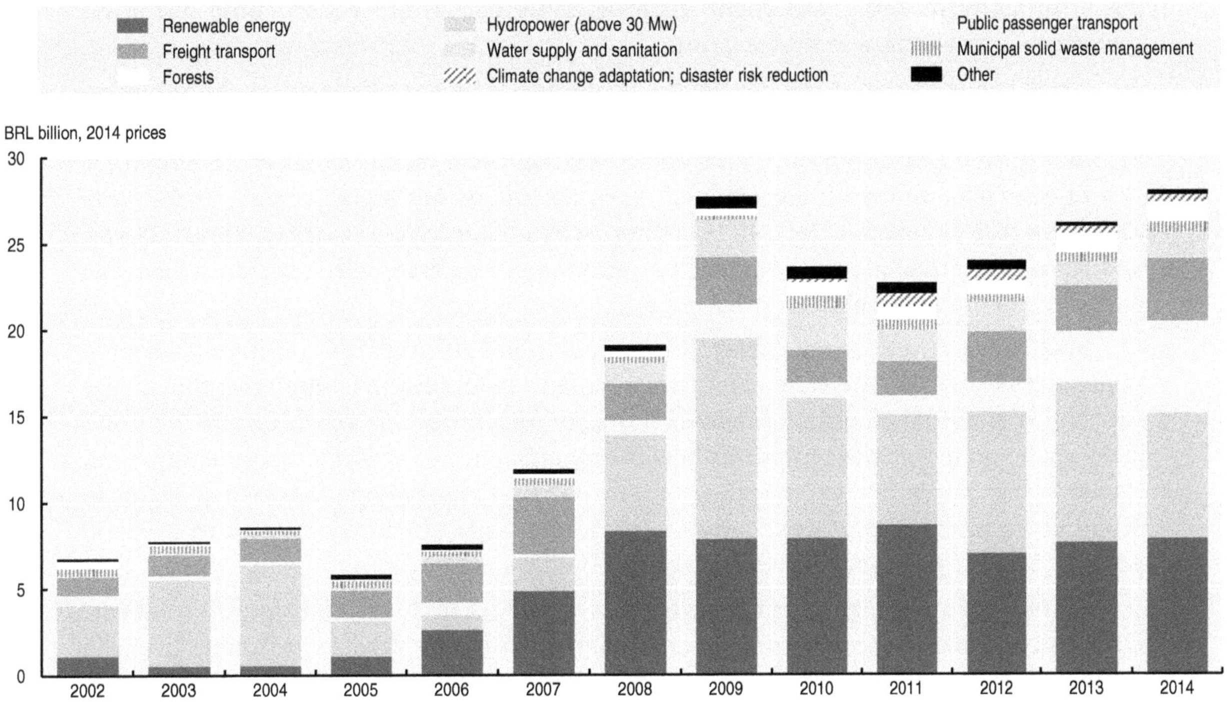

Note: Amounts disbursed prior to 2007 may be underestimated due to changes in the expenditure classification. 2014 data for renewables include investment in the energy efficiency programme PROESCO.
Source: Based on BNDES (2014), *Annual Report 2013*; BNDES (2013), *Annual Report 2012*.

StatLink http://dx.doi.org/10.1787/888933279332

More people now have access to electricity, clean water, sanitation and waste management services. Yet coverage and quality of infrastructure need to be expanded and improved, particularly for wastewater treatment, sanitary landfills and recycling (Section 1). Inadequate pricing is among the impediments to extending water and waste infrastructure and services. Most municipalities do not charge for waste collection or do so through property taxes, which do not provide any incentive to reduce waste generation or sort for recycling. On average, water tariffs allow coverage of operational and maintenance costs but a very limited share of new infrastructure investment, and there are wide variations in tariffs and operation efficiency across municipalities and service providers (MCid, 2014). As in other Latin American countries, a large share of distributed water does not generate revenue. Revenue is lower in poorer municipalities, partly due to social tariffs applied to low-income households; this may discourage investment in extending infrastructure where it is most needed. Alternatively, cash transfer programmes could be used to compensate low-income households.

Investment in clean energy and sustainable transport

In 2014, Brazil was the world's seventh largest investor in renewable energy sources (BNEF, 2015). The Energy Expansion Plan 2022 envisages maintaining the reliance on renewables (Section 1). Investment has focused on large hydropower plants, which received most of the BNDES's environment-related lending in 2008-14 (Figure 2). Various forms of support, including renewables-technology-specific power purchasing auctions, have helped increase energy supply from sources other than large hydro, especially wind. Local content rules, a condition for BNDES financing, have led to the creation of a wind power industry in Brazil, although this form of industrial protection could harm the sector's competitiveness in the long run.

Brazil has encouraged the development of large-scale sugarcane ethanol production and the use of ethanol to power road vehicles since the 1970s, including by means of mandatory blending quotas and favourable taxation. As a result, biofuels accounted for 17% of fuels used in road transport in 2012, by far the world's highest share. In the early 2010s, the government and the BNDES renewed investment support to the ethanol industry and sugarcane production in response to declining productivity in the sector, which was partly due to the artificially low price of petrol.

Brazil lunched a National Energy Efficiency Plan in 2011 and set a countrywide energy saving target to 2030. The state electricity company, Eletrobras, has implemented energy demand management programmes in industry and municipalities. Regulations and labelling programmes have improved the energy efficiency of appliances and equipment. However, the approach to energy efficiency and demand management has been piecemeal. Brazil can gain from systematically integrating energy efficiency criteria in sectoral policies, including for housing, urban planning and transport.

Passengers and freight mostly travel on roads in Brazil. Insufficient public transport infrastructure and rising user costs, in combination with relatively low taxation of vehicle ownership and use, have contributed to exacerbating urban car traffic. The 2011 Growth Acceleration Programme included expansion of the long-distance and urban rail networks, which is welcome. More emphasis could also be given to bus rapid transit systems, which have been successfully operating in some cities, such as Curitiba, and were launched in Rio de Janeiro and Brasília in 2014. They could help reduce congestion in cities and along road networks, with benefits including fewer accidents and lower GHG and air pollutant emissions.

Eco-innovation and environmental goods and services

Eco-innovation is among the priorities of Brazil's innovation strategy. Brazil has leading innovative firms and high expertise in selected high-technology fields such as renewables and agro-technology. Green research and development (R&D) expenditure is estimated to account for about 3% of total R&D expenditure (Frischtak, 2011). Eco-innovation performance has improved and Brazil has been developing a specialisation in environmental technology compared to other BRIICS economies. The number of patents in environment- and climate-related technology has grown, accounting for about 9% of all patents filed in Brazil in 2009-11 (the BRIICS average was 7.8%). Brazil has generated the world's third largest amount of certified emission reduction credits under the Clean Development Mechanism, which has been a key driver of technology transfer and has also encouraged domestically driven innovation.

Brazil would benefit from improved coherence of industrial, labour market and innovation policies and enhanced co-operation between the government, research institutions and the business sector. Eco-innovation faces barriers similar to those facing general innovation, including weak science-industry links, skill gaps, regulatory obstacles, high patenting costs and a complex system of economic and fiscal incentives. Together with public support to R&D, some demand-side policy measures have recently emerged, including sustainable public procurement, labelling programmes and policies that set sectoral environmental performance targets. However, environmental labelling is costly and sustainable products account for a negligible share of government purchases (MMA, 2015). The 2015 Biodiversity Framework Law is expected to facilitate innovation and industrial activity based on the fair use of genetic assets and traditional knowledge (Section 4).

The environmental goods and services sector seems to have grown faster than the overall economy (ABDi, 2012). Estimates indicate that it could be a significant source of growth for the country (1% to 7% of GDP). However, various forms of protection of national businesses (e.g. local content requirements and high import duties) limit competition, raise technology costs and discourage innovation and diffusion of more efficient, cleaner technology, goods and services. Brazil's leading companies invest only 1% of turnover in sustainable technology, and small and medium-sized enterprises are likely to invest even less (AHK, 2009). Nevertheless, increased adoption of social corporate responsibility practices and environmental management systems shows that business awareness of environmental issues has improved.

Development co-operation

Brazil has increased its expenditure on development co-operation and is one of the most active partners in triangular co-operation. While its co-operation has traditionally focused on health, agriculture and education, the number of environmental projects has expanded, and prospects of this growth accelerating in the near future are good. Brazil is engaging with other countries to share its expertise in forest and land-use monitoring; and the government plans to increase south-south co-operation on forest recovery (Section 4).

Recommendations on greening the economy in the context of sustainable development

Greening the system of taxes and charges

- Reform the system of environmentally related taxes and charges, possibly within the context of a broader fiscal reform, including:
  - maintaining positive rates for the federal CIDE tax on petrol and diesel and adjusting them to reflect fuel carbon content and emissions of local air pollutants; applying the CIDE to fuels used for aviation and stationary purposes (e.g. industry);
  - introducing taxes on pollution (e.g. air emissions), waste (e.g. packaging materials) and resource use (e.g. minerals), and aligning vehicle taxation to environmental performance;
  - ensuring that water abstraction and pollution charges reflect scarcity and pressures on the environment and are consistently applied across river basins and throughout the country (as required by law).
- Pursue the assessment of carbon pricing options; consider testing GHG cap-and-trade systems at state level to gain the experience needed to implement a countrywide system linked to international carbon markets.

Recommendations on greening the economy in the context of sustainable development *(cont.)*

Investment in environment-related infrastructure and services

- Systematically integrate environmental objectives into sectoral policies and public investment programmes, which should feature environmental sustainability criteria for implementation and indicators to monitor progress.
- Simplify administrative procedures and support capacity development to improve the execution of environment-related infrastructure investment programmes, especially at local level; encourage stronger intermunicipal collaboration to achieve economies of scale in providing sanitation and waste treatment services.
- Extend the use of user charges for water supply, sanitation and waste services and enforce their collection, with a view to encouraging efficient use of resources, increasing cost recovery, improving investment financial viability and leveraging private sector resources; use social transfers to ensure that low-income households have adequate access to these services.
- Strengthen measures to improve energy efficiency by introducing energy standards for buildings and appliances, integrating them into social housing programmes and using mandatory fuel economy standards and labelling to promote a shift towards more efficient vehicles.
- Continue to scale up investment in railways and urban public transport systems; consider extending the use of instruments such as road tolls, congestion charges, parking fees and restrictions on car circulation to moderate the use of private vehicles.

Eco-innovation and environmental goods and services

- Stimulate the production and diffusion of environmental technology, goods and services by:
  - raising awareness about best practices and available technology, particularly in small and medium-sized enterprises;
  - facilitating access to finance for investing in environmental, renewables and energy-saving technology;
  - monitoring the effects of local content rules on the long-term competitiveness of the emerging environmental technology industry (e.g. wind and solar);
  - regularly updating the catalogue of sustainable products for green public procurement, and training procurement managers;
  - further streamlining environmental labelling initiatives.

4. Conservation and sustainable use of biodiversity*

Brazil's biodiversity: state, trends and pressures

A megadiverse country, Brazil is home to around one-tenth of all known species and more endemic species than any other country. It is host to six terrestrial ecosystems, or biomes (Amazon, Cerrado, Caatinga, Atlantic Forest, Pantanal and Pampa) and various coastal and marine ecosystems.[1] The Amazon, the world's largest rainforest, occupies nearly half of Brazil's territory. As in most emerging economies, infrastructure development, agriculture, population growth and urbanisation are the main pressures on

* See Section 5 for details on protected areas.

biodiversity (MMA, 2015). Biodiversity conservation status varies widely across regions and states, being generally poorer in the South and South-east regions and along the coast, where most of the population lives.

Brazil has made impressive progress in reducing deforestation. In 2014, after peaking in the mid-2000s, the annual deforestation rate in the area known as Amazônia Legal[2] was 75% below the average for the previous 10 years (Figure 3). Brazil is, therefore, likely to overshoot its target of reducing deforestation in the region by 80% by 2020. However, progress has been uneven across the states in the region, and the current pace still means forest loss equivalent to the size of Slovenia (or the Brazilian state of Sergipe) every four years. Deforestation rates have also declined in most other biomes in recent years, but pressures remain high in the Cerrado. Overall, total forest area has decreased by about 5% since 2000. Unclear land tenure has historically exacerbated deforestation pressures from illegal logging and agriculture and pasture expansion.

Action to protect threatened species has increased and the conservation status of more than 100 species has improved since the previous assessment (MMA, 2015). In 2012, about half of threatened fauna species were protected under a conservation action plan, and federal protected areas now cover nearly 60% of threatened flora and fauna species. Yet the 2014 lists of threatened flora and fauna species indicate that over 45% of plant species are threatened, especially in the Atlantic Forest and Cerrado biomes, as are nearly 10% of fauna species. Several coastal and inland fish stocks are fully exploited or overexploited (MMA, 2015).

Figure 3. **Expanding protected areas has helped reduce deforestation in the Amazon**

Protected areas and deforestation rates in the Amazon, 2000-14

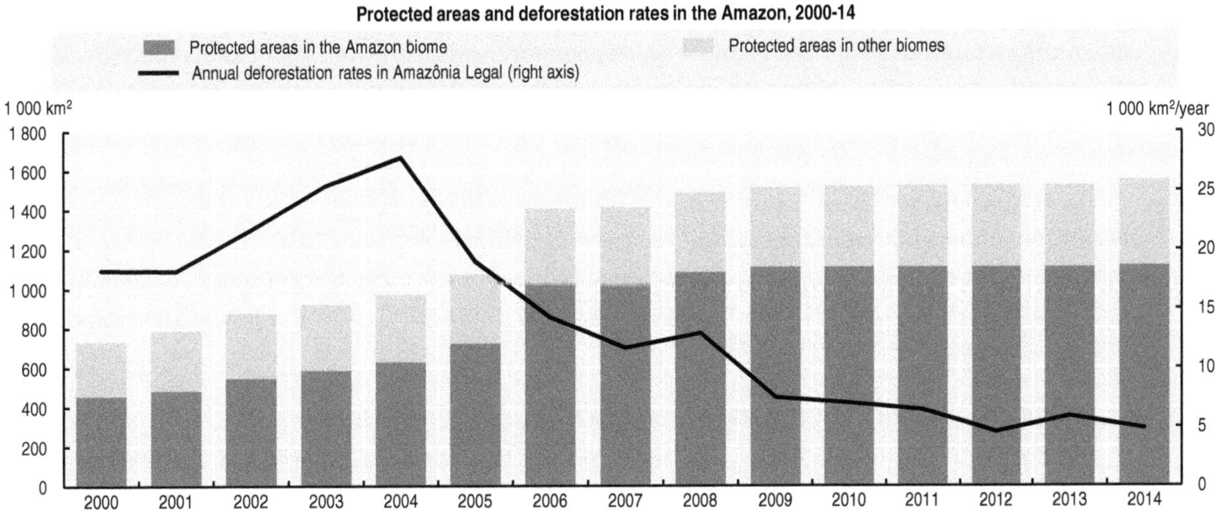

Note: The Amazônia Legal encompasses the Amazonian forest (about 4.1 million km²) and transitional vegetation (1 million km²).
Source: INPE (2015), "Projeto PRODES: Monitoramento da floresta Amazônia Brasileira por satélite"; MMA (2015), *Cadastro Nacional de Unidades de Conservaçao.*

StatLink http://dx.doi.org/10.1787/888933279342

Improving the knowledge base for biodiversity policy

Brazil has made impressive progress in improving the knowledge base on species and ecosystems and in monitoring the state and trends of biodiversity. However, the abundant biodiversity-related information remains fragmented and not always consistent. In 2010, the Ministry of Science and Technology launched the online Information System on

Brazilian Biodiversity (SiBBr), in an attempt to systematise this information and make it more accessible for research and policy design.

Brazil is a world leader in monitoring deforestation via satellite imaging, which has been a crucial factor in reducing forest clearing in the Amazon. A nearly real-time monitoring system alerts authorities if deforestation and forest degradation occur in the region. Satellite deforestation monitoring has been implemented for the other biomes, too, but it is less developed and data are not fully compatible across systems. Forest fire detection systems cover the entire country.

In 2013, the MMA launched the Brazilian Natural Capital Initiative as part of Brazil's commitment to develop a national TEEB (The Economics of Ecosystems and Biodiversity) process. This initiative could help fill Brazil's gap in economic valuation of biodiversity and build consensus on the benefits of maintaining functioning ecosystems. This, in turn, would contribute to raising the political and social support that is needed to mainstream biodiversity effectively in the development agenda.

Policy framework for biodiversity conservation and sustainable use

Since the mid-2000s, Brazil has strengthened its institutional, policy and legislative frameworks for biodiversity conservation and sustainable use. There has been a gradual shift from a strict fence-and-protect and enforcement approach to a sustainable development approach that identifies biodiversity priority regions and recognises the role of rural, traditional and indigenous communities in maintaining the provision of ecosystem services.

In 2013, the National Biodiversity Commission adopted 20 ambitious national biodiversity targets to 2020, aligned with the Aichi Targets under the Convention on Biological Diversity (CBD). It also established a multistakeholder panel, PainelBio, to define indicators to monitor progress. A midterm assessment indicates that Brazil is on the right track to achieve most of its targets, although additional efforts are required (MMA, 2015). Several states have developed biodiversity strategies and action plans, but ensuring consistency and synergy with federal biodiversity policies is challenging.

Overall, there has been a proliferation of biodiversity-related plans and programmes since 2000, often with overlapping objectives. It is unclear to what extent they have been implemented or yielded the expected results. With few exceptions, implementation of biodiversity policies and plans is not systematically monitored, and their effectiveness, costs and benefits are rarely evaluated.

An integrated strategy to combat deforestation

Understandably, Brazilian biodiversity policy has focused heavily on combating deforestation. In 2004, in response to rising deforestation rates in the Amazon, the government launched the Action Plan for Prevention and Control of Deforestation in Amazônia Legal (PPCDAm). The plan has effectively brought the fight against deforestation into other sectoral agendas, thanks to high-profile co-ordination by the Executive Office of the Presidency (Casa Civil) and the assignment of implementation responsibilities to 13 ministries. Currently in its third phase, the PPCDAm is based on a coherent set of actions such as establishment of protected areas (Section 5), land tenure regularisation (including the Terra Legal programme), advanced monitoring systems, strict enforcement, and promotion of sustainable natural resource use. Complementary instruments such as embargos and credit restrictions for illegal deforesters have spurred enforcement effectiveness.

The PPCDAm is widely recognised as an effective strategy, which can serve as a model for other countries. It has greatly helped reduce deforestation in the Amazon (Figure 3), although other factors may have contributed, including declining prices of agricultural products and voluntary private sector engagement. Building on the success of the PPCDAm, the government launched a similar programme to control deforestation in the Cerrado biome. In addition to strict monitoring and enforcement, further reducing deforestation will increasingly require making sustainable agriculture and forest management more attractive than illegal logging and land grabbing, and ensuring that sustainable practices provide a viable income source for traditional communities (CEPAL et al., 2011).

Acknowledging this need, since 2006 the government has granted concessions for sustainable harvesting of timber and non-timber forest products. Concessions still cover less than 1% of the eligible forest area, mainly because of red tape, high transaction costs, lack of infrastructure and land tenure conflicts. Many rural communities do not have the knowledge or means to adopt sustainable forest practices or to compete in concession processes.

Funding from international and bilateral co-operation has helped finance the PPCDAm and other biodiversity-related programmes and has added implementation capacity to the government machine. Much of the international finance is used through extrabudgetary funds, including the innovative Amazon Fund. Established in 2008 and managed by the BNDES in co-ordination with the MMA, the fund invests in deforestation prevention and sustainable forest use, thereby contributing to reducing GHG emissions. Norway is the largest donor, followed by Germany. Between 2009 and early 2015, the fund accumulated more than USD 970 million and supported over 70 projects. Through the Amazon Fund, Brazil has received about half the total approved international finance from Reducing Emissions from Deforestation and Forest Degradation (REDD and REDD+) (Norman et al., 2014). In June 2014, it was the first country to submit its forest reference emission level for payments under REDD+ as required by the 2013 Warsaw Framework. A national REDD+ strategy has been under discussion since 2010.

The business sector has contributed to the combat against deforestation in the Amazon through the Soya Moratorium and the Beef Slaughterhouse Pact. The moratorium involves a group of large companies that have voluntary agreed to stop using soya beans grown on Amazonian forestland that has been illegally cleared since 2008. The moratorium has proved effective, as farmers tend to adapt to market demand. There is scope to further engage the business sector in forest conservation and restoration and, more generally, in biodiversity conservation and sustainable use.

The new Forest Code and the Rural Environmental Cadastre

In 2012, Brazil approved the new Forest Code, which replaced and updated the 1965 code. The code had traditionally been the key legal instrument to protect native vegetation on private property and to regulate land use. It required landholders to set aside a share of their land for forest and soil conservation and restoration (so-called Legal Reserves and Permanent Preservation Areas). The code was hardly enforced, however, with considerable areas being deforested illegally. In response, the new code, while criticised as indulgent towards commercial interests, introduced potentially more effective enforcement instruments, which may result in a better level of protection. The new Forest Code aims to reconcile the objectives of preserving biodiversity and forests and of ensuring a good business environment for agriculture, a key sector of Brazil's economy.

In particular, the new code introduced the Rural Environmental Cadastre (CAR) to improve monitoring of, and compliance with, forest conservation requirements on rural lands: landholders must register their lands and set-aside areas in the cadastre by May 2016, and CAR registration will be a condition for access to rural credits as from October 2017. Rural plots that do not comply with the land set-aside obligations will have to join state environmental regularisation programmes. The system uses high-resolution satellite images to localise and register each rural parcel.

The CAR implementation is on track: as of April 2015, 53% of the target area had been registered. The federal government has invested in establishing the necessary information system and in building capacity at state level, as states are responsible for implementation of the cadastre. Strict enforcement of the new code is expected to greatly help reduce deforestation rates further. Although the cadastre is not designed for regularising land property rights, the authorities responsible for rural development and settlements can use the geo-referenced information about the location of rural plots (as declared by their owners or holders) to clarify land tenure.

The new Forest Code foresees to complement cadastre registration with an innovative system of tradable forest quotas called Environmental Reserve Quotas (CRAs). In practice, landholders who did not meet their set-aside obligations (prior to 2008) can either restore the tree cover or purchase an equivalent quota amount. Quotas are issued for area maintained as native vegetation in excess of the set-aside requirements. Offsetting is possible only within the same biome and, possibly, the same state. This system creates demand for forested lands and encourages forest conservation. Estimates indicate that the past deficit of compliance with forest conservation obligations is large (Soares-Filho et al., 2014). As forest restoration is costly, especially for small rural holders, the quota system could be a cost-effective way of ensuring compliance. The MMA is considering how to address the risk that only low-opportunity-cost areas are competitive in the market, leading to increased conservation of areas that do not necessarily have the highest biodiversity value.

The National Plan for Native Vegetation Recovery (PLANAVEG), developed by the MMA and currently under public consultation, aims to promote large-scale forest restoration on 125 000 km^2 within 20 years. The MMA expects the plan to generate over 190 000 direct jobs in rural areas. Meeting the restoration targets is likely to require significant financial resources and innovative finance mechanisms, such as green bonds for restoration investment. The CAR will allow to identify high-biodiversity-value areas and to prioritise restoration actions.

Payments for ecosystem services and conditional cash-transfer programmes

While the regulatory approach has traditionally prevailed, the use of economic instruments has been broadened. Most such instruments aim to reward biodiversity-friendly actions, such as good agricultural practices or sustainable forest use. The use of charges and fees, such as water charges and entrance fees to protected areas, is very limited (see also Sections 3 and 5).

Brazil has implemented several federal and state programmes of payments for ecosystem services (PES) and income support for rural communities. The Water Producer Programme, launched in 2011 by the National Water Agency and replicated by some states and municipalities, financially compensate investment in soil and water protection in river basins that provide water resources to a large population. Programmes such as Bolsa

Floresta and Bolsa Verde provide payments to extremely poor households in rural and forest communities to compensate them for environmental conservation activities and support their income. Bolsa Floresta, in Amazonas state, has helped control deforestation, although it is implemented mostly in areas experiencing little deforestation pressure (Börner et al., 2013).

Bolsa Verde is a federal programme providing payments for adoption of environmental practices and technical training to support beneficiaries in meeting their conservation commitments. It is seen as a potentially efficient way to curb deforestation, with low payments per hectare of avoided deforestation. However, implementation is complex and complementary training activities are insufficiently developed (CGU, 2014). Developing monitoring mechanisms and ensuring a link with the Rural Environmental Cadastre would help improve effectiveness and reduce management costs for Bolsa Verde and the existing PES programmes. An overarching federal PES law has been under parliamentary discussion since 2007 and could provide the basis for expanding and improving the use of such programmes.

Access to genetic resources and benefit sharing

Brazil is home to hundreds of indigenous, *quilombola*[3] and other traditional communities whose residents have considerable knowledge of how to use plant and animal species. This underlines the importance of ensuring access to genetic assets and fairly sharing the benefits derived from them. Brazil signed the Nagoya Protocol on Access and Benefit Sharing (ABS)[4] in 2011, and is discussing its ratification. After more than a decade of a transitory regime and years of debate, in May 2015 Brazil approved a comprehensive Biodiversity Framework Law. The law aims to overcome the bottlenecks associated with the previous ABS regulation, which had severely restricted access to genetic resources for both commercial and scientific purposes. The new law reduces the administrative burden, improves participation of indigenous groups and traditional communities in decision making and creates a fund for benefit sharing. It has many potential benefits, including generating innovation, business opportunities and additional resources for conservation and sustainable use of biodiversity, for example in protected areas and indigenous lands. It could encourage like-minded African and Asian countries to adopt similar ABS regulations.

Mainstreaming biodiversity consideration in agriculture, fishery and energy policies

Brazil is a major agricultural producer and exporter. Since the mid-2000s, the government has increased its focus on encouraging adoption of sustainable agricultural practices. Access to concessional rural credits is linked to environmental compliance. Some programmes target small family farms, organic farming and sustainable production practices; an example is the Low-Carbon Agriculture programme. Organic farming accounts for a very small share of agricultural output, however, and less than 1% of the agricultural land area.

Overall, support to farmers is low compared to OECD and other BRIICS economies, but it is mostly tied to production based on conventional practices (OECD, 2013), with potentially negative impact on soil and water. By stimulating production and input use, and thereby agricultural intensification and expansion, these support programmes risk increasing pressures on natural resources and encouraging deforestation. The rural land tax, although not very significant, also incentivises agricultural production over conservation, as it is lower for agricultural land. In addition, fertilisers and pesticides benefit from some tax exemptions. This has contributed to their growing use, which has health and environmental effects. The use of unauthorised pesticides is also high, and, unlike in most OECD countries, regulations do not require periodic review and renewal of pesticide licences (MMA, 2015).

Brazil's fishery management model integrates environmental sustainability and social inclusion concerns. Several measures aim to limit the environmental impact of fishing, but no formal environmental licensing of fishery activities is required. Fish catches have increased and pressures on stocks are exacerbated by resource conflicts between artisanal and industrial fishing. Most fishing is carried out by obsolete fleets and very often directed at fish stocks that are already heavily exploited. Further increasing aquaculture production could contribute to supplying seafood and fish at lower costs to the population, thereby reducing pressure on natural fishery resources. However, its potentially negative impact on aquatic ecosystems should be taken into account.

Hydropower will continue to be a major energy source, but its expansion is constrained by location: most currently available potential is located in the Amazon, which raises difficulties with environmental licensing and public acceptance. Efforts are being made to develop new approaches and techniques, including run-of-river projects in suitable conditions, as development of dams for large hydro can have an adverse impact on river ecosystems and local communities. It can also encourage road construction, migration and urbanisation, further increasing pressures on native vegetation (Barber et al., 2014). Like all infrastructure projects, hydropower plants are subject to environmental licensing and impact assessment (Section 2). Brazil would benefit from adopting a more integrated and strategic licensing process at river basin level, as well as from a clearer quantification of the impact of hydropower on biodiversity and of associated compensatory measures.

5. Protected areas

The expansion of the protected area system

Protected areas are a cornerstone of biodiversity policy in Brazil. In 2003-08, Brazil accounted for over 70% of the global new terrestrial area placed under environmental protection. The National System of Protected Areas (SNUC), established in 2000, laid the groundwork for this remarkable expansion of official protected areas, or "conservation units" as they are known in the country. It consolidated the pre-existing highly fragmented assortment of federal, state, municipal and private protected areas into one consistent framework. It introduced 12 management categories of protected areas, divided into two groups: strict protection areas, with the primary objective of biodiversity conservation; and sustainable use areas, which permit human settlement and natural resource use in accordance with sustainable management plans. In 2006, the MMA set up the National Register of Protected Areas (CNUC), a database collecting a wide range of biodiversity and management data for each official protected area, although information is often incomplete.

Between 2000 and early 2015, the number and extent of terrestrial protected areas in the SNUC more than doubled. In March 2015, 1 940 protected areas covered 17.2% of Brazil's terrestrial area and inland waters. About two-thirds of the protected area is in the sustainable use categories, reflecting the objective of bridging biodiversity conservation

Recommendations on conservation and sustainable use of biodiversity

Knowledge base and evaluation

- Build on the Information System on Brazilian Biodiversity to compile, consolidate and systematise existing and new biodiversity-related information and make it more accessible for research and policy design and evaluation; ensure that the system is regularly and timely updated.
- Continue to develop satellite-based monitoring systems that detect forest deforestation and degradation and cover all biomes, especially the Cerrado, Caatinga and Pampa, where most vegetation clearing is expected; ensure that the systems generate up-to-date and compatible data series.
- Pursue the Brazilian Natural Capital Initiative; conduct a national ecosystem assessment at the earliest opportunity to improve knowledge of the values of biodiversity and ecosystem services and of the risks associated with their loss; ensure that the values of ecosystem services are integrated in national accounts and in policy design and evaluation.

Policy framework

- Maintain the policy focus on combatting deforestation and clarifying land tenure, and extend it to all the terrestrial biomes and to marine, coastal and inland water ecosystems.
- Streamline the multitude of biodiversity-related plans and programmes with a view to eliminating overlap and duplication of efforts and increasing cost-effectiveness; systematically evaluate the implementation of policies and measures in terms of results, costs and benefits, and revise policies and programmes accordingly.

Forest conservation, restoration and sustainable management

- Strengthen implementation of the Rural Environmental Cadastre (CAR) by providing economic incentives to encourage cadastre enrolment, promote compliance and support sustainable management and restoration of set-aside areas; build on the CAR information system to improve compliance monitoring, landscape planning and policy priority setting.
- Support the development of state-level environmental regularisation programmes and enhance implementation capacity of states and municipalities.
- Consider adjusting the Environmental Reserve Quota system to allow quota exchanges within the same priority areas, in terms of biodiversity value; systematically monitor the functioning of the system and allow for the adjustments necessary to achieve its forest preservation and restoration objectives.
- Scale up support for sustainable forestry and farming practices, including in protected areas, by providing training and technical assistance to rural and traditional communities and small farms and facilitating their access to credit and product markets.
- Speed up the use of concessions for sustainable forest management, including in eligible protected areas, by simplifying procedures and improving capacity of government officials to design and negotiate concession contracts; systematically monitor the areas under concession to ensure compliance with the contract specifications and delivery of the expected environmental and social outcomes.
- Accelerate the development of the proposed National Plan for Native Vegetation Recovery, estimate its costs and identify priority areas (with high biodiversity value) for restoration; identify funding sources and assess the feasibility of extending the existing tax-free infrastructure bonds to restoration investment.

Recommendations on conservation and sustainable use of biodiversity *(cont.)*

- Further encourage the private sector to implement sustainable and traceable value chains that would minimise their impact on biodiversity and ecosystems, including deforestation.
- Adopt a national REDD+ strategy at the earliest opportunity, indicating objectives, actions, institutional arrangements, monitoring mechanisms and the necessary resource allocation.

Payments for ecosystem services (PES)

- Continue discussing the current federal legislation proposal and adopt an overarching federal PES law to provide a framework for PES implementation and improve consistency across state regulations and programmes.
- Put in place a countrywide monitoring system for PES programmes, possibly within the framework of a federal PES law, with a view to verifying their effectiveness in maintaining the ecosystem services that are being paid for.
- Scale up and improve the management of Bolsa Verde and reinforce its link with the Rural Environmental Cadastre; ensure adequate training of beneficiaries to help them meet their conservation commitments.

Mainstreaming biodiversity in sectoral policies

- Re-orient agricultural support to encourage environmental improvement and efficient use of agricultural inputs.
- Reform land taxation to encourage land conservation and gradually remove the tax exemptions on fertilisers and pesticides; use the resulting tax revenue to improve farmers' knowledge of good agricultural practices such as alternative pest control methods; review the pesticide regulations to make licences subject to periodic renewal and intensify efforts to control unauthorised pesticide use.
- Introduce measures to improve sustainability of fishing in marine and inland waters, including fish catch quotas, management plans for overexploited species and the extension of marine protected areas, particularly in coastal and marine areas where fish stocks are at their limits.
- Introduce strategic planning, including environmental assessment procedures, for hydropower development so as to identify where energy capacity could be built with the least environmental impact, take account of cumulative effects and, ultimately, reduce the costs of mitigating the environmental and social impact.
- Clarify the rules for biodiversity and finance compensations in the framework of the licensing process; improve the quantification of the impact of infrastructure projects on biodiversity and ecosystems and the definition of the associated compensatory measures.

and the development of sustainable economic activities in rural areas. In addition, indigenous lands cover about 13% of the territory, mostly in the Amazon region. Brazil thus has already exceeded the Aichi target of protecting at least 17% of its terrestrial and inland water areas by 2020.

Most new protected areas are in the Amazon biome, reflecting government efforts to fight deforestation there. The Amazon Region Protected Areas (ARPA) programme, launched in 2002, has been at the heart of this progress. One of the world's largest tropical forest conservation programmes, it created more than 500 000 km^2 of federal and state-level protected areas in the biome, including along the so-called "deforestation arc" and in areas expecting road infrastructure development. It has also effectively supported the operation of protected areas by investing in basic infrastructure and capacity building. The ARPA programme complemented the PPCDAm in reducing deforestation in the region (Figure 3) and, in turn, greatly contributed to the achievement of Brazil's climate change goals (see also Sections 1 and 4).

Coverage of protected areas also increased in the other biomes, but varies widely, from nearly 27% in the Amazon to less than 3% in the Pampa. More efforts thus are needed in areas outside the Amazon biome if Brazil is to meet its ambitious targets of protecting at least 30% of the Amazon and 17% of the other terrestrial biomes by 2020. The implementation and enforcement of the new Forest Code will contribute to achieving these targets by expanding the areas under protection within private lands (Section 4). Only 1.5% of coastal and marine areas are under environmental protection; the government is scaling up efforts to bring this share to 5% by 2020, still far from the Aichi target of 10%, however.

The institutional framework

The MMA oversees and co-ordinates the SNUC. Executing agencies at each level of government are responsible for implementation. As in many federal countries, a national agency, the Chico Mendes Institute for Biodiversity Conservation (ICMBio), is responsible for overseeing all aspects of federal protected areas. The ICMBio, established in 2007, has helped improve the transparency and effectiveness of the SNUC. The ICMBio operates regional offices that facilitate co-operation with state governments and protected area managers. Yet the large number of protected areas at all levels of government makes effective communication and co-operation challenging. International co-operation and NGOs often play complementary roles and support the planning and operation of protected areas; engagement by the business sector is still limited.

Establishment of protected areas

As in all countries, the majority of lands that are or may be included in protected areas are inhabited and intended for economic activities. In addition, some areas can be important for potential infrastructure and urban development. The SNUC law acknowledges that consideration must be given to competition among environmental, social and economic interests when establishing protected areas. It requires public consultations with local communities, stakeholders and relevant sectoral institutions to be conducted prior to the establishment of protected areas at all levels of government. As in other countries, this process can take some years. To further extend the area under environmental protection, Brazil could promote the establishment of private protected areas, formally recognised by the SNUC, notably in border zones of existing protected areas. The implementation of the Forest Code may encourage landowners to set up protected areas to effectively preserve and manage the set-aside lands (Section 4).

Some SNUC categories, including national parks, are of exclusively public domain. Establishing such a protected area requires private lands within its boundaries to be expropriated and the owners compensated. Partly because of the approach used before 2000, about 70% of federal protected areas, or 7% of their surface, include some land on which there are private property claims (Veríssimo et al., 2011). The expropriation and compensation of private properties in exclusively public protected areas is expected to require considerable financial resources. The resolution of problems related to territorial consolidation and land tenure sometimes exceeds environmental authorities' capacity and responsibility (TCU, 2013).

To help consolidate public protected areas, the 2012 Forest Code introduced an innovative offset mechanism. It will allow landholders that do not meet their forest set-aside obligations to compensate this deficit by buying private property within official protected areas on behalf of the government, thus reducing the burden of territorial consolidation on the public budget. To be operational, the offset mechanism requires the Rural Environmental Cadastre to be fully implemented. Brazil could consider using transitional contractual agreements with owners of lands within protected areas to ensure that their land use does not conflict with conservation objectives until land tenure disputes are resolved.

Effective management of protected areas

Following the remarkable expansion of protected areas over the 2000s, Brazil now faces the challenge of effectively managing them. Management efficiency has improved, especially in the areas supported by the ARPA programme. This is due in part to its result-based approach, the considerable financial resources available to the programme and the requirement that both federal and state governments contribute qualified staff to manage the ARPA areas. However, many protected areas do not yet fully meet their objectives (TCU, 2013; WWF and ICMBio, 2012).

Many protected areas have been operating without a management plan for more than 10 years, even though such plans are required by law. As the management plan is a condition for sustainable public use (such as tourism, environmental education and sustainable logging) and local community resource use (e.g. harvesting, fishing, farming), its absence reduces socio-economic development opportunities in the longer term and could hinder effective control over resource use in the area. Most federal protected areas have a management committee, composed of government officials and representatives of civil society and the private sector. Many committees still have to define their operating rules to ensure effective stakeholder participation and resolve and prevent conflicts.

Several official protected areas and indigenous lands can be integrated into a so-called mosaic, whose aim is to facilitate co-ordination among managers and achieve economies of scale, for example in monitoring, enforcement and the promotion of sustainable production and commercialisation of natural resources. The MMA has approved 14 mosaics, but there is no evidence that they have helped improve management effectiveness.

Demonstrating how protected areas can contribute to environmental conservation and sustainable development is critical for securing political and societal support and mobilising resources. For example, Brazil's protected areas significantly contribute to the conservation and provision of water resources and have high economic potential (Medeiros and Young, 2011). The ICMBio has monitored coral reefs in marine protected areas since 2002 and launched *in situ* monitoring programmes in terrestrial federal protected areas in 2012. Most protected areas, however, struggle to monitor the state and trends of biodiversity and socio-economic development outcomes. Further encouraging partnerships with civil society, research and business organisations could help develop monitoring in areas not supported by ICMBio programmes.

Human resources

A shortage of human resources is among the main causes of the generally weak management performance. Managing the vast territory covered by the SNUC requires numerous well-trained staff members. There is evidence that current staff is insufficient:

estimates indicate that in the late 2000s, staff per square kilometre of protected area was lower than in other Latin American countries (Medeiros and Young, 2011). Government estimates suggest that operating federal and state protected areas needs at least 19 000 additional workers, three-quarters of them for field activities.

Attracting staff for long periods has proved difficult in some areas, notably in remote regions of the Amazon, where working and living conditions are demanding. Strict employment regulations for the public sector are an additional obstacle. While generally highly motivated and committed, many managers and staff are not adequately trained for day-to-day management activities, although several training programmes have helped improve capacity in recent years. Realising the full environmental, social and economic potential of protected areas requires additional skills and expertise, including in financial and project management. The lack of these skills, combined with red tape, has sometimes resulted in financial resource being unspent. Experience from other sectoral programmes (e.g. for health care) can help identify strategies for attracting qualified staff for managing remote protected areas.

Financial resources

The budget of the ICMBio, the main source of SNUC finance, grew by 57% between 2008 and 2014. Overall, however, the increase in resources is not proportional to the expansion of the areas under environmental protection, resulting in a considerable financial gap – a situation common to most Latin American countries (Bovarnick et al., 2010). The operation of the SNUC heavily relies on federal and state budgets, which makes funding vulnerable to external factors and political negotiations. Resources are largely used to cover staff and other operational costs, while investment in equipment and infrastructure is relatively modest. Other sources of finance include environmental compensation, international development co-operation, private donations and revenue from tourism and sustainable forestry, although the latter are still limited.

Brazil pioneered the use of fiscal transfers as an incentive for biodiversity conservation in protected areas. About half the states redistribute a share of the revenue from the state-level value added tax (ICMS) on the basis of environmental criteria under a mechanism called Ecological ICMS. The main parameter is the extension and type of protected areas and indigenous lands. In practice, the Ecological ICMS has been used to compensate municipalities for the opportunity cost of maintaining part of their territory under nature protection. While the revenue is not necessarily used to finance expenditure in protected areas, the mechanism has helped increase the number and size of protected areas in Brazil. The impact on biodiversity conservation is not clear, however (May et al., 2012). Only one state makes the revenue transfers conditional on quality indicators of protected area status and on municipal resources dedicated to conservation actions. This mechanism is potentially more effective in encouraging good protected area management, but entails additional cost, including for periodic inspection of the areas.

Brazil has attracted substantial international finance for protected areas, especially through the ARPA programme. Germany is the largest donor to the programme. While international co-operation accounts for a limited share of the SNUC budget, it has helped leverage domestic finance and improve resource use effectiveness. However, funding from international co-operation is likely to gradually decline in the years to come. The MMA and ICMBio envisage the shift of the ARPA programme from donation based to government financed over 25 years and has set up a transition fund for the purpose. This model could be extended to the entire SNUC. Brazil would benefit from developing a comprehensive financial strategy for the SNUC and for biodiversity policy more generally. Such a strategy should consider alternative funding sources, including PES programmes, concessions for tourism services and sustainable forest management (Section 4).

Promoting public visitation

There is room to better integrate protected areas into Brazil's wider tourism strategy. Public visitation for tourism, recreation and environmental education purposes is one of the most relevant ways to enhance social and economic benefits and increase financial sustainability of, and public support for, protected areas. While expanding, public visitation is still in its infancy. The number of annual visits has increased steadily since 2006. They are largely concentrated in few major national parks where government programmes such as Tourism in the Parks and private investment allowed for developing infrastructure and provision of tourism services. It is estimated that roughly two-thirds of protected areas received visitors in 2012, often in limited numbers, although not all protected areas track and report the number of visitors. However, less than 20% of the areas generated revenue from access fees and other public visitation charges (Semeia, 2012).

Few protected areas engaged in partnerships with private businesses and non-profit organisations to manage visitation services. This is mainly due to regulatory constraints and red tape, the lack of adequate management plans, and limited resources and capacity on the part of the park management. Public-private partnerships (PPPs), including concessions, can help strengthen management capacity and increase investment. In 2011, the MMA and the Ministry of Planning, Budget and Management agreed to launch pilot PPP and concession agreements in 10 national parks with high tourism potential. Such agreements could be extended to the full management of protected areas, including environmental conservation activities. This would allow the public authorities to shift their attention from direct management to oversight of protected areas, which is less resource intensive.

Extractive and sustainable development reserves

Extractive and sustainable development reserves are inhabited by small traditional communities, which depend on natural resources (e.g. fish, wood, nuts, oils, rubber) for their livelihoods. Effective management of these areas requires offering such communities meaningful opportunities to sustainably use natural resources. Although traditional communities generally have good knowledge of the use of natural resources, they often lack sufficient expertise for sustainable farming, forestry and fishing, as well as access to markets. Programmes such as Bolsa Floresta and Bolsa Verde (Section 4) and the minimum price policy for socio-biodiversity products – a joint programme of the MMA and the ministries for agrarian and social development – aim to address these issues. As benefiting from such programmes tends to be easier in extractive and sustainable development reserves, some communities have requested this status for the area they live and work in.

In addition to viable sources of livelihood, much of the population living in extractive reserves needs better access to social services such as education, health and sanitation. Overall, this mix of issues goes beyond the responsibilities of the MMA and other environmental authorities and calls for stronger intersectoral co-ordination.

Recommendations on protected areas

Expansion and consolidation of the national system of protected areas

- Strengthen inter-institutional co-operation to ease the resolution of land tenure issues within existing or proposed new protected areas and improve social service provision to communities living in sustainable use reserves.
- Further expand the area under environmental protection to fully achieve the national 2020 targets and international commitments (including through official protected areas, indigenous lands and set-aside areas required by the Forest Code); prioritise areas with high biodiversity values and where pressures from infrastructure development, urbanisation and agriculture are the highest; expand the coverage of protected areas in marine and coastal zones to achieve the Aichi target.
- Develop a strategy for the territorial consolidation of protected areas; encourage the use of financial and land offset mechanisms provided in the protected area legislation and in the Forest Code once the Rural Environmental Cadastre is fully operational; and explore the use of transitional contractual agreements with landowners within protected areas to ensure compatible land use until property rights are clarified.

Management of protected areas

- Develop a comprehensive financial strategy for the National System of Protected Areas (SNUC), with a view to reducing dependency on the public budget and on international finance; explore alternative funding sources, including payments for ecosystem services, access fees, branding and sale of merchandise, and benefits generated from genetic resources.
- Strengthen efforts to develop the management plans of protected areas and review their implementation; ensure that the plans set clear priorities, targets and progress indicators.
- Develop targeted capacity building and skill development programmes for protected area managers and staff, with a view to enhancing management effectiveness; promote networks of protected area managers and exchange of experiences and best practices.
- Continue to periodically assess protected area management effectiveness and efficiency; further encourage protected area managers to provide accurate and timely information to the National Register of Protected Areas (CNUC), and systematically review this information to derive system-level recommendations.
- Develop standard biodiversity monitoring methods with a view to generating the information needed to assess the environmental effectiveness of protected areas; further expand federal monitoring programmes.
- Integrate protected areas into national and state tourism strategies and identify areas with high tourism potential; develop tourism products linked to protected areas.
- Extend the use of concessions and other public-private partnerships for public visitation and tourism in protected areas; simplify procedures and improve capacity of government officials and protected area managers to design and negotiate contracts; implement pilot programmes to test and develop new management models.
- Consider including regular visits to protected areas in educational programmes of schoolchildren.

Notes

1. A biome is a large naturally occurring community of flora and fauna occupying a geographic region.
2. The Amazônia Legal super-region covers an area larger than the Amazon biome, encompassing both the Amazonian forest (about 4.1 million km^2) and transitional vegetation (1 million km^2); the Amazon biome covers only the forest area. Amazônia Legal takes in the states of Amazonas, Pará, Acre, Roraima, Rondônia, Amapá and Tocantins, and part of Mato Grosso and Maranhão.
3. *Quilombolas* are inhabitants of *quilombos*, traditional communities of escaped slaves who fled inland under colonisation.
4. In full, the 2010 Nagoya Protocol on Access to Genetic Resources and the Fair and Equitable Sharing of Benefits Arising from their Utilization. It is a protocol to the Convention on Biological Diversity.

References

ABDi (2012), *Relatório de Acompanhamento Setorial: Competitividade do Setor de Bens e Serviços Ambientais [Sectoral Monitoring Report: Competitiveness of the Environmental Goods and Services Sector]*, Brazilian Agency for Industrial Development, Brasília, *www3.eco.unicamp.br/neit/images/stories/arquivos/Relatorios_NEIT/Bens-e-Servcos-Ambientais-Setembro-de-2012.pdf*.

ABEMA (2013), *Novas propostas para o licenciamento ambiental no Brasil [New proposals for environmental licensing in Brazil]*, Brazilian Association of State Environment Authorities, Brasília.

AHK (2009), *Green Technologies in Brazil. An Overview of the Sustainability Market*, AHK German Chamber of Industry and Commerce in Brazil and Roland Berger Strategy Consultants, São Paulo, *www.renewablesb2b.com/data/ahk_brazil/publications/files/GreenTechStudy_AHK_RB.pdf*.

ANA (2013), *Conjuntura dos Recursos Hídricos no Brasil [State of Water Resources in Brazil]*, National Water Agency, Brasília, *http://conjuntura.ana.gov.br/docs/conj2013_rel.pdf*.

Barber et al. (2014), "Roads, deforestation, and the mitigating effect of protected areas in the Amazon", *Biological Conservation*, Vol. 177, pp. 203-209.

BNEF (2015), *Global Trends in Renewable Energy Investment 2015*, Bloomberg New Energy Finance and Frankfurt School-UNEP Centre, Frankfurt am Main, *http://apps.unep.org/publications/pmtdocuments/-Global_trends_in_renewable_energy_investment_2015-201515028nefvisual8-mediumres.pdf.pdf*.

Börner, J. et al. (2013), *Promoting Forest Stewardship in the Bolsa Floresta Programme: Local Livelihood Strategies and Preliminary Impacts*, Center for International Forestry Research, Rio de Janeiro, Fundação Amazonas Sustentável, Manaus, and Zentrum für Entwicklungsforschung, Bonn, *http://fas-amazonas.org/versao/2012/wordpress/wp-content/uploads/2014/02/BF_report_ENG_web.pdf*.

Bovarnick, A. et al. (2010), *Financial Sustainability of Protected Areas in Latin America and the Caribbean: Investment Policy Guidance*, United Nations Development Programme and The Nature Conservancy, *www.undp.org/content/dam/aplaws/publication/en/publications/environment-energy/www-ee-library/biodiversity/financial-sustainability-of-protected-areas-in-latin-america-and-the-caribbean/financial_sus_pa_lac.pdf*.

CEPAL, GIZ e IPEA (2011), *Avaliação do Plano de Ação para a Prevenção e Controle do Desmatamento na Amazônia Legal – PPCDAm: 2007-10 [Evaluation of the Action Plan for Prevention and Control of Deforestation in the Legal Amazon]*, United Nations Economic Commission for Latin America and the Caribbean, Brasília, Institute for Applied Economic Research, Brasília, and Deutche Gesellschaft für International Zusammenarbeit (GIZ) GMbH, Bonn, *www.cepal.org/dmaah/publicaciones/sinsigla/xml/7/45887/IPEA_GIZ_Cepal_2011_Avaliacao_PPCDAm_2007-2011_web.pdf*.

CGU (2014), "Relatório de Acompanhamento n° 07/2014 Programa Bolsa Verde" [Follow-up report No. 07/2014 of the Green Grant Programme], Comptroller General of the Union, Brasília.

Frischtak (2011), "Vantagens Comparativas, Inovação e Economia Verde" [Comparative Advantages, Innovation and Green Economy], paper prepared for the BNDES National Forum, 21 September 2011. *www.bndes.gov.br/SiteBNDES/export/sites/default/bndes_pt/Galerias/Arquivos/empresa/download/inovacao_paper_05.pdf*.

IBGE (2014), *Perfil dos Municípios Brasileiros 2013 [Profile of Brazilian Municipalities 2013]*, Brazilian Institute of Geography and Statistics, Rio de Janeiro.

IBGE (2013), *Indicadores de Desenvolvimento Sustentável [Sustainable Development Indicators]* (database), Brazilian Institute of Geography and Statistics, Rio de Janeiro (accessed March 2015).

May, P. et al. (2012), "The 'Ecological' Value Added Tax (ICMS-Ecológico) in Brazil and its effectiveness in State biodiversity conservation: a comparative analysis", paper presented at the 12th Biennial Conference of the International Society for Ecological Economics, Rio de Janeiro.

MCid (2014), "Sistema Nacional de Informações sobre Saneamento: Diagnóstico dos Serviços de Água e Esgotos – 2013" [National Sanitation Information System: Diagnosis of Water and Sewerage Services – 2013], Ministry of Cities, Brasília, *www.snis.gov.br* (accessed February 2015).

Medeiros, R. and C. Young (2011), *Contribuição das Unidades de Conservação Brasileiras para a Economia Nacional: Relatório Final [Contribution of Brazilian Protected Areas to the National Economy: Final Report]*, UNEP-WCMC, Brasília.

MMA (2015), *Fifth National Report to the Convention on Biological Diversity*, Ministry of the Environment, Brasília, *www.cbd.int/doc/world/br/br-nr-05-en.pdf*.

MMA (2010), *Fourth National Report to the Convention on Biological Diversity*, Ministry of the Environment, Brasília.

Norman, M. et al. (2014), "Climate Finance Thematic Briefing: REDD+ Finance", Climate Finance Fundamentals 5, December, Overseas Development Institute, London and Heinrich Böll Stiftung North America, Washington, DC, *www.odi.org/sites/odi.org.uk/files/odi-assets/publications-opinion-files/9330.pdf*.

OECD (2013), *Agricultural Policy Monitoring and Evaluation*, OECD Publishing, Paris, *http://dx.doi.org/10.1787/agr_pol-2013-en*.

OECD (2015a), *Water Resources Governance in Brazil*, OECD Studies on Water, OECD Publishing, Paris, *http://dx.doi.org/10.1787/9789264238121-en*.

OECD (2015b), *OECD Economic Surveys: Brazil*, OECD Publishing, Paris, *http://dx.doi.org/10.1787.19390820*.

OECD (2015c), *Taxing Energy Use 2015: OECD and Selected Partner Economies*, OECD Publishing, Paris, *http://dx.doi.org/10.1787/9789264232334-en*.

Semeia (2012), *Análise 2012 – Uso Público e Parcerias para Conservação e Desenvolvimento [Analysis 2012: Public Use and Partnerships for Conservation and Development]*, Instituto Semeia, São Paulo.

Senado Federal (2015), *Portal Orçamento [Budget portal]* (database). *www12.senado.gov.br/orcamento/loa* (Accessed April 2015).

Soares-Filho, B. et al. (2014), "Cracking Brazil's Forest Code", *Science*, Vol. 344, No. 6182, pp. 363-364.

TCU (2013), *Relatório de Auditoria Operacional: Governança das Unidades de Conservação do Bioma Amazônia [Operational Audit Report: Governance of the Amazon Biome Protected Areas]*, Federal Court of Accounts, *http://portal2.tcu.gov.br/portal/pls/portal/docs/2642553.PDF*.

Veríssimo, A. et al. (eds) (2011), *Protected Areas in the Brazilian Amazon: Challenges and Opportunities*, Imazon, Belém; Socioenvironmental Institute, São Paulo, *www.socioambiental.org/banco_imagens/pdfs/10381.pdf*.

WWF and ICMBIO (2012), *Avaliação comparada das aplicações do método Rappam nas unidades de conservação federais, nos ciclos 2005-06 e 2010 [Comparative assessment based on the Rappam method in federal conservation units in cycles 2005-06 and 2010]*, World Wide Fund Brazil and Chico Mendes Institute for Biodiversity Conservation, Brasília. *www.icmbio.gov.br/portal/images/stories/comunicacao/downloads/relatrio%20rappam%202005%20x%202010%20-%20verso%20integral.pdf*.

PART I

Progress towards sustainable development

PART I

Chapter 1

Key environmental trends

This chapter provides a snapshot of key environmental trends in Brazil, highlighting some of the main achievements and remaining challenges on the path towards sustainable development and a greener economy. It reviews progress against national policy goals and international commitments, focusing on the period since 2000. Beginning with an overview of key socio-economic developments, the chapter presents Brazil's progress in moving towards i) an energy-efficient and low-carbon economy; ii) resource efficiency in material consumption, waste management and agro-chemical use; and iii) sustainable management of the natural asset base, including forests, biodiversity and water resources.

The statistical data for Israel are supplied by and under the responsibility of the relevant Israeli authorities. The use of such data by the OECD is without prejudice to the status of the Golan Heights, East Jerusalem and Israeli settlements in the West Bank under the terms of international law.

1. Introduction

Brazil's environmental performance must be seen in the context of its size, its vast natural wealth and its economic and social development since the early 2000s. The world's fifth largest country, by both land area and population, it possesses enormous biological diversity and is exceptionally rich in fertile soil, forests, water, minerals and fossil energy resources. Economic growth was strong throughout the decade to 2012 and Brazil achieved remarkable progress with respect to social development and inclusion. However, expanding economic activity, population growth and rising living standards are increasing the need for energy, food, minerals and other resources, amplifying environmental pressures in both rural and urban areas.

This chapter provides a snapshot of Brazil's main environmental achievements as well as remaining challenges on the path towards sustainable development and a greener economy. Based on indicators from national and international sources, the chapter reviews progress against national policy goals as well as international commitments and targets, focusing on the period since 2000. To the extent possible, it compares the state of the environment and key environmental trends with those of OECD member countries and the other emerging economies in the BRIICS group (Brazil, Russia, India, Indonesia, China and South Africa). The chapter provides a baseline for the rest of the report, which examines the effectiveness of Brazil's environmental policies in tackling key challenges and in using environmental objectives to generate economic and social opportunities.

2. Key economic and social developments

2.1. Economic performance

Brazil is the world's seventh largest economy, and South America's largest. It enjoyed strong economic growth over most of the 2000s, with average annual GDP growth well above the OECD average, though below the economic performance of other BRIICS economies (Figure 1.1; also see Basic Statistics). Per capita income increased by around 30% between 2000 and 2013, allowing about 40 million Brazilians to enter the middle class. The share of the population living in poverty (on less than USD 2 per day) fell from 19% in 2002 to less than 7% in 2012. However, per capita income remained at about 40% of the average income in OECD countries in 2013 (Figure 1.1), and poverty in Brazil is higher than in some other Latin American countries. Strong economic growth has been largely driven by strong domestic demand, as well as a favourable external environment (OECD, 2013a; OECD, 2015a; World Bank, 2015).

While the economy weathered the 2009 global financial crisis well, growth began decelerating in 2012 and reached almost zero in 2014. Growth is expected to remain modest in coming years due to tightening monetary and fiscal policies, weaker external demand and such persistent barriers to growth as infrastructure bottlenecks, low investment, high tax and administrative burdens (known as the "Brazil cost"), trade protection and low domestic competition, as well as a tight labour market and skills shortages (OECD, 2013a;

Figure 1.1. **Brazil's per capita income reached higher levels than in most BRIICS countries**

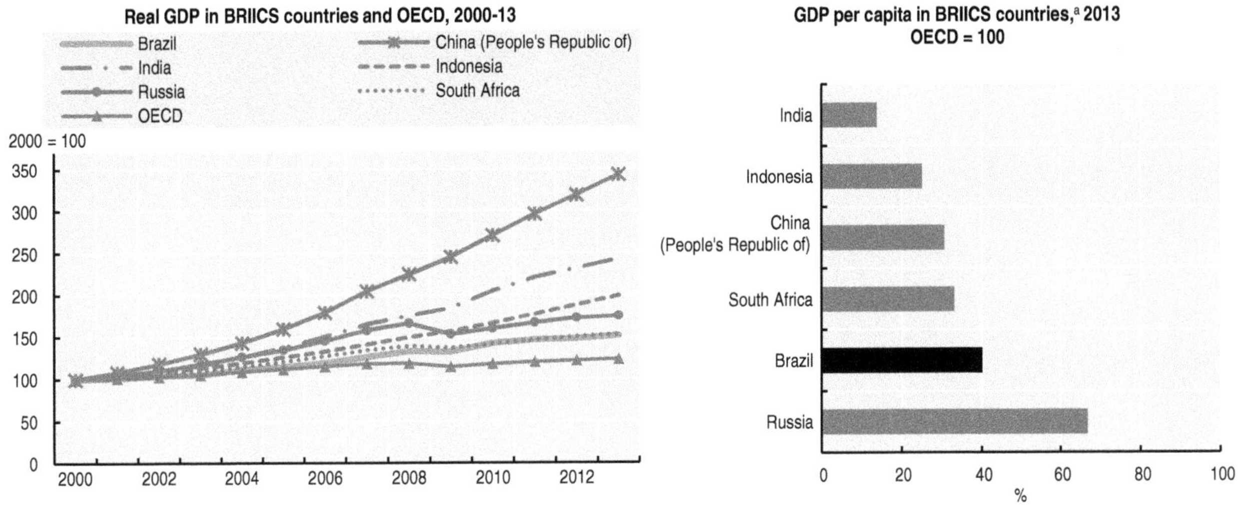

a) GDP per capita at current purchasing power parities. Data include estimates.

Source: OECD (2015), "OECD Economic Outlook No. 96", *OECD Economic Outlook: Statistics and Projections* (database); OECD (2015), *OECD National Accounts* (database).

StatLink http://dx.doi.org/10.1787/888933279350

OECD, 2015b; World Bank, 2011). The water crisis in south-eastern Brazil (Section 5.2) and the energy shortages resulting from it are further constraining the picking up of the economy.

Brazil undertook major economic reforms in the 1990s and has since enjoyed stable macroeconomic conditions. However, its well-earned reputation for solid macroeconomic and fiscal policies has weakened, as both the fiscal deficit and public debt showed significant increases in 2013 and 2014, while inflation remained elevated (OECD, 2015b; IMF, 2014). In 2013, tax revenue and government expenditure stood at levels slightly below the respective OECD averages (see Basic Statistics). Environmental taxes make up a minor share of total tax revenue, while fiscal revenue from hydrocarbons and mining was 2.4% of GDP in 2013 (OECD, 2015c) (Chapter 3).

Brazil's labour market performance has been strong. According to national statistics, the unemployment rate fell to a record low of 5.2% in 2013, down from 10.5% in 2004 (Figure 1.2). Labour market informality has receded considerably. At the same time, real wages increased by almost 60% between 2004 and 2013 (Figure 1.2). The growth in real wages accelerated after 2010, reflecting tight labour market conditions and skills shortages (OECD, 2013a). However, unemployment has been on the rise since early 2015 (OECD, 2015b).

2.2. Structure of the economy and trade

Brazil has a diversified economy and a broad industrial base, albeit one characterised by low productivity and competitiveness (OECD, 2015b). The economic structure has shifted towards stronger reliance on services in recent decades while the share of the primary sector and industry in value added has declined. Nevertheless, the primary sector accounts for a larger share of GDP than in OECD countries (see Basic Statistics) and remains a mainstay of the economy. Brazil ranks among the world's five largest agricultural producers and exporters (Section 4.3), is a major player in global mining production (including iron ore, copper, bauxite and gold manganese) and will be among the world's top

Figure 1.2. **Unemployment decreased while labour income increased**

Unemployment rates and average annual wages, 2004-13

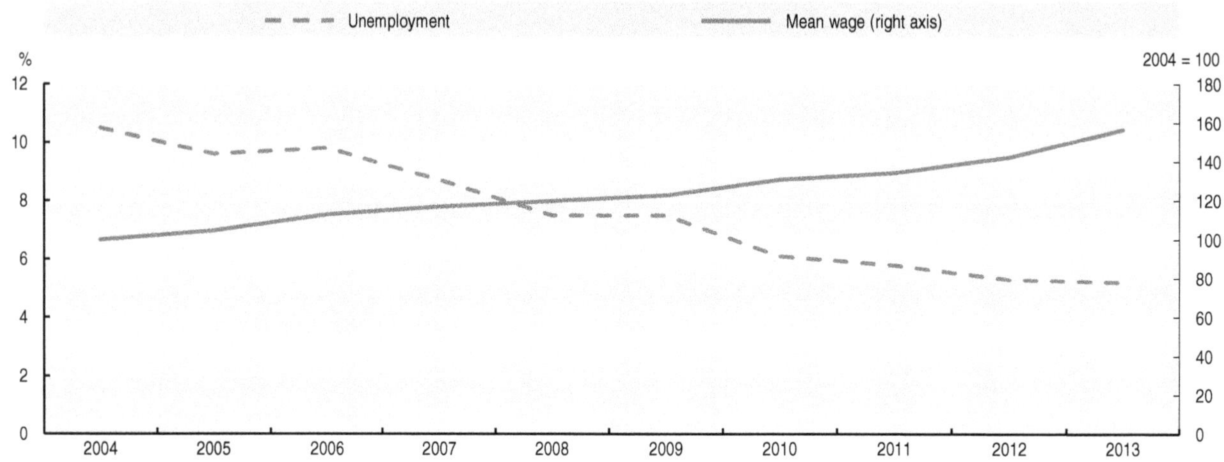

Note: Data are based on national surveys which cover persons aged of 10 years and over.
Source: IBGE (2014), *Pesquisa Mensal de Emprego.*

StatLink http://dx.doi.org/10.1787/888933279362

oil producers when large oil and gas reserves discovered in 2006 are developed over the next two decades (IBRAM, 2012; IEA, 2013). Agriculture and mining registered higher production, employment and export growth than knowledge-intensive sectors over the 2000s (IPEA, 2012).

Primary products dominate the export portfolio, accounting for roughly two-thirds of total exports in 2013 (WTO, 2014; also see Basic Statistics). While the trade volume almost quadrupled over the past decade, exports and imports together amount to only about 25% of GDP, significantly lower than in similar sized countries. Brazil is also less integrated into international value chains and has high tariff protection levels (WTO, 2014).

2.3. Regional disparities and inequality

Economic activity in Brazil is geographically highly concentrated. Most industry is located in the South-east region and, to a lesser extent, the South, while farming and other natural-resource-based activities prevail in the North, North-east and Centre-West regions.[1] The South and South-east enjoy significantly higher income (Figure 1.3) and perform better in key socio-economic indicators. Inequality among regions has been declining since 2000, mainly due to above-average growth rates in areas specialised in agriculture and mining; however, the position of the most lagging areas (most of which are located in the North-east) improved only marginally (OECD, 2013b).

Brazil is the only BRIICS economy to have experienced a decline in income inequality. As measured by the Gini coefficient, inequality fell from 58.6 to 52.7 over 2002-12, although it remains one of the highest levels in the world (World Bank, 2015; also see Basic Statistics). The fall in poverty and inequality is attributed to changes in labour income as well as direct income redistribution, including a large-scale conditional cash transfer programme, Bolsa Família (Box 3.1) (OECD, 2013a; World Bank, 2011).

Figure 1.3. **Per capita income varies widely across Brazilian states**

GDP per capita by state and region, 2000 and 2011

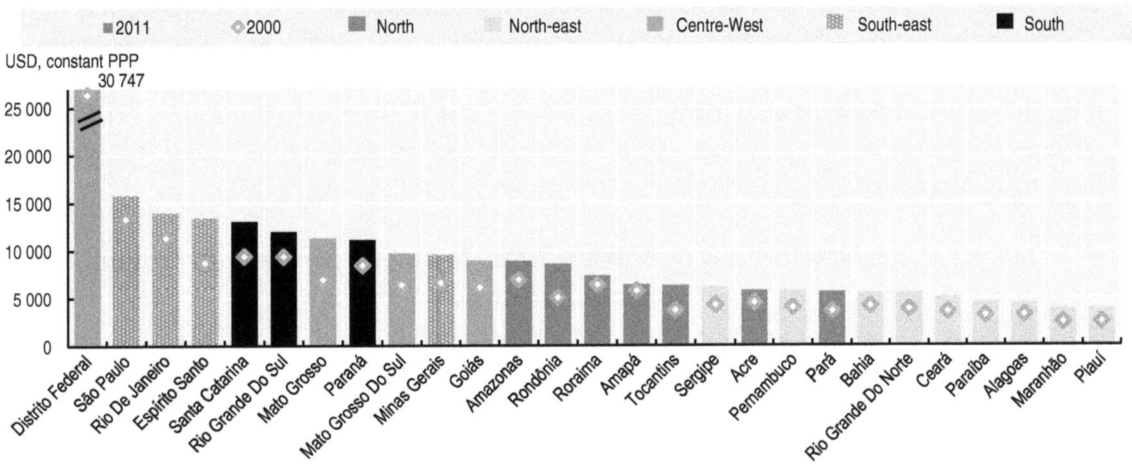

Source: OECD (2015), "Large regions, TL2: Regional accounts", *OECD Regional Statistics* (database).

StatLink http://dx.doi.org/10.1787/888933279370

2.4. Population, urbanisation and quality of life

The population is growing rapidly (see Basic Statistics), and it is projected to peak at about 230 million inhabitants by 2040 (IBGE, 2014). The country's size results in relatively low average population density, but the population is highly concentrated along the coast. Still, the proportion of the population living in predominantly rural areas is relatively high by OECD standards (see Basic Statistics). Almost 5 million Brazilians live in traditional or indigenous communities that practice extractive activities of non-timber forest products, small-scale agriculture, hunting or fishing (Fundaj, 2014).

Even though the process of urbanisation has been slower than in OECD or other BRIICS economies, most cities are experiencing increasing environmental pressures. These include traffic congestion, air pollution, waste volumes that exceed the capacity for adequate treatment and disposal, and polluted water sources due to insufficient sanitation and wastewater treatment infrastructure. Housing remains a major challenge: some 11 million Brazilians live in *favelas* (IBGE, 2011), informal urban settlements characterised by low public service delivery and high crime. Public safety remains a problem despite improvement such as progress in reducing armed violence.[2]

Access to and quality of key public services such as education and health have improved. Access to primary education is almost universal and enrolment rates for secondary and tertiary education have been increasing. Educational outcome indicators (as measured by the Programme for International Student Assessment, PISA) have also improved, especially among the young and people from low-income backgrounds (OECD, 2013a; OECD, 2013c). However, in 2012, only 13% of the working population had competed tertiary education; human capital still significantly lags behind OECD standards, which constrains growth prospects. Health services have become more accessible to poor households and improved in quality, as reflected in rising life expectancy, which remains nonetheless below the OECD average (see Basic Statistics). Regional disparities with respect to education and health services remain large.

Overall, Brazil is making progress in improving quality of life. Brazilians seem to be slightly more satisfied with their quality of life than the average person in the OECD, according to the OECD Better Life Index[3] (OECD, 2013c). In addition to a relatively low level of disposable income, education, safety and housing present the greatest constraints to life quality for much of the population (Figure 1.4). Brazilians are proud of their country's natural wealth, and awareness and concern about environmental pressures are increasing (MMA, 2012a). Deforestation, water and air pollution and waste generation and treatment are considered the most pressing environmental problems (Figure 2.3).

Figure 1.4. **Life satisfaction in Brazil is high, but some constraints remain**

OECD Better Life Index, 2013

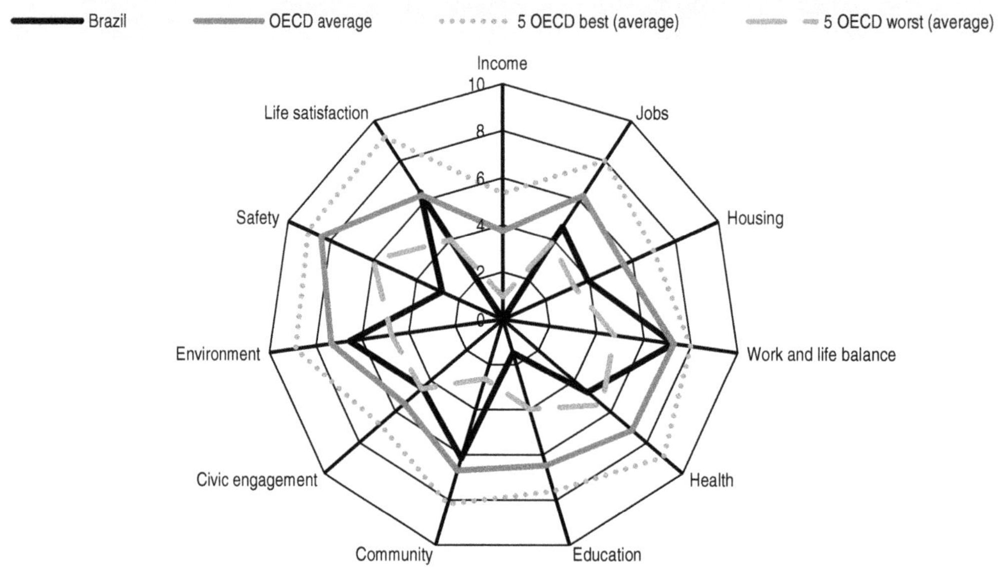

Note: Each well-being dimension is measured by one to three indicators from the OECD Better Life Index data set. Indicators are averaged with equal weights and then normalised to express all values in a range from 0 (worst) to 10 (best).
Source: OECD (2013), "Better Life Index: Better Life Index 2013", *OECD Social and Welfare Statistics* (database).

StatLink http://dx.doi.org/10.1787/888933279388

3. Transition to an energy-efficient and low-carbon economy

3.1. Energy use in Brazil

Energy mix

Brazil has a low-carbon energy mix. The use of renewable energy sources has increased steadily to reach 41% of total primary energy supply (TPES) in 2012 (Figure 1.5). This is one of the world's highest shares, more than four times the OECD average (see Annex 1.A and Basic Statistics). Renewables account for 83% of electricity generation, far above the OECD average of 21% (IEA, 2014a). Iceland and Norway are the only OECD countries that source more power from renewables (Annex 1.A). Hydropower for electricity generation and biofuels for industrial and transport uses are the main renewable sources. Brazil has encouraged the development of large-scale sugar cane ethanol production and the use of ethanol to power road vehicles since the 1970s (Chapter 3). As a result, biofuels accounted for 17% of fuels used in road transport in 2012, by far the highest share in the world and well above the OECD average of 4% (IEA, 2014a; also see Annex 1.A). Other renewables play a minor but growing role. Power generation from wind turbines increased

Figure 1.5. **Renewables make up an increasingly large share of the energy supply**

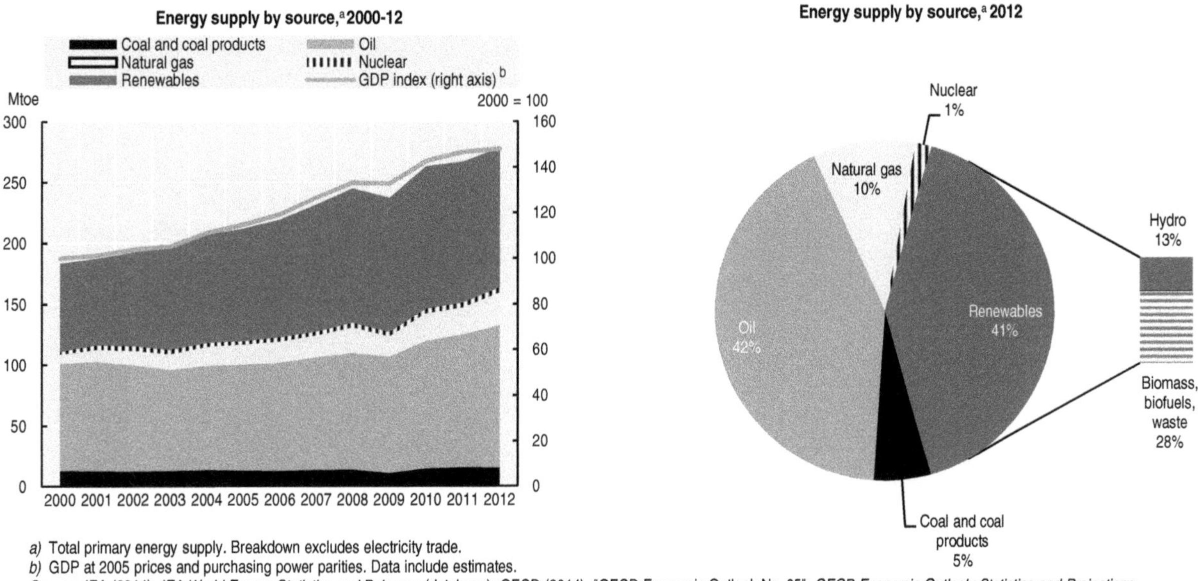

a) Total primary energy supply. Breakdown excludes electricity trade.
b) GDP at 2005 prices and purchasing power parities. Data include estimates.
Source: IEA (2014), *IEA World Energy Statistics and Balances* (database); OECD (2014), "OECD Economic Outlook No. 95", *OECD Economic Outlook: Statistics and Projections* (database).

StatLink http://dx.doi.org/10.1787/888933279391

by more than 400% over 2009-12; solar installations are also widespread, mainly in decentralised applications (IEA, 2013).

The use of petroleum products, mainly in road transport, has increased to reach more than 40% of TPES in 2012. Brazil imports a significant share of its petroleum supply, but exploitation of pre-salt reserves discovered in 2006 could triple oil production (IEA, 2013).[4] Other fossil fuels and nuclear energy play minor roles (Figure 1.5).

Energy consumption and intensity

Strong economic growth and the rise of a middle class led to a rapid increase in energy use: both total final consumption and TPES increased by about 50% between 2000 and 2012 (IEA, 2014a). More than half of the demand increase occurred in industry and transport, the sectors that are the biggest energy consumers in absolute terms (Figure 1.6). The rise in transport energy demand came almost exclusively from road transport, reflecting a rapid increase in the vehicle fleet (ANFEVA, 2015).

As the increase in energy use occurred at the same pace as GDP growth, the energy intensity of the economy (TPES per unit of GDP) remained fairly stable. Brazil's energy intensity is lower than the OECD average and significantly below that of the other BRIICS, mainly because of the relatively small amount of energy used for heating and cooling and the large share of hydropower in the energy supply.[5] Per capita energy demand increased by about 31% over 2000-12 but is still about one third of the OECD average, due in part to the remaining income gap (see Annex 1.A and Basic Statistics).

3.2. Greenhouse gas (GHG) emissions

GHG emission profile

In 2010, Brazil was the world's sixth-largest emitter of greenhouse gases (behind China, the United States, India, Russia and Indonesia), contributing 3.2% of global GHG

Figure 1.6. **Energy consumption in transport and industry has been rising rapidly**

Total final energy consumption by sector, 2000-12 **Total final energy consumption by sector, 2012**

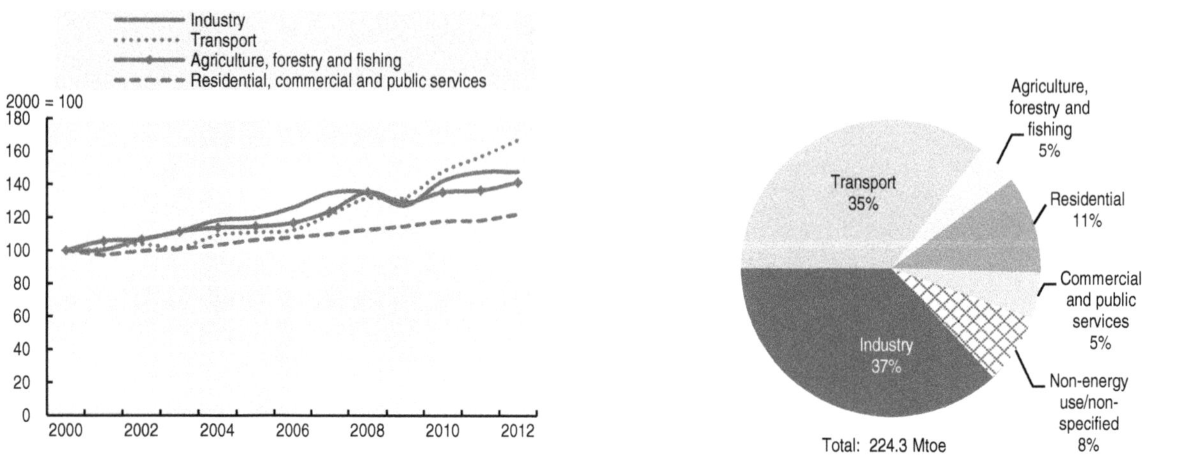

Source: IEA (2014), *IEA World Energy Statistics and Balances* (database).

StatLink http://dx.doi.org/10.1787/888933279401

emissions (IEA, 2014b). Two features distinguish its emission profile from those of most OECD or BRIICS economies. First, the large share of renewables results in relatively low emissions in the energy sector, which accounts for the bulk of GHG emissions in most OECD countries. Second, land use, land-use change and forestry (LULUCF),[6] mainly deforestation, has been a key driver of GHG emissions in Brazil. According to national estimates, 60% of net emissions stemmed from LULUCF in the first half of the 2000s (MCTI, 2014a). The IEA estimated that, in 2010, LULUCF (excluding removals) still accounted for about 35%, a share second only to that of Indonesia (IEA, 2014b; Figure 1.7).[7]

Brazil's total GHG emissions declined by 43% between 2000 and 2012, thanks to a steady decline in deforestation and associated emissions since the mid-2000s (Figure 1.7; Section 5.1). However, emissions are projected to increase. GHG emissions from sectors other than LULUCF rose steadily, by about 35% overall, between 2000 and 2012. The trend was particularly pronounced in energy-related emissions (+49%), mainly as a result of fossil fuel combustion in industry and road transport. Agricultural emissions also grew substantially (+28%). By 2012, energy and agriculture had replaced land use as the primary source of emissions, accounting for 37% of total emissions each, followed by LULUCF (15%), industrial processes (7%) and waste management (4%) (MCTI, 2014a).

In 2010, Brazil committed itself to limit emissions by between 36.1% and 38.9% compared to a business-as-usual (BAU) scenario by 2020.[8] This sets a ceiling of roughly 2 billion tonnes of CO_2 equivalents (tCO_2eq), up from about 1.2 billion tCO_2eq in 2012 (Figure 1.7). As almost half of future emissions were projected to stem from LULUCF, success in reducing deforestation puts Brazil in a good position to meet the target. However, the latest estimates suggest that both LULUCF and total emissions grew by about 8% from 2012 to 2013 (SEEG, 2014),[9] which may make reaching the target more challenging than expected.

Emission intensities

Despite a decline since the mid-2000s, Brazil's GHG emission intensity (GHG emissions, excluding LULUCF, per unit of GDP) remained in line with the OECD average in 2012 (see

Figure 1.7. **GHG emissions from deforestation declined, but emissions are rising in other sectors**

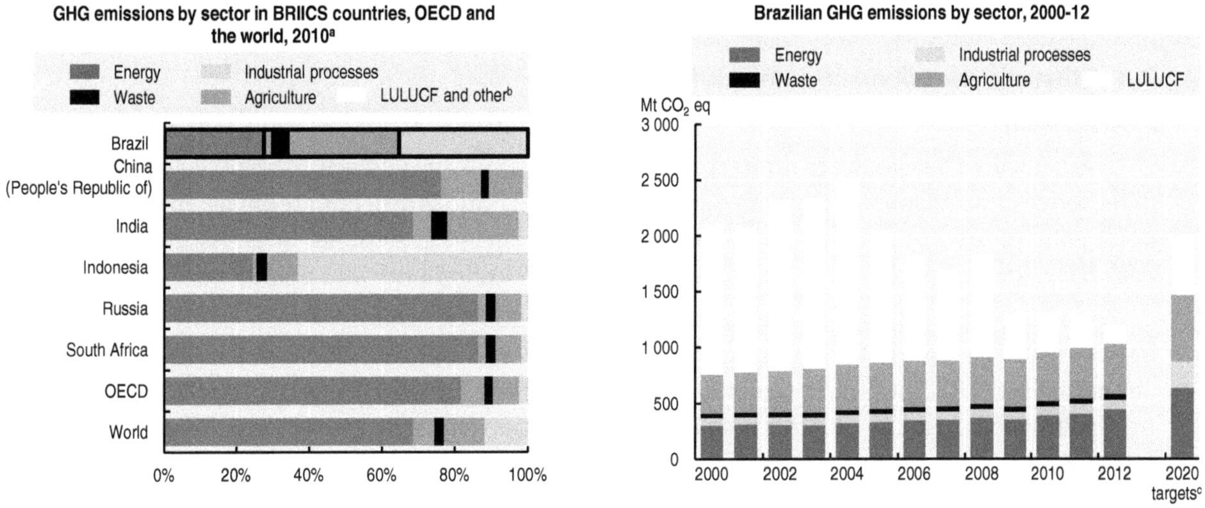

a) IEA estimates.
b) Excludes removals from LULUCF and includes emissions from: forest, peat and other vegetation fires; decay of drained peat soils and of aboveground biomass that remains after logging and deforestation (IPCC cat. 5); solvent use (IPCC cat. 3); application of agricultural lime (IPCC cat. 4); fossil fuel fires (IPCC cat. 7); some industrial processes such as methanol production (IPCC cat. 2); N_2O usage, human sewage discharge and waste incineration (non-energy), and indirect N_2O from atmospheric deposition of NO_x and NH_3 from non-agricultural sources (IPCC cat. 3, 6 and 7).
c) According to Decree n. 7.390/2010, which defines the expected GHG emissions under business-as-usual (BAU) scenario and sectoral emission reduction targets varying from 36.1% to 38.9% of the BAU. The category "industrial processes" includes emissions from waste management.
Source: IEA (2014), "Emissions of CO_2, CH_4, N_2O, HFCs, PFCs and SF_6", *IEA CO_2 Emissions from Fuel Combustion Statistics* (database); MCTI (2014; 2013), *Estimativas anuais de emissões de gases de efeito estufa no Brasil*; MCTI (2010), *Second National Communication of Brazil to the UNFCCC.*

StatLink http://dx.doi.org/10.1787/888933279419

Basic Statistics). Brazil's carbon intensity (CO_2 emissions from fuel combustion per unit of GDP) is low by international comparison in both per capita terms and per unit of GDP, partly due to the low-carbon energy mix and the fact that per capita energy use is still significantly below OECD levels (Figure 1.8 and Annex 1.B). CO_2 emissions from fossil fuel combustion increased at a slower pace than GDP, resulting in a relative decoupling from

Figure 1.8. **Brazil's carbon intensity remains low by international comparison**

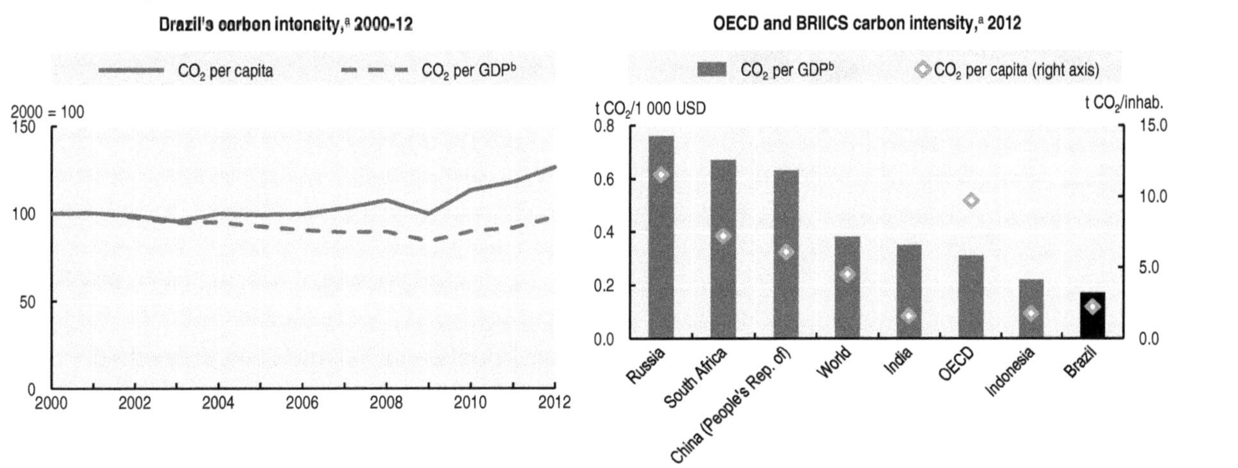

a) CO_2 emissions from energy use only; sectoral approach; excludes international marine and aviation bunkers.
b) GDP at 2005 prices and purchasing power parities. Data include estimates.
Source: IEA (2014), *IEA CO_2 Emissions from Fuel Combustion Statistics* (database); OECD (2014), "OECD Economic Outlook No. 95", *OECD Economic Outlook: Statistics and Projections* (database); OECD (2014), "Population projections", *OECD Historical population data and projections statistics* (database).

StatLink http://dx.doi.org/10.1787/888933279423

economic growth and a decline of the carbon intensity of the economy (by 2%) over 2000-12. However, energy-related CO_2 emissions per capita grew by 26% over the period (Figure 1.8), in line with the increase in per capita energy consumption.

3.3. Other air emissions and air quality

Air emissions

Data on air emissions are limited; the Ministry of the Environment has published two inventories of atmospheric emissions in transport (2011 and 2013), but air emissions from point sources are not systematically captured or aggregated at national level. As in many countries, the main sources of air pollution are transport, industry and energy generation.

Available data suggest that total carbon monoxide (CO) emissions were fairly stable between 2000 and 2010, decreasing in the energy and LULUCF sectors yet rising in agriculture (+77%). Total nitrogen oxide (NO_x) emissions increased by 15% over 2000-10, primarily due to energy-related fossil fuel combustion but also rising emissions from LULUCF (MCTI, 2014b). Emissions of volatile organic compounds (VOCs) increased by 37% over 2000-10, mainly from solvent production and use and industrial processes (Figure 1.9). There are no national, cross-sector emission inventories of other air pollutants, including sulphur oxides (SO_x) and ammonia (NH_3).

Figure 1.9. **Transport-related air emissions are decreasing, but overall emissions are rising**

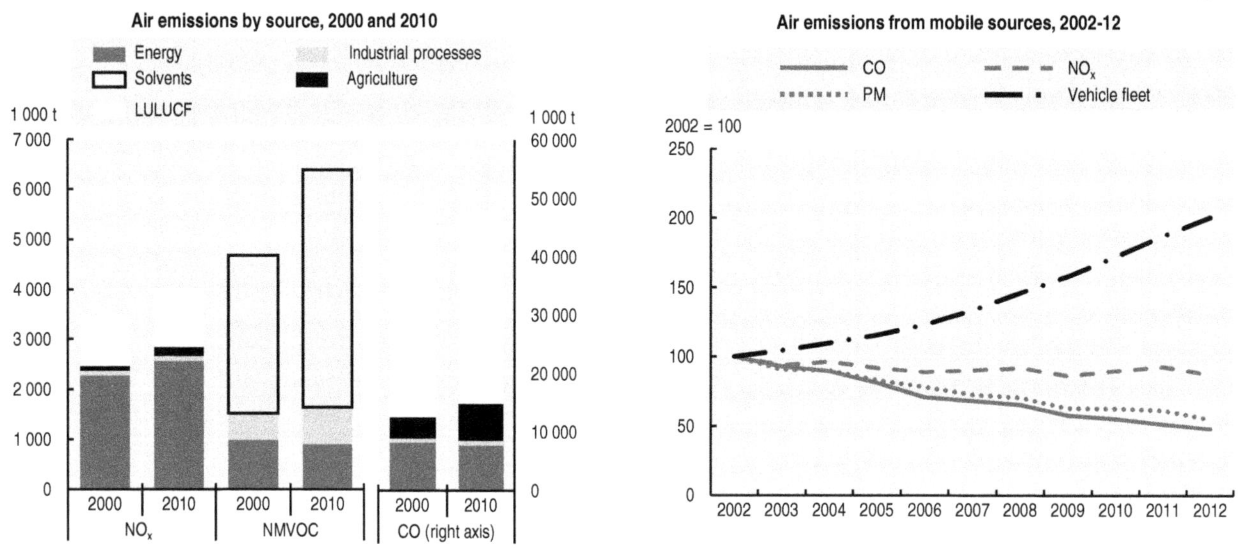

Source: ANFAVEA (2014), *Anuário da Indústria Automobilística Brasileira*; MMA (2014), *Inventário Nacional de Emissões Atmosféricas por Veículos Automotores Rodoviários, 2013*; UNFCCC (2014), *First Biennial Update Report of Brazil*.

StatLink http://dx.doi.org/10.1787/888933279431

The number of vehicles in use more than doubled between 2000 and 2014. It reached 35 vehicles per 100 inhabitants, which remains well below the OECD average and the vehicle ownership rate of most OECD countries (see Annex 1.A and Basic Statistics). Nonetheless, emissions of CO, NO_x and particulate matter (PM) from mobile sources decreased significantly, thanks to stricter vehicle emission standards, improvement in road vehicle technology and widespread use of ethanol in cars (Figure 1.9; also see Chapter 3). Transport-related PM and NO_x emissions largely stem from buses and heavy-duty diesel vehicles. Over 2002-12, PM emissions from mobile sources declined by about 45%. Transport-related NO_x emissions decreased by 13% thanks to better performance of the passenger car fleet (Figure 1.9), yet NO_x emissions from heavy trucks increased by roughly 25% (MMA, 2014a).

Air quality

Air pollution in urban areas is considered a serious environmental challenge (IBGE, 2012a), but quantitative data are scarce as Brazil lacks an effective air quality monitoring system. The law obliges the states to monitor air quality and produce annual air quality reports, but only 12 of the 27 states (including the Federal District) had some type of monitoring system installed by 2012, and few of them provide consistent, accessible data (IEMA, 2012). Less than 2% of municipalities monitor air quality (ISS, 2014).

PM_{10} emitted by industry and transport is the most serious air quality issue. At a national level, average exposure to air pollution from $PM_{2.5}$ is relatively low in Brazil compared to most OECD countries (Annex 1.B), but this average hides wide differences across urban and rural areas. PM_{10}, $PM_{2.5}$ and ozone (O_3) are the pollutants that most frequently exceed national and/or international standards, while CO, SO_2 and NO_2 seem to be somewhat better controlled. This difference may partly be linked to the distinct smog composition in Brazilian urban areas, which is related to the reliance on ethanol in road transport[10] (IEMA, 2014; MCTI, 2010); however, it may also be explained by the fact that fewer data points are available for CO, SO_2 and NO_2.

PM_{10} concentration levels have been reduced in most cities of more than 100 000 inhabitants in the past two decades, thanks largely to stronger vehicle emission control and advancements in engine technology and fuel quality (World Bank, 2015; IBGE, 2012a; also see Chapter 2). This reduction resulted in a decrease in the average annual exposure level of urban residents to outdoor PM from 46 to 36 $\mu g/m^3$ over 2000-11 (World Bank, 2015).[11] Annual average concentrations remain above this level in several metropolitan areas, however, and peak concentrations still regularly exceed national air quality standards in many cities. Rio de Janeiro, among the cities with the greatest traffic congestion problems, registered the highest levels of PM_{10} exposure in 2010: both the highest annual mean concentration (67 $\mu g/m^3$) and highest peak concentration (574 $\mu g/m^3$) among monitored cities. In São Paulo, PM_{10} concentrations decreased over the 2000s, but the city faces high O_3: concentration levels exceeded the national eight-hour average quality standard 257 times in 2010, or more than 70% of the year (IBGE, 2013).

Poor air quality poses severe health risks to Brazil's population, even in areas where pollution levels remain below national emission standards (Olmo et al., 2011). Estimates suggest that in the states of São Paulo and Rio de Janeiro alone, 135 000 people died from diseases caused by air pollution over 2006-11 (ISS, 2014).

Ozone-depleting substances

Brazil has reduced the use of ozone-depleting substances by more than 80% over the past two decades, surpassing the goals established in the Montreal Protocol (IBGE, 2013). Chlorofluorocarbons (CFCs), the main cause of stratospheric ozone depletion, and methyl bromide had been phased out by 2010, as required by the Montreal Protocol. The use of hydrochlorofluorocarbons, a common replacement for CFCs, with lower ozone-depleting potential but a high global warming potential, grew over the 2000s.

4. Transition to a resource-efficient economy

4.1. *Material consumption*

Domestic material consumption (DMC)[12] grew by more than 70% over 2000-11, faster than in any OECD country or other BRIICS country except China. As DMC grew even faster than GDP, material productivity (GDP per DMC) deteriorated by 14%, while in most OECD countries and all other BRIICS countries, it improved (Figure 1.10; Annex 1.C). In 2011, Brazil's material productivity was about one-quarter of the OECD average and below the BRIICS average. Material consumption per capita has also been growing and is high: in 2010, per capita DMC was 50% above the OECD average and well above DMC in other BRIICS countries.

Figure 1.10. **Domestic material consumption increased faster than GDP**

Domestic material consumption and productivity, 2000-11

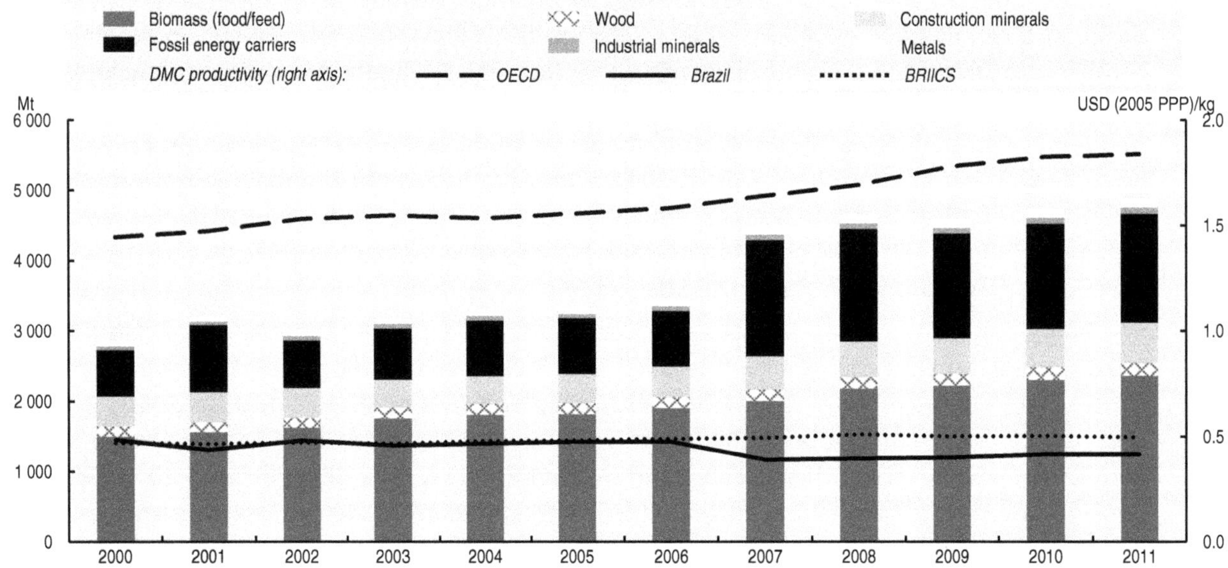

Note: Domestic material consumption (DMC) designates the sum of domestic raw material extraction used by an economy and its physical trade balance. Material productivity refers to the amount of GDP generated per unit of materials used and corresponds to the ratio of GDP to DMC. A rise in material productivity is equivalent to a decline in material intensity (i.e. DMC/GDP).

Source: OECD (2015), "Material resources", *OECD Environment Statistics* (database).

StatLink http://dx.doi.org/10.1787/888933279442

Due to Brazil's large agricultural and forestry sectors, biomass and wood extraction accounts for over half of total DMC, which is more than in any OECD country (Annex 1.C). Biomass DMC increased by 58% over 2000-11, a period in which sugar cultivation, largely for ethanol production, expanded considerably. DMC of fossil fuels and metals grew even faster due to a jump in domestic oil extraction in 2006/07 and increased metal exports (Figure 1.10). Brazil exports more materials than it imports and its trade surplus is rising, reflecting the increasing role of commodities (notably minerals and biomass) in its export portfolio (see Basic Statistics).

4.2. *Waste management*

Data on the generation, collection, treatment and disposal of solid waste are limited and hence need to be interpreted with caution.[13] According to the Brazilian Association of Public Cleaning and Special Waste Disposal Companies (Abrelpe), the amount of municipal solid waste (MSW) generated per year grew by about 10% over 2009–12, reflecting rising living standards and consumption levels. MSW has grown more rapidly than population in recent years, though slower than private consumption (Abrelpe, 2012; World Bank, 2015). Per capita waste generation remains significantly below OECD levels (see Annex 1.C and Basic Statistics).

Brazil has made noticeable progress in expanding household access to waste collection services, though with wide geographical disparity. In urban areas, access increased from 96% in 2004 to over 98% in 2012, while in rural areas it increased from 20% to 53%, although data are not fully comparable over time (Figure 1.11). Service coverage tends to be lower in small municipalities, as well as in the North and North-east regions, where only 85% and 88%, respectively, of the population had access to waste collection services. It is estimated that more than 6 million tonnes of MSW per year (almost 10% of the total) is burned, buried or dumped (Abrelpe, 2012).

Figure 1.11. **Waste management has improved, but remains challenging in rural areas**

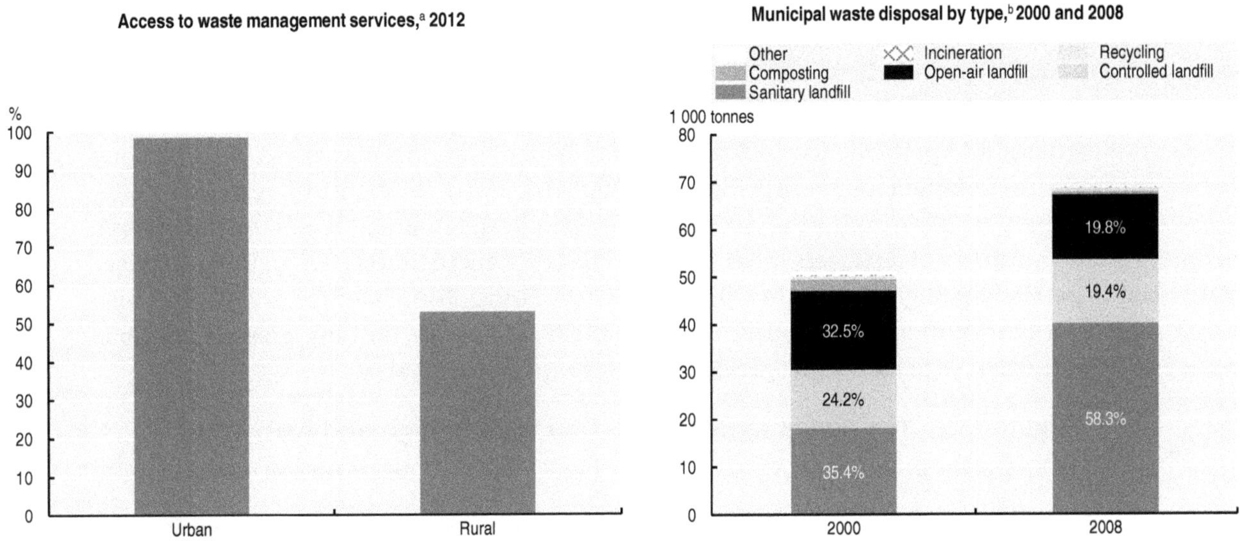

a) Estimates based on sample surveys covering about 50% of municipalities.
b) Includes waste originating from households, offices, institutions, commerce and selected municipal services (i.e. street cleaning). Controlled landfill: site operating in compliance with technical control procedures, but not requiring environmental mitigation measures. Sanitary landfill: site operating in compliance with technical control procedures and measures to reduce environmental impacts (i.e. groundwater contamination).
Source: MMA (2012), *National Plan for Solid Waste*; UNSD (n.d.), UNSD Environmental Indicators.

StatLink http://dx.doi.org/10.1787/888933279452

Appropriate MSW treatment and disposal remain a significant challenge. As in many developing or emerging economies, the main type of disposal is landfilling, which in Brazil accounted for almost 98% of treatment in 2008. Waste disposal in non-sanitary landfills (i.e. sites without measures to minimise environmental damage such as groundwater contamination) decreased over 2000-08, particularly disposal in uncontrolled, open-air dumps (Figure 1.11). Despite this improving trend, however, Brazil fell short of its national target to eliminate uncontrolled landfills by August 2014. Small municipalities, and those with large rural zones, have particular trouble complying with national legislation, usually because of limited institutional capacity and lack of economies of scale (Chapters 2 and 3). In addition, Brazil performs poorly in organic waste management, despite the very high share of such waste in total MSW (51%). In 2008, less than 2% of organic waste collected was disposed of at composting facilities, which are almost non-existent (MMA, 2012b).

Recycling is very limited. It is estimated that only 27% of recyclable collected waste is effectively recovered. As in many developing or emerging countries, recovery is dominated by waste pickers (*catadores*), who earn their living by collecting recyclables and selling them to private recycling companies (Chapter 3). Waste pickers are responsible for almost 20% of the waste separated for recycling, and for the high recycling rates of aluminium cans (98%) and PET (57%). Only about 15% of municipalities, most of which are located in the South-east and South regions, offer selective waste collection services (Cempre, 2013).

4.3. *Agriculture and nutrient inputs*

Brazil is the world's fourth-largest agricultural producer, generating 6% of global output, after China (23%), the United States (10%) and India (10%). Agriculture accounts for 15% of employment; 75% of the rural workforce (about 12 million Brazilians) is employed in small-scale, relatively unproductive family farming (IBGE, 2009). Agricultural production increased by 70% between 2000 and 2012 (MMA, 2015a), due to both enhanced productivity and, especially in the early 2000s, an expansion of land area devoted to crops and livestock. The density of livestock has increased along with livestock inventories; it was about twice the OECD average in 2013, but remains below many regions with more intensive livestock production (e.g. Korea and a number of European countries; see Annex 1.C).

Fertiliser and pesticide use in Brazil has intensified. National statistics reveal a strong increase in fertiliser consumption over 2000-10, both in absolute terms (+137%) (IBAMA, 2013) and per unit of agricultural area (Figure 1.12). Brazil is one of the world's largest consumers of fertilisers (after China, India and United States) (FAO, 2014). Fertiliser use is particularly high for certain crops, such as soya (Accioli and Monteiro, 2011). It is also higher in the South and South-east regions, where large-scale farming prevails, and has been associated with increasing pressures on water and soil quality.

Figure 1.12. **The use of agricultural chemicals is high and increasing**

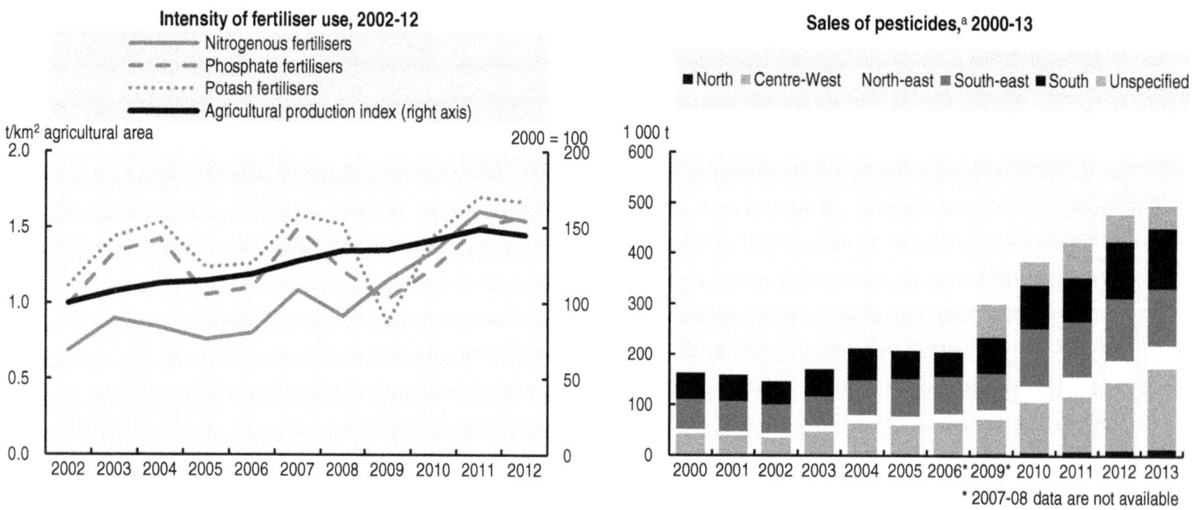

a) Pesticides and similar products according to the Decree n. 4.074 of 4 January 2002.
Source: FAO (2014), *FAOSTAT* (database); IBAMA (2013), *Agrotóxicos e Afins -Histórico das Vendas - 2000 a 2012.*

StatLink http://dx.doi.org/10.1787/888933279462

Pesticide consumption has increased even more strongly, by almost 200%, since 2000 (Figure 1.12). In 2010, pesticide sales amounted to USD 7.2 billion, 10% more than in the US market (Pelaez et al., 2013). Almost a third of pesticides consumed are considered dangerous or highly dangerous for the environment and several widely used substances have been identified as detrimental to pollinators, notably bees (IBAMA, 2013; MMA, 2015a). The widespread use of pesticides is associated with the practice of minimum-tillage and no-tillage farming. Alternative pest control practices, such as crop rotation and biological control, are rare, perhaps in part because a relatively large share of farmers (78%) have only finished elementary school (IBGE, 2012a). Low education may also explain why 20% of pesticide consumers do not use protective equipment when applying them.

The high use of agricultural chemicals, and notably the use of unauthorised pesticides, has become a public health problem. Such chemicals are second only to medical drugs as a cause of poisoning (MMA, 2010). A study revealed that 36% of food samples in 2011 and 29% in 2012 contained unauthorised pesticides and/or exceeded allowable amounts of pesticides (ANVISA, 2013).

Organic farming accounts for a very small share of agricultural output. The latest national agricultural census showed less than 2% of farms producing organically in 2006, 82% of which were family farms that might have used chemicals if they had had access to them (IBGE, 2012b). In 2014, about 7 200 registered establishments produced certified organic products (MMA, 2015a), or about 0.1% of total farms and less than 1% of agricultural land area (Figure 4.11).

5. Managing the natural asset base

5.1. *Biodiversity*

Brazil is the world's most biodiverse country, hosting about 10% to 12% of known species and more endemic species than any other country (CDB, n.d.). The world's fifth-largest country, it covers 47% of the South American continent's surface and extends about 7 500 km along the Atlantic coast. Owing to its size, its physical characteristics vary enormously, as do climate, vegetation and land-use patterns. Accordingly, it is typically divided into six large terrestrial ecosystems, or biomes:[14] Amazon, Cerrado, Caatinga, Atlantic Forest, Pantanal and Pampa (Box 4.1). The Atlantic Forest and Cerrado biomes are two of the world's 35 biodiversity hotspots (Chapter 4). Brazil also has vast coastal and marine areas: it hosts rich coral reef ecosystems and has the world's largest contiguous area of mangroves.

Despite past and current efforts to protect Brazil's natural wealth (Chapter 4), threats to biodiversity persist. Extension of agriculture and cattle farming, natural resource extraction, and infrastructure and development are the most significant causes of habitat loss (Figure 1.13). Unclear land tenure has historically exacerbated deforestation pressures, but the new Forest Code and its implementation mechanisms (notably the Rural Environmental Cadastre; see Chapter 4) promise to reduce illegal logging for land-titling purposes. Other threats to biodiversity include alien species and exotic diseases, overexploitation, pollution, fire and climate change (MMA, 2015a).

Forests and deforestation

Brazil's immense forest resources, 98.5% of which are native, include the world's largest rain forest (SFB, 2015). In 2012, 62% of the territory was covered with forests, double the OECD average (see Basic Statistics). Less than 1% of total forest area is used for timber production (SFB, 2013).[15] Brazil is a large producer and consumer of tropical timber: in 2007, the forestry sector accounted for 3.5% of GDP and 7.3% of exports, and employed about 7 million people (SFB, 2015).

About 70% of the total territory retains its original vegetation, in various degrees of conservation (MMA, 2010). The share varies widely across biomes, with the Amazon and Pantanal having more than 80% of their original vegetation and the Atlantic Forest biome, where nearly three-quarters of Brazilians live, about 20% (Figure 1.13).

Figure 1.13. **Vegetation cover has declined in some Brazilian biomes**

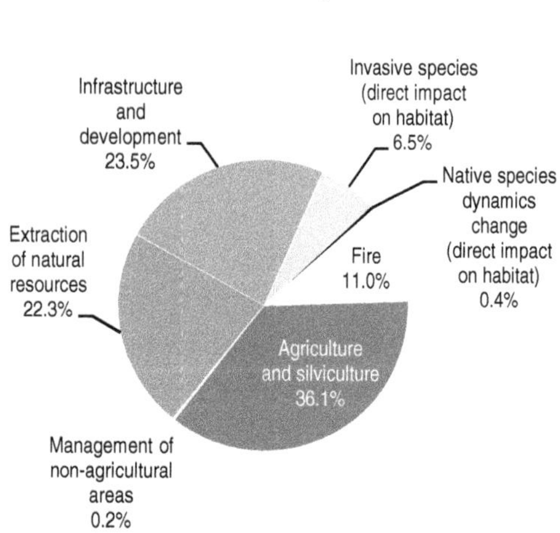

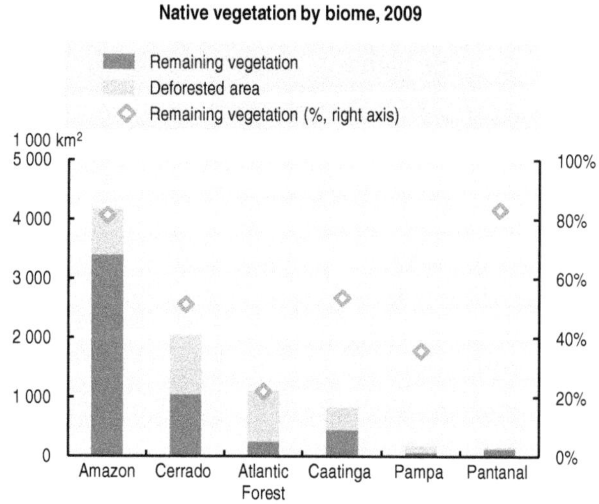

Source: Martinelli G. and M.A. Moraes (2013), *Livro vermelho da flora do Brasil*; MMA (2015), *Fifth National Report to the Convention on Biological Diversity*.

StatLink http://dx.doi.org/10.1787/888933279479

The area designated Amazônia Legal[16] was a deforestation hotspot in the 1990s and early 2000s, with deforestation peaks in 1994 and 2004, but is now recognised for successful large-scale deforestation control. A significant share of deforestation was due to illegal logging, with cleared land subsequently used for pasture (MMA, 2015a). In 2006, the government pledged to reduce deforestation in Amazônia Legal by 80% by 2020 (compared with the average of the previous ten years)[17] and has since considerably scaled up efforts to fight deforestation (e.g. creation of protected areas, land tenure regularisation, and enhanced monitoring, control and enforcement; see Chapters 4 and 5). This helped deforestation drop from 28 000 km^2 per year in 2004 to about 4 800 km^2 per year in 2014, by which time the deforestation rate was down by 75% (Figure 4.3) (INPE, 2015). Deforestation rates have also declined in other biomes in recent years. Pressures remain high in the Cerrado, however: it lost 0.4% of its total forest area in 2008-09 (IBAMA, 2015). Overall, total forest area has declined by about 5% since 2000.

Protected areas

One driver of the drop in deforestation was the rapid expansion of protected areas (Chapter 5). The number of official terrestrial protected areas (*unidades de conservação*) increased from 919 in 2000 to 1 940 in early 2015, or from 9% to 17.2% of the territory (MMA, 2015b).[18] Brazil achieved the Aichi target – protecting at least 17% of terrestrial and inland water areas by 2020, under the UN Convention on Biological Diversity – in 2010, well ahead of time. The coverage of protected areas varies across biomes, ranging from nearly 27% in the Amazon to 2.7% in the Pampa biome, and only 1.5% of marine areas are protected (Figure 1.14). In 2013, Brazil set a national target to protect 30% of the Amazon, 17% of other terrestrial biomes and 10% of coastal and marine areas by 2020.[19]

Figure 1.14. **A large share of Brazil's territory is under environmental protection**

Share of protected areas by biome and Aichi targets, 2015

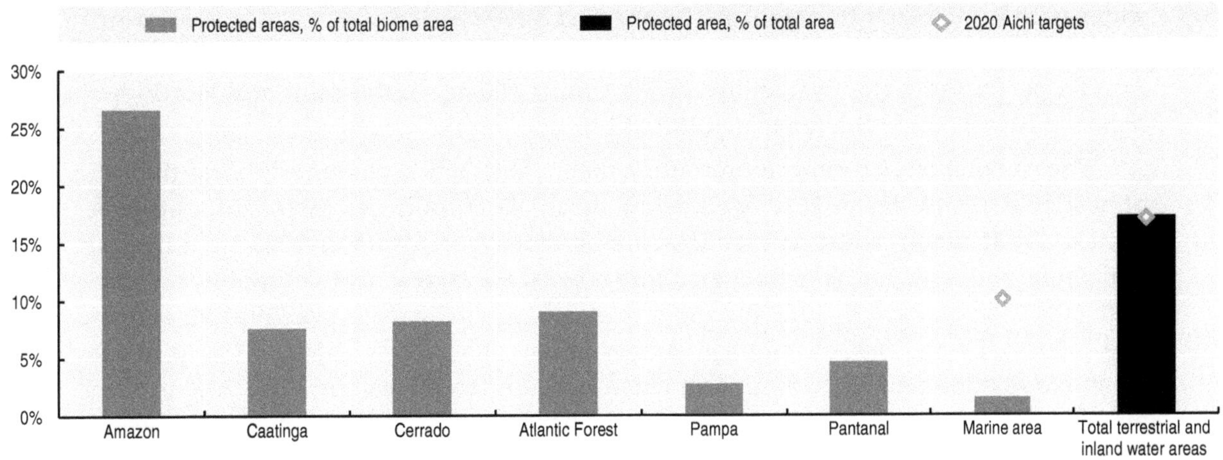

Note: Officialy protected areas according to the National System of Protected Areas (SNUC).
Source: MMA (2015), *Cadastro Nacional de Unidades de Conservação.*

StatLink http://dx.doi.org/10.1787/888933279488

In addition to the official protected areas, 13% of Brazil's territory (about 1.1 million km^2) is protected in about 600 indigenous lands, mostly located in the Amazon. Private landowners are required by law to set aside Permanent Preservation Areas (APPs) and Legal Reserves (RLs), in which original vegetation cover is maintained (Chapter 4). APPs cover 12% and RLs 30% of the territory, more than twice the area covered by official protected areas. While they have often not been respected in the past (Sparovek et al., 2010), the new Forest Code and its implementation mechanisms (Chapter 4) promise to increase effective conservation within these areas.

Terrestrial and marine species

The official list of threatened species, updated in 2014, counts more than 1 000 threatened fauna species and more than 2 000 threatened plant species (Chapter 4). The Atlantic Forest is the biome with the most threatened species, followed by the Cerrado and the Amazon. These are also the biomes with the most known species (IBGE, 2013). More than 400 marine and freshwater fish species are included in the 2014 official list of threatened species. Fishing and fish farming are the major pressure, followed by pollution from industrial, urban, agricultural and household waste, due in part to the high concentration of population and, in some areas, industry along the coastline (MMA, 2015a). Action on protection of threatened fauna species has increased: in 2012, about 50% of all threatened species were protected under a national action plan, compared with 4% in 2008 (MMA, 2014b).

Catches of marine and freshwater fish grew by nearly 15% in 2000-13 (Annex 1.D). Fish catches increased by nearly 20% in inland waters and by about 13% in marine areas. Several coastal and inland fish stocks are fully exploited, or overexploited, as a result of overfishing, generally by industrial fisheries (FAO, 2013). In many cases, declining fish stocks are associated with resource conflicts between artisanal and industrial fishing and among fishing communities (MMA, 2015a).

5.2. *Water resources*

Brazil is endowed with 12% of the world's freshwater resources and some of its largest water basins, including the Amazon, Paraná and São Francisco (ANA, 2013). Freshwater distribution is uneven, with the Amazon holding about 70% of freshwater resources. Annual per capita water availability varies from 1 460 m^3 in the semi-arid North-east region to 634 887 m^3 in the Amazon (GWP, 2013).

The size of Brazil's freshwater resources meant abstraction amounted to less than 1% of available freshwater in 2010, well below most OECD countries (ANA, 2013; also see Annex 1.D). However, water abstraction rose by more than 80% over 2000-12, reflecting population and economic growth. Agriculture is by far the largest user, accounting for more than 60% of abstraction in 2012 and more than 70% of the increase over 2000-12. Human and industrial water use, by contrast, increased only moderately (Figure 1.15). Losses in water distribution relative to total abstraction have decreased slightly since 2000 but still amounted to more than one-third of abstracted freshwater in 2012, and more than 50% in several northern and north-eastern states, primarily because of obsolete water supply and sanitation infrastructure. Per capita water consumption averaged 167 litres per day in 2013: it ranges from 126 litres in the North-east region to 193 litres in the South-east, reflecting differences in climatic conditions and consumption patterns (MCid, 2014). Overall, Brazil's yearly freshwater abstraction per capita is below the OECD average (see Annex 1.D and Basic Statistics), although with large regional variations.

Figure 1.15. **Water use, especially by agriculture, has increased considerably**

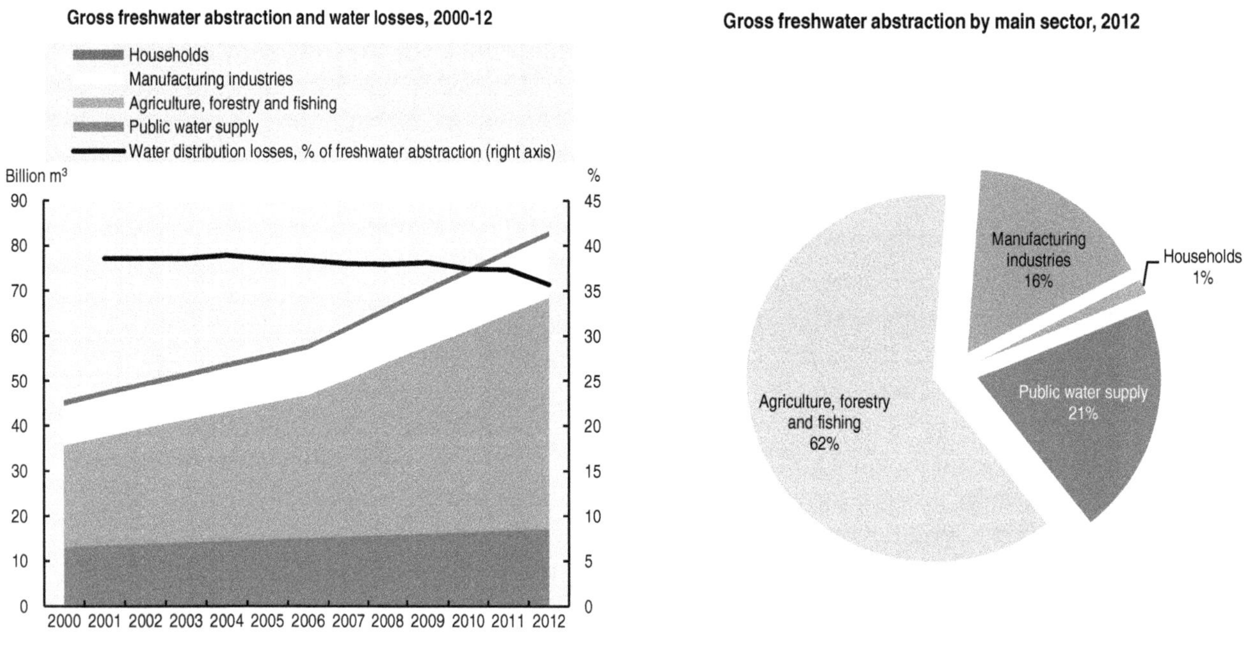

Source: OECD (2015), "Freshwater abstractions", *OECD Environment Statistics* (database).

StatLink http://dx.doi.org/10.1787/888933279491

The balance between water supply and consumption is stable in most basins, but considered worrying, critical or very critical for almost 25% of freshwater resources due to scarcity (e.g. in the North-east) and extensive use (e.g. in the densely populated South-east) (ANA, 2013). In 2013 and 2014, high temperatures, low rainfall and years of inefficient water use caused severe water shortages in the South-east, notably in São Paulo state, with a severe impact on water supply and energy generation. About 4 million people, as well as industry and agriculture, were affected by water rationing and power cuts (The Guardian, 2015).

Water quality is good or very good in about 80% of water bodies but critical in many densely populated urban areas. The national water quality index showed 44% of urban monitoring sites recording poor or very poor quality in 2011 (Figure 1.16). This means water quality after conventional treatment is insufficient for public supply, requiring advanced treatment. The main problem affecting surface water quality is wastewater discharge, both treated effluent and domestic wastewater. The deterioration of water quality is usually related to increasing wastewater volumes, reflecting population growth and urbanisation, which were not matched by investment in wastewater collection and treatment systems (ANA, 2013; MMA, 2015a; also see Chapter 3). In 2012, only 39% of wastewater was treated (MCid, 2014) and only a fraction of that received treatment to remove phosphorus, hormones and antibiotics, which affect both ecosystems and human health. Other major pressures on water quality include mining, industrial effluent, diffuse flows from urban and agricultural soil drainage, and solid waste discharge.

Figure 1.16. **Water quality is critical in many urban areas**

Water quality index, 2011

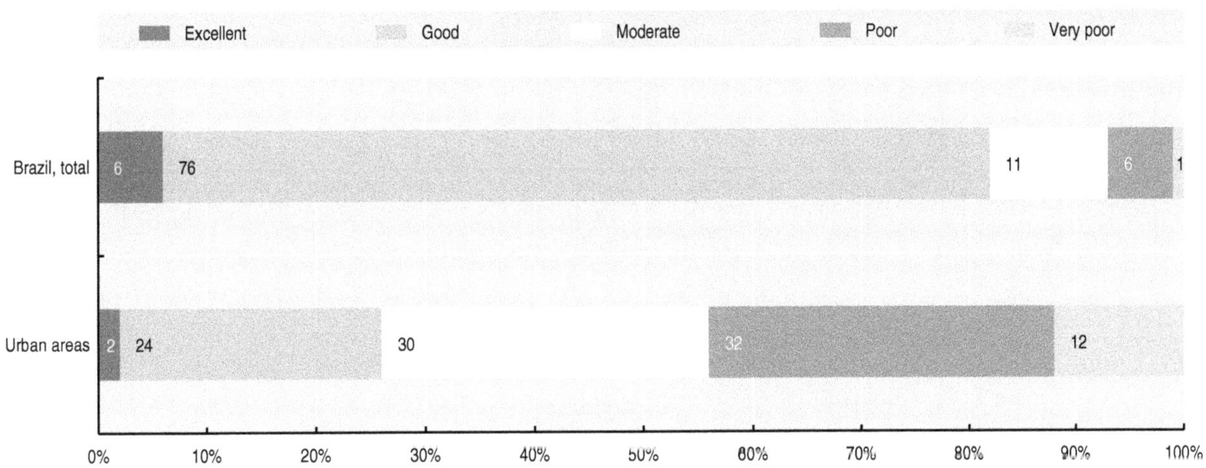

Notes: Water quality index (IQA) calculated as weighted average of nine parameters. The index varies from 0 to 100. Water classes: "excellent" (≤79); "good" (51-79); "moderate" (36-51); "poor"(19-36); "very poor" (≤19). The last two categories (index values ≤ 36) refer to unsafe drinking water.
Source: ANA (2013), *Conjuntura dos Recursos Hídricos no Brasil.*

StatLink http://dx.doi.org/10.1787/888933279503

Access to clean water supply and sanitation

Brazil has made considerable progress in providing its citizens with water supply services. The share of the population with access to improved water sources increased from 88% in 1990 to almost 98% in 2012. Water supply in urban areas is almost universal, though 15% of the rural population still lacks access to an improved water source (Annex 3.A). The share of households connected to water pipe networks reached 94% in urban areas in 2013. Regional disparity is wide, however, with most of the urban dwellers still not connected to a water network found in the North-east region and, particularly, the North, where less than 60% are connected (MCid, 2014). Countrywide, only 24% of urban water supply networks are considered satisfactory; 33% need upgrading to meet quantity and/or quality standards and 43% need expansion to adequately meet projected demand increases (ANA, 2011).

Progress on sanitation has been somewhat slower. National estimates suggest that the share of urban population with access to a sewage collection network increased from 48% to 56% over 2006-11. Coverage rates are highest in the South-east region (79% of the urban population) and lagging in the North (12%) and North-east (28%) (MCid, 2014). The countrywide share of urban population with sewage treatment (through a network or local treatment) is even lower: 35% in 2011, up from 30% in 2006 (Figure 1.17). There is a wide disparity between urban and rural areas. Only 5% of households living in rural areas had

Figure 1.17. **Access to sewage collection networks and sewage treatment needs to be expanded**

Urban population with access to sanitation services by region,[a] 2006, 2009 and 2011

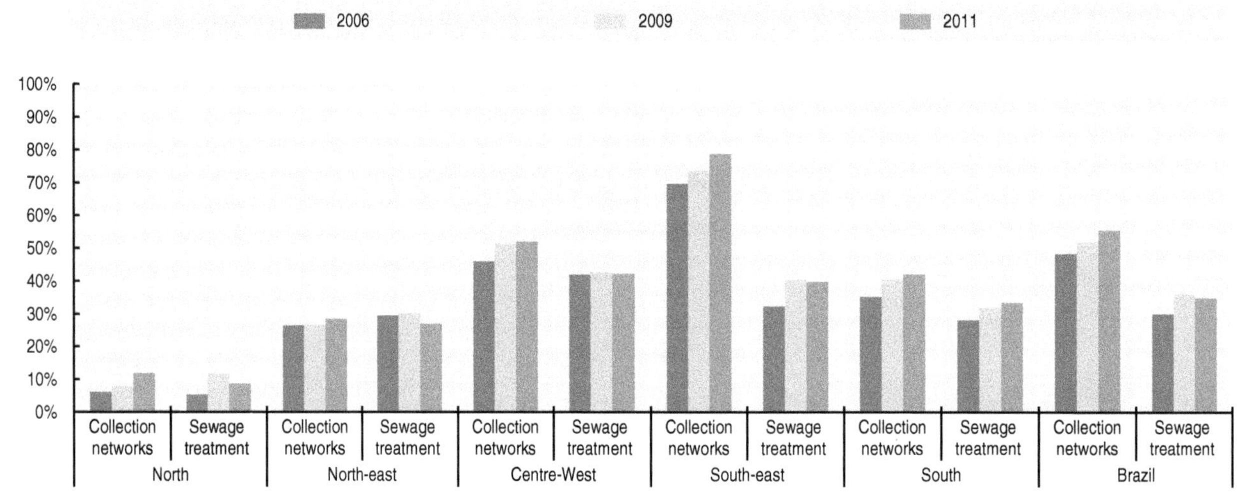

Access to sanitation, by type of service and area, 2009

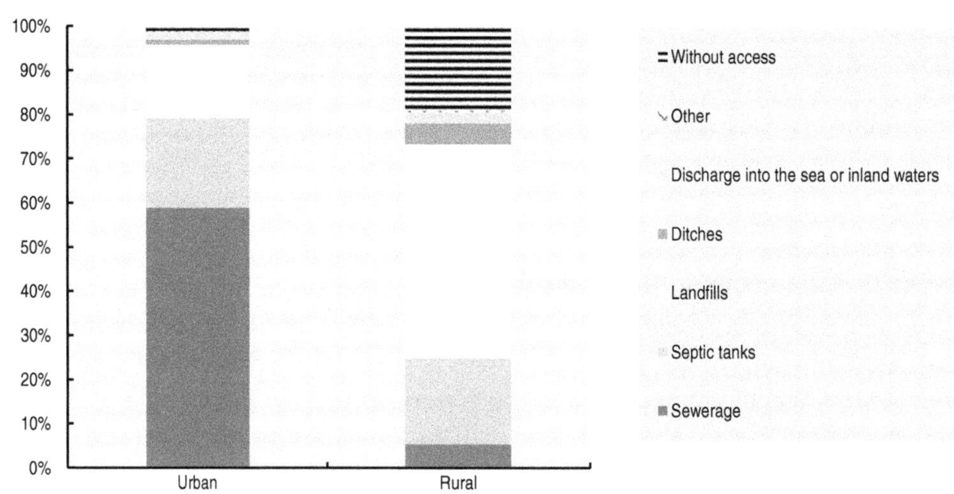

a) Data refer to the share of urban population living in municipalities served by water supply services (93% of Brazil's total urban population in 2011, according to the SNIS).
Source: MMA (2014), *PNIA 2012: Painel Nacional de Indicadores Ambientais;* IBGE (2009), *Pesquisa Nacional por Amostra de Domicílios 2009.*

StatLink http://dx.doi.org/10.1787/888933279514

access to sewage collection networks in 2009, compared to about 60% in urban areas; nearly 20% had no access to any form of sewage collection system (Figure 1.17).

Diseases related to inadequate sanitation decreased by more than 50% over 1993-2010 to 325 incidences per 100 000 inhabitants (IBGE, 2013), reflecting progress in expanding sanitation services. Not surprisingly, regional disparity is large, with 691 incidences in the North and 121 in the South-east, reflecting the overall sanitation service situation in the regions.

Recommendations on climate change policy and air, water and waste management

Climate change policy

- Rapidly implement the sectoral programmes to mitigate GHG emissions and speed up the development of the SMMARE system to monitor results; ensure that effective measures are replicated and scaled up.
- Further advance the development and implementation of the climate change adaptation plan with the involvement of all sectors, levels of government and stakeholders; ensure that the strategy adequately reflects economic, social and environmental impacts, including on biodiversity and water availability and quality.

Air pollution, water and waste management

- Develop an effective nationwide air quality monitoring system, with consistent methodologies and data collection across states.
- Establish consistent and compatible criteria for water allocation and ensure that wastewater discharge limits are set in accordance with use-based water quality standards.
- Strengthen solid waste management by:
  - better enforcing hazardous waste management regulations to eliminate the disposal of hazardous waste in municipal landfills without prior treatment;
  - establishing the National Solid Waste Management Information System, as required by law, and using it to facilitate implementation of "reverse logistics" programmes for key product waste streams.

Notes

1. Brazil is divided into five geographical regions: South-east, South, Centre-West, North and North-east. These regions enjoy no administrative or budgetary powers.
2. The homicide rate is one of the world's highest: 21 murders per 100 000 inhabitants per year, compared to the OECD average of 2.2 (OECD, 2013c).
3. The Better Life Index is an interactive web-based tool created to engage people in the debate on well-being and, through this process, learn what matters most to them. The tool makes it possible to compare well-being across countries according to the importance that each participant attaches to a number of topics (community, education, environment, civic engagement, health, housing, income, jobs, life satisfaction, safety and work-life balance). The Better Life Index is part of the OECD Better Life Initiative, which aims to develop statistics that better capture aspects of life quality. See *www.oecdbetterlifeindex.org*.
4. In 2012, proven oil reserves stood at about 15.3 billion barrels and natural gas reserves at 450 billion m^3, with roughly 90% of both resources located offshore (ANP, 2013).
5. Conversion losses in hydropower are minimal, which makes it a much more efficient form of energy generation than fossil fuel combustion.

6. Land use, land-use change and forestry, as defined by the United Nations Framework Convention on Climate Change (UNFCCC), covers emissions and removals of GHGs resulting from direct human-induced LULUCF activities. LULUCF emissions as reported under the UNFCCC are net emissions, i.e. the sum of positive emissions to the atmosphere minus removals from the atmosphere through carbon sinks. Emissions to the atmosphere can occur through forest fires, conversion of forest to cropland and decomposition of aboveground biomass that remains after logging and deforestation. Removals from the atmosphere occur, for instance, through the extension of forest cover through afforestation and reforestation.
7. National data on GHG emissions, provided by the Ministry of Science, Technology and Innovation (MCTI), are not directly comparable to data provided by the International Energy Agency (IEA), owing to different accounting and estimation methods: IEA data include positive emissions from LULUCF but exclude carbon sequestration. MCTI data presents net LULUCF emissions (see note 6). In Brazil, GHG emissions from LULUCF are higher than removals, resulting in positive net GHG emissions in the LULUCF sector.
8. Brazil's commitment to reduce GHG emissions was set in Law 12.187/2009, which establishes the National Climate Change Policy. Projected BAU emissions and respective emission targets per sector are defined in Decree 7.390/2010.
9. Official GHG emission data are available until 2012. The Greenhouse Gas Emission System, a coalition of Brazilian think tanks and NGOs, provides unofficial annual data until 2013 (*www.seeg.eco.br*). Its estimates suggest that total Brazilian GHG emissions reached 1.57 tCO_2eq in 2013 – the highest emission levels since 2008. Emissions increased in all sectors, but most strongly from LULUCF and fossil fuel combustion.
10. Ethanol in fuel combustion produces less CO than gasoline and leads to lower NO_X and possibly PM_{10} concentrations, but results in greater emission of aldehydes and higher ground-level ozone.
11. PM concentrations refer to fine suspended particulates less than 10 microns in diameter (PM_{10}), which can penetrate deep into the respiratory tract, causing significant health damage. The state of a country's technology and pollution controls is an important determinant of PM concentrations. The estimates cited are urban population weighted PM_{10} levels in residential areas of cities with more than 100 000 residents. The estimates represent the average annual exposure level of the average urban resident to outdoor particulate matter.
12. DMC is the sum of domestic raw material extraction used by an economy and its physical trade balance (imports minus exports of raw materials and manufactured products).
13. There are significant data gaps for MSW management in Brazil. Various data sources are available for urban MSW, but methodologies and samples vary enormously, resulting in different and sometimes contradictory estimates. The two most important official data sources are the 2000 and 2008 National Surveys of Basic Sanitation, conducted by the Brazilian Institute of Geography and Statistics, and the annually updated National Sanitation Information System (SNIS), managed by the Ministry of Cities. Available data are hardly comparable, however, due to methodological difference and poor statistical bases (e.g. the SNIS relies on self-reported data from municipalities, but the number of municipalities participating is low and some of the data fed into the systems are inconsistent).
14. A biome is a large naturally occurring community of flora and fauna occupying a geographic region.
15. Includes national forests, states forests and forest plantations.
16. The Amazônia Legal super-region corresponds to an area larger than the Amazon biome, encompassing both the Amazonian forest (about 4.1 million km^2) and transitional vegetation (1 million km^2); the Amazon biome covers only the forest area. The Amazônia Legal takes in nearly nine states: Amazonas, Pará, Acre, Roraima, Rondônia, Amapá, Tocantins, and part of Mato Grosso and Maranhão.
17. The commitment to reduce deforestation was later incorporated into the National Climate Change Policy.
18. These numbers refer to protected areas officially designated under the National System of Protected Areas (SNUC). They do not include indigenous lands, protected area on private land (i.e. as requested under the Forest Code) and other areas that would qualify as protected area under international conventions.
19. The 2013 target expands the definition of protected areas to also include indigenous lands and areas under the Forest Code, including APPs and RLs.

References

Abrelpe (2012), *Panorama dos Resíduos Sólidos no Brasil [Panorama of Solid Waste in Brazil]*, Brazilian Association of Urban Cleansing and Waste, *www.abrelpe.org.br/Panorama/panorama2012.pdf*.

Accioli, C. and S. Monteiro (2011), "Brazil: World's Breadbasket", *The Brazilian Economy*, Vol. 3, No. 11, FGV IBRE, Rio de Janeiro.

ANA (2013), *Conjuntura dos Recursos Hídricos no Brasil [State of Water Resources in Brazil]*, National Water Agency, Brasília, *http://conjuntura.ana.gov.br/docs/conj2013_rel.pdf*.

ANA (2011), *Atlas Brasil do Abastecimento Urbano de Agua: Panorama Nacional [Urban Water Supply in Brazil: a National Panorama]*, National Water Agency, Brasília, *http://atlas.ana.gov.br/Atlas/downloads/atlas/Resumo%20Executivo/Atlas%20Brasil%20-%20Volume%201%20-%20Panorama%20Nacional.pdf*.

ANFEVA (2015), "Production, sales and exports of vehicles" (database), National Association of Motor Vehicle Manufacturers, *www.anfavea.com.br/tabelas.html* (accessed February 2015).

ANP (2013), *Anuário Estatístico Brasileiro de Petróleo, Gás Natural e Biocombustíveis [Brazilian Statistical Yearbook of Petroleum, Natural Gas and Biofuels]*, National Agency of Petroleum, Natural Gas and Biofuel, Rio de Janeiro, *www.anp.gov.br/?dw=73191*.

ANVISA (2013), *Programa de Análise de Resíduos de Agrotóxicos em Alimentos (PARA). Relatório de Atividades de 2011 e 2012 [Programme of Analysis of Pesticides Residues in Food (PARA). Activity Report 2011 and 2012]*, Brazilian Health Surveillance Agency, Brasília, *http://portal.anvisa.gov.br/wps/wcm/connect/58a5580041a4f6669e579ede61db78cc/Relat%C3%B3rio+PARA+2011-12+-+30_10_13_1.pdf?MOD=AJPERES*.

CDB (n.d.), "Brazil – Country Profile", UN Convention on Biological Diversity, *www.cbd.int/countries/profile/default.shtml?country=br - facts* (accessed May 2015).

Cempre (2013), *Compromisso Empresarial para Reciclagem – Review 2013 [Business Commitment for Recycling – Review 2013]*, the Brazilian Recycling Commitment, São Paulo.

FAO (2014), FAOSTAT (database), *http://faostat.fao.org*, Food and Agriculture Organization of the United Nations, Rome (accessed March 2015).

FAO (2013), "Fishery and Aquaculture Country Profiles: Brazil", Food and Agriculture Organization of the United Nations, Rome, *www.fao.org/fishery/facp/BRA/en* (accessed December 2014).

Fundaj (2014), "Povos e Comunidades Tradicionais" [Traditional Peoples and Communities], Fundação Joaquim Nabuco (Fundaj), Recife, *http://basilio.fundaj.gov.br/pesquisaescolar* (accessed January 2015).

GWP (2013), *Brazil. National Consultation on Water in the post-2015 Development Agenda*, Global Water Partnership, *www.gwp.org/Global/About GWP/Publications/Reports/Country Consultation Reports/Brazil Final National Consultation Report.pdf*.

IBAMA (2015), "Projeto de Monitoramento do Desmatamento dos Biomas Brasileiros por Satélite – PMDBBS" [Project for Satellite-based Deforestation Monitoring of Brazilian Biomes], Brazilian Institute of Environment and Renewable Natural Resources, Brasília, *http://siscom.ibama.gov.br/monitorabiomas/index.htm* (accessed February 2015).

IBAMA (2013), *Agrotóxicos e Afins – Histórico das Vendas – 2000 a 2012 [Agricultural Chemicals and Related Products – Sales History – 2000 to 2012]*, Brazilian Institute of Environment and Renewable Natural Resources, Brasília, *www.ibama.gov.br/phocadownload/Qualidade_Ambiental/boletim de comercializacao_2000_2012.pdf*.

IBGE (2014), "Projeção da população do Brasil por sexo e idade: 2000-2060" [Projection of the Brazilian population by sex and age: 2000-2060], Brazilian Institute of Geography and Statistics, Rio de Janeiro, *www.ibge.gov.br/home/estatistica/populacao/projecao_da_populacao/2013/default.shtm* (accessed February 2015).

IBGE (2013), *Indicadores de Desenvolvimento Sustentável [Sustainable Development Indicators]* (database), Brazilian Institute of Geography and Statistics, Rio de Janeiro (accessed March 2015).

IBGE (2012a), *Indicadores de Desenvolvimento Sustentável [Sustainable Development Indicators]*, Brazilian Institute of Geography and Statistics, Rio de Janeiro, *ftp://geoftp.ibge.gov.br/documentos/recursos_naturais/indicadores_desenvolvimento_sustentavel/2012/ids2012.pdf*.

IBGE (2012b), *Censo Agropecuário 2006. Brasil, Grandes Regiões e Unidades da Federação. Segunda Apuração [Agricultural Census 2006. Brazil, Major Regions and Federative Units. Second Evaluation]*, Brazilian Institute of Geography and Statistics, Rio de Janeiro, *http://biblioteca.ibge.gov.br/visualizacao/periodicos/51/agro_2006.pdf*.

IBGE (2011), *Censo Demográfico 2010 [Census 2010]*, Brazilian Institute of Geography and Statistics, Rio de Janeiro, *http://censo2010.ibge.gov.br/*.

IBGE (2009), *Censo Agropecuário 2006. Agricultura Familiar. Primeiros Resultados [Agricultural Census 2006. Family Farming. First Results]*, Instituto Brasileiro de Geografia e Estatística (IBGE), Rio de Janeiro, 2009.

IBRAM (2012), *An Optimistic Outlook for Mining in Brazil. Mining Companies in Brazil. Information and Analyses on the Brazilian Mineral Economy*, 7th Edition, Brazilian Mining Association, *www.ibram.org.br/sites/1400/1457/00000364.pdf*.

IEA (2014a), *IEA World Energy Statistics and Balances* (database), *http://dx.doi.org/10.1787/enestats-data-en* (accessed February 2015).

IEA (2014b), *IEA CO2 Emissions from Fuel Combustion Statistics* (database), *http://dx.doi.org/10.1787/co2-data-en* (accessed February 2015).

IEA (2013), *World Energy Outlook 2013*, IEA/OECD Publishing, Paris, *http://dx.doi.org/10.1787/weo-2013-en*.

IEMA (2014), *1° Diagnóstico da Rede de Monitoramento da Qualidade do Ar no Brasil [First Diagnosis of the Air Quality Monitoring Network in Brazil]*, Energy and Environment Institute, *www.energiaeambiente.org.br*.

IEMA (2012), *Padrões de Qualidade do Ar. Experiência Comparada Brasil, EUA e União Europeia [Air Quality Standards. A Comparison of Experiences in Brazil, the US and the EU]*, Energy and Environment Institute, *www.energiaeambiente.org.br*.

IMF (2014), *World Economic Outlook Database, October 2014* (database), International Monetary Fund, Washington, DC, *www.imf.org/external/data.htm* (accessed February 2015).

INPE (2015), "Projeto PRODES: Monitoramento da floresta Amazônia Brasileira por satélite"[The PRODES Project: Monitoring the Brazilian Amazon forest by satellite], National Institute for Space Research, *www.obt.inpe.br/prodes/index.php* (accessed February 2015).

IPEA (2012), "Produtividade no Brasil nos anos 2000-2009: análise das Contas Nacionais" [Productivity in Brazil from 2000 to 2009: an analysis of National Accounts], Institute for Applied Economic Research, *www.ipea.gov.br/portal/images/stories/PDFs/comunicado/120203_comunicadoipea133.pdf*.

ISS (2014), *Monitoramento da Qualidade do Ar no Brasil [Monitoring Air Quality in Brazil]*, Health and Sustainability Institute, *www.saudeesustentabilidade.org.br/site/wp-content/uploads/2014/07/Monitoramento-da-Qualidade-do-Ar-no-Brasil-2014.pdf*.

Martinelli G. and M.A. Moraes (2013), *Livro Vermelho da Flora do Brasil [Red Book of Brazil's Flora]*, CNCFlora e Jardim Botânico do Rio de Janeiro, Rio de Janeiro.

MCid (2014), "Sistema Nacional de Informações sobre Saneamento: Diagnóstico dos Serviços de Água e Esgotos – 2013" [National Sanitation Information System: Diagnosis of Water and Sewerage Services – 2013], Ministry of Cities, Brasília, *www.snis.gov.br* (accessed February 2015).

MCTI (2014a), *Estimativas Anuais de Emissões de Gases de Efeito Estufa no Brasil. Segunda Edição [Annual Estimates of Greenhouse Gas Emissions in Brazil. Second Edition]*, Ministry of Sciences, Technology and Innovation, Brasília, *www.mct.gov.br/upd_blob/0235/235580.pdf*.

MCTI (2014b), *First Biennal Update Report (BUR) under the United Natiosn Framework Convention on Climate Change (UNFCCC)*, Ministry of Sciences, Technology and Innovation, Brasília, *http://unfccc.int/resource/docs/note/brbur1.pdf*.

MCTI (2010), *Second National Communication of Brazil to the United Nations Framework Convention on Climate Change*, Ministry of Sciences, Technology and Innovation, Brasília.

MMA (2015a), *Fifth National Report to the Convention on Biological Diversity*, Ministry of the Environment, Brasília, *www.cbd.int/doc/world/br/br-nr-05-en.pdf*.

MMA (2015b), "Cadastro Nacional de Unidades de Conservação" [National Protected Areas Register], Ministry of the Environment, Brasília, *www.mma.gov.br/areas-protegidas/cadastro-nacional-de-ucs* (accessed February 2015).

MMA, (2014a), *Inventário Nacional de Emissões Atmosféricas por Veículos Automotores Rodoviários, 2013 [National Inventory of Air Emissions by Road Motor Vehicles, 2013]*, Ministry of the Environment, Brasília.

MMA (2014b), *PNIA 2012: Painal Nacional de Indicadores Ambientais. Referencial Teórico, Composição e Síntese dos Indicadores [PNIA 2012: National Panel of Environmental Indicators. Theoretical Framework, Composition and Synthesis of Indicators]*, Ministry of the Environment, Brasília.

MMA (2012a), *O que o Brasileiro Pensa do Meio Ambiente e do Consumo Sustentável: Pesquisa Nacional de Opinião: Principais Resultados [What Brazilians think of the Environment and Sustainable Consumption: National Opinion Research: Key Findings]*, Ministry of the Environment, Brasília.

MMA (2012b), *Plano Nacional de Resíduos Sólidos [National Solid Waste Plan]* (draft August 2012), Ministry of the Environment, Brasília, *www.sinir.gov.br/documents/10180/12308/PNRS_Revisao_Decreto_280812.pdf/e183f0e7-5255-4544-b9fd-15fc779a3657* (accessed February 2015).

MMA (2010), *Fourth National Report to the Convention on Biological Diversity*, Ministry of the Environment, Brasília.

OECD (2015a), *OECD Economic Outlook No. 96* (database), OECD, Paris, *http://dx.doi.org/10.1787/data-00717-en* (accessed January 2015).

OECD (2015b), *OECD Economic Surveys: Brazil*, OECD Publishing, Paris.

OECD (2015c), *Revenue Statistics in Latin America and the Caribbean 2015*, OECD Publishing, Paris, *http://dx.doi.org/10.1787/rev_lat-2015-en-fr*.

OECD (2013a), *OECD Economic Surveys: Brazil*, OECD Publishing, Paris, *http://dx.doi.org/10.1787/eco_surveys-bra-2013-en*.

OECD (2013b), *OCED Territorial Reviews: Brazil*, OECD Publishing, Paris, *http://dx.doi.org/10.1787/9789264123229-en*.

OECD (2013c), "Better Life Index: Better Life Index 2013", *OECD Social and Welfare Statistics* (database), OECD, Paris, *http://dx.doi.org/10.1787/data-00703-en*.

Olmo, N.R.S. et al. (2011), "A review of low-level air pollution and adverse effects on human health: implications for epidemiological studies and public policy", *Clinics*, Vol. 66, No. 4, pp. 681-690.

Pelaez V. et al. (2013), "Regulation of pesticides: A comparative analysis", *Science and Public Policy*, Vol. 40, pp. 644-656.

SEEG (2014), "Estimativas anuais das emissões de gases de efeito estufa" [Annual estimates of greenhouse gas emissions] (database), Sistema de Estimativas Anuais das Emissões de Gases de Efeito Estufa (SEEG), *www.seeg.eco.br/emissoes-totais* (accessed January 2015).

SFB (2015), "Sistema Nacional de Informações Florestais" [National System of Forest Information], Brazilian Forest Service, Brasília *www.florestal.gov.br/snif* (accessed February 2015).

SFB (2014), "Os Biomas e Suas Florestas" [Brazilian biomes and its forests], Brazilian Forest Service, Brasília, *www.florestal.gov.br/snif/recursos-florestais/os-biomas-e-suas-florestas* (accessed February 2015).

SFB (2013), *Brazilian Forests at a Glance 2013*, Brazilian Forest Service, Brasília.

Sparovek G. et al. (2010), "Brazilian Agriculture and Environmental Legislation: Status and Future Challenges", *Environmental Science & Technology*, Vol. 44, No. 16.

The Guardian (2015), "Brazil water shortage: São Paulo devastated by its worst drought on record", *The Guardian newspaper*, London, *www.theguardian.com/world/2015/jan/23/brazil-worst-drought-history* (accessed February 2015).

World Bank (2015), *World Development Indicators* (database), World Bank, Washington, DC, *http://data.worldbank.org/data catalog/world-development-indicators* (accessed February 2015).

World Bank (2011), *Country Partnership Strategy 2012-15*, World Bank, Washington, DC, *http://documents.worldbank.org/curated/en/2011/09/15273914/brazil-country-partnership-strategy-cps-period-fy2012-2015*.

WTO (2014), *Trade Profiles 2014*, World Trade Organization, Geneva, *www.wto.org/english/res_e/booksp_e/trade_profiles14_e.pdf*.

ANNEX 1.A

Energy and transport data

Figure 1.A1. **Energy structure and intensity**

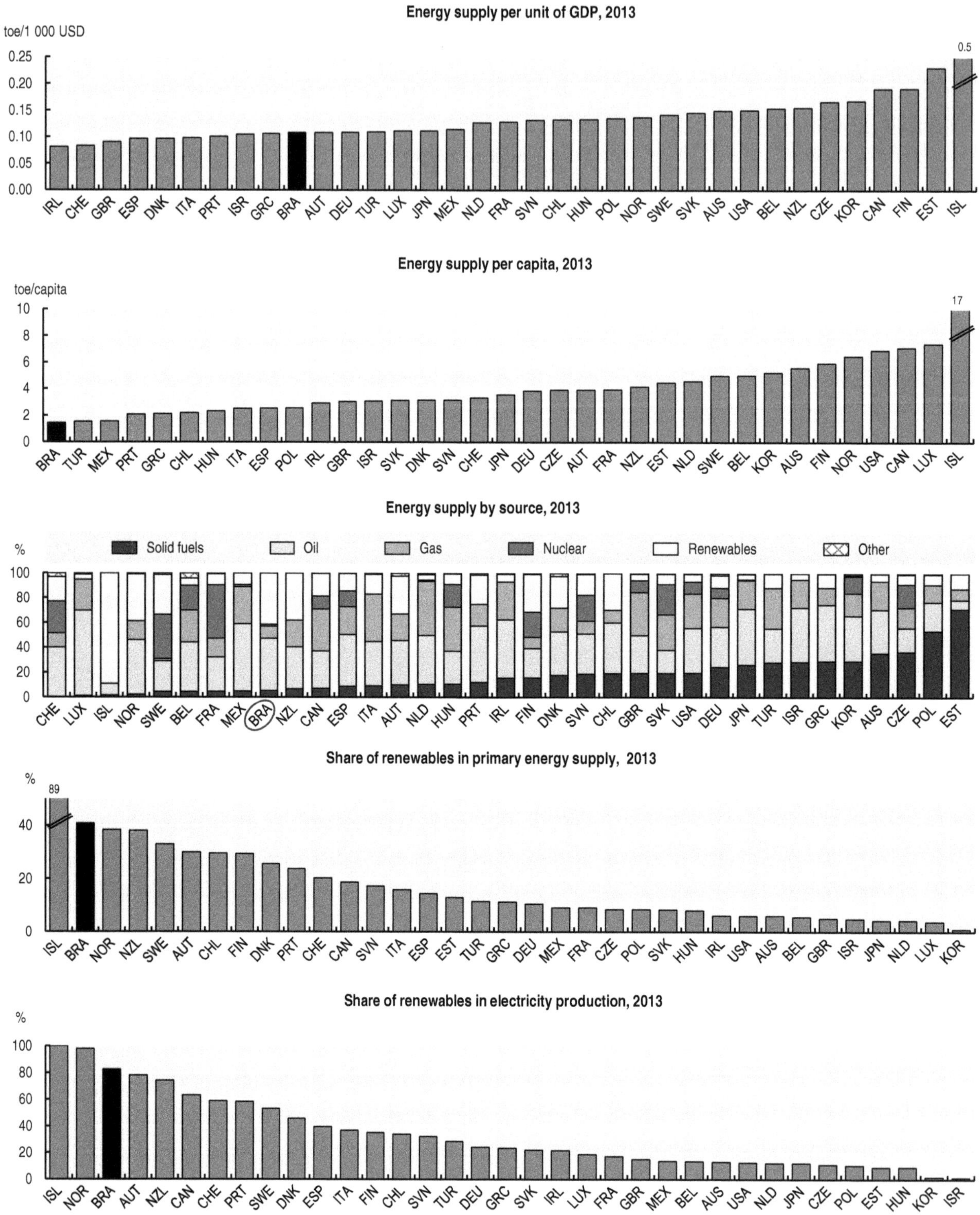

Notes: Data for Brazil refer to 2012. Data may include provisional figures and estimates.
Total primary energy supply; the breakdown excludes electricity trade. GDP at 2005 prices and purchasing power parities.
Source: IEA (2014), *IEA World Energy Statistics and Balances* (database); OECD (2014), "OECD Economic Outlook No. 95", *OECD Economic Outlook: Statistics and Projections* (database).

StatLink http://dx.doi.org/10.1787/888933279845

Figure 1.A2. **Road transport**

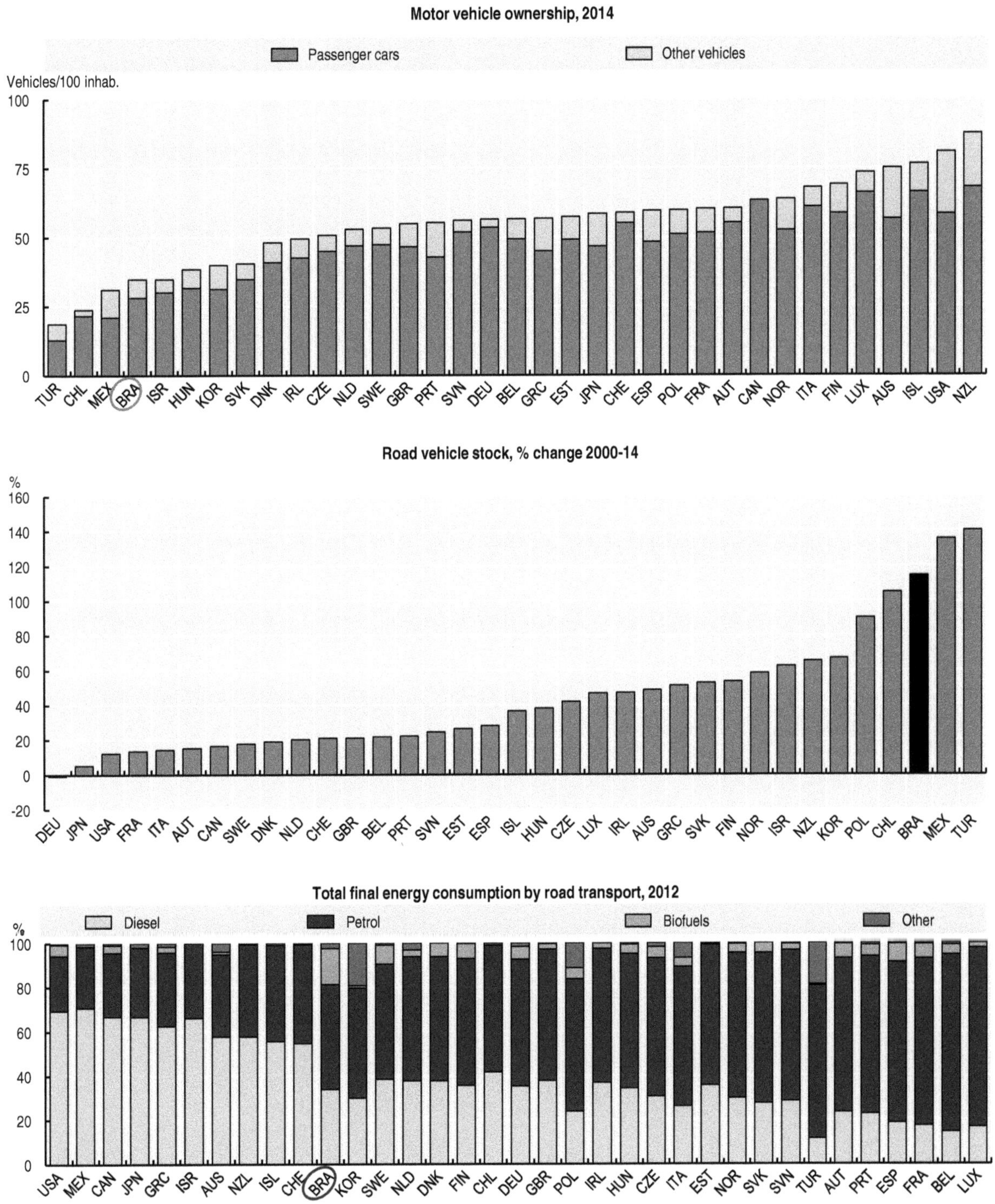

Notes: Data refer to the indicated year or to the latest available year. They may include provisional figures and estimates.
Vehicles: Motor vehicles with four or more wheels; Canada: data refer to total vehicles.
Source: IEA (2014), *IEA World Energy Statistics and Balances* (database); OECD (2015), *OECD Environment Statistics* (database).

StatLink http://dx.doi.org/10.1787/888933279855

ANNEX 1.B

Climate change and air pollution data

Figure 1.B1. **GHG emissions and intensity**

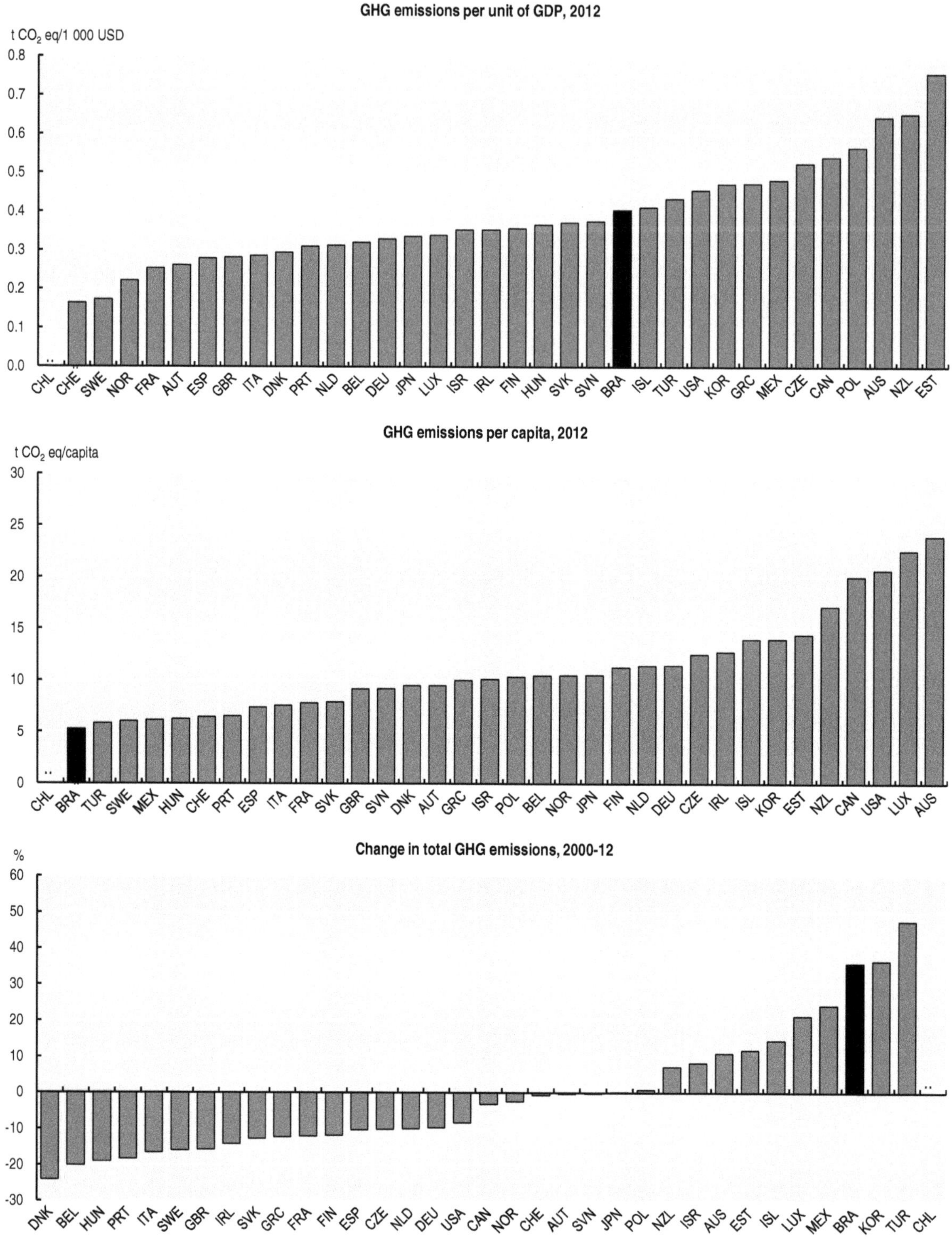

Notes: Data refer to the indicated year or to the latest available year. They may include provisional figures and estimates.
GHG emissions excluding emissions/removals from land use, land-use change and forestry. Israel: 2000 data exclude F-gases.
GDP at 2005 prices and purchasing power parities.
Source: OECD (2015), "Greenhouse gas emissions by source", *OECD Environment Statistics* (database); OECD (2014), "OECD Economic Outlook No. 95", *OECD Economic Outlook: Statistics and Projections* (database).

StatLink http://dx.doi.org/10.1787/888933279869

Figure 1.B2. CO_2 emissions and intensity

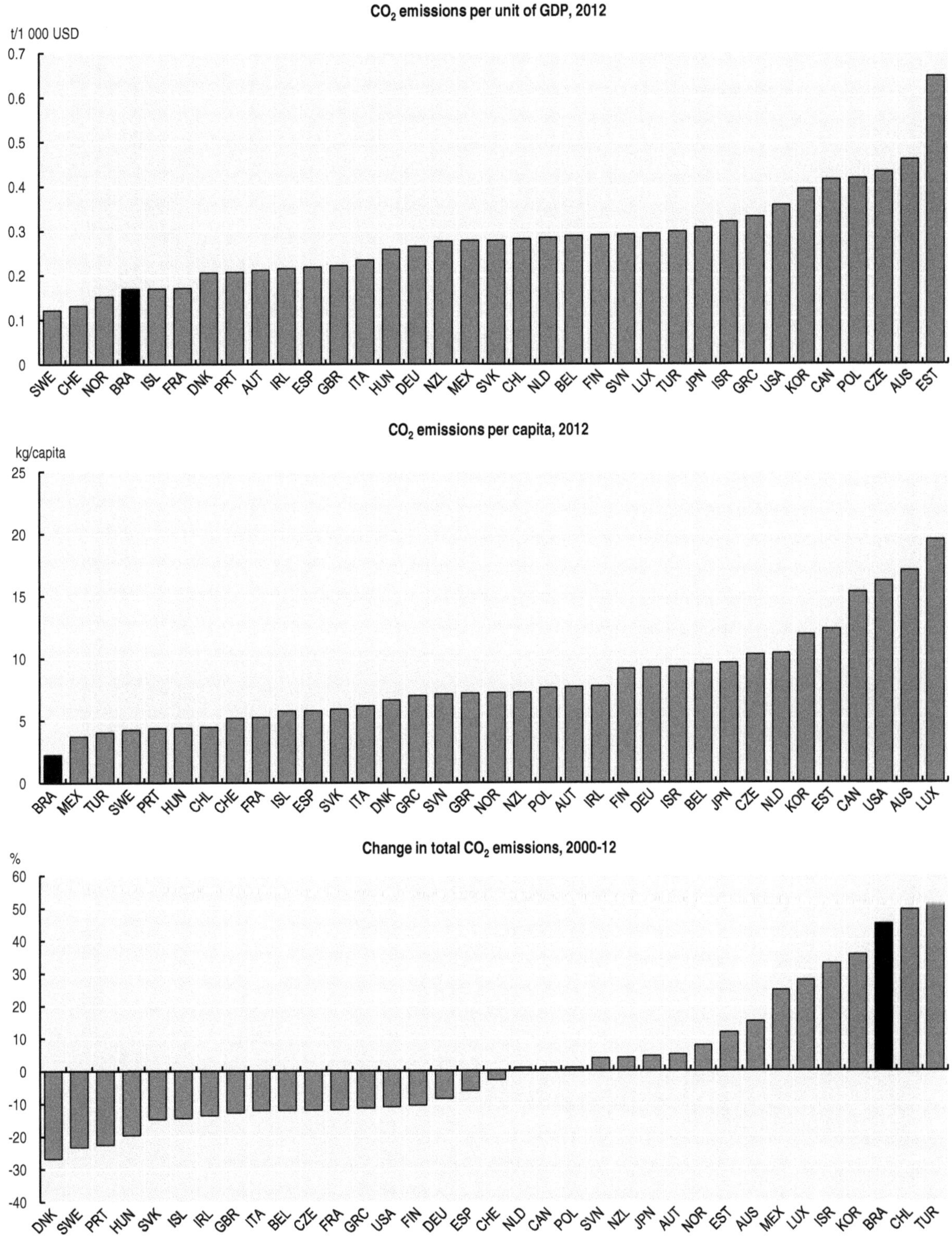

Notes: Data refer to the indicated year or to the latest available year. They may include provisional figures and estimates.
CO_2 emissions from energy use only; excluding international marine and aviation bunkers; sectoral approach. GDP at 2005 prices and purchasing power parities.
Source: IEA (2014), *IEA CO_2 Emissions from Fuel Combustion Statistics* (database); OECD (2014), "OECD Economic Outlook No. 95", *OECD Economic Outlook: Statistics and Projections* (database).

StatLink http://dx.doi.org/10.1787/888933279870

Figure 1.B3. **SO_x emissions and intensity**

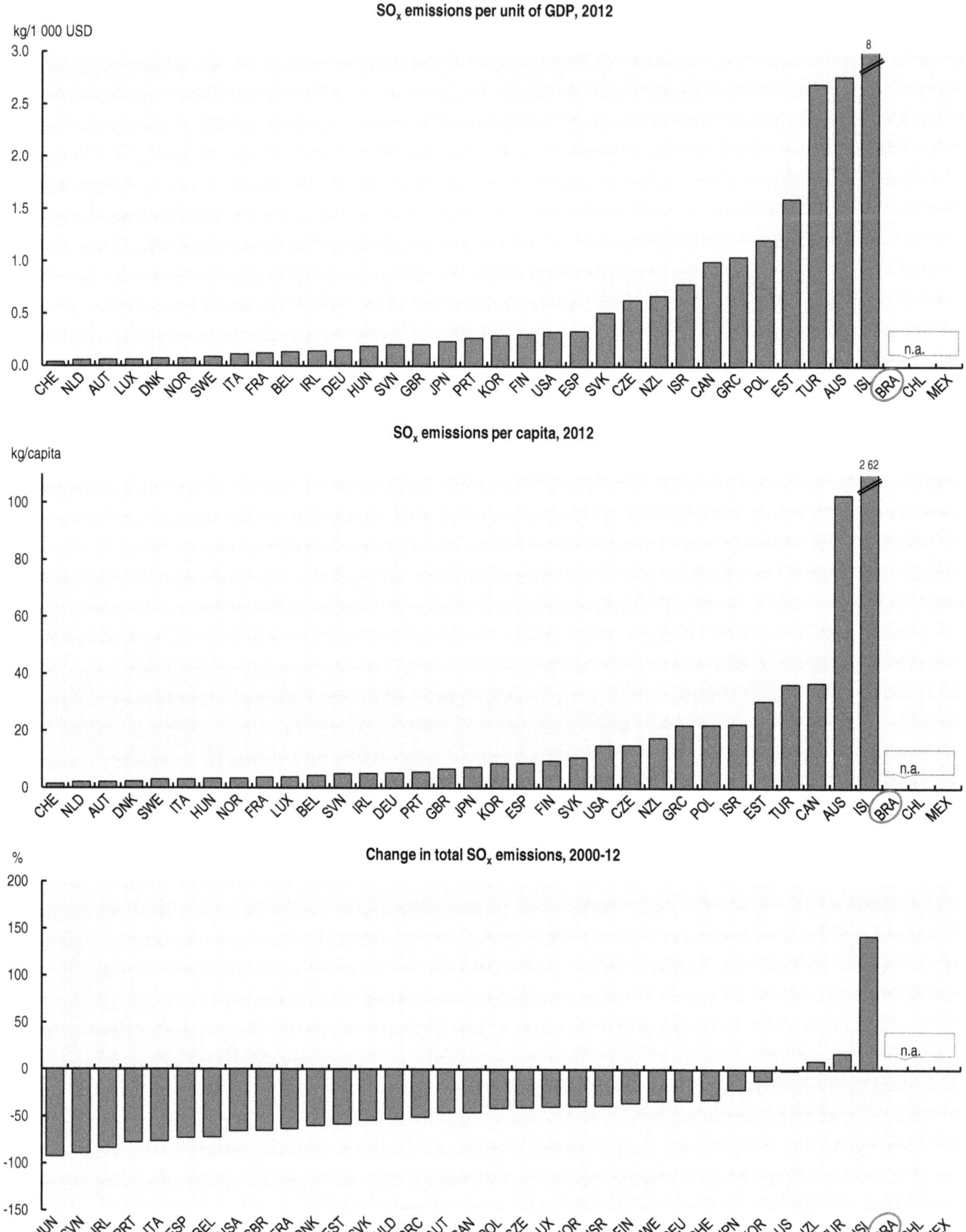

Notes: Data refer to the indicated year or to the latest available year. They may include provisional figures and estimates.
GDP at 2005 prices and purchasing power parities.
Source: OECD (2015), "Air emissions by source", *OECD Environment Statistics* (database); OECD (2014), "OECD Economic Outlook No. 95", *OECD Economic Outlook: Statistics and Projections* (database).

StatLink http://dx.doi.org/10.1787/888933279885

Figure 1.B4. NO_x emissions and intensity

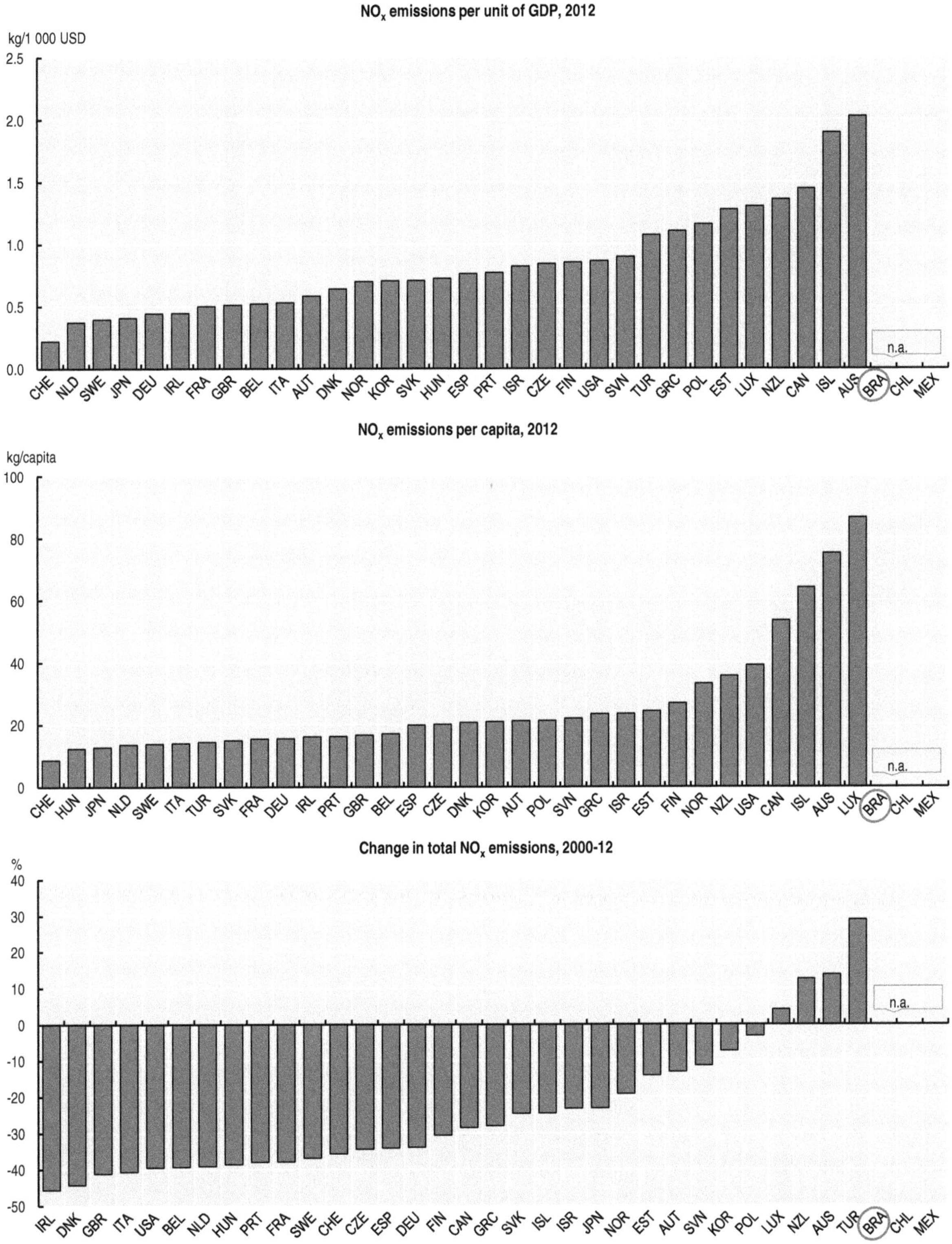

Notes: Data refer to the indicated year or to the latest available year. They may include provisional figures and estimates. GDP at 2005 prices and purchasing power parities.
Source: OECD (2015), "Air emissions by source", *OECD Environment Statistics* (database); OECD (2014), "OECD Economic Outlook No. 95", *OECD Economic Outlook: Statistics and Projections* (database).

StatLink http://dx.doi.org/10.1787/888933279896

Figure 1.B5. PM$_{2.5}$ emissions and pollution

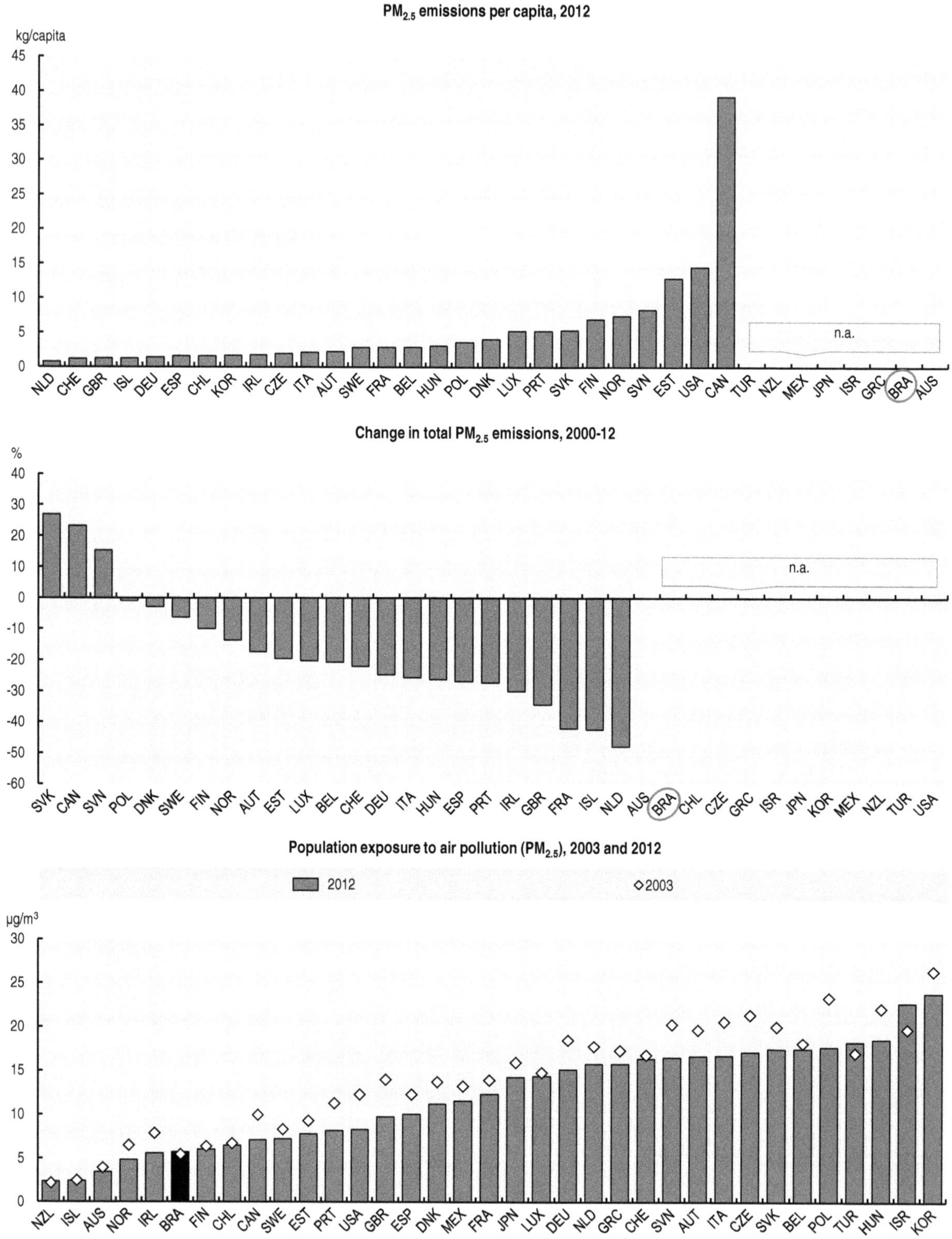

Notes: Data refer to the indicated year or to the latest available year. They may include provisional figures and estimates.
Population exposure to air pollution: estimated average exposure based on satellite imagery data; three-year average data.
Source: OECD (2015), "Air emissions by source", *OECD Environment Statistics* (database); OECD (2015), *OECD Regional Statistics* (database).

StatLink http://dx.doi.org/10.1787/888933279904

ANNEX 1.C

Waste and resource management data

Figure 1.C1. **Waste generation and management**

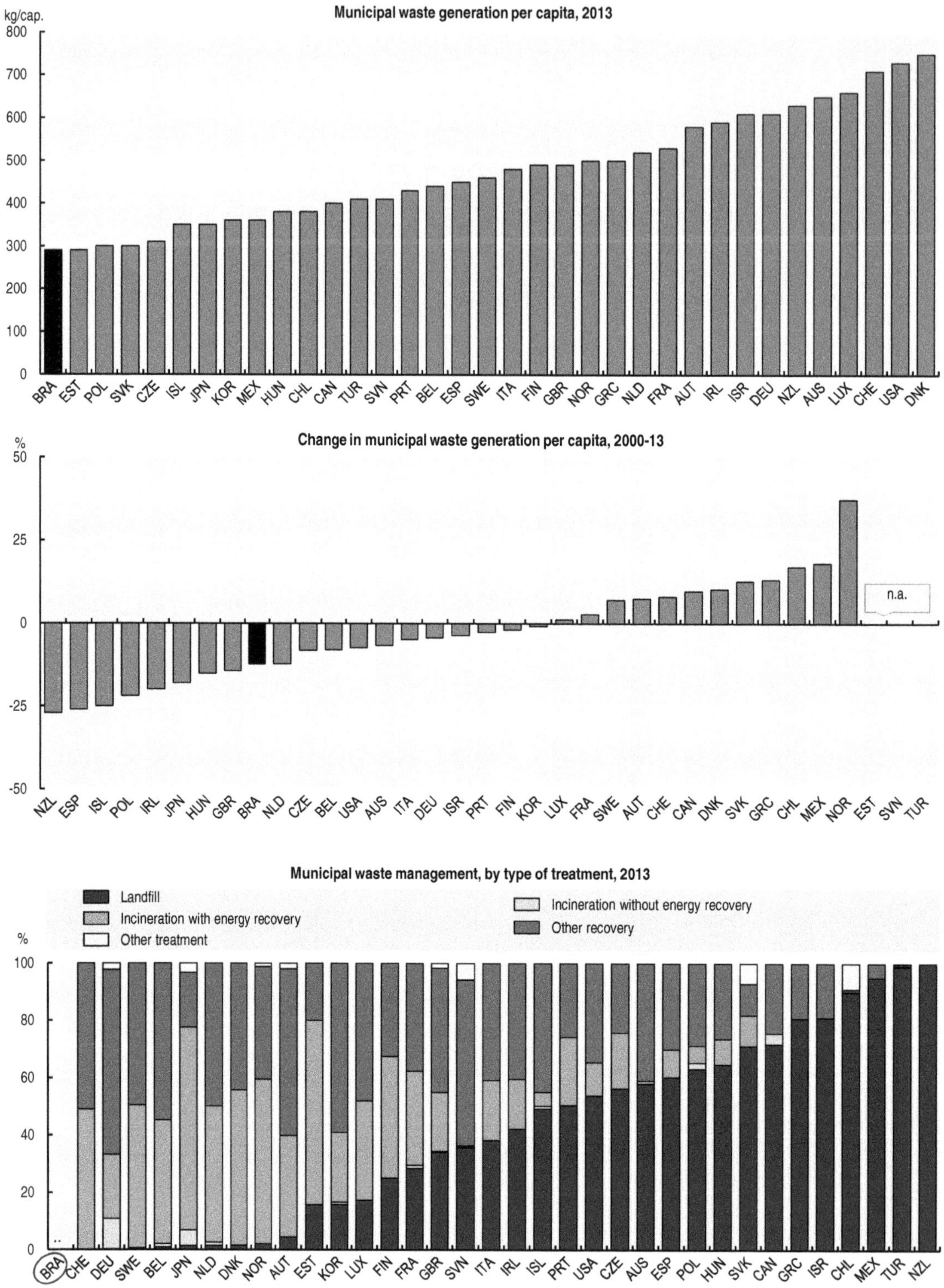

Notes: Data refer to the indicated year or to the latest available year. They may include provisional figures and estimates. Amounts per capita are rounded. Waste collected by or for municipalities. It includes household, bulky and commercial waste, and similar waste handled at the same facilities. It does not include municipal construction waste, nor waste sludges from municipal sewage treatment facilities.
Canada: household waste only and total incineration; New Zealand: landfilled waste only.
Source: OECD (2015), "Municipal waste", *OECD Environment Statistics* (database).

StatLink http://dx.doi.org/10.1787/888933279915

Figure 1.C2. **Material consumption and productivity**

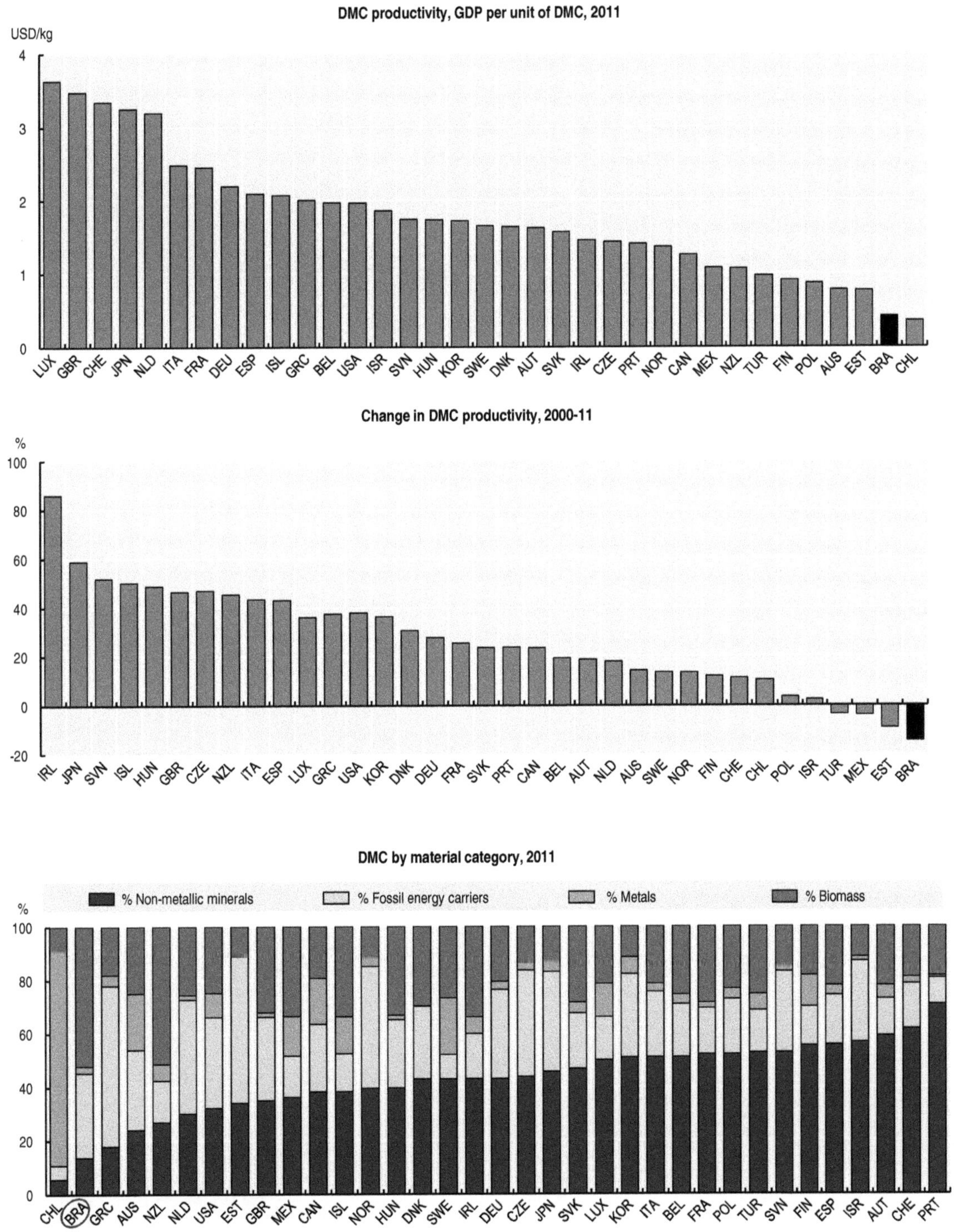

Notes: Data refer to the indicated year or to the latest available year. They may include provisional figures and estimates.
Domestic material consumption (DMC) equals the sum of domestic extraction of raw materials used by an economy and their physical trade balance (imports minus exports of raw materials and manufactured products). DMC productivity designates the amount of GDP generated per unit of materials used and is calculated as the ratio of GDP to domestic material consumption (DMC). GDP at 2005 prices and purchasing power parities.
Materials category: Non-metallic minerals: domestic extraction and trade of minerals used in industry and construction, plus trade of derived processed products; fossil energy carriers: coal, crude oil, natural gas, peat and traded-derived products; metals: domestic extraction of metal ores, plus trade of metal ores, metal concentrates, refined metals, products mainly made of metals, and scrap; biomass: domestic production from agriculture, forestry and fisheries, plus trade of raw and processed products from these sectors.
Source: OECD (2015), "Material resources", *OECD Environment Statistics* (database); OECD (2014), "OECD Economic Outlook No. 95", *OECD Economic Outlook: Statistics and Projections* (database).

StatLink http://dx.doi.org/10.1787/888933279927

Figure 1.C3. **Agricultural inputs and livestock density**

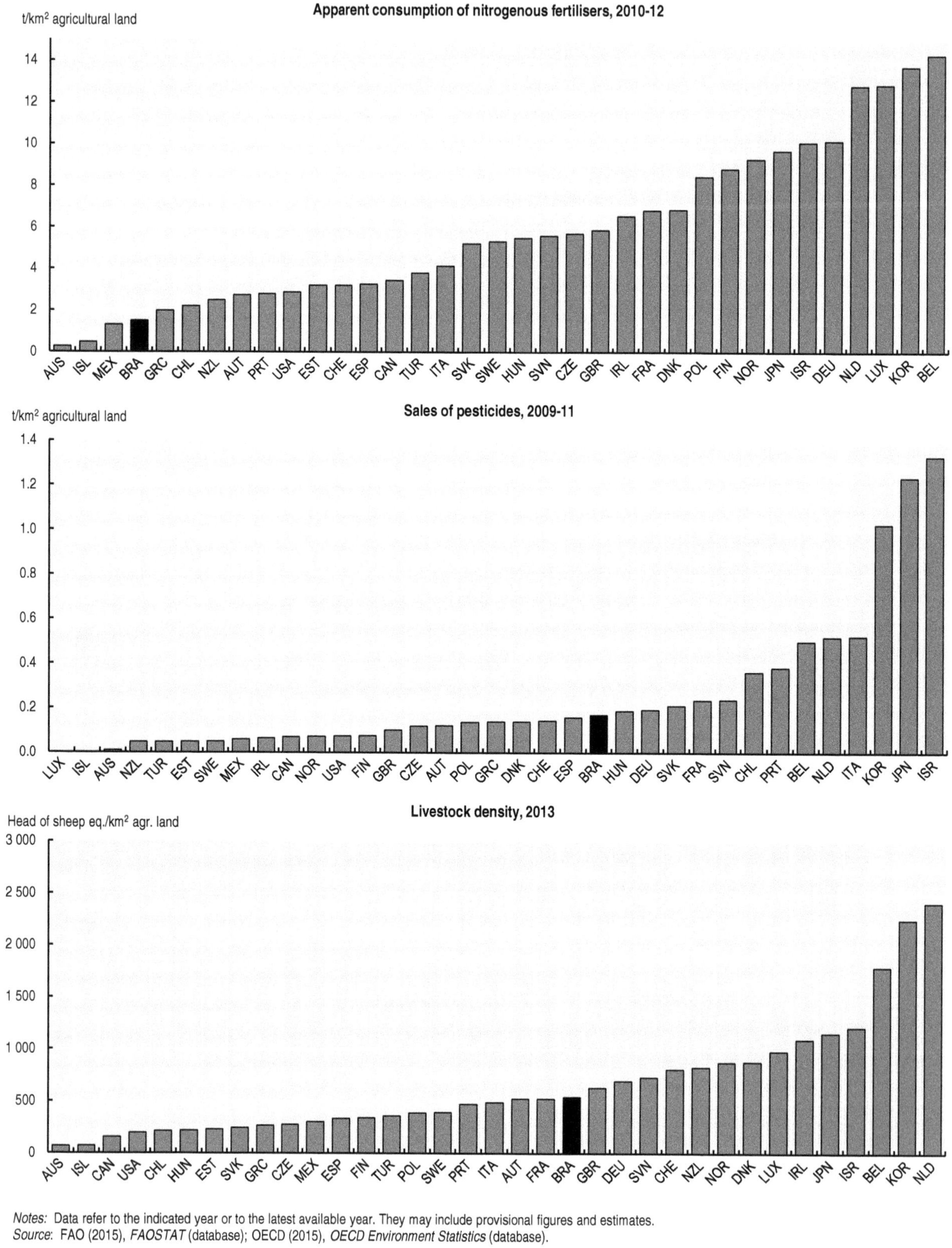

Notes: Data refer to the indicated year or to the latest available year. They may include provisional figures and estimates.
Source: FAO (2015), *FAOSTAT* (database); OECD (2015), *OECD Environment Statistics* (database).

StatLink http://dx.doi.org/10.1787/888933279935

ANNEX 1.D

Biodiversity and water data

Figure 1.D1. **Fish catches and threatened species**

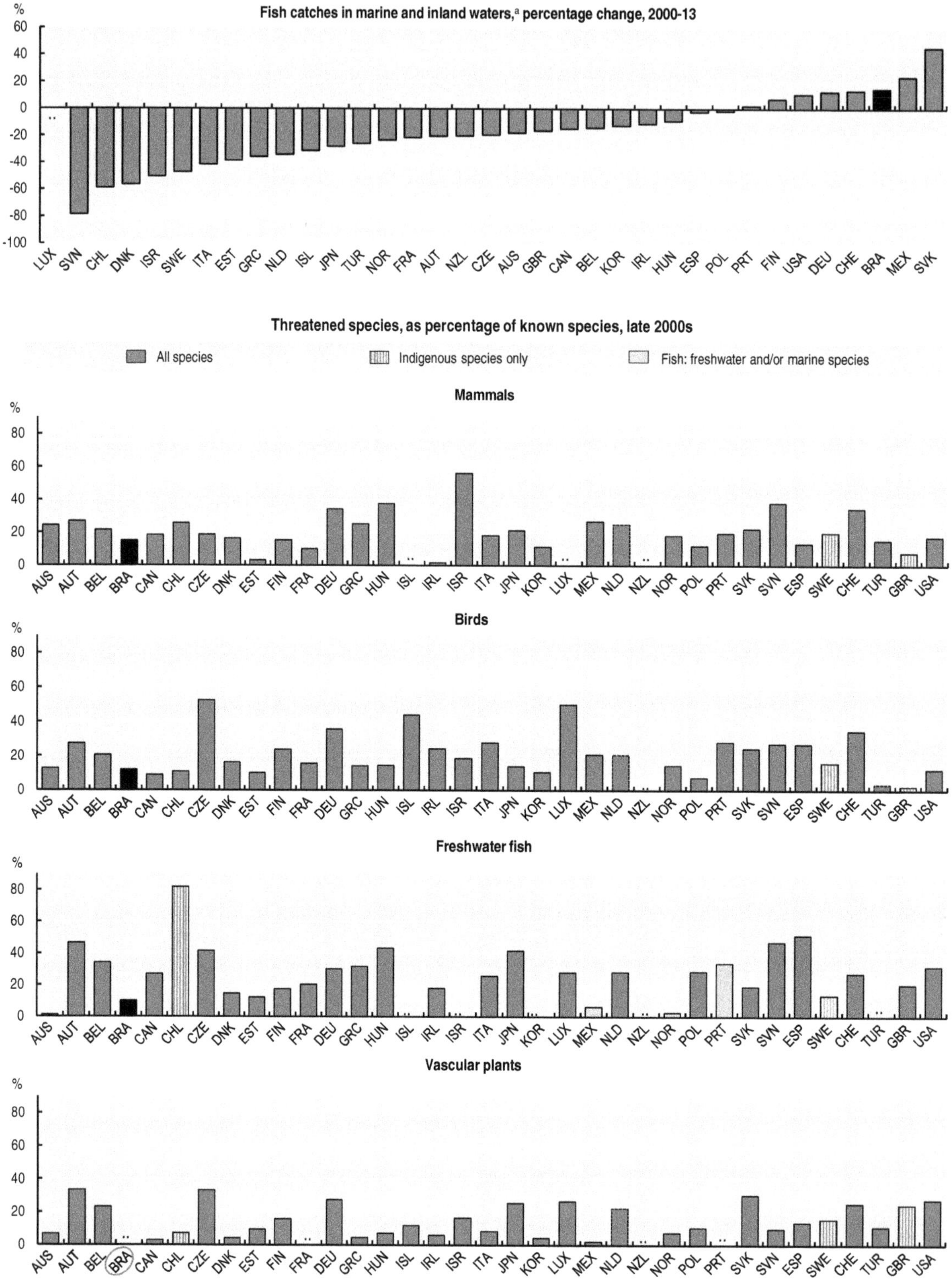

Notes: Data refer to the indicated year or to the latest available year. They may include provisional figures and estimates.

a) Includes fish, crustaceans, molluscs and other aquatic animals. Excludes marine mammals, crocodiles and alligators, and miscellaneous aquatic products.

Source: Chico Mendes Institute for Biodiversity Conservation (ICMBio) (2015), "Espécies Ameaçadas – Lista 2014" [Endangered species list 2014]; FAO (2015), *Global Capture Production* (database); MMA (2015), *Fifth National Report to the Convention on Biological Diversity*, OECD (2015), "Threatened species", *OECD Environment Statistics* (database).

StatLink http://dx.doi.org/10.1787/888933279943

Figure 1.D2. **Water abstraction and wastewater treatment**

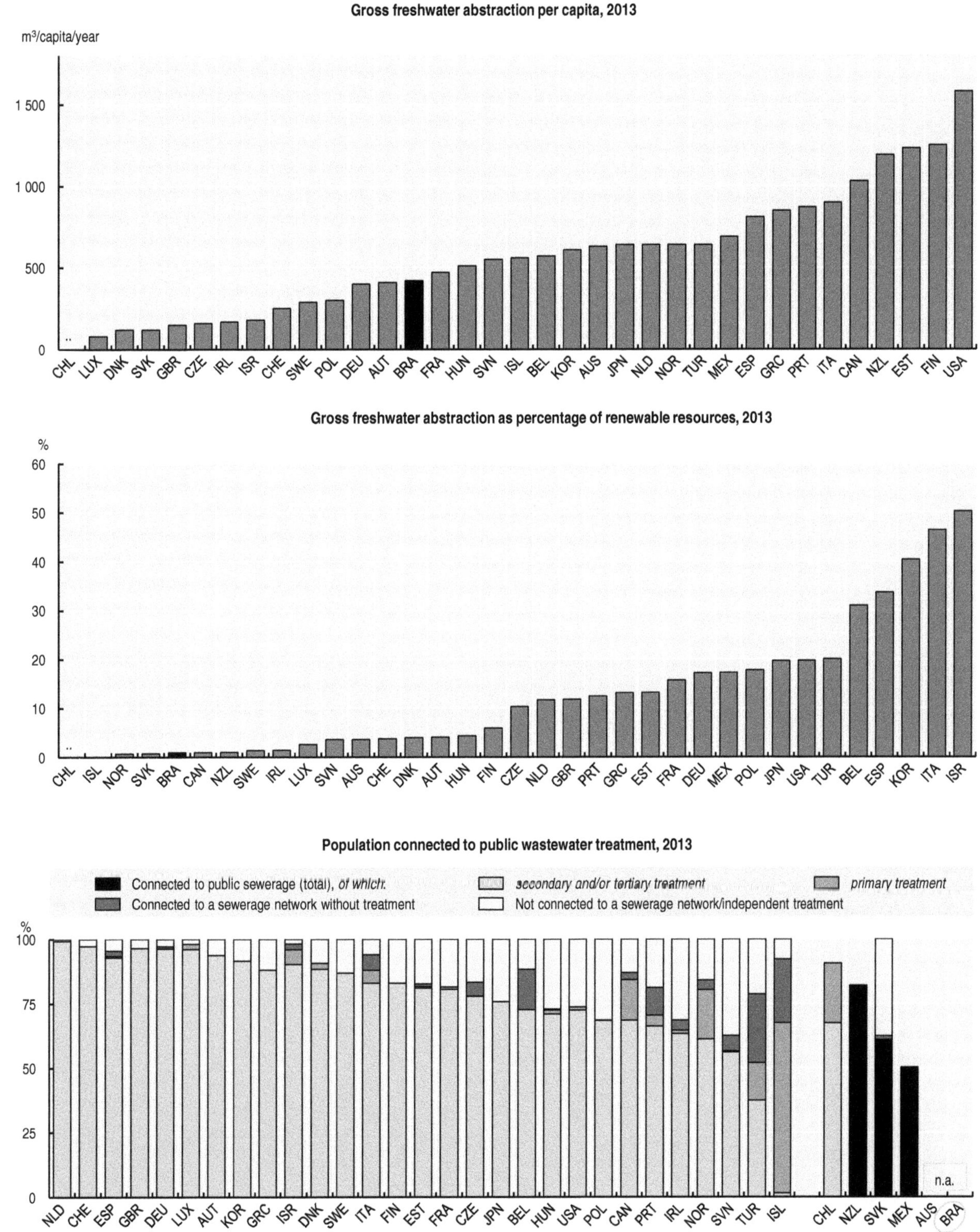

Notes: Data refer to the indicated year or to the latest available year. They may include provisional figures and estimates. United Kingdom: England and Wales only. Freshwater abstraction: for some countries, data refer to water permits and not to actual abstractions. Amounts per capita are rounded.

Source: OECD (2015), "Water: Freshwater Abstractions", "Wastewater Treatment (% Population Connected)", *OECD Environment Statistics* (database).

StatLink http://dx.doi.org/10.1787/888933279958

OECD Environmental Performance Reviews: Brazil 2015

PART I

Chapter 2

Environmental governance and management

Brazil has developed comprehensive and advanced environmental legislative framework and institutional arrangements. The country's economic and social heterogeneity and decentralised federal system, however, generate significant implementation challenges. This chapter analyses the Brazilian environmental governance system, including horizontal and vertical co-ordination mechanisms and environment authorities' budgets. It reviews the regulatory framework for air, water and waste management and for addressing climate change, as well as for environmental impact assessment and permitting. Enforcement and compliance assurance are discussed. The chapter also assesses progress in promoting public participation in decision making and access to environmental information, education and justice.

1. Multilevel institutional framework for environmental governance

Brazil has a highly decentralised federal system of governance, with 26 states and the Federal District. The 5 570 municipalities (about 70% of which have fewer than 20 000 inhabitants) enjoy very broad autonomy: the 1988 Federal Constitution gave municipalities the status of federal entities, at the same level as states. States have their own constitutions and governments and can adopt policies and laws, according to their priorities, within the general framework of federal law. Municipalities can legislate on all matters of local interest and supplement federal and state laws, except on matters falling under exclusive federal jurisdiction. While states and municipalities raise their own tax revenue, the federal government's large direct financial transfers to local governments give it significant policy leverage.

The Constitution identifies environmental policy as a "common and convergent" responsibility shared by the federal, state and municipal levels. The National Environmental System (SISNAMA), created by the 1981 National Environmental Policy (PNMA) Law, brings together relevant government institutions at all levels in a complex governance framework of councils and executive agencies (Table 2.1). Complementary Law 140/2011 and Presidential Decree 8437/2015 provided long-awaited clarification of the boundaries of federal, state and local jurisdiction over certain environmental issues, particularly with respect to environmental licensing and impact assessment (Sections 4.1 and 4.2).

Table 2.1. **SISNAMA at different government levels**

Administrative level	Council	Executive agency
Federal	National Environmental Council	Ministry of the Environment, Brazilian Institute of Environment and Renewable Natural Resources, Chico Mendes Institute for Biodiversity Conservation
State	State Environmental Council	Secretariat or state executive agency (may be integrated with other policy areas)
Municipal	Municipal Environmental Council	Executive agency (usually integrated with other policy areas)

Source: Cavalcanti (2007), "Economic Growth and Environmental Protection in Brazil: An Unfavourable trade-off", in *Environmental Governance and Decentralisation*, A. Breton et al. (eds), Edward Elgar, Cheltenham, UK.

1.1. *National institutions and horizontal co-ordination*

The main nationwide policy-making and multilevel co-ordination body is the National Environmental Council (CONAMA). Established in 1981, this high-level advisory and deliberative committee brings together representatives of all government levels and principal stakeholders.[1] To fill the wide gap in environmental regulations in the 1980s and 1990s, CONAMA went beyond its advisory mandate, adopting a large body of national regulations. Its resolutions gained increasing authority, attaining the force of law and substituting to some extent for legislative activity on the environment. While the judiciary has never challenged CONAMA's regulatory powers, the body's proactive rule making has created tension with other regulators, particularly at the state level, and damaged CONAMA's reputation for multi-stakeholder collaboration. The council is working to restore the trust of other environmental actors by reviewing its body of resolutions and assuming more of a guiding and co-ordination role.

The Ministry of the Environment (MMA), established in 1992,[2] develops, co-ordinates and oversees implementation of federal environmental policy (whereas CONAMA deals with policies at all levels of government). The MMA's responsibilities include developing proposals for economic and social strategies and instruments aimed at improved environmental quality and sustainable natural resource use. The MMA's institutional capacity has grown remarkably over the last ten years. However, its annual budget is still among the lowest of any federal ministry (Section 2), and high staff turnover remains a big problem in terms of retaining qualified personnel and ensuring institutional continuity.

The Brazilian Institute of Environment and Renewable Natural Resources (IBAMA), formed in 1989, is the federal executive environment agency. As state agencies are predominant in pollution regulation, natural resource management has become IBAMA's main emphasis, with a focus on areas of the country that are particularly rich in natural resources, such as the Amazon. In 2007, IBAMA was divided into two agencies: one maintaining the IBAMA name and the principal functions of licensing, monitoring and enforcement; and the Chico Mendes Institute for Biodiversity Conservation (ICMBio), which oversees all aspects of federal protected areas. The rationale for this change was to separate preservation and management of protected areas from compliance monitoring (Chapter 5). The Brazilian Forest Service manages activities related to public forests.

Brazil has a separate complex institutional framework for water resource management, which is loosely co-ordinated with the environment authorities (Box 2.1), an arrangement similar to that in some OECD countries, such as the Netherlands.

The new SISNAMA Strategic Information System (SEIS) aims to show how activities, projects and instruments of the MMA and its institutions are related to 15 strategic agendas established in the ministry's strategic planning. "Strategic Plan: Management by Results, 2014-2022", which the MMA issued in June 2014, established qualitative targets in each of 15 priority policy areas and outlined concrete initiatives for their achievement, though it includes no procedures for performance evaluation or outcome indicators. SEIS is still at an early stage and only accessible internally, but the MMA intends to expand it to all SISNAMA institutions.

Several of the 39 federal ministries have environment-related responsibilities, and thus are considered part of SISNAMA, including the agriculture, energy and transport ministries. Other ministries have responsibilities that in some countries fall under the environment ministry's jurisdiction: for example, the Ministry of Cities oversees waste management and sanitation, and the Ministry of Science, Technology and Innovation (MCTI) runs the greenhouse gas (GHG) emission inventory.

Brazil's institutional culture is one of silo-type ministries: each sectoral ministry pursues its own strategy at the subnational level and does not necessarily co-ordinate with other ministries. Similar systems exist in many other countries but the situation may be exacerbated in Brazil because the number of ministries is so large. Failure to mainstream environmental matters into sectoral policies and programmes was long a key sustainable development challenge for the country: sectoral ministries were reluctant to deal with environmental issues, arguing that this was the role of environmental authorities. In the

Box 2.1. **Institutional framework for water governance**

The National Water Agency (ANA) is responsible for implementing the National Water Resources Policy and regulating water use in rivers under federal jurisdiction. The National Water Resources Council (CNRH), a consulting body in parallel with CONAMA, formulates the National Water Resources Policy.[3] Its members represent federal and state government agencies, water resource users and civil society organisations. CNRH and ANA are overseen by the MMA Secretariat of Water Resources and Urban Environment.

Responsibility for water resource management is divided between the national government, for federal rivers, and the states, for state rivers – including tributaries of federal rivers – and groundwater. The National Water Resources Policy Law made river basins the main unit of water resource planning and established respective committees and agencies.

The institutional framework for water resource management at the subnational level aims to ensure decentralisation and stakeholder participation. It is complex, with the relationship between water resource management and environmental institutions varying by state. Some states (e.g. Rio de Janeiro) have adopted full integration within one organisation, while others keep water resource agencies separate from environment agencies. In Rio de Janeiro, integration has been successful due to deep awareness of water problems and a well-trained staff; in other cases the environmental agenda in merged institutions has tended to crowd out water management issues. Subnational water governance includes the following entities:

State water resource councils – consulting bodies instituted by the states to formulate state water resource policies. All states but Acre have a water resource council, though capacity varies widely among them.

State water resource management agencies – bodies that regulate resource use in rivers under state jurisdiction, which often form river basins with federal rivers. Some states have special agencies to manage water resources, while in others such bodies are part of environment authorities and subject to periodic reorganisation.

River basin committees – deliberative bodies at river basin level that include representatives of government authorities, water users and civil society. Over 200 committees have been established, covering about a quarter of the national territory, but mostly in the South and South-east, in areas with acute problems and mobilisation of water users.

Water agencies – technical bodies that act as executive agencies of the river basin committees. In practice, state water resource management agencies usually perform this role because the human and financial resources to maintain separate institutions are lacking, but this makes river basin committees dependent on state government to implement their decisions.

Source: OECD (2015), *Water Resources Governance in Brazil*, OECD Publishing, Paris.

early 2000s, the MMA was somewhat isolated and to a large degree excluded from sectoral policy making (Teixeira, 2012). As a result, sector-specific policies and programmes took little account of potentially negative environmental effects.

The situation has improved in recent years, with thematic groups on environment-related issues established in many ministries and engaging in dialogue with the MMA. Environment has taken a more important place on Brazil's economic and social agenda. Yet the MMA lacks the necessary resources and power to ensure systematic mainstreaming of environmental concerns into policy making. High-profile leadership or co-ordination would help improve policy coherence and enable a whole-of-government approach to sustainable development. Positive experiences in this respect are the co-ordination arrangements in place for climate change policy and for combatting deforestation in the Amazon, with direct involvement by the chief of staff of the President's office, which is known as the Casa Civil (Section 3.1 and Chapter 4).

Interagency collaboration has been institutionalised in many policy areas, including climate change (Section 3.1), biodiversity and forestry. Over 400 interagency committees, boards and working groups deal with various environment-related issues. These horizontal co-ordination bodies are useful in countering the ministerial "silo culture", in engaging the business community and civil society, and in raising environmental awareness in the administration. Their overabundance, however, makes it costly and time-consuming for member agencies to participate, and many are abandoned soon after their creation.

1.2. Subnational institutions

States have important regulatory and compliance assurance powers in water resource management and air pollution control, and a more limited role in the management of waste, natural resources and biodiversity. The set-up of state environmental institutions is similar to that at the national level. Each state has an environmental council and a secretariat or agency for the environment (usually also in charge of other areas, such as planning or science and technology). The councils include representatives of municipalities and non-government stakeholders. Some states (e.g. Espírito Santo) have regional environmental councils in addition to the state council. States also have fragmented sectoral ministries, and in many cases have created horizontal co-ordination systems (e.g. in water resource management; see Box 2.1).

States vary considerably in the level of development of environmental institutions. The strongest environment agencies are those of São Paulo, including the state-owned Environmental Sanitation Technology Company (CETESB), the pollution control authority, which dates back to the 1970s. On the other end of the spectrum, the Science, Technology and Environment Secretariat of the Amazonian state of Pará did not start functioning until the mid-1990s (McAllister, 2008) and remains institutionally weak. Many state agencies face a significant challenge to maintain qualified technical staff. IBAMA has tended to supplement the state agencies, taking a greater role in the states where institutional capacity is most limited, particularly in the North and North-east.

Municipalities have a high degree of constitutional autonomy. They can elaborate and enforce environmental norms, including licensing regimes; impose environmental fees and earmark their revenue to special funds (e.g. to support local conservation projects); and create protected areas of particular natural or cultural value. Municipalities are also responsible for providing water supply, sanitation and waste management services as well as for land use planning.

However, real devolution of environmental management to the municipalities, a principle embraced in the Constitution and other environmental legislation, has been difficult to achieve. Institutional capacity varies quite widely among municipalities because of differences in socio-economic development, a fact that needs to be accounted for in the design and implementation of federal environmental policies on issues such as waste management. To strengthen environmental management devolution to municipalities, São Paulo state adopted an incentive-based programme that could serve as a model for other states (Box 2.2).

Box 2.2. **São Paulo's GreenBlue Programme**

In 2007, São Paulo state's Secretariat for the Environment launched an innovative programme to strengthen devolution of environmental management to the municipal level. The GreenBlue Municipality Programme provides incentives to municipalities to develop and implement environmental plans, evaluates municipalities' performance annually and provides technical support and measures to increase environmental management capacity.

While participation in the programme is voluntary, it is a condition for access to resources from São Paulo's pollution fund, FECOP. Municipalities can join by signing a memorandum of understanding agreeing to actions and goals in ten environmental management areas: sewage treatment, solid waste management, biodiversity, urban forests, environmental education, sustainable city management, water management, air quality, environmental governance and the functioning of an environmental council.[4] The number of municipalities participating in the programme increased from 44 in 2008 to 645 in 2014.

At the end of each annual cycle, the state secretariat evaluates municipalities' performance on a set of indicators for each environmental management area, on the basis of self-reporting by municipalities. The secretariat publishes a ranking and awards prizes to the best-performing municipalities. Municipalities with high scores gain a "green seal" and priority access to funding; those that score low receive technical support. The assessment criteria may vary from year to year. For example, in the 2014 cycle, municipalities could earn 0.5 points (out of 100) for joining the UN Making Cities Resilient campaign, and 210 cities did so.

Source: São Paulo Secretariat for the Environment (2015), Project Portfolio; São Paulo Secretariat for the Environment (2015), Município VerdeAzul website, *www.ambiente.sp.gov.br/municipioverdeazul*.

The share of municipalities with a municipal environmental council has grown significantly in the last decade, although their status and activities vary greatly and about a quarter are inactive (Figure 2.1). Still, all but a very few municipalities with population over 100 000 have functioning environmental institutions (IBGE, 2014a). About 1 100 municipalities have benefited from capacity-building activities in the National Training Programme for Environmental Managers, which the MMA has run since 2005.

1.3. *Vertical collaboration mechanisms*

The federal institutions in charge of vertical relations with other administrative levels are the Under-secretariat of Federal Issues in the Secretariat for Institutional Relations, supervised by the Casa Civil, and the Federal Co-ordination Committee, aimed at facilitating dialogue between the federal and municipal levels. However, these bodies are only marginally concerned with environmental issues.

CONAMA is the principal formal mechanism for co-operative environmental governance. In reality, however, its representative composition (Section 1.1) does not correspond to the level of engagement of the various stakeholders in environmental

Figure 2.1. **Many municipalities have established an environmental institution**

Percentage of municipalities with environmental institutions, 2004, 2009 and 2013

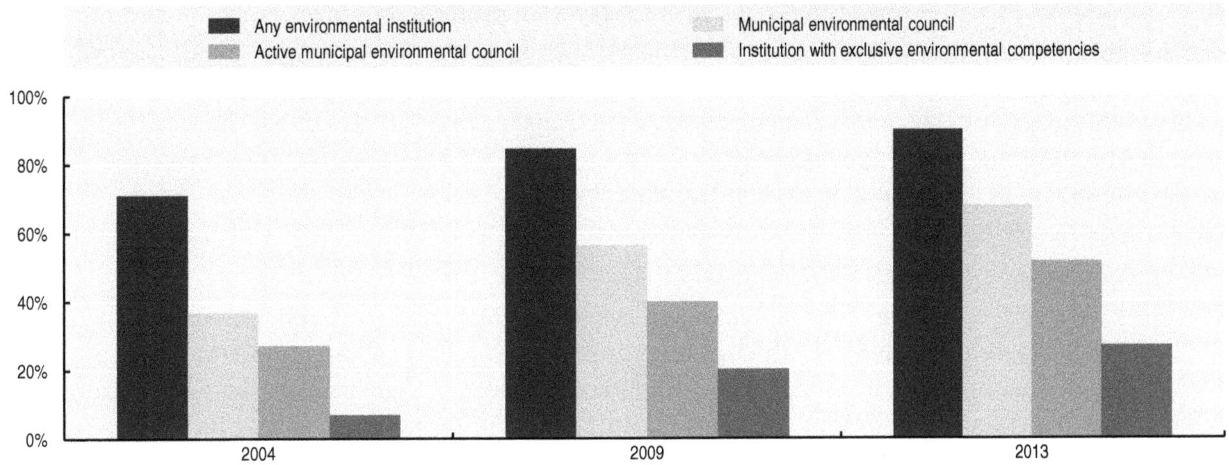

Source: IBGE (2013; 2009; 2004), *Perfil dos municípios brasileiros.*

StatLink http://dx.doi.org/10.1787/888933279525

decision making; many members routinely miss its meetings (Sano, 2012), and municipalities complain that they lack influence on its decisions. Similar problems are common in state environmental councils, which do not appear to provide an effective platform for collaboration between states and municipalities.

To complement the policy-making collaboration in CONAMA, the National Tripartite Technical Commission (CTN) was created in 2001. Its aim is to strengthen vertical co-ordination between the three levels of government to improve environmental policy implementation. Each level is represented by three CTN members. The state representatives are appointed by the Brazilian Association of State Environment Authorities (ABEMA) and the municipal delegates by the National Association of Municipal Environment Agencies (ANAMMA). The CTN plays only an advisory role and, like many similar Brazilian co-ordinating bodies, lacks the policy tools to ensure that its recommendations are implemented.

All states have State Tripartite Technical Commissions (CTEs) intended to foster dialogue between the state environment agency and municipalities. There is some evidence, however, that the CTEs are institutionally weak, lack clear working procedures and get little or no support from the federal level (Sano, 2012).

ABEMA and, to a lesser extent, ANAMMA undertake activities to promote co-operation and information exchange between their member institutions and defend at the national level their views on environmental policy design and implementation. For example, in 2013 ABEMA developed proposals to improve the environmental licensing system (Section 4.1). Both associations hold frequent issue-specific workshops; ANAMMA, for instance, held several events on sanitation and solid waste management.

Despite the abundance of federal-state collaboration mechanisms (technical co-operation agreements, partnership agreements, decentralised execution agreements, etc.), the ties between levels of government are seen as weak and riddled with conflict, leading to fragmentation of power (Costa Neves, 2012). Co-ordination challenges arise not only between the federal and state levels, but also among states (for example, those sharing a river basin) and between states and municipalities. In a 2009 report on achieving climate change goals in the Amazon, the Federal Court of Accounts (TCU) pointed out several key institutional challenges in multilevel environmental governance, including fragmented distribution of responsibilities, conflicting policy objectives, poor vertical and horizontal interaction between agencies, and lack of ownership of environmental initiatives, often due to insufficient capacity (TCU, 2009). The TCU also noted the weakness of monitoring, reporting and evaluation, stating that the federal government was often unaware of activities taking place at the state level.

2. Environmental institution budgets and environmental funds

Brazil does not yet have a system to systematically monitor public environment-related expenditure. However, in 2014 the Ministry of Planning, Budget and Management launched a project to track and better understand all federal government spending and investment on environment, in co-operation with the Brazilian Institute for Applied Economic Research (IPEA). This is of particular importance because the MMA budget is relatively small and other ministries and agencies contribute a large part of public environmental expenditure.[5] The MMA is also making an effort to track federal climate-related spending: initial estimates suggest that such spending totalled about BRL 10 billion over 2012-14. These initiatives are important steps in improving understanding of the effectiveness and efficiency of public resource allocation. They should be continued with rigor and, over time, extended to state and municipal spending.

The budget of the MMA and environmental institutions was BRL 3.6 billion (about USD 1.5 billion) in 2014, one of the lowest among federal entities, amounting to 0.15% of the federal budget (Senado Federal, 2015). The federal budget has recently been shrinking, but resources allocated to the MMA and environmental agencies increased by 16% in real terms over 2010-14. More than half the MMA budget is generally distributed to environment agencies, notably IBAMA and ICMBio (Figure 2.2). In the Treasury's budget classification by government function, allocations for environmental management grew by 48% over 2010-14 to 0.37% of the federal budget. The MMA budget amounts to about 30% of overall budget allocations for environmental management; most of the total is spent by the Ministry of National Integration, which is in charge of reducing regional disparity (Senado Federal, 2015).

A distinct feature of public environment-related expenditure in Brazil is the use of dedicated funds (budgetary and extra-budgetary) for implementation of environmental policies and programmes at the federal, state and municipal levels. This further complicates the tracking and evaluation of resource allocation. The MMA co-ordinates five federal funds of various sizes and with differing but partly overlapping objectives. Resources originate from a variety of sources, including the federal budget, royalties from oil and gas exploration (Box 3.2), donations from private and public sources (including performance-based donations) and loans (Table 2.2). Earmarking resources to funds for environmental purposes may be necessary to secure reliable, sufficient resources, but can reduce the flexibility of fiscal decisions and, therefore, efficiency of revenue allocation. It is essential to regularly monitor the activities of environment funds to ensure that they are in line with policy priorities and are transparent and cost-effective. Multiple funds with overlapping objectives should be avoided.

The two largest federal funds (Climate Change Fund and Amazon Fund) have sound monitoring systems and have been effective in securing resources for projects, including

Figure 2.2. **The federal budget allocated to environmental institutions has grown**

Federal budget outlays to environmental institutions, 2005-14

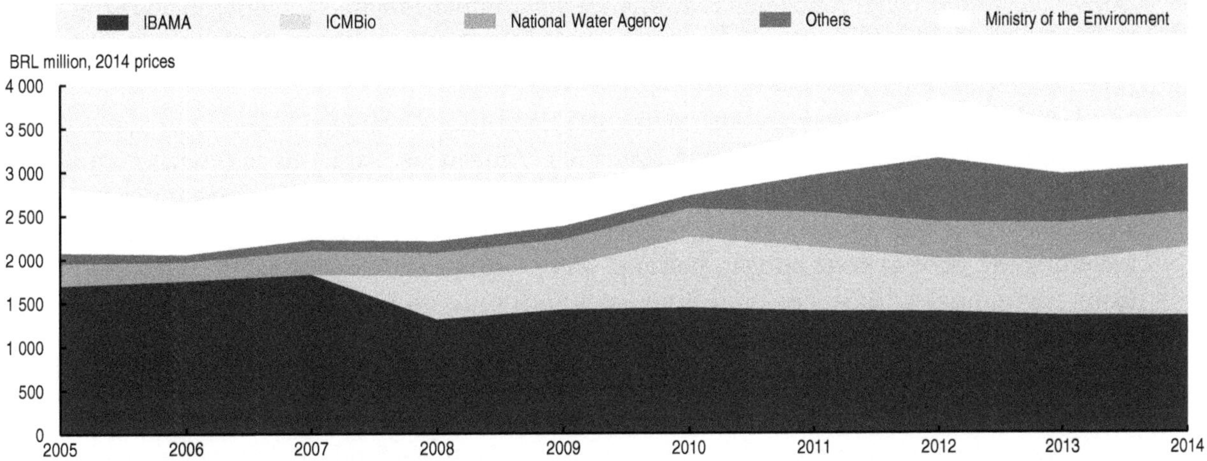

Note: Contingency reserves are excluded; others include: Brazilian Forest Service, Research Institute of Rio de Janeiro's Botanic Gardens, National Environment Fund, National Climate Change Fund and Company for the Development of Barcarena.
Source: Senado Federal (2015), *Portal Orçamento* (database).

StatLink http://dx.doi.org/10.1787/888933279535

Table 2.2. **Federal environment funds**

Fund	Objective	Governance	Funding source	Volume
Climate Change Fund (2009)	Established under the National Climate Change Policy (Section 3.1) to finance climate change mitigation and adaptation projects	Distributes loans (managed by the Brazilian Development Bank, BNDES) and non-refundable resources (managed by the MMA)	Largely funded from a special tax on oil production (Box 3.2), federal budget, donations, loans and transfer of unused government budgetary funds	Total available resources reached BRL 560 million in 2014
Amazon Fund (2008)	To invest in forest conservation and sustainable use, deforestation prevention and monitoring, and to reduce GHG emissions resulting from deforestation and forest degradation	Managed by the BNDES	Public and private donations; was originally to use a performance-based financing mechanism;[8] at least 80% of the fund's investments are earmarked for the Amazon region and up to 20% can be invested in deforestation monitoring and control in other Brazilian biomes or tropical countries	As of March 2015, the fund supported 72 projects with BRL 339 million, out of over BRL 2 billion in contracted donations (Figure 4.10)
Environment Fund (1989)	To fund public or private third-party implementation of environmental policies	Managed by the MMA	Federal budget, donations, interest from asset investments, environmental fines	Total disbursement since its creation: BRL 230 million; disbursement fell from nearly BRL 32 million in 2007 to BRL 2.4 million in 2013
Forest Development Fund (2006)	To promote sustainable forest-based activities and technological innovation in the sector	Managed by Brazilian Forest Service	Will likely receive about 20% of revenue from forest concessions in national forests and 40% of revenue from concessions in other public forests	Not yet fully operational
Atlantic Forest Restoration Fund	To finance environmental restoration and scientific research in the Atlantic Forest biome	Managed by the MMA	Federal budget, donations, income from asset investment and other money earmarked by specific legislation	Not yet operational

Source: MMA (2015), *Fifth National Report to the Convention on Biological Diversity*; MMA (2010), *Fourth National Report to the Convention on Biological Diversity*; Amazon Fund (2015), Amazon Fund website *www.amazonfund.gov.br*.

from international finance. Environment funds have also been used to secure finance for programmes or policies, for example in the Amazon Region Protected Areas Programme (ARPA; Chapter 5). Other funds that may finance environment-related activities include the Defence of Collective Rights Fund,[6] sectoral funds,[7] the Biodiversity Fund (Chapter 4) and the Protected Areas Fund (Chapter 5).

Resources available to state environmental institutions averaged 2.2% of the states' budgets in 2012 (IBGE, 2014b). In some states (e.g. Amazonas, Pará, Minas Gerais), more than 6% of the total state budget was devoted to environment, while in half the states the share was 1% or less. In most states, financial resources come from a variety of sources, including the general state budget, national and international donations, royalties, fees from environmental licences, and fines; in Rio Grande do Sul state, resources come exclusively from environmental licensing fees and fines.

In many cases, these resources are channelled through state environment funds. The Federal District and 23 of the 26 states operate such funds (IBGE, 2014b). The law requires that revenue from environmental fines be earmarked for these funds. But that defeats the main purpose of enforcement actions and sanctions, which is to deter non-compliance. In most OECD countries, revenue from fines goes to the Treasury to avoid a situation where the environmental enforcement authority is more interested in issuing fines and collecting the revenue than in preventing non-compliance.

In 2012, 21 state environment funds disbursed resources for environmental projects in such areas as environmental monitoring and education, biodiversity protection, water resource and soil management, and reforestation. The São Paulo State Pollution Prevention and Control Fund (FECOB) has disbursed BRL 327 million to over 2 000 projects since 2000, exceeding the volume of the National Environment Fund (Table 2.2). FECOB is financed through environmental fines, however, and thus its volume varies annually: it was BRL 1.2 million in 2000, and BRL 51.2 million in 2010 (CETESB, n.d.). Wide variation is also a challenge for Rio de Janeiro state, which finances its environment fund through oil and gas revenue.

Some municipalities operate environment funds, though their use is often less stringently tracked and published. As of 2013, about 43% of municipalities, mainly in the South and Centre-West regions, had such funds. Nearly all municipalities of over 500 000 inhabitants have environment funds (IBGE, 2014a). About half the states redistribute a share of the revenue from the state-level value added tax (ICMS) on the basis of environmental criteria, under a mechanism called Ecological ICMS (Chapter 5). The main parameter is extension of protected areas and indigenous lands, followed by municipal waste collection services and wastewater treatment (IBGE, 2014b). ICMS revenue is not necessarily earmarked for environment funds or to finance environment-related expenditure.

3. Key environment-related policies and regulations

The development of a comprehensive legal and institutional framework for environmental governance started with the adoption of the PNMA Law in 1981 (Box 2.3). The PNMA declared the need to protect the environment as a public heritage and to make socio-economic development compatible with ecological equilibrium. The 1988 Constitution gave environmental protection an even higher profile by dedicating an entire chapter to the subject. Its Article 225 recognised the population's right to an ecologically balanced environment as a common good essential to the quality of life.

Box 2.3. **Principal federal environment laws**

- Law 6938/1981 outlined the National Environmental Policy and established the environmental licensing process and civil liability for environmental damage.
- Law 9433/1997 set forth the National Water Resources Policy and water use regime.
- Law 9605/1998 is the main instrument of environmental criminal and administrative liability.
- Law 9795/1999 established the National Environmental Education Policy.
- Law 9966/2000 governs prevention and control of oil pollution and others hazardous substances in Brazilian waters.
- Law 9985/2000 established the National System of Protected Areas for biodiversity conservation.
- Law 12187/2009 established the National Climate Change Policy.
- Law 12305/2010 established the National Solid Waste Policy and requirements for the generation, transport, management and disposal of solid waste.
- Complementary Law 140/2011 and Presidential Decree 8437/2015 regulate shared responsibilities of the environment agencies at all administrative levels for permitting and enforcement of polluting activities.
- Law 12651/2012 on protection of native vegetation on private properties and some sensitive areas, or the new Brazilian Forest Code.
- Law 13123/2015 on access to genetic resources and traditional knowledge and benefit sharing, or Biodiversity Framework Law.

Source: Latin Lawyer (2015), "Brazil", *www.latinlawyer.com/reference/topics/51/jurisdictions/6/brazil.*

While the federal Congress has adopted major pieces of framework environmental legislation (Box 2.3), after years of political debate, most environmental norms have come through CONAMA resolutions (Section 1.1). However, many of the resolutions are of low technical quality, so regulatory requirements are either open to interpretation by subnational agencies or altogether impossible to apply (Sano, 2012), mostly because CONAMA resolutions are usually drafted by its members rather than issue-specific professionals inside or outside its technical expert groups (who are consulted only occasionally).

Federal environmental law has played a large role in establishing the legal and institutional frameworks for natural resource management, including forestry, mining and protection of natural areas, while state law has dominated in the area of pollution control. The stringency of pollution control requirements varies substantially by jurisdiction, reflecting local priorities and capacity constraints. Thus there are concerns about potential "environmental dumping", where highly polluting industries could establish new (or relocate existing) production facilities in states that lack capacity to establish and enforce environmental regulations and that might even seek to use this gap to attract industrial development.

As the following sections will show, national policies in several environmental domains (e.g. water resource and waste management) were adopted through legislation, which raised their status. Considerable attention is given to the social impact of environmental policies. At the same time, neither the policies themselves nor the implementing regulations are subject to *ex-ante* economic analysis. The TCU and state auditors conduct *ex-post* evaluation of implementation, but rarely consider cost implications.

3.1. Climate change

Brazil has developed a comprehensive policy framework to address climate change and, remarkably, embedded its national GHG emission reduction target in a law. The 2009 law establishing the National Climate Change Policy (PNMC) calls for a reduction of between 36.1% and 38.9% compared to business-as-usual projections for 2020, equivalent to a reduction of between 6% and 10% from 2005 levels (Seroa da Motta, 2011).

The PNMC is often cited as an example of successful co-operation and co-ordination across ministries and sectors. It consolidated sectoral actions already in place and assigned policy co-ordination to the Inter-ministerial Climate Change Committee (CIM), led by the chief of staff of the Casa Civil. The PNMC set out instruments to achieve the GHG mitigation target, including establishment of the federal Climate Change Fund (Section 2), and provided for a possible national carbon market linked to the international one.

The PNMC required the development of climate change action plans with quantifiable emission reduction targets, policy actions and monitoring indicators for five sectors, corresponding to the nationally appropriate mitigation actions that Brazil pledged to undertake under the United Nations Framework Convention on Climate Change. Plans for four additional sectors were finalised in 2012 (Table 2.3). The sectoral plans were developed through an open participative process. Work is in progress to develop a modular system,

Table 2.3. **Sectoral climate change mitigation and adaptation programmes to 2020**

Sector	Actions	Mitigation plan	Responsible federal ministry
	Nationally appropriate mitigation action		
Reduction in Amazon deforestation	80% reduction in annual Amazon deforestation rates, compared with 1996-2005 average	Action Plan for Prevention and Control of Deforestation in the Legal Amazon	MMA
Reduction in Cerrado deforestation	40% reduction in annual deforestation rates in the Cerrado biome, compared with the 1999-2008 average	Action Plan for Prevention and Control of Deforestation and Fires in Cerrado	MMA
Energy	Increased energy efficiency Increased biofuel use Increased supply from hydro plants Expanded supply from renewables	Ten-Year Plan for Energy Expansion	Ministry of Mines and Energy
Agriculture	Recovery of 150 000 km^2 of degraded pasture Expansion of integrated crop-livestock-forest systems on 40 000 km^2 Expansion of direct seeding practice on 80 000 km^2 Expansion of biological nitrogen fixation on 55 000 km^2 of farmland, replacing nitrogen fertiliser use Expansion of plantation forests on 30 000 km^2 Expansion of technology to treat 4.4 million m^3 of animal waste	Plan for Mitigation and Adaptation to Climate Change for the Consolidation of a Low-Carbon Economy in Agriculture	Ministry of Agriculture, Livestock and Food Supply; Ministry of Agrarian Development
Iron and steel	Increased use of charcoal from planted forests in iron and steel production, and improved efficiency in carbonisation	Plan for Reducing Emissions of the Steel Industry (Charcoal).	Ministry of Development, Industry and Foreign Trade
	Additional domestic actions under the PNMC		
Industry (aluminium, lime, cement, iron and steel, chemicals, pulp and paper, glass)	5% reduction of projected GHG emissions by 2020; gradual establishment of monitoring, reporting and verification	Industry Plan	Ministry of Development, Industry and Foreign Trade
Mining	Energy source shift, use of new technology	Low-Carbon Mining Plan	Ministry of Mines and Energy
Transport	Freight modal shift, development of public transport	Transports and Urban Mobility Plan	Ministry of Transport; Ministry of Cities
Health	Strengthened capacity of the health system to respond to climate change impact	Health Plan	Ministry of Health

Source: Country submission.

known as SMMARE, for monitoring implementation of the sectoral plans and resulting GHG emission reductions.

Progress in reducing deforestation has put Brazil in a good position to meet its target, with deforestation control in the Amazon and Cerrado biomes expected to account for over 60% of GHG mitigation. It is not clear, however, whether current sectoral programmes are of sufficient scale to significantly cut rising energy- and agriculture-related emissions and to advance towards an efficient, low-carbon economy. Important development opportunities that would yield significant reductions in the longer term (by 2030-50), such as sustainable transport infrastructure, seem to not be receiving sufficient consideration (Vogt-Schilb et al., 2014). The economic costs and benefits of the sectoral plans have not been evaluated.

Climate action is also occurring at subnational levels. Nineteen states have adopted climate change laws and targets: for example, São Paulo state established a 20% emission reduction target relative to 2005 levels by 2020 and Rio de Janeiro state set a target of reducing its carbon intensity to below 2005 levels by 2030. The city of Rio de Janeiro pledged to reduce emissions by 8% relative to 2005 levels by 2012, 16% by 2016 and 20% by 2020 (Mansell and Sopher, 2014). Both states planned to launch state-level GHG emission trading systems in 2013, but strong opposition from energy-intense industry and disagreement on emission caps have so far delayed the plans (Mansell and Sopher, 2014). The PNMC required federal climate change actions to integrate subnational actions, though a lack of institutional and legal arrangements have hindered such co-ordination (Seroa da Motta, 2011).

Brazil has generated the world's third largest number of certified emission reductions from the Clean Development Mechanism (CDM), a key driver of technology transfer (Chapter 3). It has also received about half the total approved international finance from Reducing Emissions from Deforestation and Forest Degradation (REDD and REDD+) through its innovative Amazon Fund (Norman et al., 2014). The fund was established to raise finance to invest in deforestation prevention and monitoring and in forest conservation and sustainable use in the Amazon (Table 2.2; Chapter 4). In June 2014, Brazil was the first country to submit its forest reference emission level for payments under REDD+ as required by the 2013 Warsaw Framework. A national REDD+ strategy has been under discussion since 2010, but has yet to be approved.

Brazil has put significant resources into improving scientific knowledge on climate impacts and into developing monitoring and early warning systems for floods, droughts and other natural disasters, financed partly through the Climate Change Fund. In 2010, it established a National Climate Change Panel, which published the first national climate change assessment report in 2013. The report found that extreme dry periods and prolonged droughts, particularly in the Amazon, Cerrado and Caatinga biomes, were likely to increase (PBMC, 2013). Other studies found that Brazil could lose millions of hectares of highly suitable agricultural land by 2030, particularly in the South region. Urban infrastructure is also considered particularly vulnerable. Adaptation cost estimates for urban, coastal and transport infrastructure are still lacking (Assad et al., 2013; Unterstell and Margulis, 2014).

To respond to the potentially negative impact of climate change in some economic sectors, notably agriculture and electricity production, work on a comprehensive national adaptation plan started in 2013. The draft plan covers water, energy, agriculture and food security, biodiversity and ecosystems, health, vulnerable population groups, industry and mining, urban centres, infrastructure, transport and coastal management. Following inter-institutional and public consultations, the plan is expected to be finalised in 2015.

3.2. Air pollution control

CONAMA Resolution 05/1989 established the National Air Quality Control Programme and set national air quality standards for five pollutants (Table 2.4). The standards may soon be updated in accordance with World Health Organization (WHO) guidelines for stringency and sampling methods. National air quality limits are only used in the absence of local outdoor air quality standards (mostly in smaller cities).

Table 2.4. **National air quality standards vs. WHO guidelines**

	National standards, µg/m³		WHO guidelines, µg/m³	
Particulate matter (PM)	50 (inhalable particles)	Annual mean	20 (PM_{10}), 10 ($PM_{2.5}$)	Annual mean
	150 (inhalable particles)	24-hour mean	50 (PM_{10}), 25 ($PM_{2.5}$)	24-hour mean
Sulphur dioxide (SO_2)	80	Annual mean	20	24-hour mean
	365	24-hour mean	500	10-minute mean
Carbon monoxide (CO)	10 000	8-hour mean	10 000	8-hour mean
	40 000	1-hour mean	30 000	1-hour mean
Nitrogen dioxide (NO_2)	100	Annual mean	40	Annual mean
	320	24-hour mean	200	24-hour mean
Ozone (O_3)	160	1-hour mean	100	8-hour mean

Source: Transportpolicy.net (n.d.), "Brazil: AIr Quality Standards", *http://transportpolicy.net* (accessed April 2015); WHO (2006), *Air Quality Guidelines – Golabl Update 2005*, World Health Organization Regional Office for Europe, Copenhagen.

CONAMA Resolution 382/2006, regulating air emissions from point sources, sets sector-specific standards for CO, NO_X, SO_2, PM and hydrocarbons for 13 industrial sectors. Similar rules have been adopted for emissions of four pollutants from mobile sources. Federal legislation (Decree 5472/2005) also bans the production and use of 12 persistent organic pollutants.

States are in charge of air quality regulation and monitoring and can adopt more stringent emission standards. In addition, most big cities have adopted local air pollution standards and designated areas where new point sources may be introduced only if existing emissions are reduced. However, despite the legal obligation to monitor air quality and produce annual air quality reports, only 12 of the 27 states (including the Federal District) had some type of monitoring system installed by 2012, and few of them provide consistent, accessible data (IEMA, 2012). Less than 2% of municipalities monitor air quality (ISS, 2014).

Brazil's first instrument to control air pollution from mobile sources was the Vehicle Air Pollution Control Programme (PROCONVE), a protocol signed in 1986 between the automotive industry and the government, converted into Law 8723 in 1993. Since then, increasingly stringent vehicle emission standards have been adopted, complemented by PROMOT, a motor vehicle emission certification system. The latest PROCONVE 7 regulations for diesel vehicle emissions have had a positive impact on air quality and have both reduced diesel emissions and improved fuel economy (Chapter 1). The first National Inventory of Road Motor Vehicle Emissions, published by IBAMA and industry partners in 2011, allowed the government to update information on mobile source emission reduction and to identify achievements and challenges in PROCONVE/PROMOT implementation.

3.3. Water resource management

Federal Law 9433/1997 formulated the National Water Resources Policy and created the National Water Resource Management System. Water resource plans, prepared at the national, state and river basin levels with broad stakeholder participation, lay out priorities, programmes and projects and guide water resource allocation. Only 52% of the territory is covered by river basin water resource plans. As of 2012, only São Paulo and Rio de Janeiro states had completed river basin plans for all rivers in their jurisdiction, and no plans had been developed in the Amazonian states (ANA, 2014). Even where water resource plans have been adopted, river basin committees are not held accountable for implementing the plans they develop, and state water agencies have little or no influence to get buy-in from other executive agencies or municipal governments to implement the plans (OECD, 2015).

In an approach that is fully consistent with best practices in OECD countries, Brazil has introduced a system of quality classification of surface water bodies that is based on their main uses (e.g. aquaculture and fisheries, public water supply, navigation) and establishes water quality standards corresponding to each use class. CNRH Resolution 16/2001 stipulates that limits for industrial wastewater discharge (expressed as the amount of water needed to dilute the pollutant load) should be set case by case so as to comply with the applicable water quality standard. However, CONAMA Resolution 357/2005 set sector-specific wastewater discharge standards irrespective of the use-based water quality standard, which makes them inconsistent with the general water quality classification approach.

Water use permits (for abstraction and other uses) are issued by the national or state water resource management agency, depending on the jurisdiction of the water body. Current water allocation processes are based on direct negotiation among water users and institutions with jurisdiction over the water body in question. Demand and water allocation amounts are considered fixed, and economic considerations are rarely taken into account (ANA, 2014). In addition, the federal and state water use permit systems are not integrated, hampering integrated management in shared river basins.

Another problem in regulating water use is that the national water resource management system does not establish sufficient links between water resource management and sanitation (OECD, 2015). The latter affects both quality and quantity, since polluted water can be used downstream only at a higher treatment cost. Therefore, finding effective solutions to challenges such as droughts (in the North-east) and water pollution (in large urban centres) requires close co-ordination between water resource management and the provision of water supply and sanitation services.

The National Water Resource Policy Law provides for water use charges to be associated with water use permits, with the revenue reinvested in the relevant river basin. River basin committees can set water charges, and ANA or state agencies are responsible for collection. While some states have the legal framework in place to collect revenue from the water sector, in many others the legal framework is either pending or has been approved but is not properly enforced because of political, social and organisational difficulties. In more industrial and wealthy states, like São Paulo, Rio de Janeiro and Minas Gerais, water charges are in effect because key stakeholders are more willing to pay. Yet these charges were set, without prior affordability studies, at levels too low to affect consumer behaviour or provide a significant source of water-related finance. Collection rates are also quite low (Chapter 3).

Brazil faces significant challenges in integrating the management of its water resources, particularly in integrating water, environmental and other sectoral policies as well as in integrating quantity and quality management aspects. Uneven implementation of water policies across regions is another major challenge. The mismatch of hydrological and administrative boundaries has led to tension and inconsistency in the application of water management instruments within a given river basin. In principle, states can negotiate a derogation with ANA to manage federal rivers and reservoirs if local capacity is sufficient.

São Paulo and Ceará states have done so, but São Paulo's experience has been mixed, particularly given the acute water shortages in 2014. Many state and local governments lack the financial and technical resources to design and implement water policies.

In response to these challenges, a National Water Management Pact (Box 2.4) has been adopted as a co-operation strategy involving authorities at all administrative levels. It includes time-specific medium- and long-term management targets and makes particular institutions responsible for their achievement. The pact does not aspire to address the magnitude of water governance challenges in Brazil, but, as a contractual agreement, could become an effective instrument to improve dialogue between the federal and state levels and serve as a model for other policy areas.

Box 2.4. **National Water Management Pact**

The National Water Management Pact resulted from long negotiations by ANA, state governments and state water resource councils. It aims at strengthening the institutional capacity of state water management organisations and enhancing collaboration, including information sharing, among federal agencies (especially ANA) and the multitude of river basin committees, agencies and local authorities involved in water management.

The Brasília Declaration (2011) established the pact, which was signed by state government representatives. As of mid-2014, all states but São Paulo had expressed their intention to join the pact. Its design, relying on states' self-assessment to set the level of ambition (expressed as targets to establish or improve water management instruments and procedures) for the next five years (until 2016), has assured states that they can participate without losing their autonomy or power in water resource management.

The pact relies on contractual agreements between ANA, state governments and state water resource councils that identify key water management challenges and envisage options to support more effective state water governance. In 2013, a USD 50 million fund called Progestão was created to give states performance-based incentives to achieve water resource management targets. The federal funding is contingent on the existence of state and river basin water resource plans, with targets, as well as the allocation of staff resources for implementation.

Not all states are subject to the same goals and targets, but all will receive equal payment through a package of institutional, operational, planning and decision-making support. There is no requirement for state water agencies to specify how the money is spent. While Progestão grants are somewhat marginal compared to federal water infrastructure investment in the states, they provide a strong incentive for poor states to engage more actively in water resource management. As of November 2014, 19 states had signed Progestão contracts.

Source: OECD (2015), *Water Resources Governance in Brazil*, OECD Publishing, Paris.

The sustainability of this initiative's results will largely depend on state agencies' capacity to retain recently trained staff and secure enough funding. The state water agencies should also do more to engage municipalities so as to better co-ordinate water and urban policies.

3.4. *Waste management*

Federal Law 12305/2010 established the National Solid Waste Policy and regulates the generation, transport, treatment and disposal of solid waste. Municipalities are responsible for municipal solid waste management (under the broad jurisdiction of the Ministry of Cities), while the federal law regulates hazardous waste management. States have limited powers in waste management (besides issuing and enforcing landfill licences), and most of them provide virtually no support to municipalities in this area.

The National Solid Waste Management Plan, finalised in 2011, is subject to review and revision every four years. States and municipalities were given a 2012 deadline to prepare their own solid waste plans as a condition to receive federal financial support for landfill construction.[9] Although only about a quarter of municipalities met the deadline, the federal government is not imposing sanctions on them but rather trying to provide capacity-building support. Some municipalities have pooled their limited resources to develop inter-municipal waste management plans. Over 2 200 municipalities (less than half) met the 2014 deadline for having an environmentally sound landfill (Chapter 3).

All legal entities that generate waste (including hazardous waste) must prepare a solid waste management plan and prove, as a condition of obtaining an environmental licence, that they have the technical and financial capacity to properly manage and dispose of the waste. In addition, legal entities managing hazardous waste in any way must register with the National Registry of Hazardous Waste Operators and notify the relevant environmental and sanitary authorities of the quantity, nature and temporary or final destination of waste under their responsibility as well as of any accidents related to hazardous waste.

The national policy envisaged the creation of a National Solid Waste Management Information System to integrate federal, state and municipal waste management data, including data on each type of waste generated. The system was expected to be launched in 2013, but its implementation has been delayed. Thus the federal waste statistics remain fragmented and incomplete, and the MMA and Ministry of Cities do not exchange waste-related data.

To gradually reduce landfilling as the main method of disposal, the National Solid Waste Policy Law established a "reverse logistics system", using an approach similar to extended producer responsibility systems in most OECD countries. It requires manufacturers, distributors and retailers of pesticides, batteries, tyres, lubricating oils, fluorescent lamps and electronic devices, and their components, to recover the products at the end of their useful life. The MMA has already signed agreements with producers of lamps, tyres and pesticides, specifying producers' and importers' obligations and setting recovery and recycling targets. However, sanctions for not meeting the obligations have yet to be established. A similar agreement is under preparation, co-ordinated by the Ministry of Industry and Commerce, for waste electric and electronic equipment. A lack of recycling infrastructure (except in the South-east region) and limited municipal capacity to ensure separate collection are the main bottlenecks in the implementation of these programmes.

The national policy also has an important social dimension. One goal is to insert nearly half a million waste pickers into the waste management market by creating and supporting co-operatives to collaborate with municipalities in the separate collection and recycling of municipal solid waste (Chapter 3).

4. Environmental impact assessment and licensing

4.1. *Environmental licensing*

Environmental licensing was introduced by the PNMA Law of 1981. CONAMA Resolution 237/1997 made environmental licensing a legal requirement before the construction, installation, expansion and functioning of any enterprise or activity that is deemed to be effectively or potentially polluting, or that could cause environmental degradation.

The licensing process has three stages:[10]

- A preliminary licence is granted at the initial stage of the activity, approving its location and establishing basic requirements and conditions to be met in the next stages. An environmental impact assessment (EIA) and its corresponding report may be required at this stage, as well as other environmental studies depending on the activity's environmental risk (Section 4.2). The developer should elaborate the engineering design of the project following the conditions defined in the preliminary licence.
- An installation licence authorises the construction or expansion of a facility or activity in accordance with its conditions. The local authority issues a separate building permit. Conditions cover air emissions, wastewater discharges (which generally should comply with national standards), waste management (large facilities and all hazardous waste generators must have a solid waste management plan) and a variety of environmental and social mitigation measures.
- An operating licence authorises the operation of the activity or facility after the environment authority verifies compliance with the requirements in the prior two licences.

The preliminary, installation and operating licences are of differing duration, generally not exceeding ten years. A new licence must be issued in the event of changes to the activity. An administrative fee, the TCFA, is levied by the licensing authority at a level covering licensing and inspection costs. TCFA rates vary from BRL 200 to BRL 10 000 per year per facility, depending on its size and polluting impact.

Other authorisations and permits may be required depending on the activity, such as a water use permit covering surface water or groundwater abstraction (Section 3.3), or a permit for the use of chemicals. Specific environmental permits are required for oil and gas extraction. The environment authority defines which studies must be carried out and which documents submitted by the applicant.

The licensing process must be conducted by a federal, state or local environment authority:

- IBAMA is responsible for projects with significant environmental impact at the national level as well as on indigenous lands, in offshore zones and in interstate areas or areas containing a resource that falls under federal jurisdiction, such as oil. IBAMA issues licences for about 700 activities and maintains a database that is publicly available on its website.
- State agencies license projects within state protected areas and those that affect more than one municipality. While state environment agencies play the biggest role in environmental licensing, over the years IBAMA has expanded its licensing authority somewhat at the expense of state environment agencies, at least partly because of their capacity constraints. There is no information at the federal level about the extent of state environmental licensing activities.
- Municipal agencies have responsibilities for activities with local impact or those delegated by the state through an agreement or other legal instrument, according to criteria established by the state environment council. Such agreements are most common in the North and Centre-West regions, where they cover about 15% of municipalities (IBGE, 2014a).

Complementary Law 140/2011 made more objective the division of environmental licensing responsibility between the three levels of government. In principle, a given project's scale and location, and the extent of its potential environmental impact, dictate which agency administers the licence. Precise criteria for a project or activity to be subject to a federal licence were elaborated in Decree 8437 of April 2015.

The licensing system has been subject to broad criticism (World Bank, 2008). The process is reported to be excessively burdensome (sometimes due to insufficient project preparation), delaying important infrastructure projects (especially energy-related ones) and creating competitiveness concerns. In response to demands for transparency, the process has increasingly become an arena for wide-ranging discussions on development options and their environmental, social or other consequences. This has required even more time and financial resources, leading to pressure from the private sector to accelerate the procedure and putting the environment authorities in the spotlight regarding issues beyond their jurisdiction (e.g. land tenure, resettlement, agrarian reform).

In a report on environmental licensing (ABEMA, 2013), state environment agencies criticised the overlap of federal and state licensing laws, which has now been partly addressed by Presidential Decree 8437/2015, as well as outdated and imprecise procedural norms, the technical quality of environmental impact studies (Section 4.2) and the lack of links with other policy instruments (e.g. land use and river basin planning). ABEMA identified several specific challenges in the design and implementation of environmental licensing (Table 2.5).

Table 2.5. **State perspective on environmental licensing: Challenges and proposals**

Challenges	Proposals
The absence of a "territorial dimension" is a major gap in the process.	Institutionalise location of the proposed activity as a factor in the granting of a licence.
The procedures' imprecision increases the degree of discretion of licensing officials and leads to repeated requests for additional information. This causes significant delays in the process and reduces its objectivity.	Establish a classification of activities subject to licensing and differentiate the licensing procedure by type of activity.
In the absence of a definition and a list of activities which may cause significant environmental impact, all activities are treated as having significant impact, which creates excessive administrative burden.	Clearly define the parameters characterising significant environmental impact, based on the activity's size, location and pollution potential.
Consents required from some non-environmental statutory consultative bodies lead to parallel decision making and institutional confusion.	Replace such consents by strengthening co-ordination with related instruments – water use permits, authorisations to remove vegetation, etc.
Mitigation measures set as conditions in environmental licences are often unrelated to environmental impact and represent demands of statutory consultative bodies.	Establish, by presidential decree, clear procedures for setting compensatory licence conditions.
The method used to evaluate environmental impact impairs the quality and efficiency of the licensing process. The assessment is fragmented by knowledge area, resulting in conflicting and contradictory opinions and making the licence determination more difficult.	Introduce interdisciplinary analysis of licence applications, bringing together required experts in each case. This approach would favour dialogue with the entrepreneur and the best technological options and location for the activity.
The current public consultation process often serves non-environmental (political, ideological) objectives. The format of public hearings, with very limited time for the proponent to present the project and even less time for community representatives to express their demands, is ineffective.	Allow for electronic public access to project proposals and improve procedures for public hearings to guarantee discussion of significant environmental impact and mitigation.

Source: ABEMA (2013), *Novas propostas para o licenciamento ambiental no Brasil*, Brazilian Association of State Environment Authorities, Brasília.

Corruption and interference by powerful political and economic actors are often cited as problems by environment agencies, especially at the subnational level. The practice of "negotiated non-compliance", where enterprises are allowed to continue operating without licences, is not as widespread as in the past but still exists, particularly in jurisdictions with weaker environment authorities (McAllister, 2008). In the last decade, however, IBAMA and several state environment agencies have made serious efforts to fight corruption in their ranks, firing and prosecuting hundreds of personnel.

Progress has been made in recent years to streamline the licensing system. The MMA and IBAMA issued improved licensing regulations (Box 2.5) and built technical capacity at federal level. The MMA is developing a National Environmental Licensing Portal to integrate, systematise and disseminate information on environmental licensing at all government levels, enhance transparency of public management processes and strengthen public control over licensing decisions. Since 2010 there have been no cases of federal environmental licenses being overruled by courts.

Box 2.5. **Selected environmental licensing regulations**

- Decree 421/2011 standardised criteria for fast-track processing of licence applications for certain project categories, including power transmission lines.
- Ordinances 288/2013 and 289/2013 set specific licensing standards for highways, which allowed to accelerate the licensing process of these projects. For example, in 2014, the environmental licenses for 3 400 km of highways (part of the federal Programme of Investment in Logistics) were issued in 30 days, on average.
- Inter-ministerial Ordinance 60/2015 aims at improving inter-institutional co-ordination in the environmental licensing process. It regulates the participation of the National Indian Foundation, the National Historic and Artistic Heritage Institute and the Ministry of Health, among others, in federal environmental licensing process.

There remain, however, concerns about the system's effectiveness. While IBAMA doubled the number of its technical staff working on licensing from 203 in 2008 to 428 in 2014, and issues 3.3 licenses per business day, the capacity of state and local environment authorities varies widely. Many do not have enough staff or financial resources to determine the accuracy of projected environmental impacts or the adequacy of proposed mitigation measures. Legal disputes related to environmental licences are common, entailing significant costs for applicants and authorities. The MMA has tried to address capacity constraints through the World Bank-supported National Environment Programme, whose second phase (2009-14) focused in large part on licensing issues.

4.2. *Environmental impact assessment*

For a long time, EIA was the only environmental management tool applied in the country on a large scale. EIA is obligatory for all activities with a potentially significant environmental impact and is an integral part of the environmental licensing process. EIA was introduced by the 1981 PNMA Law and later mentioned in the Federal Constitution. At the federal level, CONAMA Resolution 01/1986 established the minimum EIA scope (expanded in 1997), while most state agencies have their own requirements, usually depending on the complexity of the activity. While an EIA is required for projects with a potentially significant environmental impact, the regulation does not define what this means.

The EIA process includes the development of an environmental impact report, a non-technical summary to provide information about the EIA process to people attending public hearings. Public hearings are organised if deemed necessary by the environment agency or if requested by the prosecutor's office or by more than 50 citizens. A number of government authorities, including the Health Surveillance Secretariat as well as several institutions in charge of historic, cultural and ethnic heritage, have to be consulted as part of the EIA process.

Overall, EIA has largely become a bureaucratic process which does not consider location, scale or technological alternatives. Potential environmental impact tends to be underestimated or played down, and project proponents rarely propose adequate measures to mitigate the impact or monitoring programmes. Public hearings are often used to justify a decision that has already been made rather than to take stakeholders' views into account.

4.3. *Land use planning*

The 1988 Constitution reserved for municipalities the most important role in urban land development control by means of municipal territorial plans. In rural areas, municipal governments implement state and federal agencies' decisions. Brazil does not have an integrated system of land administration that would provide for co-ordinated actions at the different levels of government. Although the federal and state governments have concurrent power to enact laws and formulate policies and programmes on land use and territorial development, their scope is limited to very general directives or related to specific situations that cannot be solved at the local level. Few states have specific constitutional provisions on land use and development control, and even fewer have enacted urban legislation.

Incorporating the environmental dimension into urban territorial planning is a substantial challenge. Planning has historically been carried out without environmental considerations, and municipal master plans (every municipality was required to develop one by 2005) combine but do not integrate individual components on sanitation, transport, housing, etc. Even the best designed territorial master plans (e.g. in Manaus and Belém) have hardly been implemented.

Another challenge is the disconnect between land use planning and water resource management. Part of the reason for this is the mismatch between the municipal and river basin planning scales. It is important to have regional land use plans that incorporate water management considerations.

Strategic environmental assessment (SEA) of municipal territorial plans and other development programmes could also be used to integrate the economic, territorial and environmental perspectives. There is no legal requirement for SEA and no plans to introduce one. In the 1990s, institutions such as the Inter-American Development Bank and World Bank promoted SEA as a condition for financing major projects. However, despite MMA efforts to train public officials in infrastructure-related agencies to use SEA, only occasional initiatives have been attempted over the years, particularly in the states of Minas Gerais, Bahia, São Paulo and Rio de Janeiro. In recent years, Minas Gerais and Bahia have included mandatory SEA in their legislation (Oberling et al., 2013). ABEMA recently expressed support for the introduction of SEA of government programmes with a large potential environmental impact, such as those related to energy, mineral extraction and infrastructure (ABEMA, 2013).

Deforestation remains a critical issue for Brazil, despite important progress in addressing it in recent years (Chapters 4 and 5). Public and private land use in rural areas is governed by the Forest Code. Its land preservation requirements have undergone significant modifications since its adoption in 1934. The Forest Code of 2012 (the Law for the Protection of Native Vegetation) stipulates a so-called Legal Reserve requirement to preserve up to 80% of forested land on private rural properties in the Amazon, 20% to 35% in the Cerrado and 20% of native flora on private land in other biomes. Landowner compliance with these requirements had historically been low, and the lack of oversight and enforcement in remote areas (notably in the Amazon) allowed violations to go unpunished. Remote sensing surveillance, introduced in 2007, has greatly improved compliance monitoring.

In addition, the Rural Environmental Cadastre (CAR), established in the new Forest Code, is an important instrument for helping in environmental regularisation of rural property, thus supporting application of the Forest Code as well as state and municipal planning. Some 50% of properties were registered in the CAR in its first year of operation (2014/15), and the target is to cover and regularise all rural properties by May 2016 (Chapter 4). The code also created a Rural Environment Cadastre System that will integrate state CARs (many of which have already been established).

Ecological-economic zoning (ZEE), introduced in 2002, is another rural land use management instrument, aimed at allocating compatible activities in defined environmental areas so as to maintain sustainable use of natural resources and a balanced ecosystem (Chapter 4). It is primarily focused on agro-economic criteria: for example, to identify appropriate areas for sugar cane cultivation. Farmers can get access to credit only if they comply with zoning requirements for their crops. However, there is no standard methodology for producing ZEE studies, and the municipal capacity to implement zoning requirements is weak. Several state environment agencies, e.g. in Mato Grosso, have tried to assess whether rural land is used for suitable purposes (such as growing certain crops) as part of environmental licensing. This seems to be a good approach, as licences should take account of the full spectrum of environmental impact of an activity.

5. Environmental compliance assurance

5.1. *Promotion of compliance and green practices*

Government engagement in compliance promotion can reduce compliance costs for businesses by allowing them to achieve and maintain compliance as efficiently as possible. It may also reduce regulatory costs by increasing the efficiency of compliance monitoring and enforcement. Compliance promotion is particularly effective when targeted at small and medium-sized enterprises, where non-compliance is primarily caused by a lack of knowledge and capacity, and where cultural resistance to enforcement is the greatest (Mazur, 2012). Compliance promotion is only starting to receive the attention it deserves from Brazilian environment authorities.

There has been a marked increase in the number of Brazilian companies with an environmental management system (EMS) certified according to the ISO 14001 standard. The number of new ISO 14001 certificates issued in Brazil went from 2 061 in 2005 to 3 695 in 2013 (ISO, 2014). While such systems do not necessarily lead to better environmental outcomes, there is some evidence that ISO 14001 certification has had, on average, a positive impact on firms' profitability (Tognere Ferron et al., 2012). The most industrialised state, São Paulo, represents over a quarter of the national total (De Oliveira, 2010). While most large industrial companies have obtained EMS certification, smaller businesses rarely develop an ISO 14001 EMS, considering it too onerous and costly. However, neither the federal nor state government provides regulatory incentives for EMS certification, such as reduced inspection frequency, permit fees and sanctions, as several OECD countries do (Mazur, 2012).[11]

Environmental audits are emerging as a complementary tool to evaluate operators' environmental performance. At the federal level, there are technical guidelines for environmental audits in accordance with ISO 14010, ISO 14011 and ISO 14012. Audits are mandatory only in the oil and gas industry. At the state level, several states, including Rio de Janeiro and Paraná, have passed laws making environmental audits mandatory for the facilities with the highest level of environmental impact.

At the same time, the Ministry of Industry and Commerce collaborates with the National Institute of Metrology, Standardisation and Industrial Quality and business associations on developing energy and resource efficiency standards, labels and codes of good practice for key industrial sectors. In 2008, the government's industrial policy included sustainable production targets for the first time: to develop CDM projects for climate change mitigation, create incentives for sustainable agro-industrial production, support energy efficiency and cleaner production practices in industry, etc. Most were not achieved, however, partly because of the economic crisis. The 2011 Greater Brazil Plan included green practices as part of measures to improve the competitiveness of domestic industry: for example, it set a target of reducing energy consumption per unit of industrial GDP (Chapter 3).

The government promotes competitiveness and sustainable development (including resource efficiency) for micro and small businesses (with fewer than 100 employees in industry and fewer than 50 in trade and services) through the non-profit autonomous Brazilian Micro and Small Business Support Service (Sebrae).[12] In another initiative targeting small businesses, the MMA, in collaboration with the National Confederation of Industries (CNI), has developed a distance learning curriculum for young potential entrepreneurs with secondary education to train them in environmental management. The CNI is delivering the courses though its industrial training programme.

The government can stimulate diffusion of green practices by setting an example and promoting green public procurement. The Public Administration Environmental Agenda (A3P) was created in 2001 for this purpose, to promote social responsibility and environmental sustainability in government institutions at all administrative levels. Specific initiatives cover water and energy efficiency, separate solid waste collection and recycling, etc. Participating institutions sign a "terms of adherence" agreement with the MMA. A3P includes a national forum, an award for best practices, and labels (green, silver and orange) recognising sustainable management practices. About 400 government bodies at all levels are engaged in the programme, up from 84 in 2007.

Presidential Decree 7746/2012 established differentiated criteria for public procurement, giving priority to green products, those produced by small and micro businesses, or having more than 60% of local content. An inter-ministerial committee on sustainable procurement is co-ordinating development of a catalogue of sustainable products and their suppliers. Green public procurement has considerable potential to stimulate demand for, and supply of, environmental goods and services (Chapter 3). The value of sustainable public procurement almost trebled in 2010-14, but sustainable products still account for less than 0.1% of government purchases. Small and micro businesses supply almost half the volume (MPOG, 2015). Brazil is actively participating in the international initiatives on sustainable public procurement and eco-labelling of the United Nations Environment Programme (UNEP), and is reviewing related policies to further promote green business practices.

Socio-environmental responsibility in the financial sector

Socio-environmental aspects may pose significant risks to loan operations, financing, investments and insurance. In addition, there is legal uncertainty about the environmental liability of financial institutions involved in financing projects that cause environmental damage, and some Brazilian court decisions have held financing institutions responsible (GVces / FGV-EAESP, 2014). To reduce such risk and uncertainty, since 2008 the Central Bank has issued resolutions incorporating socio-environmental concerns in financial activities (Table 2.6).

Table 2.6. **Environment-related resolutions and circulars of the Brazilian Central Bank**

Resolution/Circular	Affected financial operation	Description
Resolution 3545/2008	Rural credit – Environmental compliance in the Amazon	Applies to the Amazon biome and requires financial institutions to demand from credit borrowers documentation proving environmental compliance.
Resolution 3813/2009	Rural credit – Sugar cane expansion	Links agro-industrial credit to agro-ecological zoning for expansion and industrialisation of sugar cane. It prohibits financing for crop expansion in the Amazon and Pantanal biomes and in the Upper Paraguay River Basin, among other areas.
Resolution 3896/2010	Rural credit – Low-Carbon Agriculture	To implement the Low-Carbon Agriculture programme as part of the National Climate Change Policy.
Resolution 4008/2011	Credit towards climate change mitigation and adaptation	Rules on financing of projects aiming at climate mitigation and adaptation, backed by resources from the National Climate Change Plan.
Circular 3547/2011	Internal Review Process for Capital Adequacy	Requires the institution to demonstrate how it considers the risk of exposure to socio-environmental damage in its assessment process and in the calculation of capital needed for risk.
Resolution 4327/2014W	Guidelines for Social and Environmental Responsibility Policies in Financial Institutions	Rules on guidelines to be observed upon establishing and deploying socio-environmental responsibilities by financial institutions.

Source: Adapted from GVces/FGV-EAESP (2014), "The Brazilian Financial System and the Green Economy – Alignment with Sustainable Development", prepared for UNEP and FEBRABAN in the framework of "Inquiry into the design of a sustainable financial system", FEBRABAN, São Paulo.

In particular, Central Bank Resolution 3545/2008 made access to subsidised rural credit in the Amazon biome conditional on the legitimacy of land claims and provision of information to demonstrate compliance with environmental regulations (particularly land use regulations set out in the Forest Code). This has helped reduce deforestation (Chapter 4). Assunção et al. (2013) estimated that BRL 2.9 billion in loans was not contracted due to this resolution between 2008 and 2011, nearly 90% of them linked to cattle ranching, a fact that is estimated to have avoided clearing of over 2 700 km^2 of land in 2009-11.

More recently, Resolution 4327/2014 requires financial institutions under Central Bank regulatory supervision to establish social and environmental responsibility policies, as well as governance structures for these aspects, socio-environmental risk management systems and action plans for the adequate monitoring and mitigation of the risk (GVces/FGV-EAESP, 2014). The Central Bank does not dictate the scope of the policies, which should be proportionate to the size and nature of operations. The Federation of

Brazilian Banks detailed the Central Bank's resolution even further and integrated sustainability aspects into lending policies for public and private banks, which are consistent with the international Equator Principles for assessing environmental and social risks of project financing (Box 2.6).

Box 2.6. **The Equator Principles**

The Equator Principles, which financial institutions adopt voluntarily, are a credit risk management framework for determining, assessing and managing environmental and social risk in project financing. The first three principles lay down the fundamentals of environmental and social assessment:

Principle 1: Review and Categorisation. When a project is proposed for financing, the financing institution will, as part of its internal environmental and social review and due diligence, categorise it based on the magnitude of its potential environmental and social risks and impacts.

Principle 2: Environmental and Social Assessment. For all projects with a potential adverse environmental and social impact, the financing institution will require the client to conduct an assessment of environmental and social risks. The assessment documentation should propose measures to minimise, mitigate and offset adverse impacts in a manner relevant and appropriate to the nature and scale of the proposed project.

Principle 3: Applicable Environmental and Social Standards. The assessment process should address compliance with relevant host country laws, regulations and permits that pertain to environmental and social issues.

Source: Equator Principles Association (2013), The Equator Principles, *www.equator-principles.com*.

5.2. *Environmental inspections*

Until recently, all federal, state and local environment agencies had the power to inspect and impose sanctions on polluters whenever a violation of a statute occurred within their jurisdiction. Complementary Law 140/2011 clarified the constitutional overlap in jurisdiction that had been widely interpreted to allow any environment agency to enforce any environmental law or regulation in effect within its territorial purview, enabling multiple means of enforcement in a country whose agencies are not uniformly capable. Article 17 of this law limits the enforcement power over licensed operations to the agency that issued the licence, effectively restricting the authority that IBAMA and some state agencies used to exercise to supplement or overrule the actions of lower-level agencies. A higher-level agency can still inspect a site licensed by a lower-level one, but must inform it and defer to it for imposing possible sanctions.

Inspections are usually conducted in response to complaints or incidents or to gather information as part of the environmental licensing process. CETESB in São Paulo state is one of the few environment agencies in Brazil that has the resources necessary to conduct routine, planned inspections besides those triggered by complaints and incidents, and even so they account for only one out of eight inspections (McAllister, 2008). IBAMA claims to plan 95% of its inspection activities (as part of its internal National Environmental Plan), but its inspections mainly focus on "green issues" such as deforestation, so inspectors go to problematic areas where they are certain to identify violations.

There is a significant shortage of federal, state and local environmental inspectors. In 2002, IBAMA had only one enforcement official for every 11 000 km^2 in the Amazon and one official for every 6 000 km^2 elsewhere (McAllister, 2008). The situation at IBAMA has improved significantly (more recent data on the number of inspectors are not available), but at the state and local levels it varies dramatically by region. One way to address this capacity gap would be to develop broader opportunities for "citizen enforcement" by engaging local communities or civil society organisations in compliance monitoring through enforcement hotlines, voluntary green patrols, etc.

In monitoring compliance with land use and forestry regulations, remote sensing (used since 2007) has proven to be a very effective instrument complementing inspection efforts. Rather inexpensive satellite imagery shows in real time where violations are and who may be responsible. By putting data from remote sensing online, the government enables green activists to help police the frontier between forest and farmland. For example, Brazil's moratoriums on soya and beef from the Amazon would not have worked without such data (Chapter 4).

5.3. *Enforcement tools*

The Federal Law on Environmental Crimes (9605/1998) is the main legal instrument regulating environmental criminal and administrative liabilities, which are uniform across the country. Federal Decree 6514/2008, implementing the law, establishes sanctions for over 60 types of environmental offences.

Criminal penalties may include fines, community service or imprisonment for physical persons, or suspension of activity for legal persons. Voluntary self-reporting of a violation may mitigate potential penalties. Public officials may also be prosecuted for environmental crimes, e.g. for issuing a licence that does not comply with environmental regulations. In 2005, the Superior Court of Justice admitted for the first time the possibility of criminal liability of legal entities, which can be prosecuted jointly with company managers.

Administrative enforcement may involve warnings, fines for physical or legal persons, and/or suspension of activity. The use of administrative warnings and fines is similar across the states. Upon discovering a violation, the inspector usually issues a warning. If follow-up inspections show that the situation is not rectified, the inspector issues up to three fines of increasing severity, then proceeds to impose a daily fine. If the fines fail to stop the offence, the agency may take action to close down the activity (in practice, this rarely happens). This procedure varies somewhat by state: in some (e.g. São Paulo), inspectors can impose the fines directly; in others, they must recommend the sanction to the head of the environment agency, who decides whether to issue it.

The size of administrative fines depends on the extent of environmental damage and measures taken by the polluter to prevent and remediate it. Fines may reach BRL 50 million for some violations. Environmental officials consider administrative fines to be sufficiently high, but collection rates are miserably low – less than 10%. Environment authorities are responsible for the collection of administrative fines, and benefit from their revenue (Section 2), but the instruments to enforce payment are insufficient.[13]

The weakness of administrative enforcement has led to the rise of prosecutorial enforcement, which has largely changed the climate of impunity that long prevailed in enforcement of environmental law in Brazil. Federal and state prosecutors play an active role in civil and criminal environmental enforcement.

The federal Prosecutor General's Office has stronger enforcement powers than the environment agencies: simply being under investigation by public prosecutors often leads to significant changes in the offender's behaviour. The possibility of a public civil action or criminal prosecution (reinforced by media coverage) tends to make polluters agree to a "conduct adjustment agreement", whereby the polluter commits to taking certain actions to prevent or remedy environmental harm.

There are over 10 000 federal and state prosecutors, under the auspices of the Prosecutor General's Office (with representatives in each state) and its state counterparts. Most are empowered to handle civil or criminal environmental enforcement cases, and some work exclusively in environmental protection.

Prosecutors most often use civil enforcement powers. They generally open civil investigations because of a public complaint or an administrative referral, but can also initiate one themselves. After investigating, they often seek to settle the case without formal court action, sparing everyone time and costs.[14] If the case is not resolved extra-judicially, the prosecutor has a duty to take it to court.[15] In civil cases, prosecutors usually seek a court order requiring the offender to take preventive or remedial action rather than payment of monetary damages.

Criminal investigations are usually conducted by the judicial police, which may refer cases for prosecution to the Prosecutor General. Once a prosecutor's office becomes aware of potential or actual environmental harm, it must take action to investigate the harm and pursue the case as necessary to remedy it (there is no prosecutorial discretion in Brazil, unlike in some countries).

The level of collaboration between prosecutors and environment agencies varies due to the differing degrees of political independence of state Prosecutor General's Offices and the extent to which prosecutors can rely on the state environment agency to prepare cases.

Prosecutors also have the power to oversee the work of the environment agencies. Most commonly, such oversight occurs when a prosecutor requests information or explanations from an agency about a particular problem or case. The prosecutor can find out, for example, how frequently inspections occurred, what the inspectors found and how the agency reacted. The prosecutor may also solicit a technical opinion from an outside expert to evaluate the agency's work. If the investigation identified a potentially illegal act or omission in the agency's conduct, the prosecutor can make a written recommendation to suggest changes, try to negotiate a "conduct adjustment agreement" with the agency, or take judicial action against it. The involvement of prosecutors makes environmental enforcement more effective by serving as a mechanism of accountability for environment agencies.

Prosecutorial enforcement also has its drawbacks. Most prosecutors are not trained in environmental law. Their enforcement actions, relying either on extra-judicial settlement or the judiciary, lack consistency across the country. In addition, lack of discretion forces prosecutors to spend time and resources investigating relatively minor issues, which compromises their efficiency (McAllister, 2008).

5.4. *Environmental liability*

Brazil has a strict civil environmental liability regime consistent with good international practice: there is no need to prove fault or negligence to impose responsibility for remediating environmental damage. Strict liability means, for example, that current landowners may be held liable for damage that existed when they acquired the land (but they may file a civil lawsuit against the previous landowners who caused the contamination). The Constitution provides a specific obligation for polluters to remediate environmental damage caused by mineral extraction.

In 2009, the Superior Court of Justice ruled that there was no statute of limitations on environmental damage, which means the environment must be remediated regardless of when damage occurred. CONAMA Resolution 420/2009 established a standard procedure for identifying, publicly disclosing and remediating contaminated sites. It sets out criteria and guiding principles for evaluating the degree of soil contamination. Environment agencies and other entitled parties, such as public prosecutors, non-government organisations (NGOs) or individuals, can demand that responsible parties conduct assessments, present a remediation plan (which should be approved by the environment authority) and clean up the damage. Remediation measures are imposed by court injunction.

When the damage cannot be remediated, the court may require monetary compensation. For example, in the case of air pollution, exceeding emission limits set in an environmental licence may lead to an assessment of damage compensation. This issue is regulated further at the state level.

Despite this robust legal framework, environmental liability is assigned only sporadically: environment authorities lack the capacity to pursue all environmental damage cases, so the vast majority remain unaddressed, and some liability-related legal requirements go unmet. For example, the National Solid Waste Policy Law (12305/2010) allows the environmental licensing authority to require operators that generate or handle hazardous waste to buy liability insurance covering possible damage to the environment or public health. The coverage rules and maximum limits were supposed to be established by a regulation, which has not yet been adopted.

6. Promoting environmental democracy

6.1. *Public participation in environmental decision making*

Participation of society in formulating policy is a crucial feature of the SISNAMA model. Representatives of environmental NGOs (of which there are about 400, according to the MMA's national register) are part of CONAMA and sit on state and municipal environment councils. Participation tends to be much stronger at the federal and state levels than in municipalities.

The National Environment Conference was established as a national forum to enhance civil society participation in the discussion and definition of the main elements of Brazil's sustainable development policies. Delegates to the national conference are selected at state conferences, with gender parity and allocation of 40% of seats to NGOs and social movements, 30% to the private sector, 20% to governments, 5% to indigenous communities and 5% to traditional communities. The first took place in 2003, and the conference reconvened in 2005, 2008 and 2013. The last two were dedicated to climate change and solid waste management. Conference discussions have led to the development of environment-related action plans and laws.

Stakeholder participation is also an important element of some formal procedures of environmental governance. The EIA process (Section 4.2) is intended to be a vehicle for public participation in decisions on environmental impact of investment projects. EIA hearings are frequently attended by NGOs and private citizens. However, public participation usually does not go beyond providing information to the public and generating information for decision makers. There are no procedural rules to take NGOs' position into account. Participants have limited resources to actively engage in debates about the decision to issue an environmental licence and the determination of its conditions and mitigation measures.

Article 231 of the Constitution stipulates the right of consultation of affected communities regarding exploration for mineral and hydrological resources in indigenous territory. Recent public discussions related to environmental licensing of large infrastructure projects (e.g. the Angra 3 nuclear power plant, the hydroelectric complex on the Madeira River and the Belo Monte Dam on the Xingu River) have been characterised by stark conflicts between environmental, social and economic interests, which have a strong lobby at the federal level. The lack of dialogue with local communities has caused NGOs to oppose development of natural resources. Many NGOs feel that while they have ample opportunity to express their views, government decision makers often disregard them.

Still, the government provides substantial financial support to NGOs. Law 13019/2014 streamlines procedures for partnerships between the government and civil society organisations, including financial support for NGOs. It establishes new forms of contracting allowing NGOs not only to fund specific project activities but also to cover staff salaries. This should both improve NGOs' institutional stability and increase their accountability.

6.2. *Provision of and access to environmental information*

Federal Law 10650/2003 granted all individuals access to any document or administrative procedure regarding environmental matters managed by any agency that is part of SISNAMA. Federal Law 12527/2011 extended this guarantee to information held by all public institutions, except in the case of information whose disclosure could jeopardise national defence, public health and safety, the stability of the monetary system or other national interests. Environment agencies at all administrative levels must keep public registries of certain information, such as environmental licences and EIA reports. Some states (e.g. São Paulo) have gone further and disclose other environmental information, such as registries of contaminated sites. However, in states with less institutionally developed environment agencies, even rather basic environmental regulatory data are either quite fragmented or poorly maintained.

The National Environmental Information System (SINIMA), managed by the MMA, is responsible for developing a consistent policy on the production, collection, systematisation and dissemination of environmental information. SINIMA comprises three programmes: development of tools to provide access to available information; integration of databases and information systems; and strengthening of production, systematisation and analysis of statistics and indicators related to the MMA's areas of responsibility. The MMA is working to strengthen SINIMA, including by developing a set of key indicators, the National Panel of Environmental Indicators (PNIA). A pilot version of the PNIA published in 2012 covered 34 indicators in eight thematic areas; 16 more indicators are expected to be consolidated by 2016.[16] The project does not involve generation of new data, but aims to consolidate environment-related data already existing across Brazil's numerous public institutions. The MMA is also collaborating with the statistics agency, the IBGE, to link the PNIA to the IBGE's sustainable development indicators (Box 2.7), its most comprehensive set of consolidated environment-related data and other information.

Box 2.7. **Brazil's sustainable development indicators**

Efforts to systematically track progress towards sustainable development began in 2002, with the launch of IBGE's Sustainable Development Indicators (IDS). This was the first attempt to compile data that had been collected by the IBGE, and dozens of other public institutions, so as to monitor and support progress towards sustainable development. The IDS were chosen and designed in line with recommendations by the United Nations Commission on Sustainable Development, yet were adjusted or extended to fit Brazilian circumstances. The indicators were presented in reports in 2004, 2008, 2010 and 2012; where possible, the reports show progress since the 1990s in a differentiated analysis for each region. The 2012 publication covered 62 indicators, structured along four dimensions:

- *social* (covering population, health, education, housing, security, gender and race equality)
- *environmental* (covering air, land, water, oceans and coastal areas, biodiversity and sanitation)
- *economic* (covering economic structure, macroeconomic and financial performance, use and depletion of natural resources)
- *institutional* (covering the existence of environmental institutions and institutional capacity).

Source: IBGE (2012), *Indicadores de Desenvolvimento Sustenável.*

The availability of environment-related information has improved considerably. In addition to the two initiatives cited above, a substantial amount of environment-related data is collected by line ministries and public agencies, such as the Ministry of Cities (data on waste and sanitation), the National Water Agency (on water availability, quality and use) and IBAMA, ICMBio and the Forest Service (on biodiversity, forests and forestry). Initiatives at subnational levels, many still in their infancy, include development of sustainable development indicators in Paraná and Mato Grosso states. However, gaps remain large in some policy fields, notably those where subnational entities are responsible for policy implementation and data collection (e.g. on solid waste or air quality). Many municipalities lack the resources or technical capacities to collect and process such data, resulting in large gaps and inconsistencies in national databases. As a consequence, the use of environmental or sustainable indicators remains very limited (MMA, 2014). So while citizens and NGOs are allowed access to such information, it is often lacking, contradictory or not well systematised.

6.3. *Access to justice*

Federal Law 7347/1985 on Public Civil Action has had a broad impact on environmental law and practice. It allows representation of environmental interests in court by environmental NGOs that have been established for at least one year, along with public prosecutors and government entities, and allows class action suits for compensation of conventional environmental damage to public health and property. In addition, environment-related lawsuits can be initiated by individual citizens under Federal Law 4717/1965, but only if the citizens are directly affected by the activity in question.

Many NGOs head public actions to challenge environmental licences that they feel fail to control activities' environmental impact (Box 2.8). NGOs generally do not go to court directly but file complaints with public prosecutors, who are required by law to act on them.

Box 2.8. **Litigation over the Belo Monte Dam construction**

The Belo Monte Dam is a hydroelectric complex under construction on the Xingu River in Pará state. Its planned installed capacity of over 11 GW would make it the country's second-largest hydroelectric dam complex and one of the world's largest. Its construction is part of government efforts to build hydroelectric dams to guarantee energy security.

There is strong opposition to the project within Brazil, with critics challenging its economic viability, generating efficiency and, particularly, impact on people and the environment. Opponents, who include NGOs such as Amazon Watch, claim the project will devastate over 1 500 km^2 of rainforest and cause a loss of biodiversity, a massive net increase in GHG emissions and forced displacement of over 20 000 people.

In early 2010, IBAMA granted the project a preliminary environmental licence, approving the 2008 EIA. Well over 100 Brazilian and international organisations, in a letter to the then Brazilian President in 2010, decried the decision-making process in granting the licence. With their support, 35 civil action lawsuits were filed against the project, but the courts upheld the licence.

IBAMA issued an installation licence in 2011 after additional studies were carried out and the developer consortium agreed to pay USD 1.9 billion to address social and environmental problems, including USD 40.7 million to be invested in reforestation and protected areas.

Source: Amazon Watch (n.d.), "Brazil's Belo Monte Dam", *www.amazonwatch.org/work/belo-monte-dam* (accessed May 2015); Portal Brasil (2015), "Belo Monte transforma a vida de 11 cidades do Pará", *www.brasil.gov.br* (accessed May 2015).

6.4. Environmental awareness and education

Environmental education is directed by the National Environmental Education Policy (Law 9795/1999) and Presidential Decree 4281/2002. The National Environmental Education Programme (ProNEA) is managed jointly by the MMA's Department of Environmental Education and the General Co-ordination Unit for Environmental Education in the Ministry of Education. Several states are also involved in its initiatives through technical co-operation agreements with the MMA.

The fourth edition of ProNEA was issued in 2014. Its main strategic directions include training of environmental educators (over 6 000 people participate in an environmental distance learning programme), inclusion of environmental courses in school curricula and communication on environmental issues. Two communication initiatives have been particularly well done:

- Under the Green Circuit initiative, the MMA issued a call for amateur videos on local environmental problems and selected about 50 of them, which have been shown and used as background for public debates organised in over 1 500 locations across the country.
- Over 400 "green rooms" have been set up in public spaces (e.g. libraries, official buildings) around Brazil, where a range of environmental publications have been put on display for free public use.

Other key thematic programmes include the National Strategy for Environmental Education and Communication in Conservation Units (for protected areas), the Programme for Environmental Education and Social Mobilisation in Sanitation, the Programme for Environmental Education and Family Agriculture, the Strategy for Environmental

Education and Social Communication in Solid Waste Management and the Youth and Environment Programme (which included a national conference in 2013).

Such initiatives have resulted in high awareness of environmental issues among young people. In an OECD survey, over 95% of 15-year-olds claimed to be familiar with issues related to air pollution, extinction of plants and animals, and deforestation – Brazil's main environmental problems (OECD, 2009).

Citizens' knowledge about key environmental concepts and problems seems to be increasing, although stark regional differences remain. For example, 74% in the South region know what a protected area is, but only 45% do in the North-east region. Overall, less than 15% of the population feels well informed about the environment and ecology (MMA, 2012).

Polls indicate that Brazilians are proud of their country's natural wealth, and that their awareness and concern about environmental pressures is increasing. In 2012, the environment ranked sixth in a list of the main concerns of Brazilians, after health, violence, unemployment, education and politics. This compared with 12th place in 2006 and no mention in 1992. Most Brazilians (82%) disagree that economic progress matters more than environmental preservation, or that elevated pollution levels would be acceptable if they brought more jobs or higher salaries (87%) (MMA, 2012; CNI, 2012).

Brazilians consider deforestation to be the most pressing environmental problem, followed by water pollution, air pollution, waste generation and treatment, and climate change. Waste generation, water and air pollution are the top environmental concerns of urban dwellers, for whom deforestation comes fourth (Figure 2.3). Levels of satisfaction with public action for environmental protection are decreasing, particularly as regards subnational government performance.

Figure 2.3. **Deforestation is Brazilians' top environmental concern, except among urban dwellers**

Environmental concerns, frequency of responses, 2012

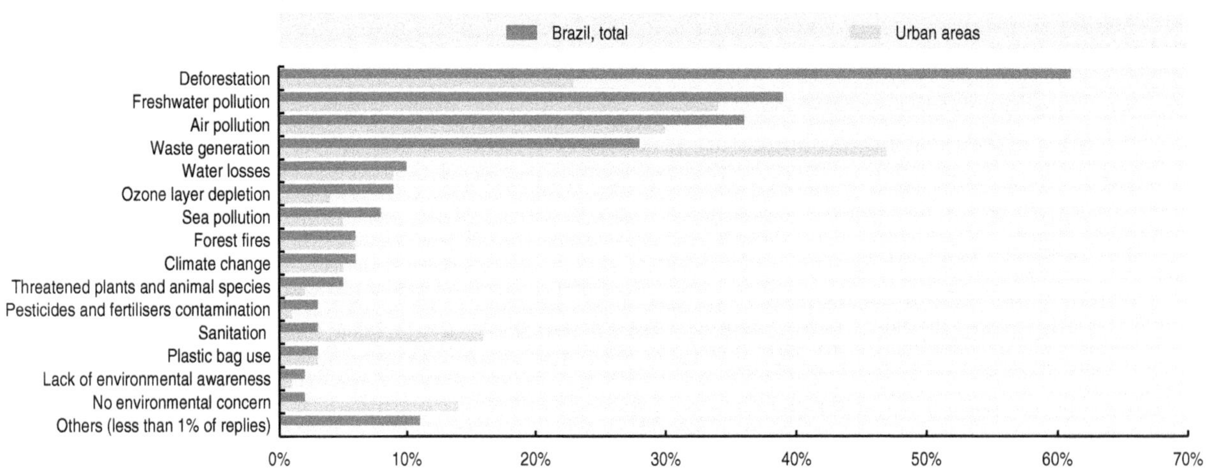

Source: MMA (2012), *O que o brasileiro pensa do meio ambiente e do consumo sustentável - Pesquisa nacional de opinião: principais resultados.*

StatLink http://dx.doi.org/10.1787/888933279547

Recommendations on environmental governance and management

Environmental governance

- Streamline the multitude of horizontal and vertical co-ordination bodies, with a view to eliminating overlaps and gaps of responsibilities and, ultimately, improving policy coherence and effectiveness; consider establishing a national system for quality control and accountability.
- Build on the associations of state (ABEMA) and local (ANAMMA) environmental agencies to create a network of regulators at all administrative levels and enhance their capacity through exchange of experiences and good practices; consider implementing a programme for strengthening capacity at subnational level.
- Consider replicating multilevel governance mechanisms such as the National Water Management Pact to other environmental policy areas to promote integration and dialogue across levels of government and reduce regional disparities in environmental performance.
- Streamline funds dedicated to environmental management and projects; systematically monitor the use of environmental funds to ensure that it is in line with policy priorities, transparent and cost-effective.
- Develop a uniform system for the collection and management of environmental data, including on environmental law implementation (input, output and outcome indicators) and economic aspects of environmental policies (expenditure and revenue accounts; environment-related goods, services and employment).

Environmental licensing, enforcement and compliance

- Introduce and enforce a legal requirement of strategic environmental assessment of municipal territorial plans and sectoral development programmes, which should be used to integrate the economic, social and environmental aspects of land use.
- Streamline the environmental impact assessment and environmental licensing requirements across and within administrative levels; clarify the boundaries of compensation actions that have socio-environmental objectives and those that pursue social objectives; develop procedural guidance for each stage of the licensing process and build capacity of licensing authorities.
- Strengthen the capacity of environmental inspectors at all government levels, emphasise proactive (planned) compliance monitoring, improve collaboration with federal and state prosecutors and develop broader opportunities for "citizen enforcement" by engaging local communities in compliance monitoring.

Notes

1. In 2010, CONAMA had 71 government representatives (41 federal, 27 state and 8 municipal), 22 representatives (11 permanent and 11 rotating) from civil society, academia and trade unions, 8 from the business sector and one honorary member. It is supported by "technical chambers" (expert groups) on various policy issues.
2. Its predecessor was the Special Environment Secretariat in the Ministry of the Interior.
3. A CONAMA/CNRH Permanent Integration Commission was created in 2006 but held only one meeting and was subsequently disbanded (Sano, 2012).
4. All proposed actions, criteria and 2014 targets are available at *www.ambiente.sp.gov.br/municipioverdeazul/*.
5. Major environment-related expenditure occurs, for example, in the Ministry of Agrarian Development, which deals with farmers (2013 budget BRL 5.3 billion); the MCTI (BRL 9.4 billion); the Ministry of

Agriculture, Livestock and Supply, which deals with agribusiness (BRL 10.5 billion); and the ministries of Mines and Energy (BRL 10.8 billion), Transport (BRL 21.4 billion) and Cities (BRL 25.6 billion).

6. This fund, linked to the Ministry of Justice, is meant to provide remedies to damage caused to the environment, to the consumer, to assets and rights of artistic, aesthetic, historical, touristic or scenic value, and to other collective interests.
7. The MCTI sectoral funds are a key instrument to strengthen the national science and technology system. Some of these funds support environment-related activities (Section 6 of Chapter 3).
8. Payment into the Amazon Fund was based on reducing GHG emissions from historical average deforestation rates, using a formula that converted estimated CO_2 emission reductions from deforestation abatement against an average rate and applied a value of USD 5 per tonne of avoided GHG emissions. The pace of decline in deforestation rates, however, was actually higher than the rate at which funding from international donors, primarily Norway, was provided, so the funding mechanism followed a pre-determined commitment and disbursement schedule instead (Birdsall et al., 2014).
9. The federal government allocated BRL 1.2 billion over four years for waste management infrastructure projects, but municipalities used only about 10% of this funding because of a lack of capacity.
10. Some states (e.g. Bahia) have established different, simplified procedures for environmental licensing.
11. Examples include reduced inspection frequency in Norway, reduced permit fees in the UK and reduced monetary penalties in the US.
12. Sebrae's budget comes from contributions of 0.3% to 0.6% of Brazilian corporations' payrolls.
13. For example, the means IBAMA uses to collect fines from violators are recording the debtor's name in the list of debtors of the federal government (CADIN) 75 days after the violator was informed of the debt; suspension of services for the debtor; registration of the violator's name in the Active Federal Debts list; or judicial collection of the fine. Registration in CADIN means the debtor cannot obtain credit from public resources.
14. Brazilian courts tend to have a long backlog, and many years are required for final decisions. Moreover, courts usually lack the expertise to deal with technically complex environmental cases (McAllister, 2008).
15. The power to bring a civil suit is not exclusive to public prosecutors, but in practice they bring over 90% of such lawsuits. Environmental groups often go to the Prosecutor General's Office rather than file lawsuits themselves.
16. See *www.mma.gov.br/pnia*.

References

ABEMA (2013), *Novas propostas para o licenciamento ambiental no Brasil [New proposals for environmental licensing in Brazil]*, Brazilian Association of State Environment Authorities, Brasília.

Amazon Fund (2015), Amazon Fund website, *www.amazonfund.gov.br* (accessed April 2015).

ANA (2014), *OECD-Brazil Policy Dialogue on Water Governance: Background report*, National Water Agency, Brasília.

Assad, E. et al. (2013), *Impactas das Mudanças Climáticas na Produção Agrícola Brasileira [Impacts of Climate Change on Brazilian Agricultural Production]*, The World Bank, Washington, DC, summary in English available at *www.profor.info/node/2061*.

Assunção, J. et al. (2013), "Does Credit Affect Deforestation? Evidence from a Rural Credit Policy in the Brazilian Amazon", CPI Technical Report, Climate Policy Initiative, Rio de Janeiro, *http://climatepolicy initiative.org/wp-content/uploads/2013/01/Does-Credit-Affect-Deforestation-Evidence-from-a-Rural-Credit-Policy-in-the-Brazilian-Amazon-Technical-Paper-English.pdf*.

Birdsall, N., W. Savedoff and F. Seymour (2014), *The Brazil-Norway Agreement for Performance-Based Payments for Forest Conservation: Successes, Challenges, Lessons*, CGD Climate and Forest Paper Series No. 4, Center for Global Development, Washington, DC.

Cavalcanti C. (2007), "Economic growth and environmental protection in Brazil: An unfavourable trade-off", in *Environmental Governance and Decentralisation*, A. Breton et al. (eds.), Edward Elgar Publishing, Cheltenham, UK.

CETESB (n.d.), "Financing Climate Action at Subnational Level São Paulo State" (presentation), São Paulo Sanitation Technology Company, *www.nrg4sd.org/sites/default/files/default/files/content/public/unfccc-cop17/presentation_nelson_bugalho_cop17_-_tcg_nrg4sd_side_event.pdf* (accessed April 2015).

CNI (2012), *Pesquisa CNI-IBOPE: Retratos da Sociedade Brasileira: Meio Ambiente [CNI-IBOPE Research: Pictures of the Brazilian Society: Environment]*, National Industry Confederation, Brasília.

Costa Neves, E.M.S. (2012), "Environmental policy, municipalities and intergovernmental cooperation in Brazil", *Estudos Avançados*, Vol. 26, Nr. 74, pp. 137-150.

De Oliveira, O., J.R. Serra and M.H. Salgado (2010), "Does ISO 14001 work in Brazil?", *Journal of Cleaner Production*, Vol. 18, Issue 18, pp. 1797-1806.

GVces/FGV-EAESP (2014), "The Brazilian Financial System and the Green Economy – Alignment with Sustainable Development", prepared for UNEP and FEBRABAN in the framework of "Inquiry into the design of a sustainable financial system", FEBRABAN, São Paulo.

IBGE (2014a), *Perfil dos Municípios Brasileiros 2013 [Profile of Brazilian Municipalities 2013]*, Brazilian Institute of Geography and Statistics, Rio de Janeiro.

IBGE (2014b), *Perfil dos Estados Brasileiros 2013 [Profile of Brazilian States 2013]*, Brazilian Institute of Geography and Statistics, Rio de Janeiro.

IBGE (2012), *Indicadores de Desenvolvimento Sustenável: Brasil 2012 [Sustainability Development Indicators Brazil 2012]*, Brazilian Institute of Geography and Statistics, Rio de Janeiro.

IEMA (2012), *Padrões de qualidade do ar. Experiência comparada Brasil, EUA e União Europeia [Air Quality Standards. A Comparison of Experiences in Brazil, the US and the EU]*, Energy and Environment Institute, *www.energiaeambiente.org.br*.

ISO (2014), *ISO Survey of Management System Standard Certifications – 2013*, International Organization for Standardization, London, *www.iso.org/iso/home/standards/certification/iso-survey.htm?certificate=ISO%20 9001& countrycode=AF*.

ISS (2014), *Monitoramento da Qualidade do Ar no Brasil [Monitoring Air Quality in Brazil]*, Health and Sustainability Institute, *www.saudeesustentabilidade.org.br/site/wp-content/uploads/2014/07/Monitoramento-da-Qualidade-do-Ar-no-Brasil-2014.pdf*.

Mansell, A. and P. Sopher (2014), "The World's Carbon Markets: A Case Study Guide to Emissions Trading – Brazil", Environmental Defense Fund and International Emissions Trading Association, Washington, DC, *www.ieta.org/assets/EDFCaseStudyMarch2014/brazil%20case%20study%20march%20 2014.pdf*.

Mazur, E. (2012), "Green Transformation of Small Businesses: Achieving and Going Beyond Environmental Requirements", *OECD Environment Working Papers*, No. 47, OECD Publishing, Paris, *http://dx.doi.org/ 10.1787/5k92r8nmfgxp-en*.

McAllister, L. (2008), *Making Law Matter: Environmental Protection and Legal Institutions in Brazil*, Stanford University Press, Reduced City.

MMA (2015), *Brazil Fifth National Report to the Convention on Biological Diversity*, Ministry of the Environment, Brasília, *www.cbd.int/doc/world/br/br-nr-05-en.pdf*.

MMA (2014), *PNIA 2012: Painal Nacional de Indicadores Ambientais. Referencial teórico, composição e síntese dos indicadores [PNIA 2012: National Panel of Environmental Indicators. Theoretical framework, Composition and Synthesis of Indicators]*, Ministry of the Environment, Brasília.

MMA (2012), *O que o Brasileiro Pensa do Meio Ambiente e do Consumo Sustentável: Pesquisa Nacional de Opinião: Principais Resultados [What Brazilians think of the Environment and Sustainable Consumption: National Opinion Research: Key Findings]*, Ministry of the Environment, Brasília.

MMA (2010), *Fourth National Report to the Convention on Biological Diversity*, Ministry of the Environment, Brasília.

MPOG (2015), *Informações Gerenciais de Contratações Públicas Sustentáveis [Information on the Management of Sustainable Public Procurement]*, Ministry of Planning, Budget and Management, *www.compras governamentais.gov.br/arquivos/estatisticas/03-apresentacao-siasg-compras-sustentaveis-_ 2014.pdf*.

Norman, M. et al. (2014), "Climate Finance Thematic Briefing: REDD+ Finance", Climate Finance Fundamentals 5, December, Overseas Development Institute, London and Heinrich Böll Stiftung North America, Washington, DC, *www.odi.org/sites/odi.org.uk/files/odi-assets/publications-opinion-files/9330.pdf*.

Oberling, D.H., E.L. La Rovere and H.V. de Oliveira Silva (2013), "SEA making inroads in land-use planning in Brazil: The case of the extreme south of Bahia with forestry and biofuels", *Land Use Policy*, Vol. 35, pp. 341-358.

OECD (2015), *Water Resources Governance in Brazil*, OECD Studies on Water, OECD Publishing, Paris, *http://dx.doi.org/10.1787/9789264238121-en*.

OECD (2013), *OECD Territorial Reviews: Brazil*, OECD Publishing, Paris, *http://dx.doi.org/10.1787/9789264123229-en*.

OECD (2009), *Green at Fifteen? How 15-Year-Olds Perform in Environmental Science and Geoscience in PISA 2006*, OECD Publishing, Paris, *http://dx.doi.org/10.1787/9789264063600-en*.

PBMC (2013), *Base Científica das Mudanças Climáticas. Contribuição do Grupo de Trabalho 1 ao Primeiro Relatório de Avaliação Nacional do Painel Brasileiro de Mudanças Climáticas [Scientific Basis of Climate Change. Contribution of Working Group 1 to the First National Assessment Report of the Brazilian Panel on Climate Change]*, Brazilian Panel on Climate Change, Brasília, *www.pbmc.coppe.ufrj.br/documentos/MCTI_PBMC_Sumario%20Executivo%204_Finalizado.pdf*.

São Paulo Secretariat for the Environment (2015a), *Project Portfolio*, São Paulo Secretariat for the Environment, São Paulo, *www.ambiente.sp.gov.br/en/files/2015/04/Portf%C3%B3lio-03.pdf*.

São Paulo Secretariat for the Environment (2015b), "Municipio VerdeAzul" website, São Paulo Secretariat for the Environment, São Paulo, *www.ambiente.sp.gov.br/municipioverdeazul*.

Sano, H. (2012), "The Brazilian National Environmental Policy: The challenge of plural environmental governance", *Development*, Vol. 55, pp. 119-125.

Senado Federal (2015), *Portal Orçamento [Budget portal]* (database), *www12.senado.gov.br/orcamento/loa* (accessed April 2015).

Seroa da Motta, R. (2011), "The national policy on climate change: regulatory and governance aspects", in Seroa da Motta, R. et al. (eds) (2011), *Climate Change in Brazil: Economic, Social and Regulatory aspects*, IPEA, Brasília, *www.ipea.gov.br/agencia/images/stories/PDFs/livros/livros/livro_climatechange.pdf*.

TCU (2009), *Auditorias de natureza operacional sobre políticas públicas e mudanças climáticas – Amazonia [Audits of operational nature on public policies and climate change – Amazon]*, Federal Court of Accounts, Brasília.

Teixeira, I. (2012), "Brazil's journey from the Earth Summit to Rio+20", in OECD, *Development Co-operation Report 2012: Lessons in Linking Sustainability and Development*, OECD Publishing, Paris.

Tognere Ferron, R. et al. (2012), "Is ISO 14001 Certification Effective? An Experimental Analysis of Firm Profitability", *Brazilian Administration Review*, Vol. 9, Special Issue, pp. 78-94, Rio de Janeiro.

Unterstell, N. and S. Margulis (2014), "Adaptation to Climate Change in Brazil: Scenarios and Alternatives", *Strategic Notes*, No. 1, March, Strategic Affairs Secretary of the Presidency of the Republic, Brasília.

Vogt-Schilb, A., S. Hallegatte and C. de Gouvello (2014), "Marginal abatement cost curves and the quality of emission reductions: A case study on Brazil", *Climate Policy*, *http://dx.doi.org/10.1080/14693062.2014.953908*.

World Bank (2008), *Environmental Licensing for Hydroelectric Projects in Brazil: A Contribution to the Debate*, Summary Report, Report No. 40995-BR, Washington, DC.

PART I

Chapter 3

Greening the economy in the context of sustainable development

In Brazil, economic growth is inseparable from sustainable use of natural resources, poverty alleviation and better access to essential services. This chapter presents Brazil's progress in mainstreaming environmental concerns into economic and sectoral policies to green its economy on the path to sustainable development. It examines the use of tax policy to pursue environmental objectives and progress in removing subsidies and other incentives that can encourage environmentally harmful activities. The chapter analyses public and private investment in environment-related infrastructure such as that for water and sanitation, waste, clean energy and transport. It reviews the promotion of environmental technologies, goods and services as a source of economic growth and jobs. The role of Brazil as both a recipient and provider of environment-focused development co-operation is also discussed.

1. Introduction

In 2014, Brazil was the world's seventh largest economy. Strong economic growth in the 2000s increased per capita income and helped halve the share of the population living in extreme poverty (Chapter 1). Sustained growth has also helped Brazil make progress towards other Millennium Development Goals, including increasing literacy rates, reducing gender disparities and child mortality, and improving housing conditions and access to basic services (Annex 3.A). Growth began decelerating in 2012, however. Low investment, persistent infrastructure bottlenecks, and domestic firms' low productivity and competitiveness are constraining growth prospects.

The country's economic growth is inseparable from sustainable use of natural resources in both the economic and social sense. Natural assets contribute to significant economic activities, such as agriculture and food production, energy generation, mining and the use of forest resources and biodiversity; they are also a primary source of employment and income for much of the rural population. Managing the trade-offs between socio-economic development and environmental sustainability has proven difficult, and growth has come at a cost to the environment.

Brazil has made remarkable progress in fighting deforestation, although agricultural expansion and intensification continue to exert pressures on forests and native vegetation, as well as on water and soil quality (Chapter 4). Population growth, urbanisation and rising income levels have resulted in increased water, energy and transport demand. Greenhouse gas (GHG) emissions from energy use have increased; the vehicle fleet doubled over the past decade, which is reflected in traffic congestion and air pollution in most major cities. Sanitation and wastewater treatment infrastructure is inadequate to meet growing volumes of industrial and domestic sewage, resulting in water and soil contamination, particularly in densely populated areas (Chapter 1). The 2014-15 water crisis in the South-east has shown how unsustainable natural resource use constrains economic development.

Brazil now faces the challenge of restoring strong, sustainable growth while continuing to eradicate poverty, reduce inequality and social exclusion, broaden access to social services and ensure conservation and sustainable use of environmental assets. Tackling these objectives in an integrated way will provide an opportunity to advance in the development of a resilient, inclusive and green economy.

2. The policy framework for sustainable development and the green economy

The government, supported by civil society and the private sector, has launched several initiatives that aim at addressing the economic, social and environmental aspects of sustainable development in an integrated manner. Several sectoral programmes integrate environmental dimensions, including the Low-Carbon Agriculture programme (Section 4.2), the Growth Acceleration Programme for infrastructure development, the Energy Expansion Plan (Section 5) and the national industrial and innovation policies (Section 6). These positive initiatives, however, do not add up to a coherent policy framework for a green and inclusive economy. With a few exceptions, integration of environmental, social and economic objectives has been ad hoc and environmental impacts are still being dealt with *ex post* rather than at the early stage of policy development.

2.1. The strategic framework for sustainable development

Brazil's president signed the sustainable development strategy, Agenda 21, in July 2002 in preparation for the World Summit on Sustainable Development. Developed through years of extensive consultation across all sectors of society, it is referred to as a social pact rather than an official government document. It notes that "the common objective ... is not restricted to the preservation of the environment alone, but to progressive and expanded sustainable development, which brings into discussion the search for balance between economic growth, social equity and environmental preservation". The pact outlines 21 objectives, including actions and recommendations in such areas as urban and rural sustainability; protection of water, biodiversity and forests; governance and ethics for the promotion of sustainability; and social inclusion.

Agenda 21 placed the onus for implementation directly on the various sectors of society, including government at all levels, private sector companies and civil society organisations. The federal government committed itself to integrating the Agenda 21 priorities throughout public policy, but this has not fully happened. In 2004, the government established the Sustainable Development Policies and Agenda 21 Council, with equal numbers of representatives from the government and civil society, to co-ordinate implementation, but it has been inactive for years. Within the framework of Agenda 21, the government has been tracking a wide range of indicators characterising sustainable development's environmental, social, economic and institutional dimensions (Box 2.7). As no quantitative targets are associated with the indicators, however, they are difficult to use in performance measurement and policy making. Agenda 21 is no longer a reference point for activities of the Ministry of the Environment (MMA) or other line ministries. At the local level, however, Agenda 21 seems to have been a successful instrument for consultation on environmental, social and economic issues in over 1 000 municipalities.

The government is looking to reinvent Agenda 21 to reflect current environmental challenges that were not seen as priorities at the time of its original adoption, including climate change and urban issues such as waste management and sustainable transport. In addition, in 2011 it approved the National Plan on Sustainable Production and Consumption (2011-14), which aims to promote green practices in public administration and the business sector. The plan set six priority areas: green commerce (promotion of eco-labelling), waste management, sustainable construction (particularly for government-funded social housing), sustainable public procurement, environmental education and the Public Administration Environmental Agenda (Chapter 2).

2.2. Aligning social policies with environmental objectives

Poverty reduction and social inclusion are pillars of sustainable development and have been priorities in Brazilian policy since the early 2000s. Several poverty reduction, income redistribution and social inclusion programmes have been introduced or expanded. These include the social protection programme Bolsa Família (Box 3.1; *bolsa* means grant or stipend), which serves as a best-practice example for poverty reduction and social inclusion and is being replicated in other countries. The government works to mainstream

Box 3.1. **Brazil's flagship social protection programme, Bolsa Família**

In 2003, the federal government launched the social protection programme Bolsa Família to consolidate four programmes into one unified conditional cash transfer programme. Beneficiaries receive, on average, BRL 70 per month in direct transfers conditional on school attendance and regular health checks. To ensure that all poor Brazilians benefit from the programme, the government launched an active search policy and established a unified social programme registry to consolidate information and statistics about income and living standards from municipal registries. In 2011, as part of Brasil sem Miséria, a new programme to eradicate extreme poverty, Bolsa Família was expanded to increase beneficiaries' income, expand access to public goods and services, and provide support for finding jobs and other income opportunities. It is now the world's largest social protection programme: in 2013 it reached 11 million families, or 50 million people, over a quarter of Brazil's population.

Bolsa Família is generally found to have made an important contribution to improvement in living standards for Brazil's poorest families. It is estimated that the programme contributed to between 33% and 50% of the drop in extreme poverty and helped reduce inequality (as measured by the Gini coefficient) by 15% to 20%. It has also been found to have a significant multiplier effect on household consumption (2.4) and GDP (1.8), and to have helped reduce regional inequality. Beneficiaries tend to have better health care provision, and children under the programme tend to have lower dropout and higher progression rates in education. Moreover, the unified social programme registry has consolidated fragmented regional and local data, allowing for identification of the municipalities with the greatest concentration of poor people and gaps in public service delivery. Despite its significant expansion, the programme's targeting remains good, and its overall cost is about 0.5% of GDP.

Source: IPEA (2014), *Bolsa Família Program: A Decade of Social Inclusion in Brazil – Executive Summary*, Institute for Applied Economic Research, Brasília.

social issues throughout public policies, including those concerning the environment, particularly for forest conservation.

Social and environmental issues are frequently addressed simultaneously, notably in forest communities. Bolsa Floresta, for example, provides monthly cash payments of about BRL 50 (about USD 20) to families living in protected areas in exchange for forest conservation efforts (e.g. for limiting the amount of forested land converted for farming). Launched in 2007 by Amazonas state, Bolsa Floresta was the first of its kind, and is now the world's largest programme of payments for ecosystem services (PES), reaching more than 35 000 people in 15 protected areas in 2013. Building on this initiative, the federal government launched Bolsa Verde in 2011 as part of the anti-poverty programme Brasil sem Miséria, extending the federal social protection system to include payments for ecosystem services and to provide an incentive to adopt environmental practices (Chapter 4).

Bolsa Floresta and Bolsa Verde are part of a wider government effort to increase income and improve living conditions of rural populations by scaling up sustainable economic use of environmental assets. Other major programmes have similar aims. One is the 2009 National Plan to Promote the Production Chain of Socio-Biodiversity Products, providing facilitated access to credit and markets, as well as technical assistance, to traditional and rural communities to promote sustainable use of biodiversity (Chapter 4). The plan, which includes minimum pricing for products such as açaí fruit, natural rubber and Brazil nuts, was recently linked to the large-scale federal Food Acquisition Programme, one of the world's largest institutional procurement programmes for smallholders' or family farmers' products. Similar initiatives have been launched at state level, e.g. in Amazonas state, where public purchasing is used to boost value chains for rural products (MMA, 2015). While there are good examples of policies and programmes that simultaneously address environmental and social objectives, many have thus far proved hard to scale up. This may be due to insufficient infrastructure and high production costs, and in many areas also to a lack of producer associations.

3. Greening the system of taxes and charges

3.1. *Brazil's tax system and the environment: An overview*

The tax system

Total tax revenue has increased steadily since 2000, reaching 36% of GDP in 2013 – above the OECD average and the highest share in Latin America (OECD et al., 2015). The tax system is fragmented, complex and characterised by a low degree of progressivity. Tax compliance costs are exceptionally high, largely due to a system of six indirect taxes, some with differing tax rules and rates across states (OECD, 2013a).

Exploitation of non-renewable natural resources such as minerals and hydrocarbons is an important source of fiscal revenue (through various forms of income and revenue taxes and royalties), although not as much as in some other Latin American countries. In 2013, fiscal revenue from non-renewable natural resources accounted for 2.4% of GDP, compared to 8% in Mexico (OECD et al., 2015). Part of this revenue is used for environmental purposes (Box 3.2).

Box 3.2. **Using oil and gas revenue for environmental purposes**

Brazil uses part of its revenue from oil and gas exploitation to fund environment-related expenditure. Until 2010, two types of oil and gas revenue accrued to the government (besides corporate income taxes): royalties and a windfall profit tax known as the Participação Especial (PE), which is applied to highly productive fields. Revenue from both sources is roughly equal, and reached over USD 16 billion in 2012 (Goldemberg et al., 2014). By law, 10% of the PE goes to the MMA, where it is an important source of National Climate Change Fund revenue (Chapter 2). The Ministry of Mines and Energy receives 40% of the revenue, state governments a further 40% and municipalities the remaining 10%. The royalty rate is 10% of gross revenue; 28% of royalty revenue is allocated to the Ministry of Science, Technology and Innovation (MCTI) and to the Navy (for coastal protection). The MCTI uses royalty revenue in sectoral funds for research and development (R&D) in various areas, including environmental ones (Section 6).

While this system has been maintained for existing production, from 2010 a new legal framework was developed for new oil exploration areas (currently pre-salt oilfield discoveries). A production sharing contract divides revenue from future petroleum discoveries between the operator and the government (aside from a portion for cost recovery), removing the PE but maintaining royalties. Given the potential increase in oil production from pre-salt fields and related revenue, discussions about revenue sharing among states – including those that lack oil production – have been animated (World Bank, 2013). Brazil established a social fund to manage a share of the expected revenue, inspired by the Norwegian model of a sovereign wealth fund. The return on investments is to be used mostly to finance education. In practice, about half the fund would be used for immediate social spending, primarily on education but also on health. The rest would be used in other areas, including environment, science and technology.

In contrast to other federal Latin American countries, a large share of revenue is collected at state level, especially through the state value added tax, called the ICMS (OECD et al., 2015). About half the states redistribute some ICMS revenue to municipalities according to environmental indicators, generally related to the extension of protected areas (Ecological ICMS, or ICMS-E; Chapter 5).

Environmentally related taxes

Revenue from environmentally related taxes is low by international comparison. In 2013, it equalled 0.7% of GDP or 1.9% of total tax revenue, below the levels in all OECD countries except Mexico (Figure 3.1; Annex 3.B). Revenue from environmentally related taxes has decreased in real terms since 2000, notably over 2011-13, when the fuel tax rate was set to zero and vehicle sales declined (Figure 3.1). As in all countries, environmentally

Figure 3.1. **Revenue from environmentally related taxes has declined**

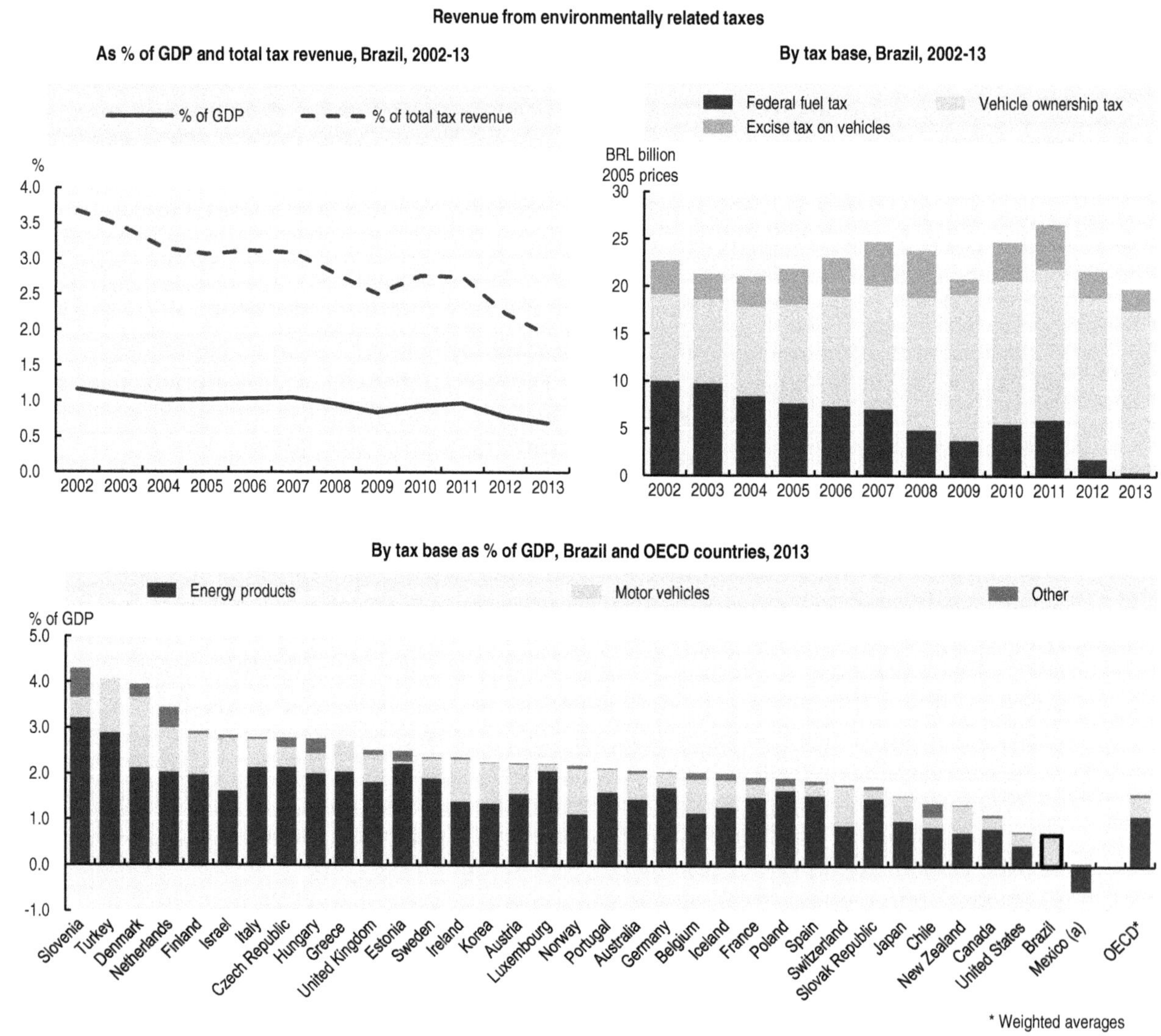

a) Until 2014, the system used to stabilise end-use prices of motor fuels caused tax revenue to turn negative (i.e. become a subsidy) in years when the international oil price was high. Mexico's 2013 Tax Reform corrected this mechanism and introduced a tax on fossil fuels based on their carbon content, which will yield positive revenue.

Source: Based on OECD (2015), *OECD Database on Instruments Used for Environmental Policy and Natural Resources Management.*

StatLink http://dx.doi.org/10.1787/888933279554

related taxes are mainly taxes on consumption of energy products and on vehicles. Several fossil fuels are exempt, however (Sections 3.2 and 4.1). Vehicle taxation accounts for over 95% of environmentally related tax revenue but is only partially linked to environmental performance of vehicles (Section 3.3). There are no taxes on natural resource use and pollution. Water abstraction and pollution charges and fees for public services such as sanitation and waste collection are inconsistently applied and often too low to stimulate efficient resource use and to finance service provision (Section 3.4).

As the 2013 OECD Economic Survey indicated, Brazil should move forward with reforming its complex tax system and shift taxation towards less distorting taxes to alleviate the burden on productivity and competitiveness. In this context, there is scope to extend and improve the use of environmentally related taxes and remove potentially harmful tax exemptions and subsidies so as to stimulate efficient and sustainable resource use. This would generate revenue that could help the government in its fiscal consolidation efforts or fund infrastructure and other high-priority areas such as education and poverty alleviation. Environmental fiscal reforms could help reduce poverty by addressing environmental problems that threaten the health and livelihood of the poor (e.g. water and air pollution) and generating resources to extend access to basic services such as electricity and sanitation (OECD, 2013b).

In addition to restructuring taxes on energy products and vehicles, Brazil could consider introducing taxes on fertilisers and pesticides to limit water pollution, on waste disposal and packaging materials, and on use of natural resources such as minerals. Such measures should be introduced in clearly defined stages to minimise uncertainty about future tax rates, help the economy adapt to changes in relative prices and facilitate long-term investment. Cash transfers in Bolsa Família could be used to address the potential impact of taxes on the large number of low-income households.

3.2. Energy taxes and charges

Brazil applies an excise duty to fossil fuels, mainly for use in transport, but the rate has gradually fallen and was set to zero between 2012 and 2015 (see below). Fuels for heating and processes are largely untaxed. Until 2012, Brazil applied relatively high charges on consumption of electricity, which is the lowest-carbon source of energy in the country thanks to the large share of hydro (Chapter 1). All this implies that Brazil's effective tax rates on energy use, expressed in terms of CO_2 emissions (as well as of energy content), are among the lowest in OECD and BRIICS economies, as Figure 3.2 shows (OECD, 2015a).

There is room to raise and restructure taxes on energy products to reflect CO_2 emissions from their consumption, encourage more efficient energy use and help reduce GHG emissions. In 2014, the finance ministry launched a comprehensive economic and regulatory impact assessment for carbon pricing options, including a carbon tax and a GHG emission trading system (Ministry of Finance, 2014). Rio de Janeiro and São Paulo states planned to introduce such system at state-level in the early 2010s, although implementation was put on hold (Chapter 2). Brazil could build on such initiatives to improve the price signal on GHG emissions.

The fuel consumption tax

A specific fuel consumption tax, the federal fuel tax, or CIDE, was introduced in 2001 and is levied on the import and domestic sale of oil and oil products, natural gas and

Figure 3.2. **Effective tax rates on CO_2 emissions from energy use are low**

Effective tax rates on energy-related CO_2 emissions by fuel type, OECD and selected emerging economies, 2012

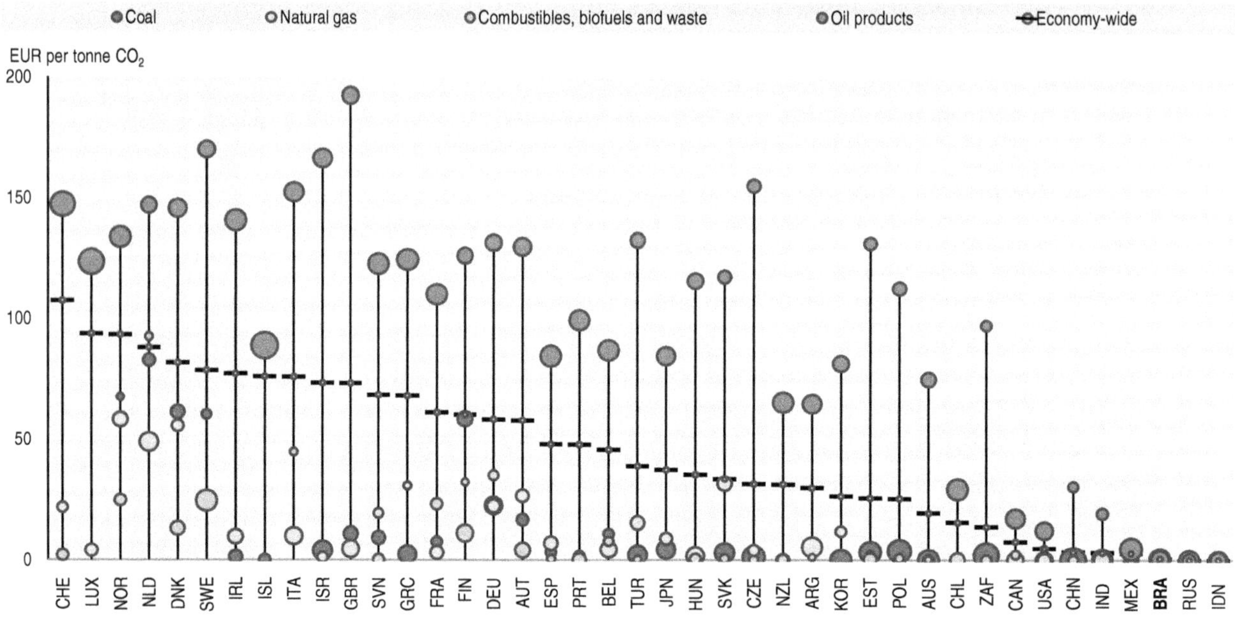

Notes: Tax rates are as of 1 April 2012 (except 1 July 2012 for AUS and BRA, and 4 April 2012 for ZAF); energy use data are for 2009 from IEA (2011). Data for CAN, IND and USA include only federal taxes.

Source: OECD (2015), *Taxing Energy Use 2015: OECD and Selected Partner Economies.*

StatLink http://dx.doi.org/10.1787/888933279561

derivatives, and ethanol.[1] The CIDE rate has been mainly used to smooth domestic fossil fuel price fluctuations. It has been zero for all fuels but petrol and diesel since 2004; tax rates for petrol and diesel were gradually lowered and also set to zero in 2012, to offset increases in fuel prices (Table 3.1). This added to the fossil fuel subsidy implicit in keeping domestic fuel prices below the world market level (Section 4.1).

Table 3.1. **Fuel consumption tax rates, 2001-15**

BRL (nominal prices)

	Dec. 2001 (Decree 10.336)	Apr. 2004 (Decree 5.060)	May 2008 (Decree 6.446)	June 2009 (Decree 6.875)	Feb. 2010 (Decree 7.095)	May 2010 (Decree 7.095)	Sep. 2011 (Decree 7.574)	Oct. 2011 (Decree 7.591)	June 2012 (Decree 7.764)	Feb. 2015 (Decree 8.395)
Petrol	860/ m^3	280/ m^3	180/ m^3	230/ m^3	150/ m^3	230/ m^3	192.6/ m^3	91/ m^3	0	100/ m^3
Diesel	390/ m^3	70/ m^3	30/ m^3	70/ m^3	0	0	0	47/ m^3	0	50/ m^3
Kerosene	92.1/ m^3	0	0	0	0	0	0	0	0	0
Fuel oil	40.9/ t	0	0	0	0	0	0	0	0	0
Liquefied petroleum gas	250/ t	0	0	0	0	0	0	0	0	0
Ethanol fuel	37.2/ m^3	0	0	0	0	0	0	0	0	0

Source: Based on Decree 8.395/2015 and previous decrees, available at *www.planalto.gov.br/ccivil_03.*

As part of its fiscal consolidation efforts, in February 2015 the government restored positive tax rates on diesel and petrol at slightly higher nominal levels than those in place prior to June 2012 (Table 3.1). Tax rates remain far below international averages and diesel is still taxed at a lower rate than petrol (Figure 3.3). This discrepancy, common in most

Figure 3.3. **CO_2 emissions from transport fuel use are taxed less than in most other countries**

Tax rates on road fuels on a CO_2 emission basis, OECD and selected emerging economies, 2012

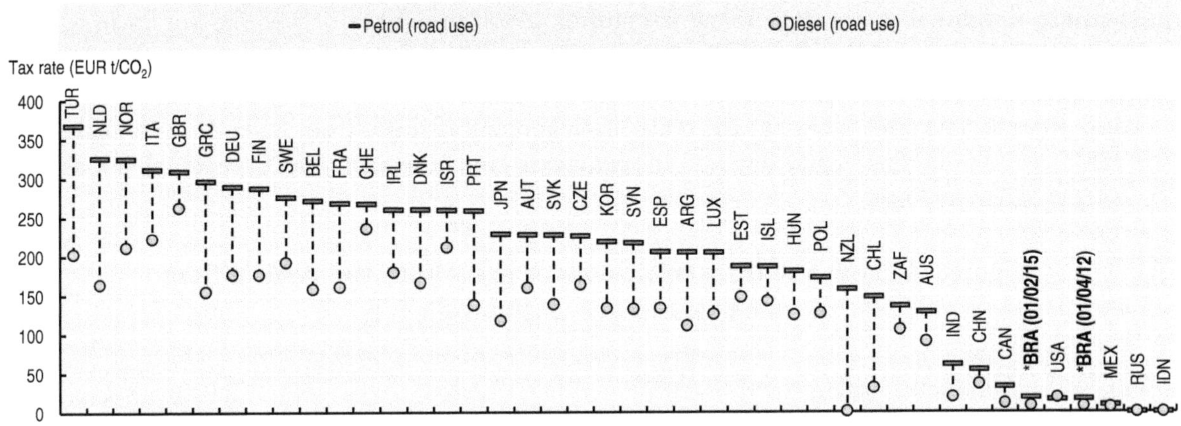

Notes: Tax rates are as of 1 April 2012, except 1 July 2012 for AUS and 4 April 2012 for ZAF. Figures for CAN, IND and USA include only federal taxes. NZL applies a road-user charge to diesel that is not included in the figure. Tax rates converted using standard carbon emission factors from the Intergovernmental Panel on Climate Change and energy conversion factors from the IEA.
*Brazilian rates are as of 1 April 2012 and 1 February 2015 to reflect changes in the tax system over time.
Source: Adapted from OECD (2015), *Taxing Energy Use 2015: OECD and Selected Partner Economies.*

StatLink http://dx.doi.org/10.1787/888933279577

countries, is not justified on environmental grounds, given diesel's higher carbon content and emissions of local air pollutants (Harding, 2014). Brazil should gradually raise the CIDE rates and consider linking them to fuel carbon content. The tax base should be gradually expanded to other fuels, including kerosene used for domestic aviation.

Special charges on electricity consumption

Electricity has traditionally been subject to a range of charges and taxes, in part used to fund socio-environmental objectives such as renewable energy sources and electrification in rural areas. The degree and complexity of taxation on electricity has led to higher end-use electricity prices than in neighbouring countries (IEA, 2013; The Economist, 2012), with taxes accounting for about 50% of final prices. In 2012, the government abolished two charges and greatly reduced the remaining charge on electricity consumption in a bid to reduce electricity tariffs (see below).[2] This can help rebalance taxation of energy products in terms of CO_2 emissions. Electricity prices have risen substantially since early 2015 and are expected to increase further (Reuters, 2015). Recent increases partly resulted from drought in south-eastern Brazil since late 2013, which has reduced hydropower generation and increased reliance on more expensive thermal power supply.

The only remaining charge on electricity consumption is the Energy Development Charge. In place since 2002, it is levied on distributors and passed on to final consumers as part of the electricity bill. The rates were significantly reduced after the 2012 reform (to 73% below the 2012 level). The revenue, managed by the national power company, Eletrobras, has been used for various purposes, including to support renewables and rural electrification programmes, and to subsidise low-income electricity tariffs and some diesel- and coal-fired power plants.

3.3. Vehicle taxes

Revenue from vehicle taxes increased between 2002 and 2013 in line with vehicle sales and ownership, though it has slightly declined since 2011 (Figures 3.1 and 3.4). These taxes include an annual motor vehicle ownership tax (IPVA) and a tax on vehicle purchase or registration. None of these taxes is differentiated according to environmental criteria, although the purchase tax is reduced for flex-fuel vehicles, which can run on both petrol and ethanol. The IPVA, levied at the state level, generally ranges from 2% to 5% of vehicle value. Its revenue has nearly doubled in real terms since the early 2000s, reaching about BRL 30 billion in 2013.

Figure 3.4. **Revenue from vehicle taxes grew with the vehicle fleet**

Motor vehicle fleet and revenue from vehicle taxes, 2002-12

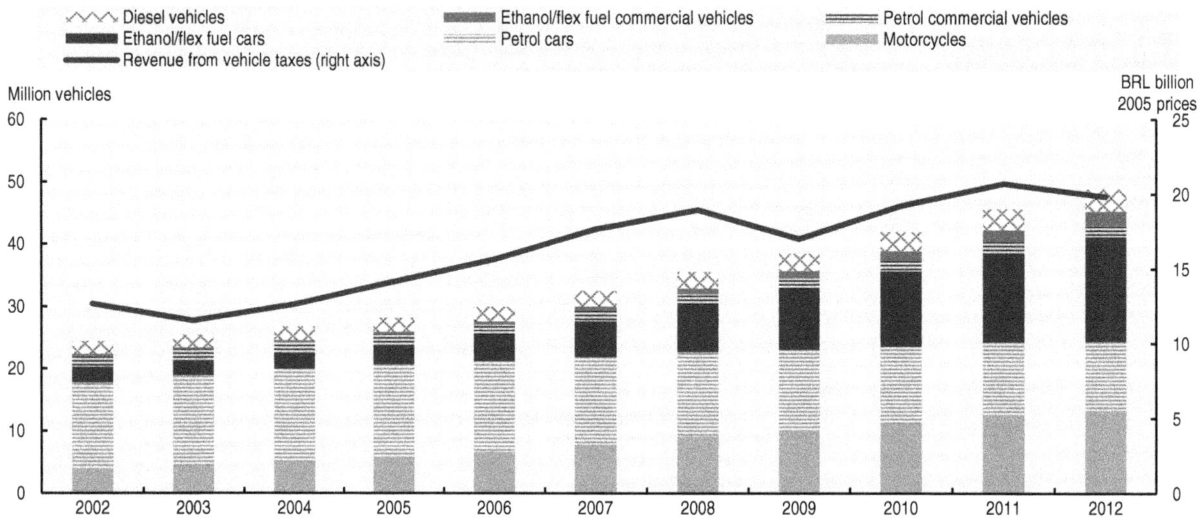

Source: Based on MMA (2013), *Painel Nacional de Indicadores Ambientais;* OECD (2015), *Database on Instruments Used for Environmental Policy and Natural Resources Management.*

StatLink http://dx.doi.org/10.1787/888933279585

The federal tax on manufactured products (IPI) is a consumption tax levied on manufactured goods, including motor vehicles. Revenue increased in real terms between 2002 and 2012, with a dip in 2009 due to the recession. It has declined since, to BRL 3.8 billion in 2013, because vehicle sales declined and the tax rate was reduced from 2012 to 2014 to stimulate the automobile industry (MMA, 2015).

The IPI is differentiated by engine capacity. It is lowest (7%) for vehicles with a 1 000 cc capacity. Above 1 000 cc, the IPI is 13% or 25% for petrol vehicles, depending on engine capacity, and reduced to 11% or 18% for flex-fuel vehicles (Barros, 2014). This differentiation has helped promote sales of flex-fuel passenger cars, which accounted for 57% of the passenger car fleet in 2012 (Figure 3.4). Electric vehicles are taxed at the same rate as combustion vehicles.

The Inovar Auto programme, aimed at promoting technological innovation in the automotive industry, imposes a 30% to 55% increase in the IPI rate (depending on vehicle engine displacement) between July 2014 and December 2017, but simultaneously grants reductions of up to 30% to manufacturers in exchange for complying with innovation targets related to emissions and fuel efficiency, R&D, safety and domestic production content (TransportPolicy, 2014). While the programme has helped improve vehicle efficiency, it has mainly boosted investment in the local auto industry, owing to local content requirements (Box 3.5). Vehicle taxes based on fuel efficiency would probably be more cost-effective in stimulating improvement in vehicle technology and would create less market distortions.

Taxes on vehicle ownership are theoretically less efficient than fuel taxes and road charges in reducing emissions of GHGs and air pollutants since they are more disconnected from vehicle use. Yet Brazil should consider differentiating vehicle taxation on the basis of environmental parameters (e.g. fuel efficiency, CO_2 emissions or emissions of local air pollutants such as NO_x), in addition to the current reduced tax rates for flex-fuel vehicles. This would provide vehicle owners with an incentive to choose lower emission vehicles and help further shift the fleet composition towards cleaner vehicles.

3.4. Other environment-related taxes and charges

Property taxes

Brazilian law allows urban property taxes, based on property value, to be raised to account for potential rises in market value resulting from improved provision of public services, including environment-related services. Payment of this so-called "contribution for improvement" can also be passed through via rent increases. The type of investment involved includes construction or expansion of rapid transit systems, drinking water supply systems, sewerage facilities, infrastructure for energy distribution, transport and communications, and infrastructure related to drought and flood protection. It is unknown how extensive the use of such contributions is, and to what extent the revenue is used to finance such investment.

Waste service charges

Municipalities can charge for the provision of environment-related services such as garbage collection, city maintenance and cleaning. Most municipalities that charge for waste collection do so through property and land taxes, with no link to the volume of waste collected, though the charges may be related to collection service frequency. The National Solid Waste Plan foresees expanding the share of municipalities that use specific charges or taxes (other than property taxes) to 75% by 2031, from 11% in 2008 (MMA, 2012). While fixed charges may be easier to administer, they provide no incentive to generate less waste or to sort for recycling.

In addition, the rates of the charges are usually too low to cover service provision costs: the 2008 National Survey for Basic Sanitation found that only 12% of the municipalities that charged for waste services recovered their costs (MMA, 2012; IPEA, 2012). As costs for waste management are likely to increase as Brazil moves from open landfills to controlled and sanitary disposal (Chapter 1), a reform of the charging system seems necessary to avoid an increasing burden on the public budget and to encourage private investment in the sector (Section 5.2).

Water charges

Legal frameworks to allow charging for water use have been in place for several decades. The 1997 National Water Resources Policy Law formally established water charges – for both abstraction and effluent discharges – as instruments that could be used for water resource management. In practice, implementation has been administratively complex (Chapter 2), and only a few river basin committees charge for water (OECD, 2012). As of March 2015, water charges were in effect in four federal river basins or levied by five state governments (OECD, 2015b). In most states that charge for water, unit prices are low, are not automatically adjusted for inflation, cover little of the water resource management costs and have had limited effect on decisions about water allocation and use (OECD, 2012; Ioris, 2008).

Rio de Janeiro is the only state in which water use is charged universally. Charges are applied by river basins for each category of water use and centralised into a water management fund, though 90% of the resources are redistributed to basins. Revenue from charges increased from BRL 3 million in 2007 to BRL 35 million in 2013. State regulations require at least 70% of the funds to be invested in collection and treatment of municipal wastewater until the target of 80% of sewage collection and treatment is reached in each hydrographic region. Nevertheless, water charges represent less than 15% of the funding needed for investment in Rio de Janeiro (OECD, 2015b). There is some evidence that water charges had a positive impact on water use efficiency in the industrial sector, though not for other users (Martinez Júnior, 2011).

In addition, the National Water Agency (ANA) receives the revenue of a 0.75% charge on the value of hydropower produced, as a compensation for flooding areas and using water resource for power generation.[3] This represents over half of its budget (OECD, 2012). The charge, however, does not reflect scarcity of water and competition to access it in the basin and does not contribute to efficient water resources management (OECD, 2015b). There is significant scope to use economic instruments in areas of water scarcity or high competition among water users. This includes water charging, used as a policy tool and not just a revenue generating mechanism, but could also include some form of trading/transferring water entitlements or allocations between users. Such measures can be accompanied with mechanisms that recognise sensitivities and legal constraints, and meet public policy objectives, such as compensation or government-facilitated transfers (OECD, 2015b).

Regulatory agencies define the watery supply and sanitation tariff regime and specify the mechanisms to periodically revise tariffs. Water supply tariffs must be set at cost-recovery levels and should allow for the necessary investment to expand service coverage and guarantee appropriate return on investment. Sanitation tariffs are often the same for collection/disposal and treatment, which tends to discourage investment in wastewater treatment services (Costa and Côrtes, 2014). Water tariffs are higher in Brazil than in other Latin American countries. On average, tariffs allow recovery of operating and maintenance costs but very little investment in new infrastructure (Figure 3.5 and Section 5.2). However, there are wide variations in tariffs and operational efficiency across states, municipalities and service providers (Ministry of Cities, 2014). As in other Latin American countries, a large share (about 40%) of distributed water does not generate revenue, due to unbilled consumption, water theft, metering inaccuracies and physical water losses (IBNET, 2015).

In most municipalities, low-income households benefit from a low social tariff on the first block of water consumption. However, this subsidy is seldom well targeted, as poorer households do not always have access to the network, especially in remote northern areas. In some places targeting has been improved using registers from the Bolsa Família programme (Box 3.1). However, the resulting cross-subsidies can hinder network expansion in rural and poor areas, as revenue may not cover associated costs (OECD, 2011). In general, a greater use of existing cash transfer programmes would be more cost-effective in supporting low-income households.

Figure 3.5. **Tariffs for water and sanitation are high enough to cover operating costs**

Operating cost coverage ratio in selected Latin American countries, 2011 or latest available year

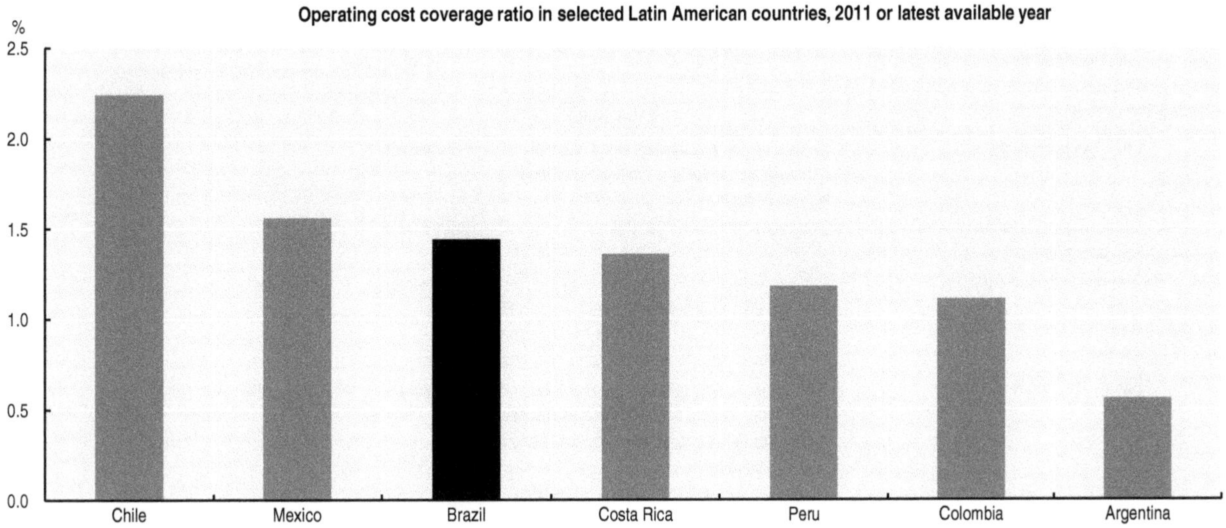

Note: Total billed revenues as percentage of total operational expenses.
Source: The International Benchmarking Network for Water and Sanitation Utilities (2015), *IB-NET Database*.

StatLink http://dx.doi.org/10.1787/888933279599

4. Reforming environmentally harmful subsidies and incentives

4.1. Support to fossil fuel consumption and production

Support to fossil fuel consumption

Brazil has a long history of subsidising production and use of energy to promote industrialisation and achieve social objectives. In the 1990s, it launched a reform agenda aimed at liberalising the energy sector and removing subsidies. The reform process culminated in the liberalisation of transport fuel prices in 2002, but has since all but stalled (De Oliveira and Laan, 2010).

In practice the government has continued to intervene in the market to limit fluctuation in domestic fuel prices: it froze prices for petrol, diesel fuel and liquefied petroleum gas (LPG) between 2006 and 2012 and repeatedly reduced fuel tax rates (Table 3.1). Fuel prices were kept below the international prices at which the stated-owned company Petrobras imported them, causing it to incur growing financial losses (OECD, 2015a). Fuel prices were raised in 2012 and 2013, but the increases were partly offset by reducing to zero the CIDE rate in June 2012 (Section 3.2). OECD (2015a) estimates that this tax adjustment resulted in BRL 5.6 billion of forgone revenue in 2012 (Table 3.2). Positive tax rates for petrol and diesel were re-established in early 2015, but the rate remains zero for other petroleum products and natural gas (Table 3.2).

The combination of government fuel pricing decisions and temporary CIDE exemptions resulted in *de facto* fossil fuel support, which has encouraged private car ownership and use and increased demand for petrol at the expense of ethanol (since flex-fuel vehicle owners tend to use the cheapest fuel). This has ultimately depressed investment in the ethanol industry (OECD, 2013a) and runs counter the government's objective of promoting ethanol production and use (Section 5.4). Other countries have implemented similar fuel price smoothing mechanisms, with different levels of government intervention and impact on prices.[4] Their experience shows that, in addition to weighing on public finances and

Table 3.2. **Examples of fossil-fuel support and related tax expenditure**

In BRL million

Support measure	Details	Type of support	Estimated support, 2011	Estimated support, 2012[a]
	Petroleum			
CIDE fuel tax reductions	Exemption for imports and retail sales of petrol, diesel, kerosene, aviation kerosene and natural gas	Consumer	817	5 632
Tax reduction on the import and retail sale of naphtha	Exemptions from PIS/COFINS	Consumer	364	429
Fuel Consumption Fund	Refunds diesel-fired power plants in the North to offset the region's high costs of electricity generation (costs of buying and transporting diesel fuel; exemptions from customs duties)	Consumer	5 482	4 854
Energy Development Fund	Support for energy consumption for low-income households, diesel- and coal-fired power plants, expansion of the natural gas network, Luz Para Todos programme	Consumer	32	36
REPENEC (tax incentive for oil company infrastructure development in the North, North-east and Centre-West regions)	Temporary exemptions from PIS/COFINS, IPI and customs duties on imports of certain capital goods	Producer	1 458	2 781
REPETRO (special tax regime for goods used in the exploration and production of oil and natural gas fields)	Exemptions from PIS/COFINS, IPI, customs duties and a tax on goods imported by sea	Producer	8 824	7 655
REPEX (special tax regime for imports of crude oil and petroleum products)	Exemptions from PIS/COFINS, IPI and customs duties	Producer	1 365	4 003
	Natural gas			
REPETRO	See above	Consumer	1146	n.a.
REPENEC	See above	Consumer	189	n.a.
	Coal			
Tax exemptions for coal and natural gas used in electricity generation	Exemptions from PIS/COFINS for purchases of coal and natural gas	Consumer	329	153
Energy Development Fund	See above	Consumer	547	627

a) Provisional data.

Source: OECD-IEA (2015), "Fossil Fuel Subsidies and Other Support", *www.oecd.org/site/tadffss.*

encouraging wasteful energy use, such mechanisms are inefficient as poverty-alleviation measures and tend to be highly regressive (OECD, 2013c). Benefits are largely captured by higher income groups which spend a larger share of their earnings on driving cars, while low-income households tend to use public transport (Section 5.3).

The CIDE rate for LPG has been set to zero since 2004. Previously, there was a targeted LPG allowance programme for low-income households, which was incorporated into Bolsa Família in 2003 (Box 3.1). As with water tariffs (Section 3.4), low-income households generally benefit from a low electricity tariff on the first block of consumption. Removing such tax exemptions and price discounts and replacing them with direct cash transfers, as was done for LPG, would provide better energy efficiency incentives.

Support to fossil fuel production

Natural gas and coal used in electricity generation – about half the total supply of these fuels – are exempt from several taxes. Oil and gas producers enjoy special tax regimes, including one for operators investing in infrastructure in certain regions (REPENEC), one for goods used in oil and gas exploration and development (REPETRO) and one for crude oil and petroleum product imports (REPEX). These regimes exempt operators from the social contributions called PIS and COFINS[5] as well as IPI and customs duties, and provide potential ICMS reductions.[6] Government budget transfers related to these programmes are significant (Table 3.2).

Sugar cane sales for ethanol production, and all ethanol fuels, are exempt from PIS/ COFINS payments. Reductions and exemptions are also available to biodiesel producers, depending on the fuel source and inputs (e.g. lower taxes are applied for palm and castor oil to encourage their use), and are designed to benefit biodiesel supply from family farmers, particularly in the North and North-east regions (Barros, 2012; La Rovere et al., 2011).[7]

Investment in oil and gas exploration and extraction has increased significantly since the discovery of vast off-shore oil and gas reserves in 2006. ODI (2014) estimated public support for oil and gas exploration and extraction at USD 530 million, through subsidies such as tax exemptions and direct support measures for R&D or skill development in the oil and gas industry. The Brazilian Development Bank (BNDES) also provides substantial finance to the domestic oil and gas sector (e.g. an estimated USD 3.9 billion in 2012), and subsidises credits for companies in the Petrobras supply chain.

4.2. Incentives to agricultural production

Agricultural support

Agriculture remains one of the pillars of the economy, accounting for 5.7% of GDP and about 15% of employment (Chapter 1; also see Basic Statistics). Brazil has moved from taxing the sector in the 1980-90s to a moderate level of support. In 2000-12, support for farmers as measured by the OECD Producer Support Estimate (PSE)[8] fluctuated around 5% of gross farm receipts, far below levels observed in OECD and other BRIICS countries (Figure 3.6), reflecting Brazil's position as a competitive agricultural exporter.

Nevertheless, a wide range of agricultural support measures are in place. The vast majority of support is based on commodity output and input use and takes the form of market price support (43% of PSE in 2012) and input subsidies (54%) (OECD, 2013d). These are the most distorting and potentially environmentally harmful forms of agricultural support, because they are tied to production. Market price support is provided through guaranteed minimum prices for a wide range of commodities,[9] as well as through direct government purchases.

Farmers have also long benefitted from concessional credit programmes, mostly under the National System of Rural Credit (SNCR).[10] Total SNCR loans reached a record BRL 111.4 billion (about USD 57 billion) in 2012, of which 85% was allocated to large-scale farmers (OECD, 2013d). Since 2008, access to subsidised rural credit in the Amazon biome has been conditional on the legitimacy of land claims and provision of information to demonstrate compliance with environmental regulations, which has effectively helped reduce deforestation. In addition, from October 2017, rural credit will be conditional on land registration in the Rural Environmental Cadastre (Chapter 4). Several policies support small family farms, including subsidised loans and insurance and special minimum price and procurement guarantees under the Food Acquisition Programme. Existing mechanisms for social protection such as Bolsa Família – or the expansion of Bolsa Floresta – could protect farmer income more effectively. Special programmes are in place to support families that sustainably extract forest products, notably under the National Plan to Promote the Production Chain of Socio-Biodiversity Products (Chapter 4).

Figure 3.6. **Support to farmers has grown but is moderate in international comparison**

Producer support estimate in Brazil, by support category, 1995-2012

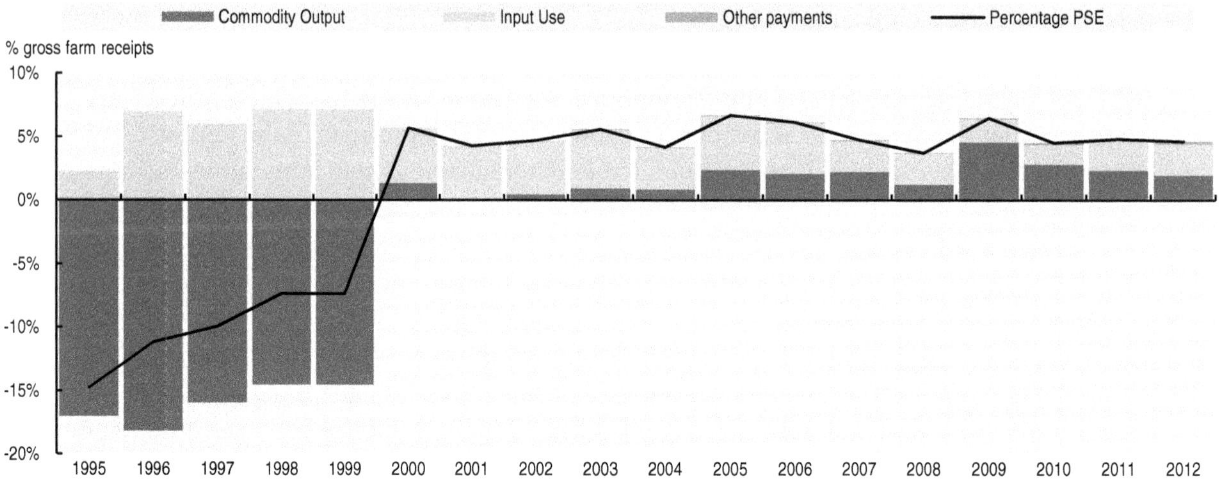

Producer support estimate, BRIICS economies[a] and OECD, 1995-97 and 2010-12

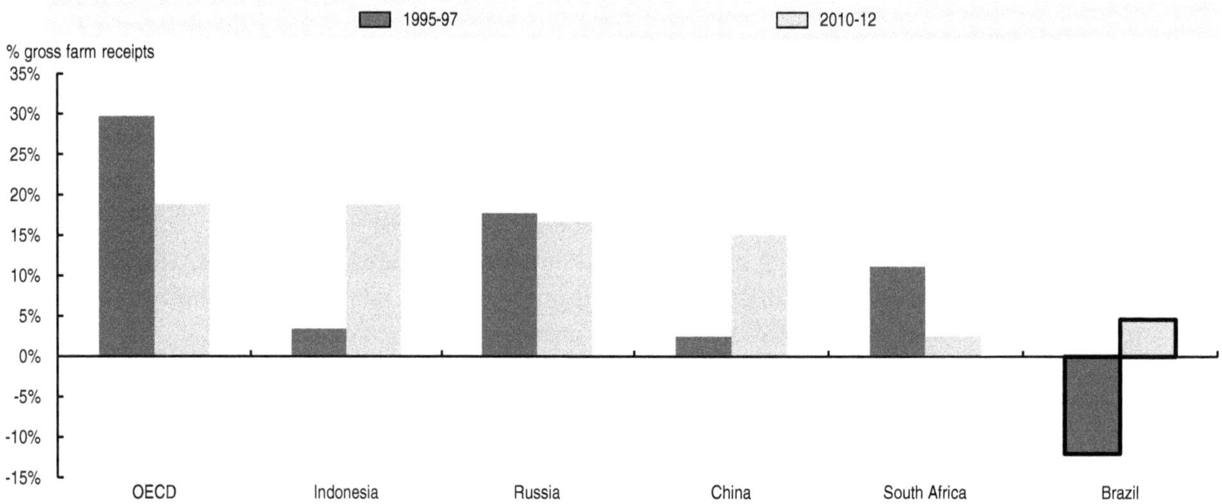

a) Data for India are not available.
Source: OECD (2015), "Producer and Consumer Support Estimates", *OECD Agriculture statistics* (database).

StatLink http://dx.doi.org/10.1787/888933279600

By stimulating production and input use, and thereby agricultural intensification and expansion, these support and credit programmes risk increasing pressures on the natural resource base. Most of these measures are based on conventional agriculture (hybrid seeds, chemical fertilisers and pesticides), with potentially negative impacts on soil and water. These policies reduce incentives to use production factors more efficiently and to innovate so as to become more competitive. They also tend to encourage agricultural production over other land uses, such as conservation, restoration and sustainable forestry. Special programmes support socio-biodiversity and organic products and sustainable production, such as the Low-Carbon Agriculture programme (Chapter 4), but their volume seems small compared to total support provided. Transfers to general services for the agriculture sector (such as research, training and infrastructure) are also much lower than support given to individual farmers. Agricultural support could be more strongly oriented to encouraging environmental improvement and efficient use of inputs, as well as to addressing infrastructure gaps that constrain agriculture development (producers are typically far from their principal markets). This could trigger agricultural growth, for both commercial farms and smallholders, more efficiently (OECD, 2015d).

Tax exemptions and other incentives

Implicit subsidies exist for input factors such as water, pesticides and fertilisers. Water is a key agricultural input: the sector consumes more than 60% of water resources (Chapter 1). Yet water abstraction is not charged for in many regions. Where charges exist, they are often too low to stimulate efficient resource use (Section 3.4). Fertilisers and pesticides are exempt from some federal and state taxes, which has increased their use and related health problems (Chapter 1). In 2010, a constitutional amendment (still under discussion) proposed to fully exempt agricultural inputs, fertilisers, agrochemicals and chemicals used for the production of food for humans and livestock from federal and state taxes, though agrochemicals were excluded after public hearings.[11] Tax exemptions for fertilisers and pesticides should be reconsidered with a view to encouraging more rational use of products that can harm human and animal health and ecosystems. Additionally, the current regulation on pesticide approval should be revised to require periodic renewal of approvals, rather than these being granted permanently.

The Rural Land Tax (ITR), although not very significant, also incentivises agricultural production over conservation. The ITR is higher for "unproductive" land than for land under agricultural production. Permanent Protection Areas and Legal Reserves on rural properties and Private Natural Heritage Reserves[12] benefit from ITR exemption (Chapter 4), which partly compensates for the opportunity cost of not engaging in more intensive land use; however, the value of the exemption is so low that the incentive is negligible (MMA, 2015). There is evidence that expansion of the agricultural frontier has been traditionally driven by the very low cost of converting areas to agriculture, rather than a need to satisfy increasing demand for food, fibre and fuels (Gurgel and Paltsev, 2013). More recently, however, agricultural output growth has been based on productivity improvements rather than on the abundance of cheap land.

5. Investing in environmental and low-carbon infrastructure

5.1. *Overview*

Brazil needs to extend and upgrade its infrastructure to ensure strong, sustainable growth and improve service delivery. In 2014, the World Economic Forum ranked Brazil 120th of 144 countries for quality of overall infrastructure, and found inadequate infrastructure to be the second most important barrier to doing business (WEF, 2014). The relatively poor state of infrastructure, including environment-related infrastructure, follows several decades of underspending (Amann et al., 2014; OECD, 2013a).

Investment in extension and renewal of infrastructure increased with the 2007 federal Growth Acceleration Programme (PAC). PAC comprised a large-scale infrastructure investment programme (BRL 504 billion) primarily targeting energy and logistics but also involving new investment in urban and social infrastructure, such as for water supply, sanitation and urban rail transport. Disbursements remained below planned investment volumes in many areas, notably in sanitation, renewables, rail and energy transmission (TCU, 2011). While massive, PAC investment appears to have been much lower than the country's needs, especially in the North-east region (OECD, 2011).

PAC was succeeded by PAC 2, which envisaged BRL 955 billion in public and private investment over 2011-14 and included a stronger environmental dimension, with increased resources for water and sanitation and a stronger emphasis on rail (Table 3.3). Project delivery and spending improved: total investment was over 70% higher than under the first plan (MPOG, 2015). Still, environmental and sustainability criteria were not systematically integrated into PAC 2, for instance in the design and location of infrastructure projects.

Table 3.3. **Investment under PAC 2**

BRL billion

Sectors	Planned spending 2011-14	Completed projects as of end 2014	Main outputs
Transport	**104.5**	**66.9**	
Road	50.2		5 188 km of highways
Rail	43.9		1 088 km of railways
Ports and water transport	7.4		19 waterways
Airports	3.0		30 port projects 37 airport projects
Energy	**461.6**	**253.3**	
Electricity generation and distribution	140.3		15.9 MW generation capacity 15 312 km transmission lines and 52 substations
Oil and gas	281.9		28 oil and gas exploration and development projects
Other[1]	39.4		21 refinery projects 11 natural gas projects 3 biofuel projects
Urban development	**57.1**	**10.7**	
Sanitation	22.1		600 sanitation projects
Urban transport	18.0		86 drainage projects and 27 slope stabilisation projects
Urban roads	6.0		31 urban mobility projects
Other[2]	11.0		46 paving projects
Urban social development	**23.0**	**5.5**	3 326 basic health units and 39 intensive care units 786 day care units and pre-schools 53 art and sport centres
Housing (Minha Casa, Minha Vida programme)	**278.2**	**449.7**	2.75 million contracted housing units 1.92 million contracts for financing housing 1 605 urbanisation projects in precarious settlements
Water and light (Agua/Luz Para Todos)	**30.6**	**10.3**	
Light	5.5		58 sewerage projects
Urban water supply	13.0		1 150 urban water supply projects
Water resources	12.1		538 518 connections to water network
Total	**955.0**	**796.4**	

1. Includes industrial shipping, renewables, energy efficiency and mineral exploration.
2. Includes control and prevention of floods, landslides and coastal erosion.

Source: OECD (2011), *OECD Economic Surveys: Brazil*; MPOG (n.a.), "PAC 2" (presentation); MPOG (2015), PAC 2: Balanço 4 Anos.

Investment in environment-related infrastructure significantly increased through lending from the BNDES, the main provider of long-term finance in Brazil (Box 3.3). Its environment-related lending increased more rapidly than its overall spending to reach BRL 28 billion in 2014, or 15% of its total lending for the year. The strongest increase occurred in the area of renewables, with large hydro projects receiving most of the support (Section 5.4). Since 2009, disbursements for water and sewerage, as well as public transport, have increased; funds have also been allocated to climate adaptation and disaster risk reduction since 2010 and, more recently, to forest restoration (Figure 3.7).

Box 3.3. **The Brazilian Development Bank's environmental safeguard policy**

The Brazilian Development Bank was founded in 1952 to stimulate the expansion of industry and infrastructure. The BNDES provides loans for long-term investment projects at below-market rates (which are generally high) for sectors such as agriculture, industry, infrastructure, trade and services.[13] The funding comes from various sources. Since 2009, the national treasury has been the largest single funding source. Brazil would benefit from gradually reducing government support to the BNDES, thereby facilitating the emergence of private lenders and the development of the private long-term capital markets. When specific government-supported lending is needed, for example to meet social objectives and develop infrastructure that the market would not serve, it should be explicit and available to all lending institutions (OECD, 2013a).

The BNDES has had an environmental policy since 2005, and has undertaken social and environmental screening of all direct and large indirect lending projects since 2010. For lending in sectors considered to have a significant environmental impact, it developed sector-specific policies, such as the 2009 environmental safeguard policy for the meat processing industry, requiring a traceability system to ensure that the ranches from which cattle are purchased meet labour laws and do not drive deforestation. Similar criteria to ensure that agri-business loans do not encourage deforestation have applied to the sugar and ethanol industries since 2010, and to soya growers since 2011. An environmental safeguard policy for loans for fossil-fuelled power plants has applied since 2009. Social and environmental guidelines were put in place for water supply and wastewater treatment in 2011.

Source: BNDES (2015), "Social and Environmental Responsibility" website.

The legal framework for private participation in infrastructure investment is in line with those observed in most OECD countries. Private investment in infrastructure appears to be higher in Brazil than in other Latin American countries (OECD, 2011). To minimise budgetary cost for infrastructure development, the government has sought to promote private participation through the use of concessions, supported by subsidised credit, tax-free infrastructure bonds and other tax incentives.[14] Private participation has increased significantly in the energy and transport sectors, but remains low in water and sanitation. It has mostly taken the form of concessions rather than public private partnerships (PPPs) (OECD, 2011).[15] PPPs have been successfully developed for health and education sectors in Brazil.

Despite the recent massive infusion of funds and incentives for infrastructure investment, problems persist in project delivery. Weaknesses in planning, implementation and monitoring, as well cumbersome regulations and procedures for project selection and evaluation and environmental licensing (Chapter 2), delay the execution of investment programmes and discourage private-sector engagement. This is especially true for environment-related infrastructure, such as sanitation and urban transport, which is the responsibility of local governments. Often municipalities are unable to spend the federal funds allocated for infrastructure development and maintenance, partly due to weak administrative capacity and insufficient finance at local level.

Figure 3.7. **BNDES environment-related disbursements have increased significantly**

Disbursements by sector, 2002-14

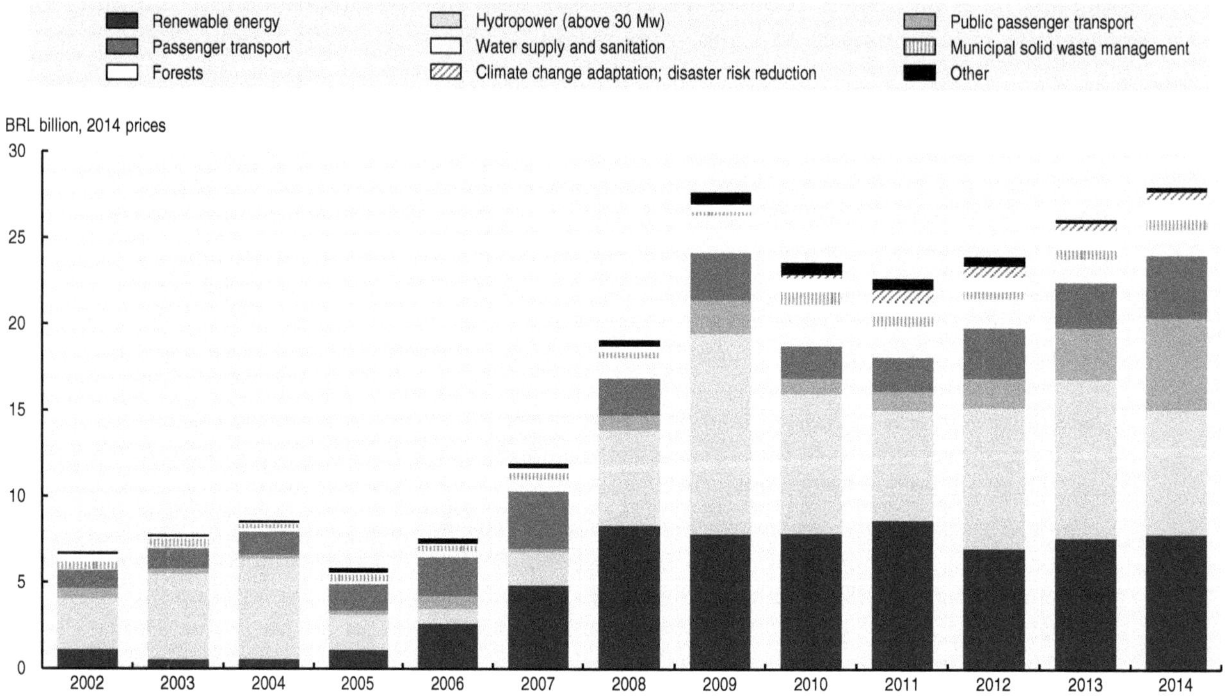

Notes: Amounts disbursed prior to 2007 may be underestimated due to changes in the expenditure classification. 2014 data for renewables include investment in the energy efficiency programme PROESCO.
Source: Based on BNDES (2014), *Annual Report 2013*; BNDES (2013), *Annual Report 2012*.

StatLink http://dx.doi.org/10.1787/888933279614

5.2. *Investment in water supply, sanitation and waste*

Water supply and sanitation

Access to water and sanitation has improved markedly over the past two decades (Annex 3.A). Nevertheless, water and sanitation remains the sector where investment is probably the most needed. Coverage and quality of sanitation need to be expanded and improved, particularly in rural areas and the North and North-east regions (Chapter 1). Water and sanitation began to receive more funding under PAC and, especially, PAC 2 (Table 3.3). Disbursement has been met with delay, however.[16] Under PAC 2, investment in water and sanitation was integrated in the second phase of the public housing programme Minha Casa, Minha Vida (My House, My Life), under which funds were successfully disbursed. Water supply in rural areas was extended under the Agua Para Todos (Water for All) programme, which installed more than 750 000 water tanks in 1 200 municipalities under PAC 2.

Investment in water infrastructure is largely public (notably from the BNDES); concessions to private water companies and PPP agreements are used for individual water systems but cover less than a third of the urban population (WWC and OECD, 2015). To support investment in wastewater treatment, ANA introduced Brazil's first output-based aid programme in 2001: under the River Basin Clean-up Programme (PRODES), public funds were granted to wastewater treatment facilities only after construction was completed and operations were under way, with environmental requirements achieved. From 2001 to 2011,

55 sewage treatment plants were contracted. Similarly, the Water Producer Programme, launched the same year, financially compensates investment in the protection and restoration of water sources (Chapter 4). As of 2011, 14 projects had been implemented in nine states (Solutions for Water, 2011).

Ensuring a stable source of funding to expand water supply and sewerage networks and manage water resources has proved challenging. While the 2007 National Sanitation Law mandated independent regulatory agencies and defined rules for service provision and tariff setting, revenue from water and sanitation tariffs does not cover the large investment cost of new infrastructure (Section 3.4). This contributes to discouraging private participation in the sector.

Waste management

Investment in municipal solid waste has increased under the 2010 Municipal Solid Waste Policy (Chapter 2) and PAC, but remains well below needs. States and municipalities were supposed to prepare solid waste plans by 2012 as a condition for federal financial support for landfill construction, but only about a quarter complied. Over 2 200 municipalities (less than half) met the 2014 deadline for having an environmentally sound landfill. The governments in compliance are mostly concentrated in the south-east. For example, Rio de Janeiro state launched an ambitious project to replace irregular landfills with licensed ones through partnerships between the state government, municipalities and private entities. However, most states do not have enough properly engineered landfills, and illegal waste dumping is an acute problem, particularly in the North and North-east regions (Chapter 1). Some recently constructed sanitary landfills have degraded into dumps due to a lack of local capacity to maintain them. Moreover, there is a lack of hazardous waste landfills, and many municipalities tolerate the illegal practice of disposing of hazardous waste in municipal landfills. Most states also lack recycling infrastructure.

The BNDES has stepped up efforts to disburse funds in this area, and is focusing on developing municipal capacity for them to better access these funds. Most solid waste management costs are associated with maintenance of disposal sites, underlining the importance of an effective cost-recovery mechanism (World Bank, 2010a). As Section 3.4 indicates, most municipalities do not charge for collection and disposal, while others charge too little. Lack of cost recovery means there is little incentive for investment in proper operations, as private concessionaires cannot generate sufficient profit. The formation of municipal consortia needs to be encouraged for achieving economies of scale, the lack of which is another key barrier to private investment. The development of more specialised business lines in the waste sector, such as recycling and treatment of special waste, could make waste operations more financially attractive (World Bank, 2010a). The potential business opportunity is large: it is estimated that Brazil loses as much as USD 3.5 billion a year by landfilling waste that could be recycled (IPEA, 2010a).

As in many developing or emerging economies, waste recovery is dominated by waste pickers (*catadores*), who earn their living by collecting and selling waste to private recycling companies. The activity is legally recognised as a profession, but most of Brazil's 400 000 to 800 000 *catadores* (including the 10% organised in informal associations or co-operatives) lack access to workers' rights. The 2010 National Solid Waste Law, which requires municipalities to adopt selective waste collection, supports the involvement of *catadores* in shared responsibility for product life cycles and prioritises recycling co-operatives in formal programmes. The Pro-Catador programme aims to strengthen co-operatives through capacity building and technical training, improve working conditions and expand opportunities for social and economic inclusion (MMA, 2012).

5.3. *Investment in sustainable transport*

Road transport

Road infrastructure in Brazil is inadequate, with a limited share of paved roads and wide disparity among states. This hurts competitiveness and economic development, particularly since a large share of freight is transported by road. Investment in road infrastructure has increased since the 1990s, when the government introduced concession agreements with private operators to manage the road network. However, concessionaires have little incentive to invest in improvement and expansion of roads, partly because concession contracts are awarded on the basis of the lowest tolls charged to recover investment and operating costs (OECD, 2011). On all tolled road stretches (mostly in São Paulo and Rio de Janeiro states) tolls are based on vehicle size and weight, but do not take account of environmental parameters (ABCR, 2015).

Rail transport

Privatisation of the railway network from the late 1990s stimulated investment in the network (which averaged some BRL 1.8 billion a year over 1997-2009) and an increase in the volume of goods transported (OSEC, 2010). However, the railway sector is underdeveloped and long-distance rail services are currently used exclusively for freight transport, with commuter passenger rail transport concentrated in the megacities of São Paulo and Rio de Janeiro. This poses economic constraints and has contributed to the acute pressure experienced by the highway and airport infrastructure (Amann et al., 2014).

In a welcome move, expanding the rail network has recently been included in infrastructure investment programmes. The National Logistics and Transport Plan sees rail-related investments shifting from 31% of total transport investment to 65% by 2015. In the long term, this could help Brazil reduce road network congestion, with benefits in terms of reduced accidents and emissions of GHGs and air pollutants. Future investment should ensure the long-term sustainability of the rail system. Current rail freight transport is diesel-based, and expanding the use of diesel fuel entails environmental and economic consequences. Full consideration should be given to options regarding biodiesel blending, hybrid diesel-electric engines and the potential for electrification, particularly for passenger transport.

Urban public transport

Insufficient urban public transport infrastructure and rising user costs, combined with a strong domestic automotive industry and the relatively low taxation of vehicle ownership and use (see below and Section 3.3), have led to greater private vehicle use (Figure 3.4). In most urban areas, the growth of private car use has been greater than that of buses (Amann et al., 2014). There are significant socio-economic discrepancies in vehicle ownership; in 2012, 28% of the poorest households had an automobile, whereas 88% of the richest households owned at least one. Underinvestment in public transport has, therefore, penalised low-income households and led to negative social outcomes.

Urban mobility infrastructure is primarily a municipal responsibility. Cities of more than 500 000 are supposed to develop integrated urban transport plans. Most, however, lack the necessary financial resources and technical capacity. This has delayed investment and project delivery for decades (Amann et al., 2014). In response, injection of federal funds and lending from the BNDES for urban mobility projects increased in the late 2000s and early 2010s, including for subway systems (Table 3.3).[17] The host cities for the 2014 FIFA World Cup also received funding to upgrade their public transport. Investment needs remain large, however. The BNDES (2012b) estimated that BRL 113 billion was needed for public transport in 38 metropolitan areas simply to make up for deficiencies, not counting future needs.

While increased investment in urban railways and subways is welcome, more emphasis may also be given to bus rapid transit (BRT) systems, which can deliver a high-quality mass transport service with much lower capital costs. The development of a comprehensive and integrated BRT system in Curitiba has proven effective in expanding public transport at moderate costs (Box 3.4). Most existing bus corridors in Brazil need renovation and BRT systems may offer an opportunity of increasing transit productivity. However, Lindau et al. (2014) identified several barriers to BRT expansion, many common to other infrastructure investment, including insufficient local technical capacity, conflicts among stakeholders and regulatory uncertainty (Section 5.1).

Box 3.4. **Bus rapid transit in Curitiba**

Curitiba's BRT system is renowned as pragmatic, integrated, cost-effective and efficient. Despite the city's above-average rate of car ownership, the BRT service, combined with parking policies, has reduced automobile trips per year, and ambient air pollution is among the lowest in Brazil.

Starting in the 1970s, Curitiba's bus system evolved from conventional buses in mixed traffic to the world's first BRT system with separate bus corridors, at-level boarding, electronic ticketing and high-capacity bi-articulated buses. The Green Line, launched in 2009, incorporated several environmental innovations, including the operation of 100% biodiesel articulated buses.

Bus operations are contracted to private companies. Since 2010, the Integrated Transport Network (RIT) has brought together feeder and inter-district buses, with transfer stations and a single fare, and has considerably improved coverage and efficiency. Fare revenue is pooled and paid to operators on the basis of service provided. The complete RIT system, with its range of buses and integrated flat passenger fare, is reported to operate without subsidy. RIT covers 14 of the 26 cities that make up the metropolitan area.

The development of an efficient BRT system has been the result of successful co-operation between the urban transport planning authority (URBS) and the urban development authority, which is in charge of land use planning. URBS is responsible for the planning, management, operation and control of the system. It defines routes, capacity and schedules, regulates and controls the system, and collects all fares.

Source: Lindau et al. (2010), "Bus Rapid Transit in Curitiba, Brazil – A Look at the Outcome After 35 Years of Bus-Oriented Development".

Public transport revenue derives almost entirely from user fees, with a much smaller share of city budgets allocated to public transport than in most cities in OECD countries.[18] Public transport systems are largely operated by private concessionaires, with routes awarded on the basis of the lowest user fares proposed. However, fares can be automatically raised if costs increase, which does not provide incentives to improve efficiency and reduce operating costs (Amann et al., 2014).[19] In addition, the financial and operational performance of private bus operators is barely monitored.[20] From 2005 to 2014 the overall cost of vehicle ownership rose by 7% and petrol prices by 16%, while the consumer price index went up by 160% and the average bus fares in six major metropolitan areas increased by 170% (Amann et al., 2014).

Policy changes are needed to attract greater investment in public transport and make it more attractive. This may include politically unpopular measures such as congestion charging and restrictions on circulation, to balance the relative costs of public transport and private vehicle use. Brazil should also ensure that municipalities have adequately staffed regulatory agencies to apply and review rules for public transport and monitor financial and operating performance under concession contracts.

5.4. *Investment in renewable energy sources and energy efficiency*

Renewables

The government is committed to maintaining Brazil's clean energy mix. The Energy Expansion Plan 2013-22 (PDE) is the overarching framework for energy policies and investment. While it includes new nuclear, coal and natural gas power plants, it aims to maintain a high share of renewables in the energy mix and to reduce GHG emissions from the energy sector by about 27% by 2020. The PDE relies on significant expansion of large hydro capacity to meet rising electricity demand, but envisages expansion of capacity from other renewables, especially wind.[21] Expansion of large hydro is constrained by location: most potential is located in the Amazon region, which raises difficulties with environmental licensing and public acceptance (Box 2.8). New techniques are being deployed to minimise environmental and social impacts and most new projects are designed as run-of-river, albeit at the cost of generating less electricity (IEA, 2013). Overall, it is estimated that achieving the renewables capacity target will require investment of the order of BRL 120 billion (FEBRABAN, 2014).

In 2014, Brazil was reported to be the world's seventh largest investor in renewables (BNEF, 2015) (Figure 3.8). Total investment, excluding large hydro, reached USD 7.6 billion, a significant rise from 2013 (which had seen the lowest level since 2005). Investment in renewables fluctuated in the last decade following shifts in the biofuels sector, the timing of renewables auctions and infrastructure construction delays (Figure 3.8). Most investment occurred in biofuels until 2009; in 2010 wind power emerged as a significant sector and has dominated investments since 2011 (BNEF, 2014; 2013). In 2014, wind attracted 84% of investment, driven by finance made available to winners of power auctions held in 2013.

Various sources have contributed to investment in renewables, including the BNDES, the Climate Change Fund (Chapter 2) and several state funds and programmes. The BNDES has spent about BRL 6-7 billion annually since 2010 on renewables. Large hydro (above 30 MW) has been the primary beneficiary of BNDES funding, accounting for 25% to 35% of its environment-related spending in 2010-14 (Figure 3.7). Brazil began supporting electricity generation from wind, small hydro and biomass in 2002 through feed-in tariffs, with the cost of the programme being included in electricity tariffs (except for low-income customers). Overall, installing the targeted 3.3 GW of new capacity took over four years longer than planned.

Figure 3.8. **Brazil is among the world's leading investors in renewables**

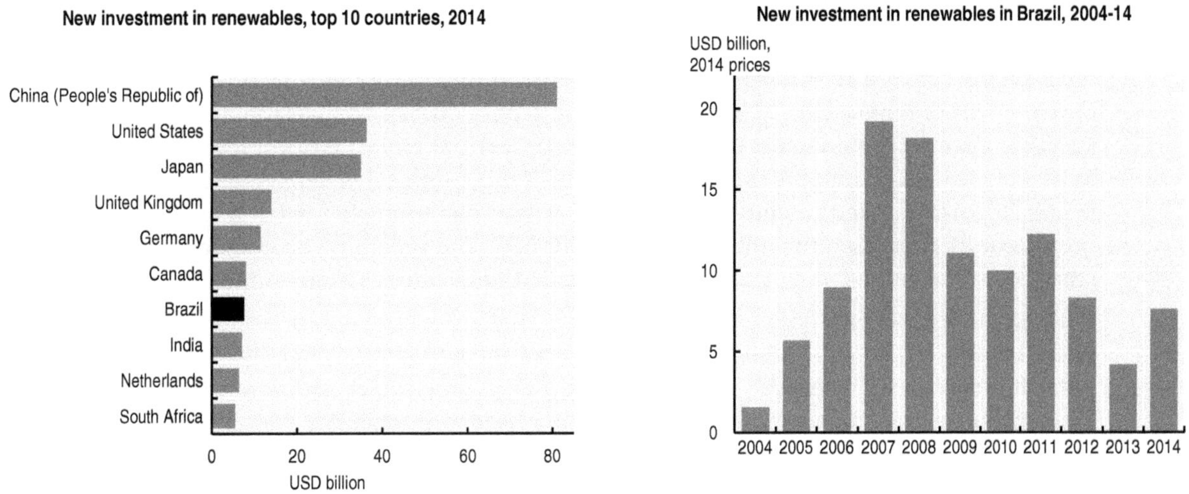

Source: Adapted from BNEF (2015), *Global Trends in Renewable Energy Investment 2015.*

StatLink http://dx.doi.org/10.1787/888933279626

Since 2009, power auctions have been used, and have proven more effective than feed-in tariffs in expanding wind power capacity. Average prices of wind power were lower than prices of electricity produced by natural gas plants in 2011, although the lower prices also reflected indirect support measures such as low-interest financing from the BNDES, reduced transmission and distribution costs, and tax reductions (Moarif and Patodia Rastogi, 2012). Brazil's first solar power auction took place in October 2014. There is huge potential for solar photovoltaic, particularly for the residential sector. Microgeneration has been permitted since 2012 but a lack of adequate credit and the incidence of the ICMS tax have made it unfeasible in most states, though tax exemptions exist in Minas Gerais and Tocantins (FEBRABAN, 2014).

Grid inadequacy, however, has led to delays in completing renewables-based power plants and putting them online, particularly in the North-east region, where the wind power potential is strongest. Investment in the national energy grid thus is needed (OECD, 2013a). As with other infrastructure investment, differences in environmental regulations across states and conflicts of jurisdiction between environmental regulatory bodies often result in delays and additional transaction and administrative costs for project developers (OECD, 2015c).

Part of BNDES financing is conditional on local content requirements (LCRs): developers and investors must source a specified share of inputs locally to be eligible for funding (Box 3.5). As almost all wind farms operating in Brazil have benefited from BNDES support, this has led to the creation of a domestic wind power industry, which will likely expand as higher LCRs are phased in to 2016 (Larive International, 2014). The BNDES has also imposed LCRs for solar photovoltaic financing to spur development of local manufacturing capacity and expects to further increase such requirements (Barth et al., 2014). However, in the long term LCRs limit industry productivity and financing capacity (Box 3.5). Brazil should consider gradually phasing out LCRs for renewables and other emerging environmental technology (Section 6.3). Where LCRs are implemented, they should be time limited and carefully designed not to harm long-term competitiveness.

Box 3.5. Local content requirements in renewable energy markets

The potential of clean energy to create local employment, added value and exports has led several OECD and emerging economies to impose LCRs as a way to support development of renewables. LCRs typically require developers and investors to provide a specified share of components, equipment, services or total project costs or jobs locally to be eligible for policy support (such as feed-in tariff programmes) or public tenders. As of March 2015, LCRs linked to wind and solar photovoltaic had been planned or implemented in at least 21 countries, including 16 OECD countries and emerging economies, mostly since 2009. This has led to at least five World Trade Organization disputes since 2010.

OECD (2015e) has produced empirical evidence that LCRs have a detrimental effect on global investment flows in renewable energy sectors and hamper the effectiveness of feed-in tariff programmes. They also have a negative impact on local job creation, added value and technology transfer when the full value chain is taken into account. By raising the cost of inputs for downstream businesses, LCRs can lead to increased overall costs, reduced price competitiveness, less international investment and higher wholesale electricity prices.

The OECD therefore advises countries with a nascent or uncompetitive solar or wind-turbine industry that, rather than imposing LCRs, they should address local impediments to the domestic manufacturing sector's competitiveness. Other options include well-targeted R&D support, which can stimulate innovation across segments of the value chains, build local manufacturing capability and encourage technology transfer from imports and FDI; training programmes and promotion measures to improve manufacturers' technological skills, build local capability of downstream firms and encourage innovation; and demand-side instruments, or more cost-effective carbon pricing instruments, to increase domestic demand and eventually support domestic manufacturing.

Source: OECD (2015c), *Overcoming Barriers to International Investment in Clean Energy*, OECD Publishing, Paris.

Biofuels

Brazil first directed public support towards developing sugar cane ethanol in the mid-1970s as a response to the 1973 oil shock. The Brazilian Alcohol Programme largely contributed to the development of large-scale sugar cane ethanol production.[22] The ethanol industry received a significant boost starting in 2003 with the development of flex-fuel cars (La Rovere et al., 2011). A mandatory blending rate is the main measure now supporting demand for ethanol, along with favourable taxation (Section 3.2). The OECD (2013e) estimates the biofuel mandatory blending cost at EUR 200 per tonne of CO_2 abated.

In the early 2010s, the government and the BNDES renewed investment support to the ethanol industry and sugar cane production in response to declining productivity in the sector (Moarif and Patodia Rastogi, 2012). The ethanol industry suffered from higher sugar prices and low petrol and diesel prices, partly due to favourable taxation of these fuels (Sections 3.2 and 4.1). This has depressed investment in the sector and run contrary to tax incentives to promote flex-fuel cars (Section 3.3). The need to improve productivity led to a new emphasis on support for R&D and innovation in the sector (Section 6.2).[23]

In 2004, the government launched the Biodiesel Production and Use programme, including various forms of financing to stimulate biodiesel production, partly with a view to reducing dependence on diesel imports. The BNDES began offering special credit lines for biodiesel, with preferential rates for biodiesel certified as containing a minimum percentage of raw material from family farms (Moarif and Patodia Rastogi, 2012). This programme was followed by mandatory blending of biodiesel into diesel starting in 2008. Both measures had a significant impact: production was non-existent in 2005 but reached 2.7 million m^3 in 2012 (Castanheira et al., 2014).

Access to electricity

Public investment programmes have provided access to electricity to millions of households over the past two decades under the Luz no Campo (Light in the Countryside) programme since 1999 and Luz Para Todos (Light for All) since 2003. Access to electricity now covers 98.8% of the population (World Bank, 2015); the remaining households lacking electricity are mostly in hard-to-reach rural areas. The cost of providing electricity to isolated communities increased the per household cost of Luz Para Todos by nearly 90% between 2004 and 2010. Technical and financial difficulties have encouraged the use of off-grid solutions such as solar panels, but also small diesel generators, with their associated fuel costs and negative health impacts. The programme has been funded primarily by general public revenue, in part through electricity charges (Section 3.2).

Energy efficiency

Brazil can largely gain from investing in energy efficiency and systematically integrating energy efficiency criteria in sectoral policies, including in the built environment, urban planning and transport (Box 3.6). Energy efficiency is included in sectoral plans under the National Climate Change Policy, and the 2011 National Energy Efficiency Plan set a target of achieving energy savings of 106 TWh by 2030 while the PDE calls for energy savings of 48 TWh by 2022. However, measures to spur investment in energy efficiency have not been significant to date. As in many countries, regulations and labelling programmes have improved the energy efficiency of appliances and equipment, and contributed to shifts in these markets. The PROCEL energy conservation programme (BRL 34 million in 2013), operated and partly funded by Eletrobras, provides energy management training and services in industry, sanitation and municipalities (Eletrobras, 2014).

The main source of funding for these programmes is a share of the net operating revenue of electricity generation, transmission and distribution companies. This obligation, included in concession contracts, requires companies to invest 1% of revenue in energy efficiency or related R&D. Revenue thus raised also supplies the Sectoral Fund for Energy, managed by the Brazilian Innovation Agency (Finep) to fund applied energy research projects with an emphasis on energy efficiency.[24]

The BNDES established a low-interest loan facility in 2006 to stimulate investment in energy efficiency and renewables with a view to encouraging development of energy service companies. Known as PROESCO, the programme at first financed few projects, largely due to its complexity and administrative burden (Moarif and Patodia Rastogi, 2012); it disbursed less than BRL 10 million a year until 2012, though annual disbursements have more than doubled since. Under PAC 2, BRL 1.1 billion was allocated for energy efficiency, though none had been disbursed by the end of 2013 (TCU, 2014).

Box 3.6. **Brazil's energy efficiency potential**

The IEA (2013) analysed energy use in key end-use sectors – industry, transport and buildings – to assess the remaining potential for energy savings using technically and economically viable energy efficiency measures and technologies. In the buildings sector, measures include building codes for new buildings and minimum energy performance standards, enhanced over time, for major appliances and equipment. In industry, measures include adoption of best available technology for new equipment and better energy management. In the transport sector, measures include mandatory fuel economy standards and labelling to promote use of the most efficient vehicles.

The analysis found that final energy consumption in 2035 would be 11% lower than what is projected if Brazil implemented existing measures, including those only announced. The IEA estimated that electricity demand would drop by some 100 TWh by 2035 (roughly equivalent to 2012 production from the massive Itaipu hydropower plant), reducing the need for new capacity. Oil demand would also fall considerably, which would help reduce GHG emissions.

The largest savings would be in transport, mainly through improved fuel economy. The analysis validated the importance of policies to raise the efficiency performance of cars sold in Brazil. Moreover, the study did not reflect all of Brazil's potential in the transport sector, as there is still huge scope to move freight transport off roads and onto rail or waterways (Section 5.3). In industry, significant savings are available in the less energy-intensive sectors such as food processing, where opportunities are often overlooked because of lack of know-how or access to finance. In the residential sector, energy use is already relatively low by international standards, largely because of low heating requirements, so the impact of new measures would be smaller than in the other sectors; the largest impact would come from stringent application of standards for a range of energy-using equipment.

Source: IEA (2013), *World Energy Outlook*, IEA/OECD Publishing, Paris.

6. Promoting eco-innovation and environmental goods and services

6.1. *Innovation policy and performance*

Innovation gained importance in Brazilian policy over the 2000s. The government recognises it as a critical factor in increasing economic performance and trade competitiveness and has made efforts to expand the R&D and innovation (RD&I) system through legislative, institutional and budgetary changes (Box 3.7). Brazil has well-known leading innovative firms and high expertise in selected high-technology fields such as deep-water oil extraction, aviation, renewables and agro-technology. Agricultural R&D under the public research body Embrapa has contributed to the development of a competitive agribusiness sector, making better technology available to producers and agro-industry, notably tropical technology that allowed for the incorporation of Brazil's *cerrados* (savannahs) into productive use (OECD, 2015d).

This leadership, however, is concentrated in relatively few firms and has so far not spilled over to the overall economy. Small and medium-sized enterprises (SMEs) in particular have very low records of RD&I expenditure and innovate very little. Most RD&I activities focus on basic research and are conducted in public universities and research institutions; there is a wide disconnect between such research institutions and the commercialisation of innovative technology and products. Several bottlenecks constrain innovation, including restrictive and cumbersome regulations, a complex tax system, high tariffs and expensive long-term credit (OECD, 2015d). As a result, despite increased R&D expenditure (Box 3.7), innovation performance indicators are weak by international standards: the number of patents and trademarks, although increasing, remain significantly below those of OECD countries and BRIICS economies such as China and India (OECD, 2014). The low patent numbers have been related to a lack of incentives for patenting in public institutions as well as to regulatory obstacles and high patenting costs (Frischtak, 2011).

Box 3.7. **General innovation policies**

The Ministry of Sciences, Technology and Innovation (MCTI) plans and co-ordinates national RD&I activities. Several efforts have been undertaken to strengthen the policy framework and improve co-ordination across relevant public institutions and stakeholders. These include the 2004 Innovation Law, which aimed to foster co-operation between research centres and businesses, and the 2005 Goodwill Law, which introduced fiscal incentives to foster innovation in production (OECD, 2014).

The policy framework is set by the National Strategy for Science, Technology and Innovation 2012-15 (ENCTI), which aims to i) close the technological gap with developed economies; ii) support Brazil's leadership in areas of the knowledge economy that take advantage of the country's rich natural resources, such as green innovation, agro-business and other natural resource-based activities; iii) strengthen the internationalisation of the national research system; iv) foster the development of a green economy; and v) address the country's substantial social and regional inequality. ENCTI is integrated into the industrial development plan Plano Brasil Major 2011-14 (aka the Greater Brazil Plan), which gives innovation a central role and includes proposals for significant changes in legislative frameworks.

The focus of innovation policy has shifted to increasing business participation in RD&I. A major initiative is the 2011 Innovate Company Plan, which targets business innovation in nine strategic sectors.[25] The plan increases support for projects of technological risk and establishes measures to increase public-private co-operation. These include reducing red tape, adding new support modalities such as decentralised credits and grants to better reach microenterprises and SMEs, and providing combined credit, grant and equity financing. In 2013, the government established the Brazilian Research and Industrial Innovation Company (Embrapii) to facilitate the translation of technological research into product innovation. Based on the model of the agricultural research institution Embrapa, Embrapii intends to better link technological research to demand from the productive sector, e.g. by establishing public-private RD&I networks.

Gross domestic expenditure on R&D increased to 1.2% of GDP in 2012. This is higher than in other Latin American countries and all other BRIICS except China, but remains significantly below both the OECD average of 2.4% and the ENCTI target of investing 1.8% by 2014 (OECD, 2014; MCTI, 2011). Public investment has grown slightly faster than private investment and reached 55% of total R&D expenditure in 2012. Sectoral technology funds have been a major source of R&D support since the late 1990s. There are funds for each major sector (fourteen in total) as well as two cross-cutting ones. In 2011, the sectoral funds disbursed BRL 1.6 billion for RD&I projects.

6.2. Eco-innovation policy framework and performance

Brazil does not have a formal eco-innovation strategy, even though environmental dimensions are identified in all strategic policy documents on industrial RD&I. Two of the five key objectives of the innovation strategy ENCTI have an environmental focus (Box 3.7). ENCTI targets various areas related to the green economy (e.g. bio- and nanotechnology, renewables, climate change, biodiversity, and oceans and coastal zones) and, for each area, elaborates objectives and key steps, albeit without quantified goals. To strengthen eco-innovation in companies, the government created the Innovate Sustainability programme as one of nine strategic sectoral programmes under the 2011 Innovate Company Plan (Box 3.7). Innovate Sustainability plans to invest BRL 2 billion over 2014-16 in four thematic green innovation areas (BNDES, 2014). As of August 2014, 126 companies had presented business plans. However, links between the strategic planning of industry, innovation, climate change and environmental policies more broadly remain weak.

The overall financial volume devoted to eco-innovation is difficult to determine, as such spending is not explicitly tracked. MCTI estimated public expenditure in "environmental control and protection" R&D at 0.8% of total public R&D disbursements in 2010 (MCTI, 2014a), which is low by OECD standards (though the data are not fully comparable).[26] Some sectoral funds (Box 3.7) are a significant source of funding for the green economy, including those for agribusiness, energy and the Amazon.[27] In 2010, 40% of projects financed by the funds related to the green economy (Frischtak, 2011). However, estimates indicate that total public and private expenditure in green R&D declined from 6% of total R&D expenditure in 2000 to 3% in 2010. The bulk of this volume targets renewables (45%), of which 80% for biofuels; low-carbon agriculture (23%) and sustainable use of biodiversity (17%), largely for natural cosmetics; and ecosystem protection (10%) (Frischtak, 2011).

Following the general pattern of innovation performance in the country, investment in environment-related RD&I primarily occurs in multinationals and very large national companies (Embrapa and Petrobras stand out in this context). An industry survey conducted by the Brazilian statistics institute, IBGE, revealed that the number of industrial companies generating environment-related innovations had grown significantly, but remained small compared to the total number of industrial enterprises (IBGE, 2013). By contrast, several multinationals have established RD&I centres in Brazil, most of them directly or indirectly linked to natural resources (including renewables, minerals, agriculture and biodiversity), according to a survey among multinationals conducted by the OECD with the BNDES in 2011. The survey also found that research in this field tended to be sophisticated and that natural resources and selected green technologies could drive Brazil's participation in global innovation dynamics (Arbache et al., 2012).

Increased policy efforts, partly accompanied by targeted public R&D funding, have helped improve some performance indicators related to environment- and climate-related technology. The number of patent applications per capita filed in these technology fields quadrupled between 2001 and 2010. The growth in environmental patenting has been concentrated in renewables, followed by water and air pollution abatement, waste management, and emission abatement and fuel efficiency in transport (Figure 3.9). Patenting remains very limited in other environment-related fields where Brazil may have a comparative advantage, however (e.g. agro-technologies like soy and sugar cane or biodiversity knowledge).

Figure 3.9. **Patenting in environment- and climate-related technology increased**

Patents in general environmental management technologies, 2000-11

Patents in selected energy- and climate-related technologies, 2000-11

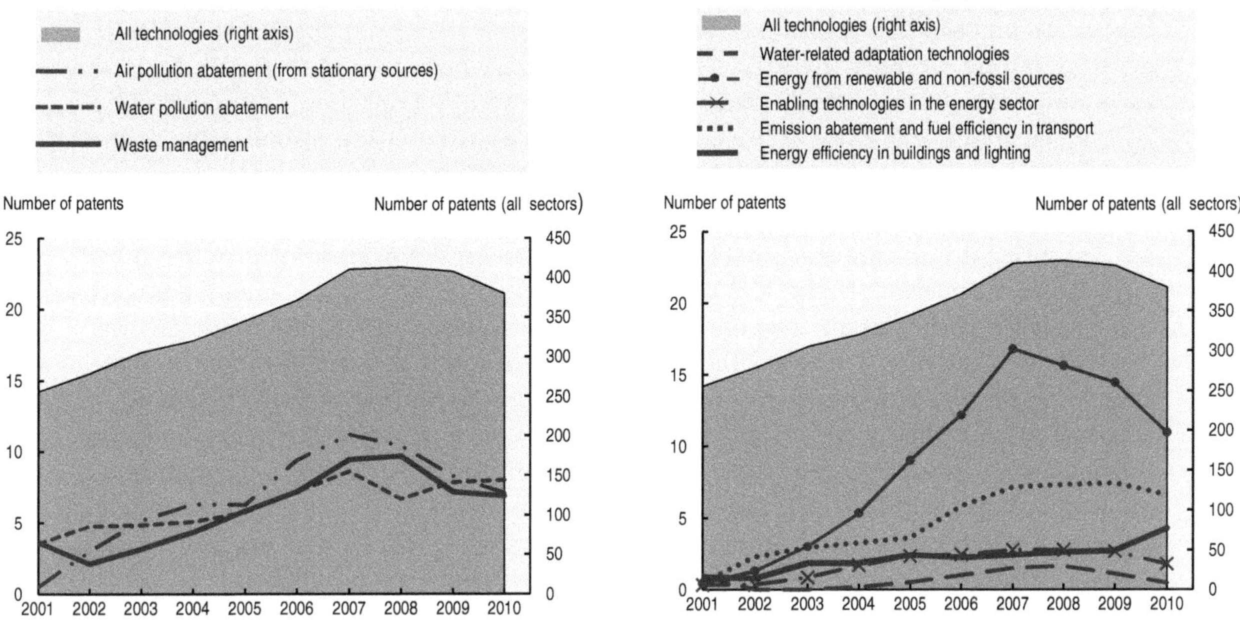

Notes: Higher-value inventions that have sought patent protection in at least two jurisdictions. Data refer to fractional counts of patent applications based on the priority date and the inventor's country of residence. Three-year moving average data.

Source: Based on: OECD (2015), "Patents in environment-related technologies: Technology development by inventor country", *OECD Environment Statistics* (database).

StatLink http://dx.doi.org/10.1787/888933279631

Environment- and climate-related technology accounted for about 9% of all patents filed in Brazil in 2009/11, compared to the OECD average of 11% and the BRIICS average of 7.8%. Brazil's specialisation in environmental technology, as measured by the revealed technology advantage (RTA) index, increased between 2000/03 and 2009/11.[28] Brazil's RTA index in environmental technology is above the BRIICS average but below the OECD median. For bio- and nanotechnology, Brazil displays a revealed technology advantage with respect to both the BRIICS and the OECD (OECD, 2014).

Brazil has effectively used the Clean Development Mechanism (CDM) under the United Nations Framework Convention on Climate Change to encourage good practices, knowledge and technology dissemination and the adoption of more sustainable production standards.[29] It ranks third, after China and India, in the generation of CDM-certified emission reduction credits worldwide, focusing on methane avoidance (27%), hydro (25%), landfill gas (13%) and biomass energy (12%). The CDM has been an important source of technology transfer, notably for biomass energy and biogas recovery in breeding farms and landfills, even though the share of Brazilian CDM projects involving technology transfer, compared to all CDM projects, is lower than in other host countries (25%, compared to an average of 40%); the absolute number of projects involving technology transfer has been declining since the mid-2000s. A significant number of CDM projects were sponsored domestically, which suggests that the CDM has created incentives for endogenous technology-based initiatives (UNFCCC 2010; Seroa da Motta, 2009).

Overall, eco-innovation faces similar barriers as general innovation, including weak science-industry links, skill gaps, regulatory obstacles, high patenting costs and a complex system of economic and fiscal incentives. Various forms of protection of national businesses, including LCRs (Box 3.5) and high import duties, limit competition and discourage innovation and the adoption of more efficient, cleaner technology. Brazil's innovation and eco-innovation policies have been largely based on supply-side measures such as public support for R&D. However, the link between R&D and industrial development and commercialisation of new technology is particularly weak. As a consequence, the employment impact of eco-innovation activities, for example on the supply chain, is limited (Arbache et al., 2012).

Some demand-side policy measures have recently emerged, including policies that set sectoral environmental performance targets and sustainable procurement requirements. For example, the 2011 Greater Brazil Plan set specific environmental targets (e.g. to reduce energy intensity of the industrial sector by 9% by 2014), the first industrial development strategy to do so. In 2012, the government launched its sustainable procurement policy to prioritise green products, among others, thereby stimulating demand for, and offer of, environmental goods and services (Chapter 2).[30] There is scope to broaden the use of demand-side measures, for example by setting more ambitious environmental performance requirements for economic activities and products (e.g. vehicles and appliances) and promoting environmental labelling (see next section), as well as by ensuring strict enforcement of existing environmental regulations (Chapter 2). This would help expand the markets for environmental technology, goods and services (Section 6.3).

6.3. *Expanding the market for environmental technology, goods and services*

Brazil could build on international experience to improve its information base about the market for environmental goods and services (EGS) and to develop a clear concept of green economic activities and related indicators. This would help assess the effects of environmental policies and their socio-economic outcomes, and facilitate the development and evaluation of policies aimed at accelerating the transition towards a sustainable and green economy.

According to Environmental Business International, Brazil's EGS market reached USD 15.9 billion in 2010 (0.7% of GDP), which represents 47% of the Latin American or 2% of the global EGS market (ABDi, 2012). A study by the US Commercial Service (2014) suggests that Brazil's market volume in environmental technology (which excludes non-industrial EGSs such as eco-tourism or the use of natural products and biodiversity) amounted to USD 12 billion in 2014. Water, sanitation and solid waste account for the bulk of the market, reflecting the government's efforts to expand the coverage of these services in recent years (Section 5.2).

Few studies have attempted to quantify employment in green sectors. The International Labour Organization (ILO) estimated that about 3 million Brazilians were occupied in the green sector in 2008 (almost 7% of formal employment); other studies point to between 1.4 million and more than 16 million green jobs (ILO, 2010; Nonato and Maciente, 2012). The International Food Policy Research Institute (2006) estimated that Brazil's biofuels programme alone created 1.3 million jobs in rural areas. The World Bank (2010b) estimates that the adoption of low-carbon technologies could increase employment in Brazil by 1.1% annually over 2010-30. The experience of other countries, for example Spain, shows that the expansion of green sectors such as renewables, water and waste management can create new job opportunities (OECD, 2015e). Yet the large job creation potential, for example linked to Brazil's renewables targets (Section 5.4), is not yet envisioned or adequately reflected in official studies and government policies (Bowen, 2012).

Brazil's EGS market is expected to expand considerably in coming years. The US Commercial Service (2014) estimates the market potential of environmental technology to be between 1% and 7% of GDP. Indeed, the EGS sector seems to have grown faster than the overall economy (ABDi, 2012). Domestic demand for environment-related technology and consultancy services will likely increase along with advancing environmental legislation, more stringent law enforcement and new investment needs related to economic development and urbanisation in areas such as water, air, waste, energy and transport. Brazil can also benefit from increasing foreign demand for certified natural products (e.g. sustainable forestry, sustainable agriculture, natural cosmetics) and position itself as an EGS supplier to Latin America, given the relatively early stage of market development of the sector across the continent.

At present, EGS-related markets in Brazil are extremely heterogeneous. Some are well developed, such as those for hydropower technology, first generation biofuels, biomass to charcoal conversion, biomass gasification, cogeneration, and hydrogen and fuel cell systems for small businesses (Jannuzzi and Poppe, 2014). However, the domestic supply of technology related to emission reduction, energy and resource efficiency, process optimisation, waste treatment and recycling is limited and access to import markets relatively constrained. This results in high costs and discourages businesses from opting for more sustainable technology and production modes. The cost of air pollution equipment, for example, is 45% to 50% higher in Brazil than elsewhere due to the lack of domestic products and to high taxes and import duties (IEMA, 2014).

Responding to growing external demand, Brazilian companies have become more active in product certification and environmental labelling. However, the lack of national certification bodies for several product lines forces companies to seek international certification, and the related costs are often prohibitive, especially for SMEs. The MMA launched the Brazilian Environmental Labelling Programme in 2002 with the aim of contributing to the increased demand for products with less environmental impact. The programme was intended to co-ordinate and better articulate environmental labelling initiatives, but it has not provided many advances (IPEA, 2010a).

Large companies, new companies and those with high productivity tend to invest more in environmental technology (ADBi, 2012). Yet a survey conducted in 2009 among the 100 leading Brazilian companies suggested that they invested only 1% of turnover in sustainable technology, with insufficient availability and high prices, as well as lack of information and knowledge about sustainable technology, being identified as the main barriers (AHK, 2009). This points to a lack of technical capacity in industry, which impedes the development of green industry. Skill development activities related to greening the economy exist, but are not embedded in an overall policy strategy or framework (ILO, 2010). New policies for skills development and better alignment between environmental, industrial and labour market policies are needed to respond to new demands from green sectors and reduce possible knowledge and skills shortages. Labour and social policy systems should accommodate the shift to more environment-related jobs to limit any unintended impact on inequality.

6.4. *Voluntary green business practices*

Brazilian companies practice corporate social responsibility (CSR) with a high degree of sophistication when compared to other Latin American countries (Scharf, 2009; Galego-Álvarez et al., 2014). The business sector has developed innovative and far-reaching initiatives to address social and environmental impacts, and some fast-growing companies, such as Natura (Box 3.8), are based on innovative, sustainable business models. However, Brazilian business performance is heterogeneous; socially unacceptable labour conditions, resource-inefficient and environmentally harmful behaviour still occur in a non-negligible number of companies. Still, overall CSR activities seem to have increased over the 2000s, particularly but not only in large enterprises (Ethos, 2008).

Box 3.8. **Sustainability as the business model: Natura**

The Brazilian cosmetics company Natura, founded in 1969, ranks among the world's top 20 beauty companies. It has a market share of about 20% in Brazil, operates in a dozen other countries and recorded revenue of BRL 5.5 billion in 2011. Its business strategy is based on innovation for sustainability and market differentiation. The company seeks to minimise its environmental impact throughout product life cycles and works with family producers and traditional communities to promote sustainable income generation.

In 2010, Natura launched a strategic sourcing programme aimed at increasing sustainability of the supply chain. Suppliers are assessed not only on the basis of product prices, but also on a "shadow price" that includes social and environmental costs and benefits (e.g. CO_2 emissions, waste generation, water use, employee education and training, social inclusion, direct investment in society). The sourcing programme initially engaged 50 of the company's largest suppliers and provided them with training on Natura's methodology and data collection. By 2014, the programme had engaged almost 90% of suppliers. Natura estimates that the socio-environmental benefits of selecting suppliers based on high sustainability performance was worth over USD 750 000 in 2012.

To develop new sustainable products, Natura established research partnerships consisting of research institutions, suppliers, local producers and NGOs. The company benefited from public support worth USD 43 million in 2012 for innovation, training, logistics and information technology.

Source: UNEP (2014), *The Business Case for Eco-innovation*, United Nations Environment Programme, Paris; WRI (2013), "Aligning profit and environmental sustainability: Stories from industry", World Resources Institute, Washington, DC.

Brazil's socio-environmental challenges have triggered the creation of associations such as Corporate Commitment for Recycling and the Brazilian Corporate Council for Sustainable Development. There are examples of successful co-operation between Brazilian business associations and public institutions, such as the 2006 Soya Moratorium, which aimed to stop soya cultivation on deforested areas in the Amazon biome. Under the moratorium, the associations for the vegetable oil industry and cereals exporters worked with the MMA and the National Institute for Space Research (INPE) to register Amazonian farms and to map and monitor cleared land areas (Chapter 4).

There has been a marked increase in the number of Brazilian companies with environmental management systems certified as meeting the ISO 14001 standard

(Chapter 2). While such systems do not necessarily lead to better environmental outcomes, there is some evidence that ISO certification has had, on average, a positive impact on the profitability of Brazilian firms (Tognere Ferron et al., 2012).

Brazilian firms, mostly large companies, have also been active in climate change mitigation. In 2009, 20 major companies committed to reducing GHG emissions per unit of production or revenue; this was before a national climate change policy or target was adopted. About 100 Brazilian companies participate in the Greenhouse Gas Protocol initiative[31] and voluntarily prepare GHG emissions inventories; some have gone even further and started assessing and managing their carbon footprints.

7. Environment and development co-operation

7.1. Brazil as a recipient of development assistance

Despite being a middle-income country, Brazil receives significant volumes of official development assistance (ODA). The volume of ODA disbursed increased over the 2000s, peaking at USD 1.4 billion in 2012, making Brazil the largest ODA recipient in South America in that year (Figure 3.10). However, due to the size of its domestic economy, Brazil's relative dependence on foreign aid is low. Between 2000 and 2013, ODA fluctuated between 0.01 and 0.06% of gross national income (GNI) per year; per capita ODA averaged roughly USD 2 per year and just recently increased to over USD 5 in 2012-13 (OECD, 2013e).

Environment and the green economy are key areas for ODA to Brazil. In 2013, USD 300 million was channelled to the Amazon Fund alone; projects targeting renewable energy and water and sanitation amounted to more than USD 400 million each (OECD, 2015f). The OECD Creditor Reporting System[32] shows that about 60% of bilateral ODA commitments to Brazil over the past decade targeted environmental sustainability. Total environment-related ODA commitments reached about USD 1.8 billion in 2012, though they decreased in 2013. A rather small share of these resources is devoted to the environment sector per se[33] (on average USD 83 million in 2011-13); most of the aid is aimed at other sectors but has environmental co-objectives (Figure 3.10). The latter category more than tripled between 2011 and 2012, driven by large-scale projects in the water supply and sanitation, forest, transport, and energy sectors. Overall, ODA related to objectives of the Rio Conventions increased in recent years, especially for climate change mitigation (Figure 3.10). The largest donors for environmental sustainability were Germany, Norway and the United Kingdom.

Brazil has also received substantial financial support from multilateral funding mechanisms established under international environmental initiatives, such as the Global Environment Facility (GEF).[34] Some major environmental projects, such as the National Biodiversity Project and the Amazon Region Protected Areas programme (Chapter 4), are financed through the GEF, though Brazil's project portfolio is large and diverse. Of the current 55 national projects, 23 target biodiversity (accounting for 45% of total GEF grants received) and 13 climate change (24% of grants); the rest involve international waters, land degradation and persistent organic pollutants. Brazil has participated in 34 GEF-sponsored regional and global projects in Latin America. The GEF Country Portfolio Evaluation attested that such funding had sustainably helped develop institutional capacity and that it triggered significant private sector involvement in climate change projects (GEF, 2012).

Figure 3.10. **Environment is a key area for official development assistance to Brazil**

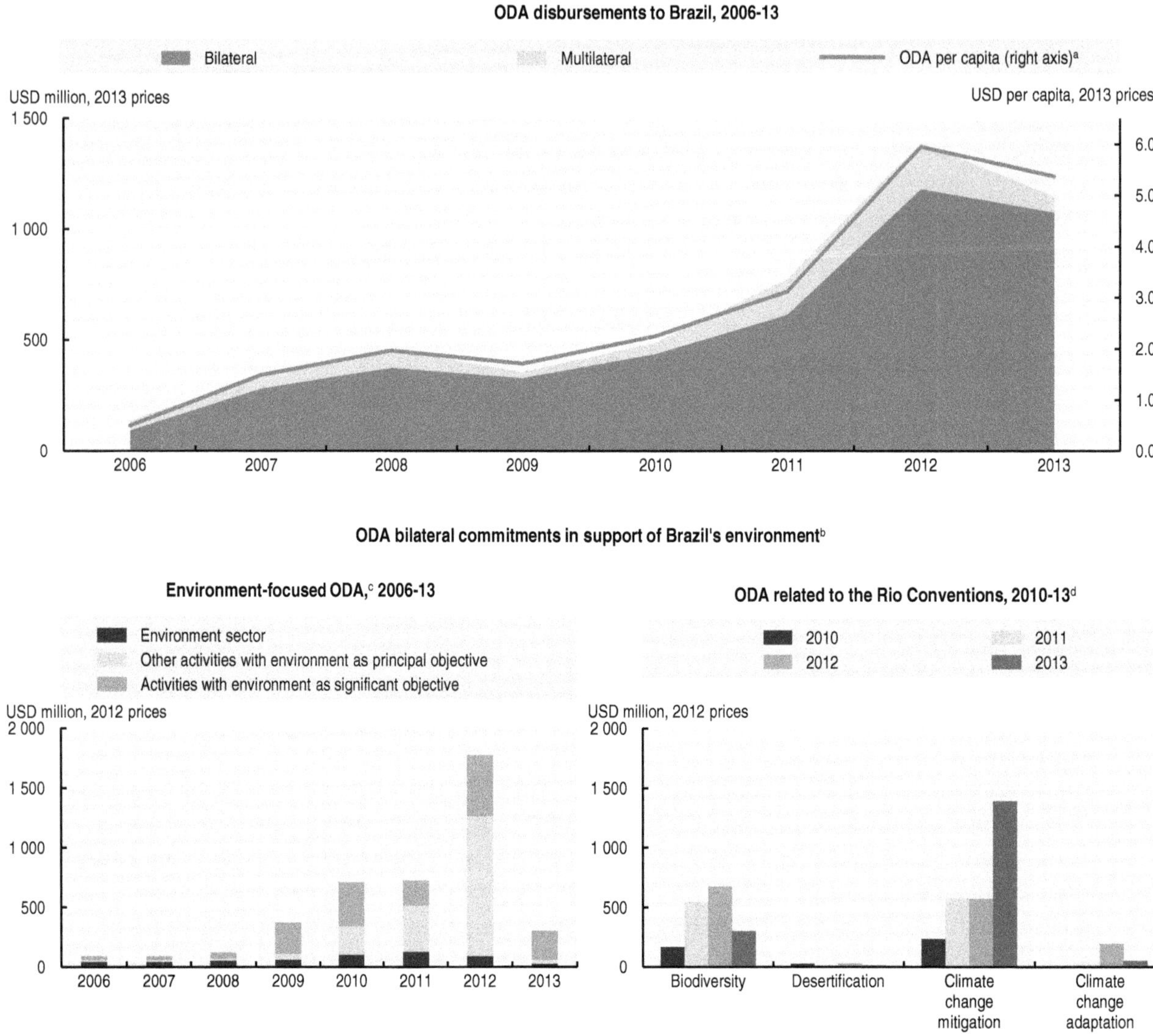

a) Bilateral official development assistance from DAC members.

b) The marker data do not allow exact quantification of amounts allocated or spent in support of the environment. They give an indication of such aid flows and describe the extent to which donors address these objectives in their aid programmes.

c) Environment sector: aid in direct support of general environmental protection activities. Other activities with environment as principal objective: aid activities where environment protection is an explicit objective of the activity and fundamental in its design. Activities with environment as significant objective: aid activities where environment protection is an important, but secondary, objective of the activity.

d) Most activities targeting the objectives of the Rio Conventions fall under the definition of "environment-focused aid" but there is no exact match of the respective coverages. An activity can target the objectives of more than one of the conventions, thus respective ODA flows should not be added.

Source: OECD (2015), *OECD International Development Statistics* (database).

StatLink http://dx.doi.org/10.1787/888933279649

7.2. Brazil as a provider of development co-operation

Brazil plays an increasing role as a provider of development co-operation. According to official estimates, federal expenditure on development co-operation increased from BRL 384 million in 2005 to BRL 724 million in 2009, and this may underestimate expenditure from all public institutions (IPEA, 2010b).[35] About two-thirds of the volume spent over 2005-09 consisted of contributions to international organisations, with regional funds, notably the Mercosur Structural Convergence Fund, being the main channels. New, more complete estimates indicate that Brazil's development co-operation reached

BRL 1.6 billion (USD 927 million) in 2010 (IPEA, 2014).[36] The OECD estimated that USD 500 million of the 2010 flows may qualify as ODA, and 60% of this was channelled through multilateral organisations (OECD, 2015g).[37] Overall, the number of projects increased from 69 in 2005 to over 400 in 2010. Bilateral projects concentrates on technical co-operation. While Latin American and Portuguese-speaking African countries were initially the focus, Brazilian co-operation now extends to some 70 developing countries in Africa, Asia and Latin America.

Technical co-operation is overseen and co-ordinated by the Brazilian Co-operation Agency (ABC) of the Ministry of External Relations, with delivery carried out by more than 170 federal institutions (IPEA, 2014). Brazilian public institutions are increasingly involved in the negotiation and design of technical co-operation projects, often through their own international affairs units, and sometimes with limited ABC involvement. Collaboration between the ABC and MMA seems to be looser than in other policy areas, such as health and social protection.

Thematically, Brazil's co-operation has focused on health, agriculture and education, which accounted for about half of its technical co-operation in 2003-10. Environment has been less prominent, with environmental projects accounting for 7.5% and energy projects for 3.5% in 2010 (Cabral and Weinstock, 2010). The number of environment projects has recently expanded, and prospects of this growth accelerating in the near future are good; the government plans to expand south-south co-operation on forest recovery, for example (MCTI, 2014b). There is no provision ensuring systematic screening of technical co-operation projects for potentially negative environmental impacts.

Many of Brazil's flagship initiatives have been in agriculture. The largest is ProSavana, a programme by Brazil, Japan and Mozambique for agricultural development of Mozambique's savannah, based on Brazil's *cerrado* development. Several other agricultural projects have been launched in Africa and elsewhere, many of which aim to stimulate agro-energy. The 2010 Africa-Brazil Agriculture Innovation Marketplace is a joint research initiative aimed at stimulating agricultural innovation in Africa in areas including pasture rehabilitation, natural resource management and clean energy production. Brazil also signed various bilateral biofuel co-operation agreements with African countries, providing technology transfer enabling them to develop their own biofuel industries.

Brazil is engaging with other countries to share its expertise in forest and land use monitoring. The National Institute for Space Research, which developed remote sensing techniques for monitoring deforestation in the Amazon (Box 4.4), runs a training centre on satellite rainforest monitoring in Belém (INPE, 2014). In addition, Brazil's Amazon Fund has begun funding projects outside Brazil, providing about USD 10 million to the Amazon Cooperation Treaty Organization for a project to expand systematic monitoring of forest coverage to the other seven countries sharing the Amazon biome.

Brazil is one of the most active partners in triangular co-operation (OECD, 2013f). The government considers such co-operation a key tool to scale up and improve the impact of Brazilian technical co-operation. Its main partners in triangular co-operation are bilateral providers and international organisations (OECD 2013f; OECD, 2015g). An example of environment-related triangular co-operation is Amazonia Sem Fogo (Amazon Without Fire), a project of Brazil, Italy and Bolivia to reduce deforestation by developing alternatives to the use of fire in agriculture, thus contributing to environmental protection and improvement of living conditions in rural communities. The BNDES signed agreements in 2013 with development institutions in the BRIICS countries to promote collaboration among them, including "initiatives to foster a low-carbon economy and to develop infrastructure on the African continent" (BNDES, 2013b).

Recommendations on greening the economy in the context of sustainable development

Greening the system of taxes and charges

- Reform the system of environmentally related taxes and charges, possibly within the context of a broader fiscal reform, including:
  - maintaining positive rates for the federal CIDE tax on petrol and diesel and adjusting them to reflect fuel carbon content and emissions of local air pollutants; applying the CIDE to fuels used for aviation and stationary purposes (e.g. industry);
  - introducing taxes on pollution (e.g. air emissions), waste (e.g. packaging materials) and resource use (e.g. minerals), and aligning vehicle taxation to environmental performance;
  - ensuring that water abstraction and pollution charges reflect scarcity and pressures on the environment and are consistently applied across river basins and throughout the country (as required by law).
- Pursue the assessment of carbon pricing options; consider testing GHG cap-and-trade systems at state level to gain the experience needed to implement a countrywide system linked to international carbon markets.

Investment in environment-related infrastructure and services

- Systematically integrate environmental objectives into sectoral policies and public investment programmes, which should feature environmental sustainability criteria for implementation and indicators to monitor progress.
- Simplify administrative procedures and support capacity development to improve the execution of environment-related infrastructure investment programmes, especially at local level; encourage stronger intermunicipal collaboration to achieve economies of scale in providing sanitation and waste treatment services.
- Extend the use of user charges for water supply, sanitation and waste services and enforce their collection, with a view to encouraging efficient use of resources, increasing cost recovery, improving investment financial viability and leveraging private sector resources; use social transfers to ensure that low-income households have adequate access to these services.
- Strengthen measures to improve energy efficiency by introducing energy standards for buildings and appliances, integrating them into social housing programmes and using mandatory fuel economy standards and labelling to promote a shift towards more efficient vehicles.
- Continue to scale up investment in railways and urban public transport systems; consider extending the use of instruments such as road tolls, congestion charges, parking fees and restrictions on car circulation to moderate the use of private vehicles.

Recommendations on greening the economy in the context of sustainable development *(cont.)*

Eco-innovation and environmental goods and services

- Stimulate the production and diffusion of environmental technology, goods and services by:
  - raising awareness about best practices and available technology, particularly in small and medium-sized enterprises;
  - facilitating access to finance for investing in environmental, renewables and energy-saving technology;
  - monitoring the effects of local content rules on the long-term competitiveness of the emerging environmental technology industry (e.g. wind and solar);
  - regularly updating the catalogue of sustainable products for green public procurement, and training procurement managers;
  - further streamlining environmental labelling initiatives.

Notes

1. The revenue raised through the CIDE is collected by the federal government, with about 30% being allocated to states in shares proportional to the length of their roads, their fuel consumption and their population.
2. The 2012 reform eliminated the Fuel Consumption Charge (CCC) and General Reserve Reversion Charge (RGR). The CCC was paid by electricity distributors and passed on to end customers. Its revenue was used by the state electricity company, Eletrobras, to subsidise electricity generation using diesel fuel in isolated systems in the North. The RGR was not levied on electricity consumption, but paid by electricity generators and transmitters at a rate of 2.5% of the value of fixed assets in service or up to 3% of annual company revenue. It was earmarked to fund the rural electrification programme Luz Para Todos (Section 5.4) and an efficient public lighting programme.
3. This is part of the Financial Compensation for Use of Water Resources: hydroelectric power generators are charged at 6.75% of the value of electricity produced. The revenue from the 6% part of the charge rate is shared between the federal government and the state and municipal governments affected by the plants. Revenue are not earmarked for water infrastructure and environmental purposes (OECD, 2012). In 2013, revenue from this source was about BRL 1.5 billion.
4. For example, prior to the 2013 tax reform, Mexico applied a floating-rate excise tax on petrol and diesel. The tax rate varied according to a formula linked to international benchmark fuel prices. In practice, when this international price was high, the tax rate became negative so that domestic prices fell below the import cost of petrol and diesel. Conversely, a lower international price triggered an increase in the tax rate (OECD, 2013b).
5. The PIS/COFINS social contributions are levied on gross revenue from fuel sales, generally at rates higher than the standard.
6. The ICMS is the state-level value added tax, levied on imports and on intra- and interstate transactions of goods and services. The standard rate varies between 17% and 19%. In general, electricity is subject to a higher rate (25%), while oil and gas operations are subject to the standard intrastate rate and natural gas at a rate of 12%. Petroleum and its derivatives are exempt from interstate operations, while natural gas is generally taxed at 12%, though in the North and North-east regions this falls to 7%. Rates for ethanol and biodiesel vary by state and may be reduced for interstate operations.
7. Biodiesel producers can opt for fixed PIS/COFINS rates per cubic metre of fuel.
8. The PSE is the annual monetary value of gross transfers to agricultural producers arising from policy measures that support agriculture, including market price support, budgetary payments and budget revenue forgone. It is expressed as a percentage of gross farm receipts.
9. Market price support arises from policy measures that create a gap between domestic market prices and border prices of a specific agricultural commodity. In Brazil, price levels vary by year and by region, with support often targeting regions that are distant from main consumer markets; they usually do not diverge much from international prices.

10. The SNCR incorporates federal, state and co-operative banks providing government-supported credit to agriculture.
11. Constitutional Amendment 491/2010.
12. The Forest Code obliges rural landowners to set aside a percentage of their land to be maintained as a permanent forest reserve (Legal Reserve) and forbids the clearing of primary vegetation on steep slopes and along the margins of rivers and streams (which are classified as Areas of Permanent Protection) (Chapter 4). Private Reserves of Natural Heritage are private areas declared as conversation units (Chapter 5). To qualify, the property must meet certain environmental requirements, such as high biodiversity, scenic looks or ecological relevance.
13. The BNDES lent at a subsidised rate of 5.5% in January 2015, compared to the central bank's short term rate of 11.75% (Financial Times, 2015).
14. The special incentive regimes for infrastructure development (Regime Especial de Incentivos para o Desenvolvimento da Infraestrutura, REIDI) grant tax exemptions for infrastructure projects in areas of public interest (e.g. transport, ports, electricity, sanitation, irrigation). The 2012 law on infrastructure bonds introduced tax breaks for buyers of bonds issued to finance approved transport and energy infrastructure. While the tax breaks have proved successful in areas such as telecommunications and renewables, the infrastructure bonds have had a slow start and are still a small part of the corporate debt market.
15. Concessions are awarded for projects that are financially viable without any public payment to the private operator (i.e. they rely on user charges alone); PPP agreements are used for projects requiring public subsidies to be financially viable.
16. In PAC's first phase only 4% of planned investment for sanitation was disbursed; by 2013 about 20% of funding was disbursed and 54% of sanitation projects scheduled as part of PAC 2 had been granted formal approval (Amann et al., 2014; TCU, 2014).
17. The BNDES has increased low-interest lending for urban mobility projects, and total lending volumes have grown since 2008. In addition, PAC channelled special funds to urban mobility projects starting in 2011, targeting both medium and large cities (Table 3.3). Since 2010, the Ministry of Cities, working with Brazil's second largest public bank – Caixa Econômica Federal, has run a low-interest loan programme for urban transport investment, financed by a levy on wages.
18. São Paulo city's budget covers about 20% of the funds needed for bus and subway transport (Amann et al., 2014).
19. The fare-setting model is based on a profit margin applied to baseline costs per passenger kilometre. Any increase in input costs (such as fuel or salaries), or reduction in number of passengers, automatically leads to a fare increase.
20. The automatic adjustment in bus fares and the lack of regulatory control sparked mass demonstrations in São Paulo and other cities in 2013 (The Economist, 2013).
21. The PDE expects to add 22.7 GW of power capacity from renewable sources other than large hydro by 2022. Wind will account for the bulk of this (15.6 GW), followed by biomass (5 GW) and small hydro (2 GW); an expansion of solar photovoltaic capacity (2 GW) was recently added.
22. The Brazilian Alcohol Programme included price control measures, investment support, preferential financing and fiscal incentives. The state oil company, Petrobras, has facilitated blending, storage and distribution.
23. In 2011, the BNDES and the Brazilian Innovation Agency (Finep) launched a programme to support RD&I in the ethanol sector, funding 42 projects for a total of USD 1.6 billion (BNDES, 2013a).
24. Established in 2002, the Sectoral Fund for Energy had launched seven public calls for tender by 2009, the majority focusing on increasing electricity supply efficiency (BRL 47.8 million), education and dissemination (BRL 1.3 million), demand-side energy management (BRL 4 million) and small-scale solar PV and wind power (BRL 4 million).
25. The sectoral programmes under the plan are i) sustainable production (energy efficiency, solid waste and wastewater treatment in industry); ii) recovery of biomes and sustainable production of forest-based activities; iii) environmental sanitation (energy generation from waste, reverse logistics and municipal waste management, and contaminated soil); and iv) monitoring systems.
26. As a benchmark, in 2011, government budget appropriations and outlays for R&D with environmental objectives was 2% of the total, on average, in OECD countries (OECD, 2014). However, Brazil does not report to the OECD Research and Development Statistics Database, and the data cannot be directly compared.

27. The sectoral funds that provide finance for environment-related innovation are CT-Agribusiness (BRL 5 million disbursed in 2010), CT-Amazônia (BRL 1.7 million), CT-Waterways (BRL 1.6 million), CT-Biotechnology (BRL 1.3 million), CT-Energy (BRL 2.7 million) and CT-Hydro (BRL 2 million).
28. The "revealed technology advantage" is defined as a country's share of patents in a particular technology field divided by its share in all patent fields. The index is equal to zero when the country holds no patents in a given sector; 1 when the country's share in the sector equals its share in all fields (no specialisation); and above 1 when a specialisation is observed (OECD, 2014).
29. The CDM was developed following a Brazilian proposal in the 1997 Kyoto Protocol negotiations.
30. The value of sustainable public procurement more than tripled over 2010-13, but sustainable products still account for less than 0.1% of government purchases (MMA, 2015).
31. The GHG Protocol, developed by the World Resources Institute and the World Business Council on Sustainable Development, sets the global standard for how to measure, manage and report GHG emissions. More information can be found at www.ghgprotocol.org.
32. Within the OECD Creditor Reporting System Aid Activity Database, countries use a policy marker to identify activities that have environmental objectives. Over the past decade, roughly 80% of projects have been screened under the Creditor Reporting System.
33. The category "environmental sector" includes ODA flows directed towards environmental policy and administrative management (e.g. regulations, institutions and practice), biosphere protection, biodiversity, site preservation, flood prevention and control, environmental education and training, and environmental research.
34. The GEF has provided USD 427 million in grants to Brazilian environmental protection since its establishment in 1991 (complemented by USD 1 400 million of co-financing) (GEF, 2014).
35. The 2005-09 estimates were a first attempt to quantify official Brazilian development co-operation and there is a general idea that this number underestimates the actual volume devoted to international co-operation due to the loose co-ordination of data collection and the dispersed pattern of project delivery (most of Brazil's technical co-operation projects are implemented by public institutions which do not charge for their participation and expertise); moreover, IPEA's estimates only include federal government expenses and exclude concessional loans by federal banks like the BNDES, as well as credit exports and debt relief.
36. The 2010 estimate attempted to include technical co-operation projects implemented by public institutions, which partly explains the significantly higher number. The rise over 2009-10 is also linked to a BRL 460 million increase in expenditure for peacekeeping operations.
37. The significant divergence between the official estimate for Brazil's development co-operation in 2010 and the OECD estimate is linked to different accounting methodologies. The OECD estimates are based on Brazil's official data, which may exclude some activities that would qualify as development co-operation in OECD statistics. In addition, the OECD estimates include only activities in low and middle-income countries and contributions to multilateral agencies whose main aim is promoting economic development and welfare of developing countries, and they exclude bilateral peacekeeping activities.

References

ABCR (2015), "Tarifas de Pedágio" [Toll Rates], Brazilian Association of Highway Concessionaires, *www.abcr.org.br/TarifasPedagio/TarifaPedagio.aspx* (accessed May 2015).

ABDi (2012), *Relatório de Acompanhamento Setorial: Competitividade do Setor de Bens e Serviços Ambientais [Sectoral Monitoring Report: Competitiveness of the Environmental Goods and Services Sector]*, Brazilian Agency for Industrial Development, Brasília, *www3.eco.unicamp.br/neit/images/stories/arquivos/Relatorios_NEIT/Bens-e-Servcos-Ambientais-Setembro-de-2012.pdf*.

AHK (2009), *Green Technologies in Brazil. An Overview of the Sustainability Market*, AHK German Chamber of Industry and Commerce in Brazil and Roland Berger Strategy Consultants, São Paulo, *www.renewablesb2b.com/data/ahk_brazil/publications/files/GreenTechStudy_AHK_RB.pdf*.

Amann, E. et al. (2014), "Infrastructure and its Role in Brazil's Development Process", *IRIBA Working Paper 10*, International Research Initiative on Brazil and Africa (IRIBA), University of Manchester, Manchester.

Arbache, J., A. Goldstein and F. Marquesurce (2012), "O Brasil e a nova geografia da inovação" [Brazil and the new geography of innovation], *Pontes*, Vol. 8, No. 2.

Barros, S. (2014), "Brazil Biofuels Annual – 2014", *GAIN Report No. BR14004*, US Department of Agriculture, Global Agricultural Information Network, Washington, DC.

Barth, B. et al. (2014), *Framework Assessment for the Photovoltaic Business Opportunities in Brazil*, BSW Solar and eclareon GmbH, report for the Deutsche Gesellschaft für Internationale Zusammenarbeit (GIZ) GmbH, Berlin.

BNDES (2015), "Social and Environmental Responsibility", *www.bndes.gov.br/SiteBNDES/bndes/bndes_en/Institucional/Social_and_Environmental_Responsibility* (accessed July 2015)

BNDES (2014), "Plano Inova Sustentabilidade" [Innovate Sustainability plan], *www.bndes.gov.br/SiteBNDES/bndes/bndes_pt/Institucional/Apoio_Financeiro/Plano_inova_empresa/inovasustentabilidade.html* (accessed January 2015).

BNDES (2013a), "The BNDES and the Sugar-ethanol Industry in 2012: Innovation as Priority", *Sectorial Report*, Industrial Division, June 2013 No. 25, BNDES, Rio de Janeiro.

BNDES (2013b), "BNDES and other development banks in the BRICS sign cooperation agreements", BNDES, *www.bndes.gov.br/SiteBNDES/bndes/bndes_en/Institucional/Press/Noticias/2013/20130327_brics.html* (accessed March 2014).

BNEF (2015), *Global Trends in Renewable Energy Investment 2015*, Bloomberg New Energy Finance and Frankfurt School-UNEP Centre, Frankfurt am Main, *http://apps.unep.org/publications/pmtdocuments/-Global_trends_in_renewable_energy_investment_2015-201515028nefvisual8-mediumres.pdf.pdf.*

BNEF (2014), *Climatescope 2014*, commissioned by the Multi-lateral Investment Fund of the Inter-American Development Bank, the UK Department for International Development, Power Africa, Bloomberg New Energy Finance, New York.

BNEF (2013), *Climatescope 2013*, commissioned by the Multi-lateral Investment Fund of the Inter-American Development Bank, Bloomberg New Energy Finance, New York.

Bowen, A. (2012), "'Green' Growth, 'Green' Jobs and Labor Markets", *Policy Research Working Papers*, No. 5990, World Bank, Washington.

Cabral and Weinstrock (2010), "Brazilian technical cooperation for development. Drivers, mechanics and future prospects", Overseas Development Institute, London, *www.odi.org/sites/odi.org.uk/files/odi-assets/publications-opinion-files/6137.pdf.*

Castanheira, E.G. et al. (2014), "Environmental Sustainability of Biodiesel in Brazil", *Energy Policy*, Vol. 65, pp. 680-691.

Costa, S.A.B and L.S. Côrtes (2014), "Tariff Disincentives: Obstacles to the Expansion of Sewage Treatment Services in Brazil", paper presented at the European Consortium for Political Research (ECPR) 5th Standing Group on Regulatory Governance, Barcelona Institute of International Studies, 25-27 June, Barcelona.

De Oliveira, A. and T. Laan (2010), *Lessons Learned from Brazil's Experience with Fossil-Fuel Subsidies and their Reform*, Global Subsidies Initiative, International Institute for Sustainable Development, Winnipeg, *www.iisd.org/pdf/2010/lessons_brazil_fuel_subsidies.pdf.*

Eletrobras (2014), *Executive Summary: Procel Results 2014 – Base year 2013*, Eletrobras Procel, Brasilía.

Ethos (2008), *Practicas e Perspectivas da Responsabilidade Social Empresarial no Brasil 2008 [Practices and Prospects of Corporate Social Responsibility in Brazil in 2008]*, Ethos Institute of Business and Social Responsibility, São Paulo, *www3.ethos.org.br/wp-content/uploads/2012/12/1Sum%C3%A1rio-da-Pesquisa-Relat%C3%B3rio-publicado.pdf.*

FEBRABAN (2014), *The Brazilian Financial System and the Green Economy Alignment with Sustainable Development*, Brazilian Federation of Banks, São Paulo.

Financial Times (2015), "BNDES: Lender of first resort for Brazil's tycoons", 11 January, *Financial Times*, London.

Frischtak (2011), "Vantagens Comparativas, Inovação e Economia Verde" [Comparative Advantages, Innovation and Green Economy], paper prepared for the BNDES National Forum, 21 September 2011, *www.bndes.gov.br/SiteBNDES/export/sites/default/bndes_pt/Galerias/Arquivos/empresa/download/inovacao_paper_05.pdf.*

Galego-Álvarez, I., H. Formigoni and M.T. Pompa Arunes (2014), "Corporate social responsibility practices at Brazilian firms", *Revista de Administração de Empresas*, Vol. 54, No.1, 2014.

GEF (2014), "Country Profile for Brazil", Global Environment Facility, *www.thegef.org/gef/country_profile* (accessed March 2015).

GEF (2012), *GEF Country Portfolio Evaluation. Brazil (1991-2011)*, Global Environment Facility, *www.thegef.org/gef/sites/thegef.org/files/documents/CPE-Brazil-v1.pdf.*

Goldemberg, J. et al. (2014), "Oil and natural gas prospects in South America: Can the petroleum industry pave the way for renewables in Brazil?", *Energy Policy*, Vol. 64, pp. 58-70, *http://dx.doi.org/10.1016/j.enpol.2013.05.064.*

Gurgel, A.C. and S. Paltsev (2013), "Costs of reducing GHG emissions in Brazil", *Climate Policy*, Vol. 14, No. 2, pp. 209-223, *http://dx.doi.org/10.1080/14693062.2013.835655.*

Harding, M. (2014), "The Diesel Differential: Differences in the Tax Treatment of Gasoline and Diesel for Road Use", *OECD Taxation Working Papers*, No. 21, OECD Publishing, Paris, *http://dx.doi.org/10.1787/5jz14cd7hk6b-en.*

IBGE (2013), *Pesquisa de Inovção [Innovation Research]*, Brazilian Institute of Geography and Statistics, Rio de Janeiro, *www.pintec.ibge.gov.br/downloads/pintec2011%20publicacao%20completa.pdf.*

IBNET (2015), *The International Benchmarking Network for Water and Sanitation Utilities* (Database), *http://database.ib-net.org/Default* (accessed April 2015).

IEA (2013), *World Energy Outlook 2013*, International Energy Agency, IEA, Paris, *http://dx.doi.org/10.1787/weo-2013-en.*

IEMA (2014), *1° Diagnóstico da Rede de Monitoramento da Qualidade do Ar no Brasil [First Diagnosis of the Air Quality Monitoring Network in Brazil]*, Energy and Environment Institute, São Paulo.

ILO (2010), "Skills for green jobs in Brazil". Unedited background country study, ILO Skills and Employability Department, International Labour Organization, *www.ilo.org/wcmsp5/groups/public/---ed_emp/---ifp_skills/documents/publication/wcms_142300.pdf.*

International Food Policy Research Institute (2006), "Bioenergy and Agriculture: Promises and Challenges. Brazil's Experience with Bioenergy", International Food Policy Research Institute Brief No. 8/2006, *www.ifpri.org/sites/default/files/publications/focus14_08.pdf.*

Ioris, A. (2008), "The limits of integrated water resources management: A case study of Brazil's Paraíba do Sul River Basin", *Sustainability: Science, Practice & Policy*, Vol. 4, Issue 2, Proquest, Maryland.

IPEA (2014), *Brazilian cooperation for international development: 2010*, Institute for Applied Economic Research, Brasília.

IPEA (2012), *Diagnóstico dos Resíduos Sólidos no Brasil [Diagnosis of solid waste in Brazil]*, Institute for Applied Economic Research, Brasília.

IPEA (2010a), *Sustentabilidade Ambiental no Brasil: biodiversidade, economia e bem-estar humano [Environmental Sustainability in Brazil: Biodiversity, Economy and Human Well-being]*, Institute for Applied Economic Research, Brasília, *www.ipea.gov.br/agencia/images/stories/PDFs/livros/livros/livro07_sustentabilidadeambienta.pdf.*

IPEA (2010b), *Cooperação brasileira para o desenvolvimento internacional: 2005-2009 [Brazilian Co-operation for International Development: 2005-2009]*, Institute for Applied Economic Research, Brasília.

Jannuzzi, G. and M Poppe (2014), "Development, Cooperation and Transfer of low carbon technologies" in Seroa da Motta, R. et al. (eds) (2011), *Climate Change in Brazil: Economic, Social and Regulatory Aspects*, Institute for Applied Economic Research, Brasília, *www.ipea.gov.br/agencia/images/stories/PDFs/livros/livros/livro_climatechange.pdf.*

Larive International (2014), *Market Study: Wind Energy in Brazil*, Ministry of Economic Affairs of the Netherlands, The Hague, Larive International, Zeist, and Transfer LBC, Rotterdam.

La Rovere, E.L., A.S. Pereira and A.F. Simões (2011), "Biofuels and Sustainable Energy Development in Brazil", *World Development*, Vol. 39, No. 6, pp. 1026-1036.

Lindau, L., D. Hidalgo and A. de Almeida Lobo (2014), "Barriers to planning and implementing Bus Rapid Transit systems", *Research in Transportation Economics*, Vol. 48, pp. 9-15.

Lindau, L., D. Hidalgo and D. Facchini (2010), "Bus Rapid Transit in Curitiba, Brazil. A Look at the Outcome After 35 Years of Bus-Oriented Development", *Transportation Research Record*, Vol. 2193, pp. 17-27.

Martinez Júnior, F. (2011), "A eficiência da cobrança pela utilização da água para o uso racional e o financiamento do sistema de gestão do recursos hídricos na bacia do Rio Paraíba do Sul" [Efficiency of water charges for rational use and financing of the water resources management system in the Paraíba do Sul River Basin], paper presented at the XIX Brazilian Symposium on Water Resources, *www.abrh.org.br/sgcv3/UserFiles/Sumarios/11e152b6915be81e862115107a899557_0d84c07b909d1b9527de2d55fedfa7ac.pdf.*

MCTI (2014a), "Indicadores Nacionais de Ciência, Tecnologia e Inovação" [National Indicators of Science, Technology and Innovation], Ministry of Sciences, Technology and Innovation, *www.mcti.gov.br/indicadores* (accessed October 2014).

MCTI (2014b), *First Biennial Update Report (BUR) under the United Nations Framework Convention on Climate Change (UNFCCC)*, Ministry of Sciences, Technology and Innovation, *http://unfccc.int/resource/docs/natc/brbur1.pdf.*

MCTI (2011), *Estratégia Nacional de Ciência, Tecnologia e Inovação (ENCTI) 2012-2015. Balanço das Atividades Estruturantes 2011 [National Strategy for Science, Technology and Innovation 2012-2015. Structural Activities in 2011*, Ministry of Sciences, Technology and Innovation, Brasília.

Ministry of Cities (2014), *Diagnóstico dos Serviços de Água e Esgotos. 2013 [Diagnosis of Water and Sewerage Services. 2013]*, Ministry of Cities, Brasília, *www.snis.gov.br/diag2013/Diagnostico_AE2013.zip.*

Ministry of Finance (2014), *Market Readiness Proposal*, report under the Partnership for Market Readiness Program, Ministry of Finance, Brasília, *www.thepmr.org/system/files/documents/Final%20MRP%20Brazil_29-08-2014.pdf.*

MMA (2015), *Fifth National Report to the Convention on Biological Diversity*, Ministry of the Environment, Brasília, *www.cbd.int/doc/world/br/br-nr-05-en.pdf.*

MMA (2012), *Plano Nacional de Resíduos Sólidos [National Solid Waste Plan]* (draft August 2012), Ministry of the Environment, Brasília, *www.sinir.gov.br/documents/10180/12308/PNRS_Revisao_Decreto_280812.pdf/.*

Moarif, S. and N. Patodia Rastogi (2012), *Market-based Climate Mitigation Policies in Emerging Economies*, Center for Climate and Energy Solutions, Arlington.

MPOG (2015), *PAC 2. Balanço 4 Anos [PAC 2. Assessment after 4 years]*, Ministry of Planning, Budget and Management, Brasília, *www.pac.gov.br/pub/up/relatorio/f9d3db229b483b35923b338906b022ce.pdf.*

MPOG (n.a.), "PAC 2" (presentation), Ministry of Planning, Budget and Management, Brasília, *www.pac.gov.br/pub/up/relatorio/c9fba67e144c9237b839e2c5adf32e99.pdf.*

Nonato, F. and A. Maciente (2012), "A identificação de empregos verdes, ou com potencial verde, sob as óticas ocupacional e setorial no Brasil" [Identification of green jobs in Brazil, or jobs with green potential, from an occupational and sectoral view], newsletter *Radar: tecnologia, produção e comércio exterior*, Institute for Applied Economic Research, *www.ipea.gov.br/agencia/images/stories/PDFs/radar/121217_radar23_cap5.*

ODI (2014), *The fossil fuel bailout: G20 subsidies for oil, gas and coal exploration*, Overseas Development Institute, London, *www.odi.org/sites/odi.org.uk/files/odi-assets/publications-opinion-files/9234.pdf.*

OECD (2015a), *Taxing Energy Use 2015: OECD and Selected Partner Economies*, OECD Publishing, Paris, *http://dx.doi.org/10.1787/9789264232334-en.*

OECD (2015b), *Water Resources Governance in Brazil*, OECD Studies on Water, OECD Publishing, Paris, *http://dx.doi.org/10.1787/9789264238121-en.*

OECD (2015c), *Overcoming Barriers to International Investment in Clean Energy*, Green Finance and Investment, OECD, Paris, *http://dx.doi.org/10.1787/9789264227064-en.*

OECD (2015d), *Innovation, Agricultural Productivity and Sustainability in Brazil*, OECD Publishing, Paris, *http://dx.doi.org/10.1787/9789264237056-en.*

OECD (2015e), *OECD Environmental Performance Reviews: Spain 2015*, OECD Publishing, Paris, *http://dx.doi.org/10.1787/9789264226883-en.*

OECD (2015f), *OECD International Development Statistics* (database), *http://dx.doi.org/10.1787/dev-data-en* (accessed June 2015).

OECD (2015g), *Development Co-operation Report 2015: Making Partnerships Effective Coalitions for Action*, OECD Publishing, Paris, *http://dx.doi.org/10.1787/dcr-2015-en.*

OECD (2014), *OECD Science, Technology and Industry Outlook 2014*, OECD Publishing, Paris, *http://dx.doi.org/10.1787/sti_outlook-2014-en.*

OECD (2013a), *OECD Economic Surveys: Brazil*, OECD Publishing, Paris, *http://dx.doi.org/10.1787/eco_surveys-bra-2013-en.*

OECD (2013b), *Putting Green Growth at the Heart of Development*, OECD Green Growth Studies, OECD Publishing, Paris, *http://dx.doi.org/10.1787/9789264181144-en.*

OECD (2013c), *OECD Environmental Performance Reviews: Mexico 2013*, OECD Publishing, Paris, *http://dx.doi.org/10.1787/9789264180109-en.*

OECD (2013d), *Agricultural Policy Monitoring and Evaluation*, OECD Publishing, Paris, *http://dx.doi.org/10.1787/agr_pol-2013-en.*

OECD (2013e), Effective Carbon Prices – Country Note on Brazil, OECD Publishing, Paris, *www.oecd.org/env/tools-evaluation/Effective-Carbon-Prices-in-Brazil.pdf.*

OECD (2013f), "Triangular co-operation: What can we learn from a survey of actors involved?", report prepared by the OECD Development Co-operation Directorate, May 2013, OECD, *www.oecd.org/dac/dac-global-relations/OECD%20Triangluar%20Co-operation%20Survey%20Report%20-%20June%202013.pdf.*

OECD (2012), *A Framework for Financing Water Resources Management*, OECD Studies on Water, OECD Publishing, Paris, *http://dx.doi.org/10.1787/9789264179820-en.*

OECD (2011), *OECD Economic Surveys: Brazil*, OECD Publishing, Paris, *http://dx.doi.org/10.1787/eco_surveys-bra-2011-en.*

OSEC (2010), *The Brazilian Market for Railway Technologies*, December, Osec Business Network Switzerland, Zurich.

OECD et al. (2015), *Revenue Statistics in Latin America and the Caribbean 2015*, OECD Publishing, Paris, *http://dx.doi.org/10.1787/rev_lat-2015-3-en-fr.*

Reuters (2015), "Brazil power rates may jump 60 pct on drought, subsidies – source", 16 January, Reuters, *www.reuters.com/article/2015/01/16/brazil-electricity-rates-idUSL1N0UV1VX20150116* (accessed April 2015).

Scharf, R. (2009), "Why Brazil leads the region in CSR", *Americas Quarterly*, Vol. 2(1), No. 68.

Seroa da Motta, Ronaldo (2009), "Eco-Innovation in Brazil", presentation held at the OECD Global Forum on Environment on Eco-Innovation, Paris 4-5 November 2009, *www.oecd.org/env/consumption-innovation/44053422.pdf.*

Solutions for Water (2011), "1974 – Payment for Environmental Services in Water Resources Management in Brazil", 26 December, Solutions for Water Platform, 6th World Water Forum 2012, Marseille.

TCU (2014), *Relatório e Parecer Prévio sobre as Contas do Governo da República Exercico de 2013: Programa de Aceleração do Crescimento (PAC) - Tabelas* [Report and Preliminary Opinion on the Accounts of the Government of the Republic, 2013: Growth Acceleration Programme – Tables], Federal Court of Accounts , Brasília.

TCU (2011), *Relatório e Parecer Prévio sobre as Contas do Governo da República Exercico de 2010: Ficha 6.1 – Programa de Aceleração do Crescimento* [Report and Preliminary Opinion on the Accounts of the Government of the Republic, 2011: Brief 6.1 – Growth Acceleration Programme], Federal Court of Accounts, Brasília.

The Economist (2013), "Taking to the streets", 22 June, The Economist Newspaper, London, *www.economist.com/news/americas/21579857-bubbling-anger-about-high-prices-corruption-and-poor-public-services-boils-over.*

The Economist (2012), "Untangling the custo Brasil: Electricity taxes in Brazil", Americas View, 20 August, The Economist Newspaper, London.

Tognere Ferron, R., et al. (2012), "Is ISO 14001 Certification Effective? An Experimental Analysis of Firm Profitability", *Brazilian Administration Review*, Vol. 9, Special Issue, pp. 78-94.

TransportPolicy (2014), "Brazil: Light-duty: Fiscal Incentive", updated August 2014, TransportPolicy.net, The International Council on Clean Transportation, Washington, DC.

UNEP (2014), *The Business Case for Eco-innovation*, United Nations Environment Programme, Paris, *www.unep.org/resourceefficiency/Portals/24147/Business-Ressource%20Efficency/BCFOREIFORWEB.pdf.*

UNFCCC (2010), *The Contribution of the Clean Development Mechanism under the Kyoto Protocol to Technology Transfer*, United Nations Framework Convention on Climate Change, Bonn, *http://cdm.unfccc.int/Reference/Reports/TTreport/TTrep10.pdf.*

U.S. Commercial Service (2014), "Doing Business in Brazil – Country Commercial Guide for U.S. Companies", U.S. & Foreign Commercial Service and U.S. Department of State.

WEF (2014), *The Global Competitiveness Report 2014-15*, World Economic Forum (WEF), Geneva.

World Bank (2015), *World Development Indicators* (database), World Bank, Washington, DC, *http://data.worldbank.org/data-catalog/world-development-indicators* (accessed May 2015).

World Bank (2013), *Impact and Implications of Recent and Potential Changes to Brazil's Subnational Fiscal Framework*. Report No. ACS5885, Washington, DC, *http://siteresources.worldbank.org/EXTPREMNET/Resources/EP147.pdf*.

World Bank (2010a), "Brazil – Integrated Solid Waste Management and Carbon Finance Project – Project Appraisal Document", Report No. 50292-BR, 29 September, World Bank, Washington, DC, *www.wri.org/sites/default/files/pdf/aligning_profit_and_environmental_sustainability_stories_from_industry.pdf*.

World Bank (2010b), *Brazil Low-carbon Country Case Study*, World Bank, Washington, *http://siteresources.worldbank.org/BRAZILEXTN/Resources/Brazil_LowcarbonStudy.pdf*.

WRI (2013), "Aligning profit and environmental sustainability: Stories from industry", Working Paper, February 2013, World Resources Institute, Washington.

WWC and OECD (2015), "Water: Fit for finance? catalyzing national growth through investment in water security", report of the High Level Panel on Financing Infrastructure for a water-secure World, World Water Council and OECD, Marseille, *www.worldwatercouncil.org/fileadmin/world_water_council/documents/mailing/mail_wwf7_documents/WWC_OECD_Water-fit-to-finance_Report.pdf*.

ANNEX 3.A

Progress towards the Millennium Development Goals

Table 3.A.1. **Selected Millennium Development Goals, targets and indicators**

Selected Millennium Development Goals, targets and indicators		Brazil, baseline		Brazil, latest available year		LAC, latest available year
GOAL 1:	**Eradicate extreme poverty and hunger**					
Target 1.A:	***Halve between 1990 and 2015 the proportion of people whose income is less than USD 1.25 a day***					
Indicator 1.1	Population below USD 1.25 (PPP) a day (%)	1990	17.2	2010	6.1	5.5
Indicator 1.2	Poverty gap ratio (%)	1990	7.2	2009	3.6	2.9
Indicator 1.3	Share of income or consumption to the poorest quintile (%)	1990	2.2	2009	2.9	..
Target 1.B:	***Achieve full and productive employment and decent work for all including women and young people***					
Indicator 1.4	Annual growth rate of GDP per person employed (%)	1993	2.82	2009	-0.7	
Indicator 1.5	Employment-to-population ratio (%)	1990	54.7	2011	61.7	62.1
Indicator 1.6	Proportion of employed people living below USD 1.25 a day (% of total employment)	1992	10.1	2009	3.3	2.9
Target 1.C:	***Halve between 1990 and 2015 the proportion of people who suffer from hunger***					
Indicator 1.9	Proportion of population below minimum level of dietary energy consumption (%)	1991	14.8	2013	5	7.9
GOAL 2:	**Achieve universal primary education**					
Target 2.A:	***Ensure that by 2015 children everywhere boys and girls alike will be able to complete a full course of primary schooling***					
Indicator 2.2	Percentage of pupils starting grade 1 who reach last grade of primary (%)	1992	70.3	2009	53.7	76.7
Indicator 2.3	Literacy rate of 15-24 year-olds both sexes (%)	2000	94.2	2012	98.6	97.8
GOAL 3:	**Eliminate gender disparity in education and empower women**					
Target 3.A:	***Eliminate gender disparity in primary and secondary education preferably by 2005 and in all levels of education no later than 2015***					
Indicator 3.2	Women's in wage employment (non-agricultural sector) (%)	1990	40.2	2012	47.2	43.8
Indicator 3.3	Proportion of seats held by women in national parliament (%)	1990	5.3	2014	8.6	25.9
GOAL 4:	**Reduce child mortality**					
Target 4.A:	***Reduce by two thirds between 1990 and 2015 the under-5 mortality rate***					
Indicator 4.1	Under-5 mortality rate (per 1 000 live births)	1990	61.5	2013	13.7	19
Indicator 4.2	Infant mortality rate (per 1 000 live births)	1990	51.4	2013	12.3	16
GOAL 5:	**Improve maternal health**					
Target 5.A:	***Reduce by three quarters between 1990 and 2015 the maternal mortality ratio***					
Indicator 5.1	Maternal mortality ratio (per 100 000 live births)	1990	120	2013	69	85
Target 5.B:	***Achieve by 2015 universal access to reproductive health***					
Indicator 5.4	Adolescent birth rate (per 1 000 adolescent women aged 15-19)	1996	83.9	2011	64.8	75.9
Goal 6:	**Combat HIV/AIDS malaria and other diseases**					
Target 6.A:	***Halt by 2015 and begun to reverse the spread of HIV/AIDS***					
Indicator 6.9	Incidence prevalence and death rates associated with tuberculosis (cases per 100 000 population) (mid-point)					
	Incidence	1990	84	2012	46	43
	Prevalence	1990	140	2012	59	61
	Death	1990	7	2012	2.5	3
Goal 7:	**Ensure environmental sustainability**					
Target 7.A:	***Integrate the principles of sustainable development into country policies and programmes and reverse the loss of environmental resources***					
Indicator 7.1	Forest area (% of land area)	1990	68.8	2010	62.4	47.4
Indicator 7.3	Consumption of Ozone-Depleting Substances (ODP metric tonnes)					
	All Ozone-Depleting Substances	1990	3 9337	2012	1 388	5 166
	Ozone-Depleting CFCs	1990	8 539	2012	0	
Indicator 7.6	Terrestrial and marine areas protected (% territorial area)	1990	7.06	2012	25.97	20.3
Target 7.C:	***Halve by 2015 the proportion of people without sustainable access to safe drinking water and basic sanitation***					
Indicator 7.8	Population using an improved drinking water source total (%)	1990	88	2012	98	94
	Urban (%)	1990	96	2012	100	97
	Rural (%)	1990	68	2012	85	82
Indicator 7.9	Population using an improved sanitation facility (%)	1990	67	2012	81	82
	Urban (%)	1990	79	2012	87	87
	Rural (%)	1990	31	2012	49	63
Target 7.D:	***By 2020 to have achieved a significant improvement in the lives of at least 100 million slum dwellers***					
Indicator 7.10	Urban population living in slums (%)	1990	36.7	2009	26.9	23.5
Goal 8:	**Develop a global partnership for development**					
Indicator 8.12	Debt service as a percentage of exports of goods and services (%)	1990	18.6	2012	4	6.6
Indicator 8.15	Mobile-cellular subscriptions (per 100 inhabitants)	1990	0	2013	135.3	109.1
Indicator 8.16	Internet users (per 100 inhabitants)	1992	0.01	2013	51.6	43.4

Source: UN (2015) *Millennium Development Goals Indicators* (database); UN (2014) *The Millennium Development Goals Report 2014*.

ANNEX 3.B

Data on green growth performance

Figure 3.B1. **Environmentally related taxes**

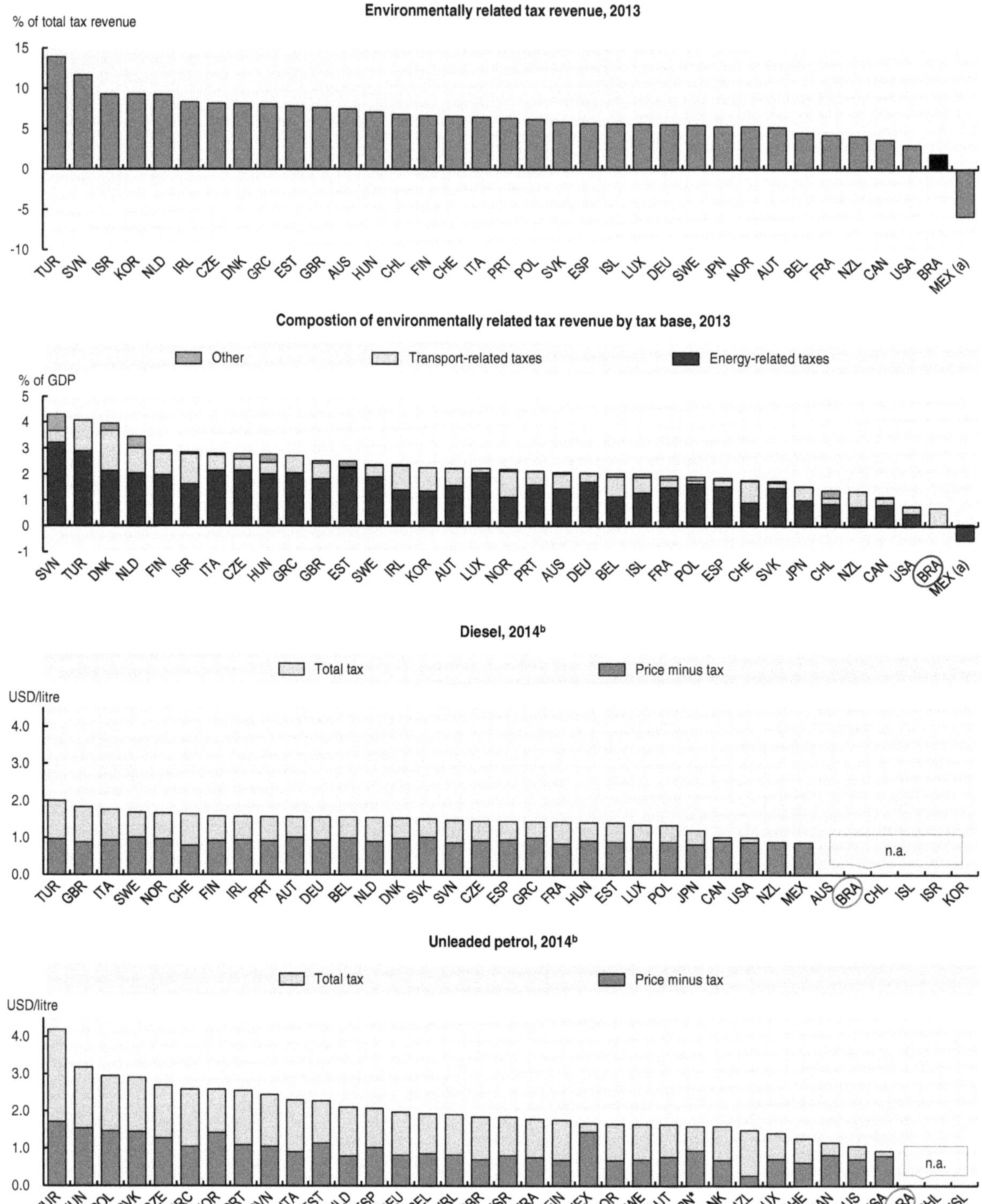

Notes: Data refer to the indicated year or to the latest available year. They may include provisional figures and estimates.

a) Until 2014, the system used to stabilise end-use prices of motor fuels caused tax revenue to turn negative (i.e. become a subsidy) in years when the international oil price was high. Mexico's 2013 Tax Reform corrected this mechanism and introduced a tax on fossil fuels based on their carbon content, which will yield positive revenue.

b) Diesel: automotive diesel for commercial use, current USD; unleaded petrol: unleaded premium (RON 95), except Japan (unleaded regular), USD at current prices and purchasing power parities.

Source: IEA (2015), *IEA Energy Prices and Taxes Statistics* (database); OECD (2015), *OECD Database on Instruments Used for Environmental Policies and Natural Resource Management* (database).

StatLink http://dx.doi.org/10.1787/888933279963

Figure 3.B2. **Green innovation**

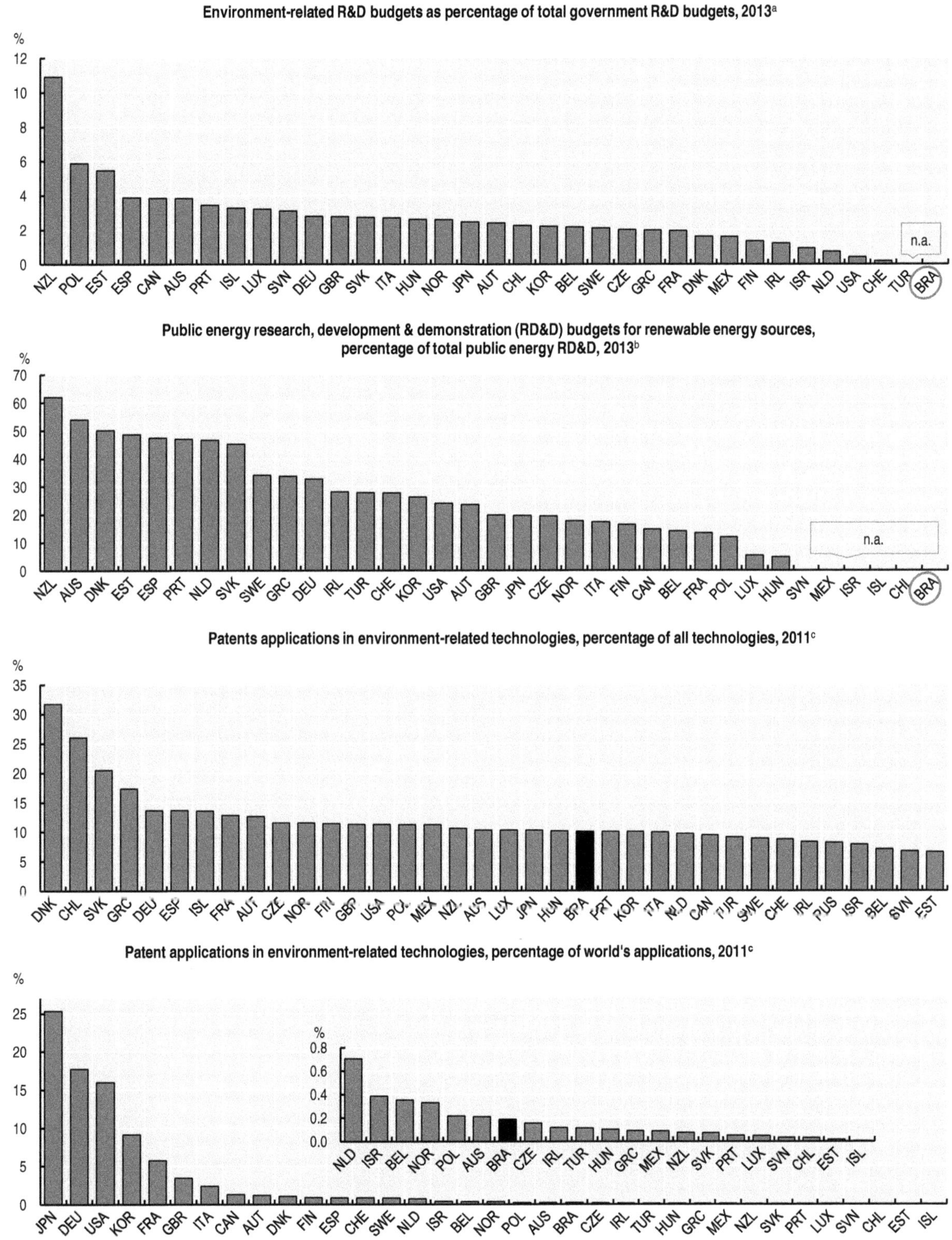

Notes: Data refer to the indicated year or to the latest available year. They may include provisional figures and estimates.

a) Government budget appropriations or outlays for R&D; breakdown according to the NABS 2007 classification.

b) Public energy technology budgets for research, development and demonstration (RD&D).

c) Higher values inventions that have sought patent protection in at least two jurisdictions. Data are based on patents applications filed under the Worldwide Patent

StatLink http://dx.doi.org/10.1787/888933279973

PART II

Progress towards selected environmental objectives

PART II

Chapter 4

Conservation and sustainable use of biodiversity

Brazil is the world's most biodiverse country. This chapter reviews the current status and trends of Brazil's biodiversity, as well as pressures stemming from a range of sources. It examines Brazil's biodiversity policy and institutional framework, including its integrated strategy to combat deforestation. The chapter assesses progress in financing biodiversity conservation, mainstreaming biodiversity into sectoral policies and enhancing the knowledge base and economic valuation of Brazil's biodiversity and ecosystems.

1. Status and trends in Brazil's biodiversity

The world's most biologically diverse country, Brazil is home to around one-tenth of known species and more endemic species than most other countries (CBD, n.d).[1] It is the world's fifth-largest country, its territory spanning close to half of South America (8.5 million km^2). Its extensive coastline (about 7 500 km) borders a vast marine area (more than 4.5 million km^2). The Brazilian population is concentrated along the coast, where average population density is around six times the national average (see Basic Statistics).

Given the size of the country's territory, its physical characteristics vary enormously, as do climate, vegetation and land-use patterns. Brazil is host to six large terrestrial ecosystems, or biomes:[2] Amazon, Cerrado, Caatinga, Atlantic Forest, Pantanal and Pampa. The Amazon is the largest biome, occupying nearly half of Brazil's territory, followed by the Cerrado (Box 4.1). The Atlantic Forest and Cerrado biomes are two of the world's 35 biodiversity hotspots, which are defined as significant reservoirs of biodiversity confronted by high levels of threat (Conservation International, 2015).

1.1. *Terrestrial ecosystems*

Despite efforts to protect Brazil's natural wealth, pressures on terrestrial biodiversity persist. Agriculture and cattle farming, natural resource extraction and infrastructure development together have contributed to more than 80% of habitat loss. Other pressures include alien species and exotic diseases, overexploitation, pollution, fire and climate change (Figure 1.13). Overall, about 70% of the total territory still has its original vegetation, in various degrees of conservation (MMA, 2010). The share of original vegetation varies widely across biomes, with the Amazon and Pantanal having more than 80% and the Atlantic Forest biome, where nearly three-quarters of Brazilians live, about 20% (Figure 1.13).

Biodiversity conservation status varies widely across regions and states (Figure 4.1). The Biodiversity Conservation Index indicates that biodiversity in the North region is generally better preserved, owing to the larger native vegetation cover and extension of protected areas and indigenous lands, while many states in the South-east and South display lower index values (MMA, 2015). The index, however, does not consider the actual status of ecosystems within protected areas (Chapter 5).

Deforestation

Brazil has the second largest forest area in the world, second only to Russia (Figure 4.2), and is home to the world's largest rainforest (SBF, 2013). Its immense forest resources extend almost 5 million km^2 and almost two-thirds of its territory is covered with forest or other wooded land. Nearly all of Brazil's forests (98.5%) are natural, non-planted forests. While the rate of deforestation has significantly declined, Brazil is the country with the highest average annual reduction in total forest cover (Figure 4.2). Overall, total forest area has decreased by about 5% since 2000 and by 10% since 1990 (FAO, 2015).

Box 4.1. **Brazil's six terrestrial biomes**

Brazil's ecosystems have been mapped into six major terrestrial biomes by the Brazilian Institute of Geography and Statistics (IBGE). Each is briefly described below.

Amazon (49% of the territory): a moist broadleaf forest that represents about 30% of the world's tropical rainforest. It hosts more than 600 types of terrestrial and freshwater habitats and a vast stock of commercial timber and carbon. It is home to hundreds of indigenous peoples and traditional communities, such as rubber tappers, non-timber forest product harvesters and riverine people. The Amazon biome has been the world's most active agricultural frontier in terms of forest loss and CO_2 emissions. In 2009, total forest loss exceeded 18% of the original extent. In addition to agriculture and cattle ranching, pressures include forest fires, land grabbing, timber extraction, road construction, hydropower and mining projects.

Source: IBGE (2004), Map of terrestrial biomes.

Cerrado (24%): the most biologically rich tropical savannah in the world. It is also the location of important shares of Brazil's soya (50%), corn (20%), rice (15%) and Brazilian bean production (11%). Together with forest fires, these activities pose a serious threat to species and ecosystems. The Cerrado has been losing original vegetation cover at a faster rate than all other biomes and it has suffered a vegetation loss amounting to an area roughly the size of Egypt.

Caatinga (10%): a semi-arid ecosystem consisting mainly of steppe savannah along with enclaves of humid tropical forest. It is one of the richest xeric shrub lands in the world and the only biome exclusive to Brazil. It has suffered high deforestation rates due to timber extraction, overgrazing and conversion to pasture, as well as soya and sugar cane production. Irrigation for fruit production has contributed to desertification affecting 15% of this biome.

Atlantic Forest (13%): a biome along the east coast of Brazil. It is made up of tropical, subtropical and dry or moist broadleaf forests, savannahs, scrublands and mangroves and is home to a large number of species, many endemic. About 80% of its original vegetation has been lost due to colonisation, urbanisation and resource extraction and the remainder is highly fragmented. About 70% of the country's population and industrial activity are concentrated here, along with the production of most of the domestically consumed agricultural products.

Pantanal (2%): the world's largest tropical freshwater wetland. It has a wealth of terrestrial and aquatic biodiversity. Pantanal is well preserved, but it is under pressure from the expansion of unsustainable farming and ranching, erosion and siltation, and pollution of rivers due to pesticides.

Pampa (1.8%): a subtropical grassland characterised by extensive cattle raising and rice, corn, wheat and soya production, which has degraded soil fertility and caused erosion. Urban expansion is another important threat to biodiversity in the Pampa.

Source: MMA (2014), "Biomas", *www.mma.gov.br/biomas*; MMA (2010), *Fourth National Report to the Convention on Biological Diversity*; Pinto et al. (2012), "Mata Atlantica"; SFB (2014), "Os Biomas e Suas Florestas", *www.florestal.gov.br/snif/recursos-florestais/os-biomas-e-suas-florestas*.

Figure 4.1. **The status of biodiversity conservation varies widely across Brazil**

Biodiversity conservation index by state and region

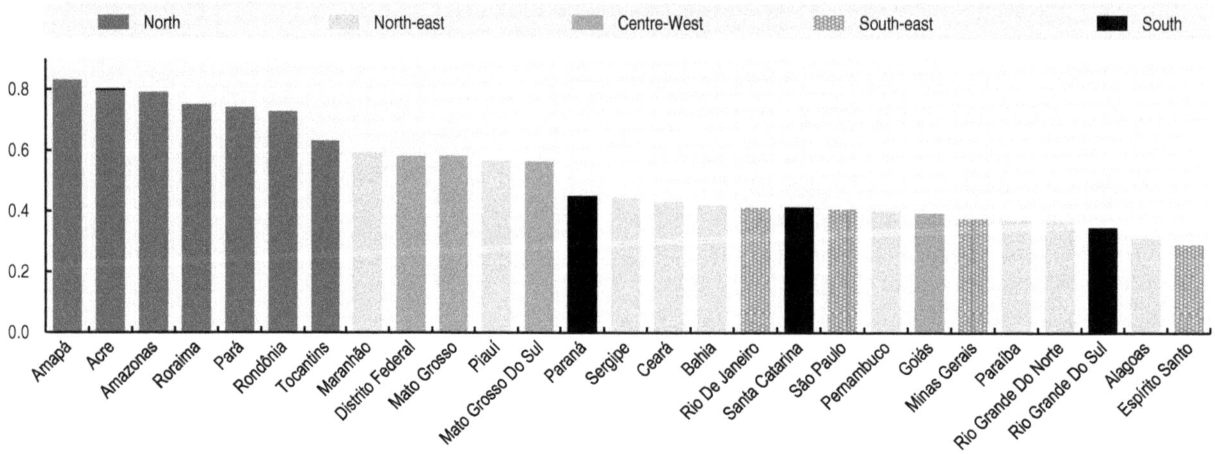

Note: The Biodiversity Conservation Index is based on number of threatened species, area covered by official protected areas and indigenous lands, remaining vegetation cover and number of *ex situ* biodiversity conservation sites. The index varies from 0 (very poor conservation status) to 1 (very good conservation status).
Source: MMA (2015), *Fifth National Report to the Convention on Biological Diversity.*

StatLink http://dx.doi.org/10.1787/888933279653

Figure 4.2. **Brazil has the world's second largest forest area and the highest deforestation rate**

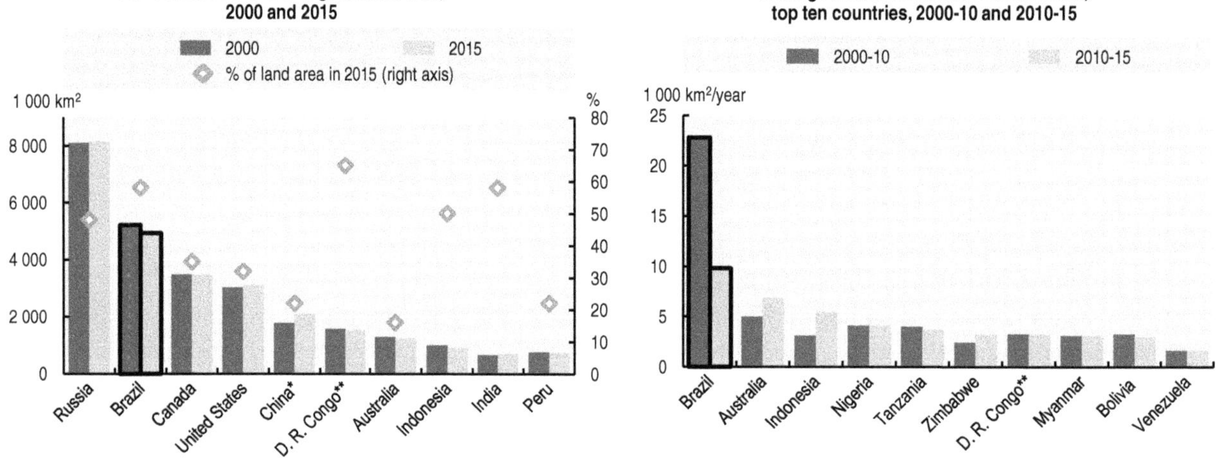

* China (People's Republic of); ** Democratic Republic of the Congo.
Source: FAO (2015), *Global Forest Resources Assessment 2015.*

StatLink http://dx.doi.org/10.1787/888933279661

Illegal logging and land grabbing made the area known as Amazônia Legal (Legal Amazon)[3] a deforestation hotspot in the 1990s and early 2000s, with deforestation peaks in 1994 and 2004 (Figure 4.3). About two-thirds of the cleared land had been converted into pasture by 2010 (MMA, 2015). Unclear legal tenure, especially in the Amazon, has been a major driver of deforestation, as property rights can be acquired by land-use conversion. This encourages illegal land grabbing by clearing new areas (Seroa da Motta, 2011). In addition, converted areas have a higher market value than forest areas, which encourages deforestation for speculative purposes (WWF, 2015). In 2011, only 4% of the Amazon area (or 11% of the non-public land areas) had a valid private property title (Figure 4.4).

Figure 4.3. **Annual deforestation rates have declined in most Brazilian biomes**

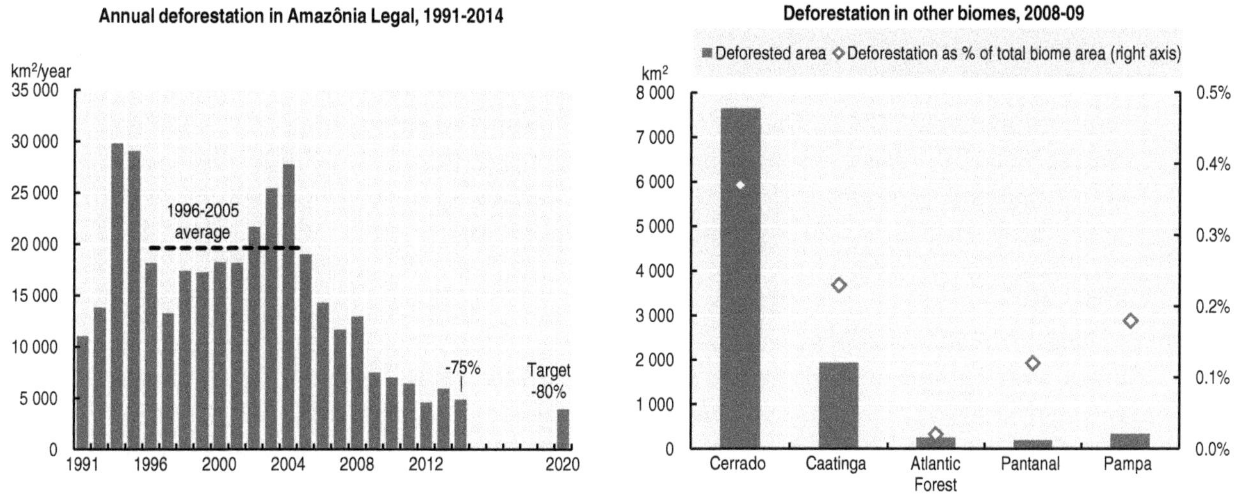

Source: Based on IBAMA (2015), "Projeto de Monitoramento do Desmatamento dos Biomas Brasileiros por Satélite – PMDBBS"; INPE (2015), "Projeto PRODES: Monitoramento da floresta Amazônia Brasileira por satélite".

StatLink http://dx.doi.org/10.1787/888933279678

Figure 4.4. **Property rights are still unclear for a large part of Amazonian lands**

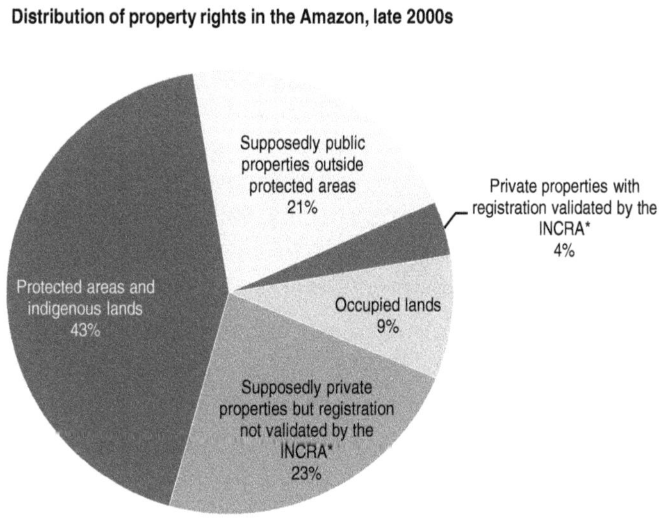

* INCRA: National Institute for Colonization and Agrarian Reform.
Source: Brito B. and P. Barreto (2009), "Os riscos e os princípios para a regularização fundiária na Amazônia", *Imazon No. 10*, March 2009.

StatLink http://dx.doi.org/10.1787/888933279686

In 2006, the government pledged to reduce deforestation in Amazônia Legal by 80% by 2020 (compared with the average of the previous 10 years) and has since considerably scaled up efforts to fight deforestation (Section 4; also see Chapter 5 on protected areas). This helped reduce deforestation from 27 700 km^2 to 4 800 km^2 per year between 2004 and 2014. By 2014, the annual deforestation rate had dropped by 75% (Figure 4.3) (INPE, 2015), which has helped cut GHG emissions (Chapter 1). However, the current pace of deforestation still means forest loss equivalent to the size of Slovenia (or the Brazilian state of Sergipe) every four years. Systematic implementation of the new Forest Code and the Rural Environmental Cadastre (Section 5.2) is expected to greatly contribute to controlling deforestation.

Deforestation rates have also declined in most, but not all, other biomes in recent years.[4] In the Atlantic Forest biome, for example, deforestation is estimated to have decreased by about 80% in the past 20 years. Pressures remain high in the Cerrado, however. It had the highest absolute and relative deforestation rates in 2008-09 (IBAMA, 2015; Figure 4.3). Some estimates indicate that annual deforestation in the Cerrado more than doubled between 2009 and 2012 (Soares-Filho et al., 2014a).

Forest fires

Uncontrolled human-caused forest fires are a major factor in degradation in many biomes, with the Amazon and Cerrado particularly affected. In the Amazon, fire occurrences have been closely related to logging and land conversion for agriculture (MMA, 2015; 2010). Forest fire occurrences have fluctuated between 100 000 and 250 000 per year since 2000. They are monitored daily by federal institutions through satellite images. The government has increased efforts to control forest fires in recent years, with additional equipment and trained firefighters, and is developing a national policy, expected to be launched in 2015.

1.2. Marine and aquatic ecosystems

Brazil hosts rich coral reef ecosystems and the world's largest contiguous area of mangroves. Its marine waters are home to a vast range of fishery resources, vertebrates, invertebrates, mammals, birds and chelonians. Estimates suggest around 25% of mangrove ecosystems have been lost (MMA, 2015). The major drivers of marine and coastal biodiversity loss include deforestation of riparian forests and mangroves; urban development along the coasts; oil and gas development; overfishing and unplanned aquaculture; introduction of exotic species; water pollution and littering; and climate change (Prates, 2014). Currently, only 1.5% of Brazil's marine areas (including the exclusive economic zone) are under protection (Chapter 5).

Pollution from industrial, agricultural and urban effluents and infrastructure development are the main drivers of freshwater habitat loss. Dams for large-scale hydropower generation, the main source of electricity in Brazil, can cause river fragmentation and affect the habitats of aquatic species. This can also have an impact on local communities, which are often dependent on small-scale agriculture and fishing. Attempts have been made to mitigate the impact of single dams, for instance by using fish ladders. However, the cumulative impact of a series of dams built on the same river has been rarely assessed (MMA, 2015) (Section 7.4).

Fish resources and aquaculture

Marine and freshwater fish catches grew by nearly 15% in 2000-13 (Figure 4.5). Several coastal and inland fish stocks are fully exploited or overexploited as a result of overfishing, generally by industrial fisheries (FAO, 2013). Excessive fishing effort and declining fish stocks are associated with resource conflicts between artisanal and industrial fishing and among fishing communities. Artisanal fishing dominates capture production, with more than 60% of total landings, and an even higher share in inland fisheries (OECD-FAO, 2015).

Figure 4.5. **Fish production has considerably increased since 2000**

Fish production in inland waters and marine areas, 2000-13

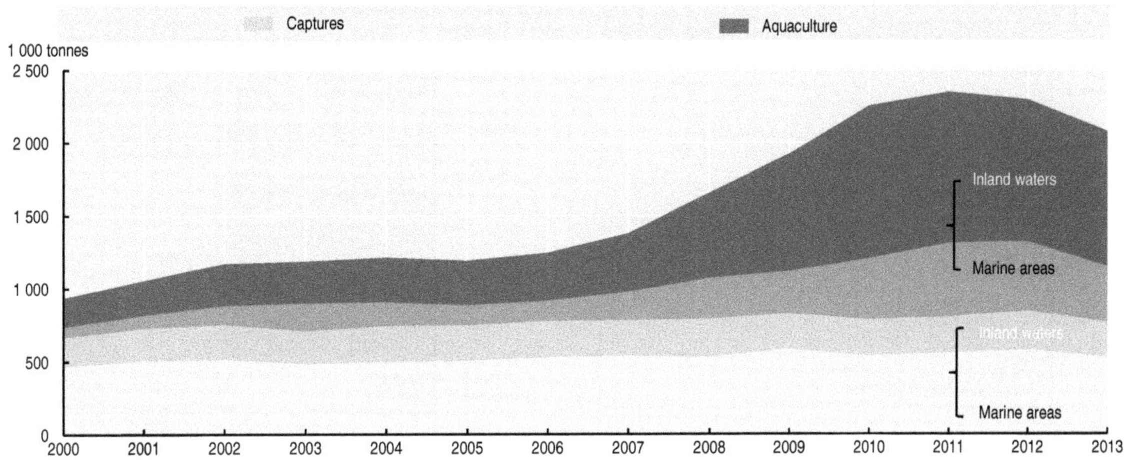

Note: Includes fish, crustaceans, molluscs and other aquatic animals; excludes marine mammals, crocodiles and alligators, and aquatic plants.
Source: FAO (2015), *FAO Global Capture and Aquaculture Production Statistics* (database).

StatLink http://dx.doi.org/10.1787/888933279699

Aquaculture increased by almost 400% over 2000-13, with a particularly strong rise in inland water aquaculture (Figure 4.5), accounting for over 60% of total fish production in 2013. While aquaculture may have a large potential to increase fish supplies and reduce pressure on natural fishery resources, its rapid expansion can pose challenges for biodiversity and ecosystem services.

1.3. *Species*

Brazil hosts nearly 44 000 plant species and more than 104 500 vertebrate and invertebrate species (MMA, 2015).[5] Several Brazilian native species are important as a source of food at the regional and local scale.[6] Studies have attempted to quantify the number of known species by biome, but the data are not fully comparable (Table 4.1).

Table 4.1. **Species estimates in Brazil's terrestrial biomes**

	Amazon	Atlantic Forest	Caatinga	Cerrado	Pantanal	Pampa
Number of species	**18 026**	**21 156**	**5 512**	**15 454**	**4 818**	**2 564**
Plants	13 993	18 951	4 508	13 014	3 500	1 675
Mammals	399	298	153	251	159	102
Birds	1 300	1 020	510	837	656	476
Reptiles	284	197	107	202	98	110
Amphibians	250	340	49	150	53	50
Fish	1 800	350	185	1 000	352	151

Note: As many species occur in more than one biome, the number of species should not be added across biomes.
Source: MMA (2015), *Fifth National Report to the Convention on Biological Diversity.*

The 2014 list of threatened flora species indicates that 46% of the nearly 4 600 evaluated plant species are threatened under various risk categories.[7] The Atlantic Forest biome hosts the largest share of threatened plant species, among those that have been assessed, which reflects high pressures from urbanisation, development and habitat fragmentation; the Cerrado biome, where agricultural pressures have intensified, follows (Figure 4.6).

Figure 4.6. **Conservation plans cover about half of threatened fauna species**

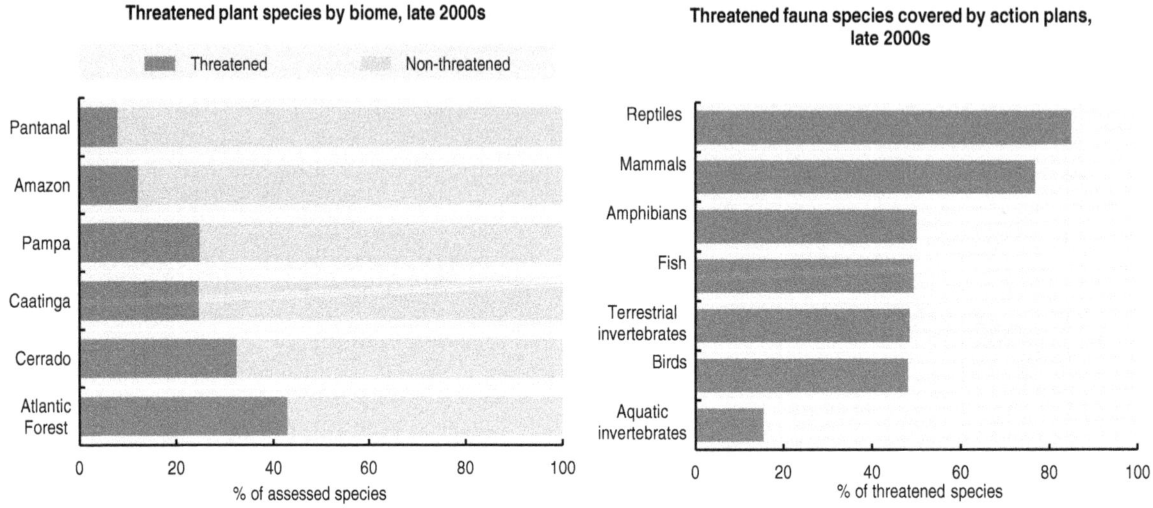

Source: MMA (2015), *Fifth National Report to the Convention on Biological Diversity.*

StatLink http://dx.doi.org/10.1787/888933279708

The 2014 list of threatened fauna species indicates that, out of over 12 000 assessed species, 1 173 species are threatened, including 110 mammal, 234 bird and 409 marine and freshwater fish species (ICMBio, 2015). This represents nearly twice the number of threatened species identified in the previous assessment, which is mostly due to improved scientific knowledge and a more extensive assessment.

Action to protect threatened species has increased. As of end 2013, Brazil had launched 48 action plans to preserve endangered species, including coastal and marine species. In 2012, about 50% of all threatened fauna species were protected under a conservation action plan, compared with 4% in 2008, with differing coverage across taxonomic groups and levels of implementation (Figure 4.6). In addition, federal protected areas now cover nearly 60% of threatened flora and fauna species (Chapter 5). Overall, the conservation status of 126 species has improved since the previous assessments (MMA, 2015).

The illegal traffic of wild animals is estimated to generate about USD 2.5 billion per year. About 38 million wild animal specimens are removed from nature every year, of which about 4 million are sold. Brazil has made progress in addressing illegal trade of endangered species with the introduction of strict regulations and improved inter-agency co-ordination. However, challenges remain, including insufficient staff, equipment and training.

Some 330 alien invasive species have been identified, mostly in the Atlantic Forest biome. It is estimated that three-quarters of alien invasive species were purposefully introduced, mostly for economic activities (including agriculture, but mainly for ornamental use of animals and plants) (IBGE, 2013; MMA, 2010). The introduction of alien plant species has led to the transformation of entire landscapes, increasing forest fragmentation and habitat degradation.[8] The presence of invasive species is estimated to cause an annual loss of USD 43 billion (MMA, 2015). Brazil has not yet developed comprehensive policies and measures for the control and monitoring of invasive species, but has implemented species-specific programmes (e.g. for the golden mussel).

2. Main actors in biodiversity policy

2.1. Institutions

In the 2000s, Brazil strengthened its institutional framework for biodiversity policy. The Ministry of the Environment (MMA) is responsible for biodiversity conservation, restoration and sustainable use. Federal executive agencies include the Chico Mendes Institute for Biodiversity Conservation (ICMBio), the Brazilian Institute of Environment and Renewable Natural Resources (IBAMA), the National Water Agency (ANA), the Rio de Janeiro Botanical Garden's Institute of Research (JBRJ) and the Brazilian Forest Service (SFB). ICMBio, established in 2007, is responsible for the implementation of the national policy on federal protected areas and endangered species. IBAMA is mainly responsible for law enforcement and licensing, in co-operation with ICMBio in protected areas and with state and municipal agencies (Chapters 2 and 5).

The National Biodiversity Commission (CONABIO) co-ordinates the design of the national biodiversity policy, oversees its implementation and monitors progress towards Brazil's commitments under the UN Convention on Biological Diversity (CBD). Established in 2003, CONABIO is chaired by the MMA and includes representatives of nine ministries, civil society, the private sector and academia. Several other federal ministries and co-ordination bodies are involved in biodiversity policy.[9] As with other environmental policy areas, however, responsibilities across institutions and levels of government often overlap and effective co-ordination is challenging (Chapter 2).

2.2. Non-government organisations and international co-operation

Non-government organisations (NGOs) and co-operation with international organisations and partner countries play a key role in supporting the design and implementation of biodiversity policy in Brazil. They provide technical capacity, expertise and advice, and leverage funding. They have also helped adopt innovative approaches for biodiversity conservation and sustainable use, and the protection of traditional communities' rights. NGOs often support the implementation of policies and programmes on the ground when institutional capacity is insufficient (Chapter 2).

As of December 2011, Brazil was a party to 233 bilateral and multilateral co-operation agreements, 22% of which had environmental themes. In 2010-13, the largest donors for environmental sustainability were Germany and Norway (Chapter 3). Co-operation with Germany and Norway has focused on the protection of tropical forests and the prevention of Amazon deforestation. Both countries are among the largest donors to the Amazon Fund (Section 6.2). Of the current 55 projects financed by the Global Environment Facility (GEF) in Brazil, 23 target biodiversity, accounting for 45% of total GEF grants received. They include the National Biodiversity Project and the Amazon Region Protected Areas (ARPA) programme (GEF, 2012).

3. The strategic policy framework for biodiversity conservation and sustainable use

Brazil was the first CBD signatory in 1992, and since then it has developed a comprehensive policy framework that is consistent with its commitments under the convention. As a result, Brazil's biodiversity policy has gradually shifted from a strict fence-and-protect and enforcement approach to a sustainable development approach, which identifies biodiversity priority regions and recognises the role of rural, traditional and indigenous communities in preserving ecosystems.

In 2002, Brazil approved its National Biodiversity Strategy and Action Plan, setting out 51 targets to 2010, some more ambitious than the global CBD targets at the time. Only modest progress was made towards these targets. The MMA acknowledges that weaknesses in the criteria and process to define the targets and a lack of monitoring indicators were major obstacles to the success of the strategy (MMA, 2015).

Following the definition of the 20 Aichi Targets at the 2010 CBD Conference of the Parties, Brazil conducted a broad consultation process to define new national biodiversity targets to 2020.[10] In 2013, CONABIO approved 5 strategic objectives and 20 national biodiversity targets, closely aligned with those of the CBD Strategic Plan 2011-20 (Annex 4.A). In addition, the MMA launched a multisector dialogue to develop a Government Action Plan for the Conservation and Sustainable Use of Biodiversity in 2014.

To overcome the implementation difficulties of the 2002 strategy, the multistakeholder panel PainelBio has been conducting a participatory process to define indicators to monitor progress towards the 2020 targets. A mid-term assessment indicates that Brazil is on the right track to achieve most of its targets, although additional efforts are required (MMA, 2015). Impressive progress has been made in reducing habitat loss and degradation and in extending the area under protection in the Amazon (Annex 4.A).

Brazil has developed a comprehensive and stringent legislative framework for biodiversity conservation and sustainable use and launched several biodiversity-related policies and programmes. Among the key laws are the 2000 law establishing a system of protected areas (Chapter 5) and the 2012 Forest Code (Law for the Protection of Native Vegetation), which regulates the protection of forests in private properties and sets up the Rural Environmental Cadastre (Section 5.2), along with comprehensive legislation on access to genetic resources and benefit sharing (Section 5.8).

Some states, including São Paulo, Paraná and Rio Grande do Sul, have developed biodiversity strategies and action plans or programmes (Box 4.2). However, ensuring consistency and synergy with the federal biodiversity policies, programmes and targets is challenging.

Brazilian biodiversity policy has heavily focused on combating deforestation, including through the creation of a protected area system, in part in response to international pressure. While Brazil should maintain the high level of attention on this area, more policy emphasis is needed on marine, coastal and inland water ecosystems. Overall, there has been a proliferation of biodiversity-related plans and programmes since the 2000s, often with overlapping objectives. It is unclear to what extent they have been implemented or yielded the expected results. With few exceptions, implementation of biodiversity policies and plans is not systematically monitored; evaluation of their effectiveness, costs and benefits is rarely conducted.

4. An integrated strategy to combat deforestation

Rising deforestation rates in the Amazon in the early 2000s prompted increasing pressure from civil society and the international community to take decisive action. In response, the Brazilian government considerably scaled up efforts to control deforestation. In 2004, it launched the Action Plan for Prevention and Control of Deforestation in Amazônia Legal (PPCDAm). In 2006, the government pledged to reduce deforestation in Amazônia

Box 4.2. **The biodiversity action plan of São Paulo state**

São Paulo was a pioneer in developing a state-level plan to support the implementation of the CBD. The Action Plan of the State of São Paulo 2011-20, launched in 2013, consolidated existing initiatives contributing to the 20 targets of the convention, and identified further actions needed. The São Paulo Biodiversity Commission oversees its implementation.

To facilitate and structure the plan's implementation, existing and proposed activities have been assessed against three criteria – generation of positive impacts, measurable results and simplicity – and grouped into seven action streams: i) awareness raising for biodiversity; ii) evaluation of São Paulo's biodiversity; iii) reducing the pressure on São Paulo's biodiversity; iv) support for sustainable production and consumption; v) instruments for biodiversity conservation; vi) ecological restoration; and vii) knowledge management. For each action stream, a project line with several concrete goals and outputs has been established. Examples of specific actions under the plan include the creation of a biodiversity portal (*www.portaldabiodiversidade.sp.gov.br*), the development of biodiversity indicators and projects on zero deforestation, forest fire control, invasive species, green economy and sectoral sustainability and protected areas, as well as the development of a support system for forest restoration. The state environment secretariat estimates that the plan's projected value exceeds BRL 100 million.

Source: MMA (2015), *Fifth National Report to the Convention on Biological Diversity*; SMA (2013), *Action Plan of the State of São Paulo. Aichi targets 2020.*

Legal by 80% by 2020 (compared with the average of the previous 10 years). This commitment was later incorporated into the National Climate Change Policy as a key element of Brazil's strategy to curb greenhouse gas (GHG) emissions (Chapter 2). It was also reinforced as part of the national biodiversity targets (target 5; see Annex 4.A).

The PPCDAm set forth an integrated strategy and an innovative governance structure, which put deforestation on the agenda of other sectors (CEPAL et al., 2011). Programme implementation was undertaken by 13 ministries and co-ordinated by the Executive Office of the Presidency (Casa Civil). The plan, currently in its third phase (2012-15), is based on three main streams of work, discussed below.

The first stream aims at clarifying land tenure in the Amazon to reduce incentives for deforestation (Section 1.1; Figure 4.4). In combination with the ARPA programme (Chapter 5), more than 500 000 km^2 of federal and state-level protected areas have been created since the start of the programme, mostly along the so-called "deforestation arc" (comprising the eastern and southern edges of the forests in the states of Rondônia, Mato Grosso and Pará) and in areas expecting road infrastructure development. This was essential in slowing the advance of deforestation for land speculation purposes (CEPAL et al., 2011; Pires, 2014). In addition, 100 000 km^2 of indigenous lands have been granted legal status and thousands of rural land holdings have been geo-referenced under the Terra Legal programme (Box 4.3).

The second work stream focuses on strengthening monitoring, enforcement and compliance. The environmental monitoring systems have been significantly enhanced to reach world-class levels (Box 4.4). This has been crucial in supporting the identification of priority locations for the creation of protected areas and allowing for informed planning of enforcement actions.

Box 4.3. **The Terra Legal programme**

The Terra Legal programme was launched in 2009 by the Ministry of Agrarian Development. It aims to regularise the occupation of federal public lands in the Amazon, fight land grabbing, control deforestation and promote sustainable development initiatives. The programme aims to provide land titles to around 300 000 rural properties occupied prior to 1 December 2004, corresponding to an area of 674 000 km^2. This regularisation gives farmers much needed legal security, as the new land titles effectively prevent future disputes over the ownership of the property.

The regularisation process involves periodic inter-institutional consultation meetings and is based on reliable spatial data. By 2014, more than 60 000 plots (covering 390 000 km^2) had been geo-referenced, and more than 10 000 titles on over 55 000 km^2 of lands had been granted (MDA, 2014). These achievements are noteworthy, and pave the way for continued implementation. In addition, about 50 000 km^2 of federal public land was assigned to the MMA for the creation of protected areas (Chapter 5).

Source: MDA (2014), "Programa Terra Legal".

Hundreds of enforcement operations have been carried out in an integrated manned by IBAMA, the Federal Police, the National Security Force and the Army, based on technical criteria and territorial priorities. Since 2008, inspections have also resulted in the economic embargo of illegally deforested areas: landholders are forbidden to sell products originating from these areas and the environmental liability extends to buyers along the market chain. Inspections have resulted in more than BRL 7 billion in fines, prison sentences for over

Box 4.4. **Brazil's deforestation monitoring systems**

The National Institute for Space Research (INPE) has monitored forest cover in the Legal Amazon region annually since 1988. This monitoring system was improved in 2002 with the adoption of digital classification of satellite images using the Amazon Programme on Deforestation Monitoring (PRODES) methodology. This new approach drastically improved the precision of deforestation monitoring. INPE also runs the Real Time Detection Programme (DETER), a deforestation monitoring system in the Amazon, which shows alerts every two to three days and has been a key support to strategic law enforcement actions. In addition, the DEGRAD system monitors forest degradation and the TerraClass analysis assesses land-use change in previously deforested areas (MMA, 2015). According to TerraClass data, about one-third of the Amazon cleared forest land has been recovering.

In addition to annual monitoring of the Amazon forest cover, in 2008 IBAMA started a satellite monitoring programme (Programme on Satellite Monitoring of Deforestation in Brazilian Biomes, or PMDBBS) for the other five terrestrial biomes. However, PRODES is more precise than the systems used by PMDBBS. Therefore, INPE and IBAMA are collaborating to develop a monitoring system for the entire national territory to generate continuous and compatible data series on deforestation, vegetation cover and land use for all biomes.

Civil society has also played a central role in supporting monitoring. For example, the NGO SOS Mata Atlântica supported monitoring vegetation cover in the Atlantic Forest biome and the NGO Imazon recently launched a new deforestation and forest degradation monitoring system for the Amazon.

600 people, the seizure of about 860 000 cubic metres of illegally logged wood and an embargo on 600 km^2 of land used for illegal activities (WWF, 2015).

Restrictions to credit from public financial institutions to landholders in municipalities with critical deforestation levels have spurred enforcement effectiveness and improved compliance. Since 2007, the MMA has maintained a blacklist of such municipalities. This has encouraged rural landholders and local authorities to work together to get their municipalities off the blacklist. In addition, a 2008 resolution of the Brazilian Central Bank made access to subsidised rural credit in the Amazon biome conditional on the legitimacy of land claims and provision of information to demonstrate compliance with environmental regulations, especially with the Forest Code (Section 5.2). As a result of this resolution, Assunção et al. (2013) estimated that BRL 2.9 billion in loans were not contracted between 2008 and 2011, roughly 90% of which were linked to cattle ranching. This is estimated to have avoided clearing of over 2 700 km^2 of land in 2009-11.

The PPCDAm's third work stream promotes sustainable production chains that provide alternatives to deforestation, as well as technology and innovation for sustainable development in the Amazon (Box 4.5). Actions taken include training and capacity building for sustainable forestry, agricultural and livestock production practices, sustainable timber logging concessions and minimum guaranteed price policies for Amazonian food products (Sections 5.7 and 7.2).

Box 4.5. **The National Institute for Amazon Research**

The National Institute for Amazon Research (INPA), founded in 1952, is one of the world's largest and most important research institutions on tropical biology. It originally focused on plant and animal inventories, but its current mission is to increase scientific knowledge of the Amazon biome with a view to promoting the economic use of its natural resources and forest conservation.

INPA runs a wide range of research groups around four major thematic clusters: biodiversity; environmental dynamics; technology and innovation; and society, environment and health. It also runs several graduate and post-graduate programmes and operates as a major training centre to respond to increasing demand for qualified personnel. As of 2014, more than 1 500 professionals have been trained.

INPA is also working with local communities to improve the sustainable use of biodiversity. This takes the form of educational workshops, technical training and other forms of capacity building to disseminate knowledge generated. Topics covered include dissemination of knowledge on sustainable agricultural practises for enhanced soil quality and agricultural output; water purification; alternative construction woods; and alternative forms of biomass for energy generation.

Source: Based on INPA (2015), INPA website, *http://portal.inpa.gov.br/.*

The PPCDAm is widely recognised as an effective strategy, which can serve as a model for other countries (WWF, 2015). The combination of this plan, rural credit restrictions and economic embargo of illegally deforested areas has greatly contributed to reducing deforestation in the Amazon. As a result, Brazil is likely to overshoot its 2020 target (Section 1; Figures 4.3 and 4.7). Assunção et al. (2013) estimate that these policies avoided 62 000 km^2 of deforestation between 2005 and 2009. Other factors may have also contributed, including declining prices of agricultural products. Building on the success of PPCDAm, the government launched a similar programme to control deforestation in the Cerrado biome (Box 4.6).

Box 4.6. **Action Plan for the Prevention and Control of Deforestation and Fires in the Cerrado**

The Action Plan for the Prevention and Control of Deforestation and Fires in the Cerrado (PPCerrado) aims to reduce deforestation by 40% by 2020 compared to historical deforestation rates. Implementation of the plan started in 2009. It was extended to involve several government agencies in early 2010 with its integration in the National Climate Change Policy (Chapter 2). It is structured around the same three work streams as the PPCDAm.

An important feature of the PPCerrado is the development of a priority list of deforestation areas, which includes 52 municipalities. The list is based on deforestation levels observed in 2009-10, remaining native vegetation cover and the presence of protected areas in the municipality. The municipalities on the priority list correspond to only 4% of the total number of municipalities in the Cerrado biome, but accounted for 44% of deforestation and 22% of the remaining native vegetation cover in 2009-10. To improve the monitoring and evaluation of the plan's effectiveness, IBAMA and INPE are working on the definition of a baseline and on the enhancement of the vegetation monitoring system (Box 4.4).

Source: MMA (2015), *Brazil Fifth National Report to the Convention on Biological Diversity*.

Challenges in the Amazon still remain. Progress has been uneven across the states that share the Amazon. The states of Pará, Mato Grosso and Rondônia are among the top contributors to deforestation (Figure 4.7). In 2014, for example, about 12% of Amazon deforestation in Mato Grosso and 16% in Pará occurred illegally in so-called Legal Reserve areas (Gibbs et al., 2015). These areas are required to be set aside by the forest legislation (Section 5.2). The lack of clarity in land tenure remains a major issue (Figure 4.4), keeping deforestation for speculative purposes attractive.

The command-and-control pillar of the PPCDAm has been the most successful so far. However, the more monitoring systems and enforcement actions improve, the more sophisticated the strategies for illegally clearing the land become (e.g. by deforesting small parcels of land or selectively logging high-value timber). This, in turn, requires increasing costs for upgrading the monitoring systems, investing in equipment (e.g. vehicles) and training the inspectors (WWF, 2015). Brazil should continue to reinforce the satellite-based deforestation monitoring systems (Box 4.4), especially for the Caatinga and Cerrado biomes where most future deforestation is expected, as well as adapting them to detect forest degradation. While the full implementation of the Rural Environmental Cadastre will further improve enforcement and compliance (Section 5.2), it is challenging for the government and its agencies to keep pace with thousands of small-scale deforestation events occurring in the huge Brazilian Amazon area.

Accompanying monitoring and enforcement actions with promotion of sustainable activities is, therefore, essential to effectiveness of the PPCDAm and PPCerrado (Box 4.6). There is a need to make sustainable logging and production chains more attractive than illegal logging and land grabbing and to promote practices that can offer alternative

Figure 4.7. **Policy measures have effectively helped curb deforestation**

Annual deforestation in Amazônia legal, 2000-14

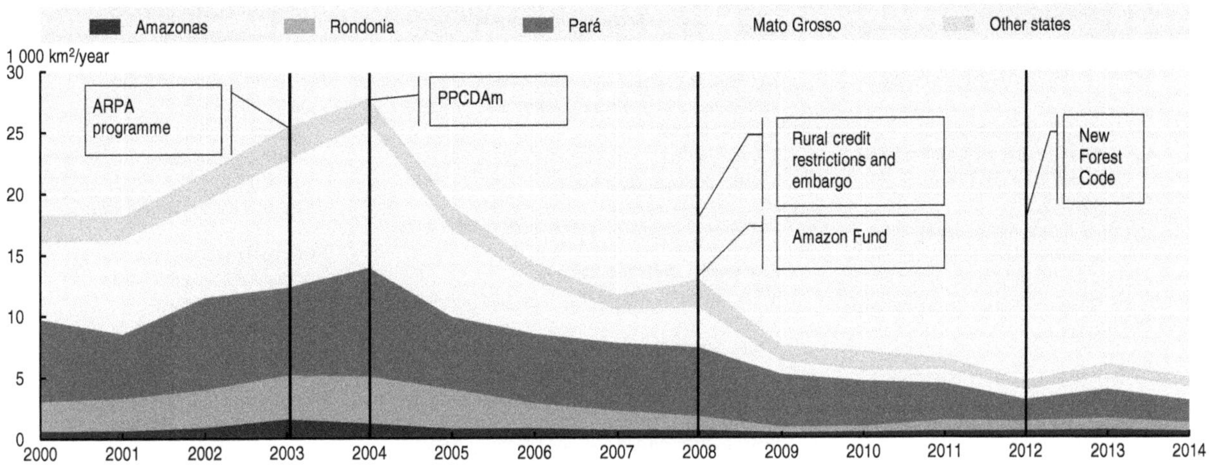

Source: Based on INPE (2015), "Projeto PRODES: Monitoramento da floresta Amazônia Brasileira por satélite".

StatLink http://dx.doi.org/10.1787/888933279713

income sources to local and traditional communities. Illegal logged wood is up to 40% cheaper than legal wood, which makes sustainable forest management uncompetitive (Nogueron and Cheung, 2013). The transaction costs involved in sustainable forest management are still too high, and many rural families do not have the knowledge or the means to adopt sustainable forestry and farming practices (WWF, 2015) (Section 7.2). This requires an integrated approach to promote research, training, technology supply, credit, technical assistance and market access, as well as more active engagement of the business sector (CEPAL et al., 2011).

5. Policy instruments for biodiversity conservation and sustainable use

Brazil has implemented a wide set of policy instruments to promote the protection, restoration and sustainable use of biodiversity. Following the categories used by the OECD (2013), these policy instruments can be classified as regulatory, economic, and voluntary and information approaches. Table 4.2 shows the key instruments in each category that Brazil has implemented and indicates where in the report they are discussed.

Overall, Brazil's biodiversity policy largely relies on regulatory approaches, but the use of economic instruments for biodiversity conservation and sustainable use has been broadened. Most such instruments aim to reward biodiversity-friendly actions, such as the use of good agricultural practices (Section 7.1). Such positive incentives can be effective because most rural private properties are small and rural people are among the poorest in the country and depend on the use of natural resources.

The use of taxes, charges and fees is very limited. The 1997 National Water Resources Policy Law introduced water abstraction and effluent charges as water resource management tools. However, only a few states and river basins charge for water. When charges exist, unit prices are often too low to affect decisions about water allocation and use (Chapter 3). National parks can charge entrance fees, but only a few of them have done so and have the capacity to collect such fees (Chapter 5).

Table 4.2. **Main policy instruments for biodiversity conservation and sustainable use in Brazil**

Regulatory instruments	Economic Instruments	Information and voluntary approaches
Restrictions or prohibitions on use or on access: • Protected areas (Chapter 5) • Set-aside native vegetation areas, as foreseen in the 2012 Forest Code (Section 5.2) • Rural Environmental Cadastre (Section 5.2) • Regulation on access to genetic resources and benefit sharing (Section 5.8) • Embargo on illegally deforested areas (Section 4) Planning and licensing instruments: • Ecological-economic zoning (Section 5.1) • Environmental licensing (Chapter 2) Permits and quotas • Concessions for sustainable timber logging (Section 7.2)	Payment for ecosystem services systems and conditional cash-transfer programmes (Section 5.5), including: • Bolsa Floresta • Bolsa Verde • Water producer programme Tradable environmental reserve quotas (Section 5.3) Biodiversity offsets (Section 5.4) • Environmental reserve offsets, as foreseen in the 2012 Forest Code • Environmental compensation in the framework of environmental licensing (Chapters 2 and 5) • Financial compensation for water and mining resources. Water abstraction and pollution charges (Chapter 3) National park entrance fees (Chapter 5) Subsidies (e.g. for good agricultural practice) (Section 7.1) Rural credit restrictions (Section 4). Removal of environmentally harmful subsidies.	Eco-labelling and certification: • Certification of organic products (Section 7.1) • Timber certification (Section 7.2) • Life certification (Section 5.6) Green public procurement: • National Plan to Promote the Production Chain of Socio-Biodiversity Products (Section 5.7) Voluntary agreements • Soya Moratorium (Box 4.9)

Source: Adapted from OECD (2013), *Scaling-up Finance Mechanisms for Biodiversity*.

Some progress has been made in mainstreaming biodiversity considerations in financial support policies, such as linking the access to concessional rural credits to compliance with environmental regulations (Section 7.1). However, little progress has been made in identifying and phasing out subsidies that can be detrimental to biodiversity and ecosystems as foreseen by the national biodiversity target 3. These include implicit subsidies such as tax exemptions for fertilisers and pesticides (Section 7.1). Brazil would benefit from improving the analysis of subsidies that can be environmentally harmful, with a view to gradually removing those subsidies that are not justified on economic, social and environmental grounds. Sound information about the magnitude of subsidies and their impact is needed to build support for subsidy reforms.

5.1. *Ecological-economic zoning*

The National Environment Policy introduced environmental or ecological-economic zoning (ZEE) as a landscape-scale planning and management tool, aimed at allocating compatible activities in defined environmental areas so as to maintain sustainable use of natural resources and a balanced ecosystem. ZEE has been effectively used since 2002; in 2013, the MMA released methodological guidelines to support the preparation of ZEEs at the subnational level and their co-ordination with other territorial planning instruments (e.g. water resource plans).

The MMA led the development of a macro ZEE of the Legal Amazon, approved in 2010; the macro ZEEs of the Cerrado biome and the São Francisco river basin were under development at the time of writing. Several states have also developed state-level ZEEs. By 2013, ZEEs covered 73% of Brazil's territory (Figure 4.8), including the entirety of the Amazon and Pantanal biomes. ZEEs also cover about 62% of the Cerrado biome and 22% of the Atlantic Forest biome, but less than 2% of the Caatinga (MMA, 2015).

Figure 4.8. **The area under ecological-economic zoning has expanded**

Total surface covered by ZEE projects, 2005-11

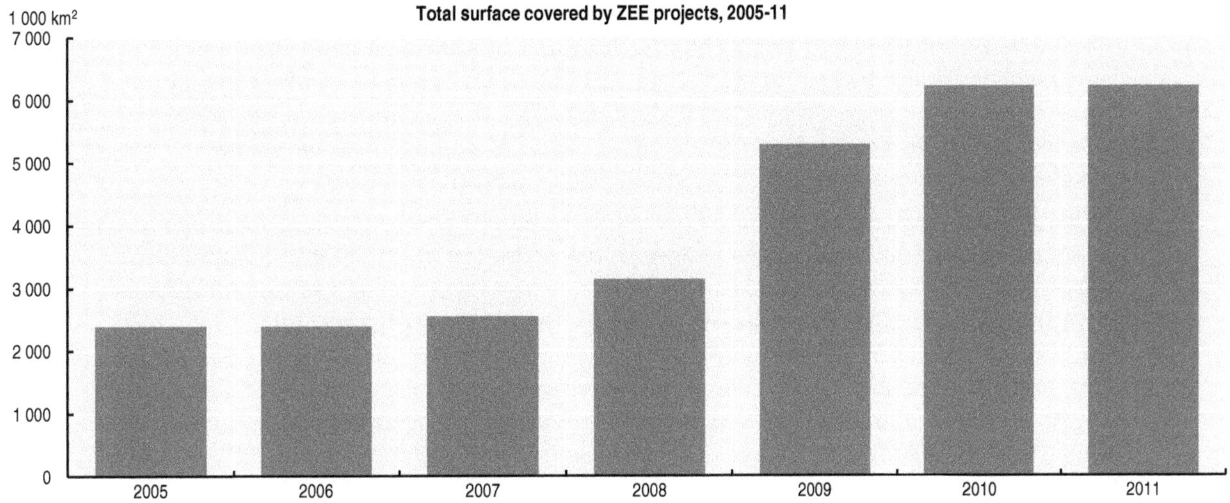

Note: The overlapping of areas of state and federal initiatives is not considered.
Source: MMA (2014), *PNIA 2012: Painel Nacional de Indicadores Ambientais. Referencial teórico, composição e síntese dos indicadores.*

StatLink http://dx.doi.org/10.1787/888933279724

ZEE maps and guidelines are made available as territorial and development planning tools, but there is no evidence that they have been effectively used in spatial planning and policy making. In addition, the municipal capacity to implement zoning requirements is weak (Chapter 2). In a welcome move, the 2012 Forest Code (Section 5.2) required all states to approve their ZEEs by 2017.

5.2. *Forest conservation and restoration obligations on private properties*

In 2012, Brazil approved the new Forest Code (Law for the Protection of Native Vegetation), which replaced and updated the 1965 code. The new Forest Code aims to reconcile the objectives of preserving biodiversity and forests and of ensuring a good business environment for agriculture, a key sector of Brazil's economy.

The Forest Code, modified several times, had traditionally been Brazil's most important legal instrument to protect native vegetation on private properties. The 1965 code required landowners to maintain native vegetation on a proportion of their properties – the so-called Legal Reserve (RL) – and along water bodies and sensitive areas to protect water resources and prevent soil erosions – the so-called Permanent Preservation Area (APP). However, levels of compliance have historically being low, with considerable areas being deforested illegally.

In response, the new and updated Forest Code introduced more effective enforcement instruments, although some of its elements have been criticised as being too indulgent towards commercial interests and less protective than the old code (Box 4.7). The new law maintained the requirements to conserve or restore vegetation cover in RL and APP areas, although it changed the definitions of these areas. The percentage of rural properties to be maintained as RL varies according to biome: up to 80% in the Amazon, 20% to 35% in the Cerrado biome and 20% in the Atlantic Forest and other biomes.

To improve monitoring of, and compliance with, the forest conservation requirements, the new code introduced the Rural Environmental Cadastre (CAR). The system uses high-

Box 4.7. The new Forest Code: Some critical elements

The 2012 Forest Code was approved after long and intense national debate and it has been highly criticised by environmentalists. Among the criticised elements of the law are a partial amnesty granted on illegal deforestation that occurred before 2008, the broadening of possibilities for offsite compensation of damage to ecosystems and the transfer of legislative autonomy to the state level (Leitão, 2014).

The new law reduced the total area previously required to be set aside as APPs and RLs by adjusting their definition. The changes in the definition of hilltop preservation areas (part of APPs), for example, reduced their total area by 87%. About 90% of rural properties (covering less than 30% of rural areas) qualify as "small" properties according to the new law,* and benefit from the amnesty on illegal deforestation in RL and APP areas before 2008. Under the previous Forest Code, landowners would have been required to restore the illegally deforested areas at their own expense. Overall, the changes to the forest code reduced by 58% the total forest area to be restored (to about 210 000 km^2), affecting mainly the Amazon, Atlantic Forest and Cerrado biomes (Soares-Filho et al., 2014b).

* The law defines small properties as those whose size ranges from 20 ha (0.2 km^2) in southern Brazil to 440 ha (4.4 km^2) in the Amazon.

resolution satellite images, which are the basis for localising and registering each rural parcel. Registration in the CAR is mandatory for all rural properties and holdings, including information about the RL and APP in each area, by May 2016. The rural properties that do not comply with the land set-aside obligations will be required to join a state-level environmental regularisation programme. As required by the Brazilian Central Bank, CAR registration will be a condition to access rural credits, from both public and private banks, as from October 2017. Although the CAR is not designed for regularising land property rights, the authorities responsible for rural development and settlements can use the geo-referenced information about the location of rural plots (as declared by their owners or holders) to clarify land tenure.

The CAR implementation is on track: as of April 2015 about 53% of the private rural area to be registered actually had been. States are responsible for the implementation of the cadastre, but in many states less than 20% of the target rural area has been registered, especially in the North-east region (SFB, 2015a). The delay is caused in large part by a lack of staff and resources at the state and municipal levels. The federal government has invested in establishing the necessary information system and in building implementation capacity at state level. It developed a detailed plan for the implementation of the CAR, including appropriate budget, timeline and targets.

Strict enforcement of the new code, as well as clarification of land tenure, is expected to greatly help reducing deforestation rates further. More efforts are needed to raise awareness about the CAR – e.g. by launching information campaigns to encourage registration – and to develop capacities of states and municipalities to implement the system. States need also to quickly develop their environmental regularisation programmes, which non-compliant rural holders need to adhere to. More incentive-based measures, such as payments for ecosystem services (Section 5.5) and the REDD+ mechanism, could be considered to encourage registration and reward compliant landowners.

5.3. Tradable forest quotas

The new Forest Code also introduces an economic instrument, Environmental Reserve Quotas (CRAs), to facilitate compliance with the land set-aside obligations. CRAs can be issued for each hectare of area maintained as native vegetation in excess of the RL requirement and be used to offset a RL deficit in a different property within the same biome, preferably within the same state. In practice, landholders who do not meet the RL obligation can either restore the tree cover of the area or purchase an equivalent amount of CRAs. Only properties which had a RL deficit prior to 2008 are allowed to use this mechanism. The system, therefore, creates demand for forested areas and enables the emergence of a market for conservation of private land. The system ultimately encourages maintaining the forest cover on areas in excess of the RLs (which could be legally deforested), instead of restoring the tree cover in areas that have been deforested (Soares-Filho et al., 2014b).

Four million of the about 5.6 million rural properties do not meet the legal vegetation cover obligations. While the size of the "deficit" in native vegetation will be known only after full implementation of the CAR, it is estimated at between 160 000 and 300 000 km^2, concentrated in the Amazon, Atlantic Forest and Cerrado biomes (BV Rio, 2014). Restoring a hectare of the Amazon forest can cost up to BRL 15 000 (in addition to the opportunity costs of alternative land use), which can be prohibitively high for small rural holders (Financial Times, 2012). Soares-Filho et al. (2014b) estimate that compensating the RL deficit by purchasing CRAs would be cheaper than restoration for about 92 000 km^2. The demand for CRAs is, therefore, potentially large and could be a cost-effective way of ensuring compliance with the forest legislation. For example, Bernasconi (2013) estimates a 76% reduction in the compliance costs in São Paulo state.

CRA transactions need to be registered in the CAR, which is still under implementation. Therefore, no CRA has been issued yet. The Bolsa Verde do Rio de Janeiro, a non-profit organisation, launched a platform to make the exchange of future CRAs possible. As of end-2013, this platform had registered 1 600 participants and more than 15 000 km^2 of rural properties offering CRAs, which signals good market prospects (BV Rio, 2014).

While the CRA system is promising, there is a risk that only low-opportunity-cost areas may be competitive in the market, leading to increased conservation of areas that do not necessarily have the highest biodiversity value. Adjusting the system design to allow CRA exchanges within the same priority areas, in terms of biodiversity value, would likely raise compliance costs, but environmental effectiveness would improve (Bernasconi, 2013). Thus, it may be necessary to provide additional incentives to ensure that high-biodiversity-value areas are restored. The functioning of the system should be systematically monitored and allow for the adjustments necessary to achieve its forest preservation and restoration objectives.

5.4. Environmental offsets

In addition to the CRA market, the legislation allows compensation of the RL deficit by buying private properties within official protected areas on behalf of the government, i.e. paying owners of land within protected areas and transferring the tenure title to the government. This offset mechanism would allow the consolidation of protected areas, many of which include extensive private lands (Chapter 5).

An offset mechanism is in place within the environmental licensing procedure. An environmental licence is required before the construction, installation, expansion and functioning of any enterprise or activity that is deemed to be effectively or potentially polluting, or that could cause environmental degradation (Chapter 2). In addition to meet the environmental impact mitigation requirements indicated in the licence, project developers can be required to pay an environmental compensation, whose amount varies according to the severity of the environmental impact of the project. Clear mechanisms for monetising the environmental impact and the amount of the compensation are still missing. All revenue from environmental compensation is earmarked for protected areas (Chapter 5).

In addition, financial compensation requirements apply to operators of hydropower plants (6.75% of the value of electricity produced) and mines (between 1% and 3% of turnover) to compensate for the use of water and natural resources. The amounts are substantial and are shared between the federal government and the state and municipal governments affected by the installations. These charges, however, do not reflect the value of resources (e.g. water scarcity) and do not contribute to their efficient use (OECD, 2015). Revenue is not earmarked to compensate for environmental degradation. In some other countries, such as Colombia, revenue from hydropower financial compensation is partly earmarked for environmental and watershed protection (OECD, 2015b).

5.5. *Payments for ecosystem services and conditional cash-transfer programmes*

Brazil has implemented several payments for ecosystem services (PES) and conditional cash-transfer programmes that integrate environmental requirements, at both federal and state levels; examples include Bolsa Floresta and Bolsa Verde, discussed below. Another example is the Water Producer Programme, launched in 2011 by the National Water Agency to financially compensate investment in soil and water protection in river basins that provide water resources to a large population. Conservation activities include building terraces and infiltration basins, restoring and protecting riparian vegetation, and adopting sustainable farming practices.

A legislative proposal to establish a national PES policy and a federal PES programme has been under parliamentary discussion since 2007. While Brazil does not yet have a national legal framework governing PES, the new Forest Code opens the possibility of using such instruments at federal level. In the absence of an overarching national framework, several states and municipalities have elaborated their own laws and PES programmes. Table 4.3 provides some examples. Guedes and Seehusen (2011) identified 78 such programmes for water conservation, carbon storage and biodiversity protection in the Atlantic Forest biome.

The PES and cash-transfer programmes and legislation currently in place vary widely across states and federal agencies in terms of payment and valuation methods,

Table 4.3. **Examples of state-level PES laws**

Region/ State	Law
North	
Acre	State System of Incentives for Environmental Services (SISA; Law 2308/2010)
Amazonas	Law of the State Climate Change Policy, Environmental Conservation and Sustainable Development of the Amazon (Law 3135/2007 and Law 3184/ 2007)
Mato Grosso	The State System for Reducing Emissions from Deforestation and Forest Degradation, Conservation, Sustainable Management of Forests and Enhancement of Forest Carbon Stocks (REDD+)
South-east	
Espírito Santo	Law of PES (Law 8995/2009)
Minas Gerais	Law of Green Grant (Law 17.727/2008)
São Paulo	Law of the State Climate Change Policy (Law 1/2009)

Source: Adapted from Guedes and Seehusen (2011), *Pagamento por Serviços Ambientais na Mata Atlântica, Lições Aprendidas e Desafios*.

socio-environmental safeguards, institutional arrangements and sources of funds. Beneficiaries are mostly rural family producers and settlers, traditional communities and indigenous peoples. These programmes have rarely established sound monitoring systems and their effectiveness is not systematically evaluated. For example, the Water Producer Programme has generated income for over 1 000 rural people (MMA, 2015), but the extent to which this has resulted in an additional level of protection of water resources is unclear.

Most PES and conditional cash-transfer programmes are government financed. As the costs of these programmes, including investment in field activities and administrative costs, can be high, it is necessary to identify alternative source of funding to expand the scale and scope of PES and cash-transfer systems and reach more beneficiaries (Guedes and Seehusen, 2011). Developing more standardised programmes would also help lower the transaction costs. Brazil would benefit from developing framework PES legislation to improve consistency of programmes across the country. Establishing a sound monitoring system is also necessary to verify the delivery of the ecosystem services that are being paid for. Such a system could be helpfully linked to the CAR, which represents an important source of information to improve monitoring.

Bolsa Floresta

Bolsa Floresta (*bolsa* means stipend or grant) is a pioneer PES programmes launched by the state of Amazonas in 2007. It is mainly a cash-transfer system based on some environmental requirements. It aims to compensate traditional and local families living in state-level sustainable development reserves for their environmental conservation efforts, mainly to limit the amount of forested lands cleared and converted to farming (Box 4.8). It is the first internationally certified programme of its type in Brazil, and one of the largest REDD+ pilot projects in the world, providing income to more than of 35 000 people scattered in hundreds of communities. Resources for this programme are provided through a partnership between the government of the state of Amazonas and some large companies.

Börner et al. (2013) found evidence of positive impacts of Bolsa Floresta on local quality of life and biodiversity conservation in selected sustainable use areas. Income and access to health and education had increased for 86% of the surveyed families; with better income, households were also able to better resist to deforestation pressures coming from people outside the communities. Deforestation decreased faster in the protected areas participating in the programme than in the others.

The programme has been implemented so far in areas where there is relatively low pressure over forest resources and beneficiaries are homogeneous. The opportunity cost of complying with the rules of the programme is relatively low for most participants. Börner et al. (2013) suggest that scaling up the programme and extending it to areas under higher deforestation pressures would require stronger and more differentiated incentives and greater involvement of the participants in monitoring activities and in protection against external threats.

Bolsa Verde

Building on the Bolsa Floresta initiative, in 2011 the federal government launched Bolsa Verde as part of Brasil Sem Miséria (Chapter 3), extending the federal social protection system to include payments conditional on the use of environmentally sustainable practices. The programme is also intended to promote participation of beneficiaries in environmental, social and technical training.

Box 4.8. **Bolsa Floresta and Bolsa Verde**

The **Bolsa Floresta programme** has four components:

i) The Income Forest Stipend (Bolsa Floresta Renda) is an incentive to sustainable income-producing activities (e.g. fish farming, non-timber forest products or ecotourism), and invests BRL 140 000 per year in each protected area.

ii) The Social Forest Stipend (Bolsa Floresta Social) has the objective of enhancing community development, public service provision and quality of life of isolated communities, investing BRL 140 000 per year in each protected area according to a participatory work plan.

iii) The Family Forest Stipend (Bolsa Floresta Familiar) is an incentive to families to reduce deforestation, paying a monthly reward of BRL 50 to mothers living inside protected areas who commit to environmental conservation and sustainable development (mainly a commitment not to deforest and not to use resources unsustainably).

iv) The Association Forest Stipend (Bolsa Floresta Associação) grants the equivalent of 10% of the total amount paid for the Family Forest Stipend to strengthen local producer associations composed of families living in protected areas. Funds are also used to promote social control over the Forest Stipend programme.

The **Bolsa Verde programme** has four main objectives: i) promoting ecosystem conservation and sustainable use; ii) promoting community participation and improvement of participants' quality of life; iii) increasing the income of people living in extreme poverty who carry out activities for the conservation of natural resources in rural areas; and iv) promoting the participation of beneficiaries in environmental, social, technical and professional capacity-building activities.

Bolsa Verde provides quarterly grants of BRL 300 to extremely poor families living in some categories of federal protected areas and other designated areas,* in return to commitments to certain conservation efforts and sustainable use activities. By including territories occupied by traditional and indigenous communities, the programme recognises these communities' role in preserving environmental services. To participate in the programme, families must be beneficiaries of Bolsa Família and registered in the Single Registry (Box 3.1). Payments through Bolsa Verde are additional to benefits received through Bolsa Família. The benefit may be granted for two years, with the option of renewal.

* The federal areas include sustainable use protected area, environmentally distinctive settlement projects, territories occupied by traditional peoples and communities, and other rural areas defined as priority by decree. Families in extreme poverty are defined by the federal government as those receiving no more than BRL 77 (USD 33) per capita per month.

The number of households enrolled in the programme has steadily grown, mostly in the Amazon biome and in the state of Parà (Figure 4.9). As of 2014, 30% of beneficiaries were living in federal protected areas. The government estimates that there are 213 000 potential beneficiary families living in 1.45 million km^2 of priority areas and that reaching all of them would imply paying BRL 1.72 per hectare per year (MMA, 2015). This is a low price for the potential outcomes in terms of improved living conditions and conservation of natural resources, provided that the beneficiaries effectively make additional conservation efforts thanks to the programme.

However, the programme faces difficulties in maintaining the database of beneficiaries, and no monitoring process or criteria for assessing compliance with conservation commitment are yet in place (CGU, 2014). No training activities had been conducted as of

Figure 4.9. **Participation in the Bolsa Verde programme has steadily grown**

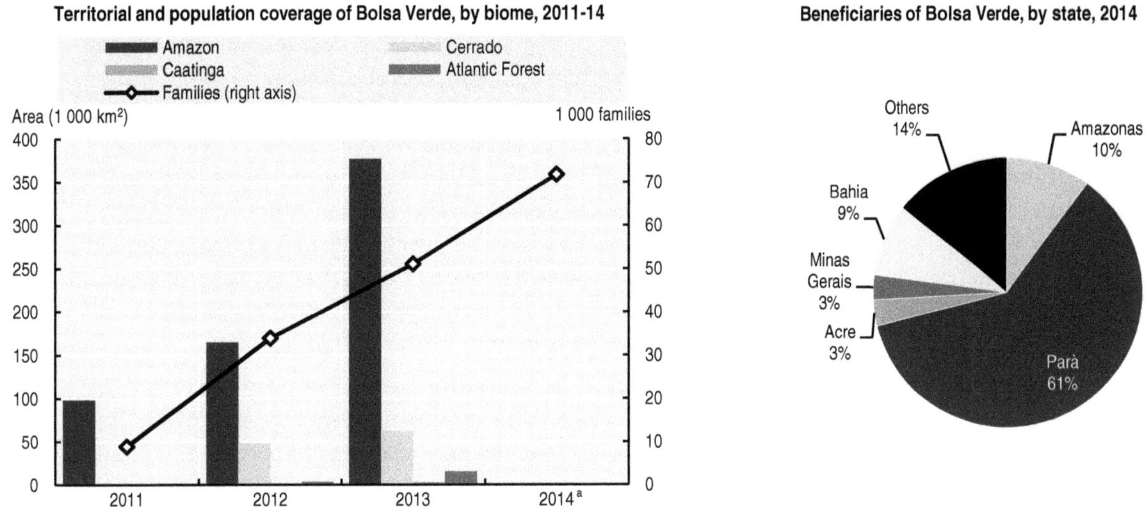

a) Number of beneficiary families as of 25 January 2015.
Source: MMA (2015), "Bolsa Verde", MMA em Números (website); MMA (2014), *PNIA 2012: Painel Nacional de Indicadores Ambientais. Referencial teórico, composição e síntese dos indicadores.*

StatLink http://dx.doi.org/10.1787/888933279736

July 2014, despite such training likely being essential to support beneficiaries in meeting their commitments. In addition, the programme seems complex from an administration point of view, with many institutions involved and managed at central level, far from the beneficiaries. Viana (2015) suggests delegating the management of the programme to the states as a way to improve execution and reach a larger part of the target population.

The lack of monitoring impedes evaluation of the effectiveness of the payments in promoting the conservation of biodiversity in the target areas. Developing a monitoring process, including conservation-based indicators, is necessary to ensure that the programme generates environmental benefits that are additional to the social benefits generated by the Bolsa Família programme (Box 3.1).

5.6. *Voluntary agreements and company certification*

The business sector, especially large companies, has been progressively more active in supporting biodiversity conservation and sustainable use initiatives and in providing related finance.[11] An increasing number of farmers and ranchers have adhered to voluntary registries that require commitments to improving social and environmental performance (Soares-Filho et al., 2014b). Yet as of 2014, only two Brazilian businesses had been certified under Life Certification, a voluntary process to assess a company's environmental management and impact on biodiversity (Instituto Life, 2014).[12]

The business sector has helped combat deforestation in the Amazon. In 2006, following a report from Greenpeace and under pressure from consumers, a group of large companies, in co-operation with the MMA, implemented a supply chain governance agreement called Soya Moratorium, agreeing to stop using soya grown on cleared forestland in the Brazilian Amazon. This initiative was one of the first voluntary zero-deforestation agreements in the world (Box 4.9). A similar initiative, the Beef Slaughterhouse Pact, involves the cattle industry.

The Soya Moratorium has proved effective, as farmers respect the requirements of the demand of the market. According to Gibbs et al. (2015), farmers are five times less likely to

Box 4.9. The Soya Moratorium

In 2006, large companies including McDonald's and Wal-Mart decided to stop buying soya grown on cleared forestland in the Brazilian Amazon, thereby launching the so-called Soya Moratorium. This put pressure on commodity traders, such as Cargill, who in turn agreed to no longer purchase soya from farmers who cleared rainforest to expand soya fields. In all, 47 companies associated with the Brazilian Association of Vegetable Oil Industries (ABIOVE – 12 companies) and the Cereal Exporters National Association (ANEC – 35 companies) joined the moratorium. From the start, the initiative also had strong support and participation from eight civil society organisations: Conservation International, Greenpeace, IPAM, TNC, WWF-Brazil, Amigos da Terra Amazônia Brasileira, Imaflora and STTR Santarém. Since 2008, the MMA has also been part of the initiative.

A study to evaluate the agreement analysed satellite-based imagery covering the Brazilian Amazon forest and the Cerrado from 2000 to 2014 to measure how much land had been cleared to grow soya. The study shows that the moratorium helped to drastically reduce the amount of deforestation linked to soya production. In 2004 and 2005, nearly 30% of soya expansion occurred through deforestation. By 2014, this rate had fallen to only ~1% in the Amazon biome. The study also found there is enough already-cleared, suitable land in the Amazon to allow the soya production area to expand by 600%. In the Cerrado biome, where the Soya Moratorium does not apply, the annual rate of soya expansion into native vegetation remained sizeable, ranging from 11% to 23% over 2007-11 (Gibbs et al., 2015).

Source: Gibbs et al. (2015), "Brazil's Soy Moratorium. Supply-chain governance is needed to avoid deforestation".

violate private sector agreements than they are to violate government policy. This points to the opportunity of further developing voluntary initiatives like the Soya Moratorium after its expiration (in 2016), as well as extending them to the Cerrado biome, where deforestation rates are high. More broadly, there is scope to further engage the business sector in biodiversity protection by promoting sustainable production and consumption plans.

5.7. Green public procurement

In 2012, the government launched its sustainable procurement policy to prioritise environmental goods and services, among other areas (Chapter 2). In addition, a national procurement programme targeting specifically biodiversity-related products exists and similar initiatives have been launched at state level, e.g. in the state of Amazonas (MMA, 2015).

The 2009 National Plan to Promote the Production Chain of Socio-Biodiversity Products (PNPSB) aims to strengthen the production and commercialisation of 30 traditional non-timber products from sustainably managed forests (Section 7.2), thereby providing a source of income for rural communities.[13] It provides facilitated access to credit and markets as well as technical assistance. The PNPSB includes a minimum price programme for selected socio-biodiversity products (PGPMBio), such as açai fruit, natural rubber and Brazil nuts, aimed at supporting producer income. This was recently linked to the large-scale federal Food Acquisition Programme, one of the world's largest institutional procurement programmes for smallholder or family farm products.[14]

The quantity of subsidised production and the number of "extractivists" benefitting from the programme has fluctuated since its establishment in 2009, but the trend is increasing; in 2013, PGPMBio reached 12 000 extractivists in six states, mostly in the Amazon and Atlantic Forest biomes. Subsidy payments reached USD 2.6 million, about 25% of the available budget, which is linked to high market prices (above guaranteed price levels) but also to difficulties in the operationalisation of payments (Viana, 2015).[15] Overall, the subsidy still benefits only a small fraction of total production of the targeted products.[16] Nevertheless, the PGPMBio support has led to an increase in production and commercialisation of socio-biodiversity products and helped increase competition among buyers, with positive income effects for extractive workers (MMA, 2015).

The PNPSB and PGPMBio have been implemented in selected areas, including sustainable use protected areas (Chapter 5). Many producers currently not in such areas have requested a protected area status for the lands they live and work on, in particular that of extractive reserve, because of the potentially higher accessibility to the PNPSB, PGPMBio and other public services.

5.8. Access to genetic resources and benefit sharing

Indigenous lands make up over 13% of Brazil's territory and the country is home to thousands of *quilombolas* and members of traditional communities (Box 5.2), who have considerable knowledge relating to plant and animal resources and how to manage them. This underlines the importance of ensuring access to genetic resources and the fair sharing of the benefits deriving from it for both the effective protection and sustainable use of the resources and the well-being of these communities.

Brazil signed the Nagoya Protocol to the CBD on Access and Benefit-Sharing (ABS) in 2011 and started the process for its ratification. Until May 2015, the Brazilian regulation was included in a provisional emergency rule dating back to 2001, when a business proposal to access and develop Brazil's genetic heritage sparked public concerns about "bio-piracy". This provisional rule severely restricted access to genetic resources for both commercial and scientific purposes (Cabrera et al., 2014).

The emergency rule introduced a highly bureaucratic and time consuming licensing process for accessing genetic resources and traditional knowledge. If access was required for commercial purposes, a bilateral contract was to be signed to set out how the benefits arising from the commercialisation were to be shared. Despite efforts to clarify the terms and scope of the provisional rule, regulatory uncertainty remained high, resulting in only a few benefit-sharing contracts being approved and a large number of pending cases (IEEP et al., 2012). This also constrained research and innovation.[17]

Acknowledging the need to improve regulations, broad public consultations were initiated in 2006, with a view to replacing the interim rule with a comprehensive law. In May 2015, the Parliament approved the Biodiversity Framework Law, which aims at reducing the administrative burden and at improving the participation of indigenous groups and traditional communities in decision making. It sets clear rules and creates a fund for benefit sharing. This could reduce the transaction costs previously associated with bilateral benefit-sharing contracts, including those due to the fact that various indigenous and traditional communities often share resources and knowledge (IEEP et al., 2012). Implementing regulations are due to be issued by November 2015.

Brazil needs to quickly implement the new legislation so as to overcome the bottlenecks associated with the previous ABS regulations while ensuring effective engagement of the indigenous and traditional communities. This could have multiple benefits, notably resulting in innovation and business opportunities, helping vulnerable populations that depend on genetic resources to use them sustainably and providing resources for conservation and sustainable use of biodiversity, for example in protected areas and on indigenous lands.

6. Financing biodiversity conservation and sustainable use

6.1. *The federal budget for biodiversity-related activities*

Several sources contribute to the financing of biodiversity conservation and sustainable use. Comprehensive and consistent information on public and private biodiversity-related spending is not available, however, and Brazil would benefit from developing a resource mobilisation strategy for achieving its national biodiversity targets. The federal budget allocated to selected biodiversity-related programmes, including for managing protected areas and monitoring deforestation in the Amazon, provides an indication of public resources available for biodiversity conservation, although these amounts are probably an underestimate (Table 4.4). Between 2010 and 2014, the federal budget outlays for these biodiversity-related programmes grew by nearly 50% in real terms, in line with the overall growth of the federal budget outlays for environmental management (according to the Treasury's budget classification by government function; see Chapter 2). In 2014, 9% of the budget related to environmental management was allocated to these biodiversity-related programmes.

Table 4.4. **Federal budget outlays for selected biodiversity-related programmes**

BRL million (nominal values), 2010-14

Programme	2010	2011	2012	2013	2014
Integrated information for Amazon protection	99.9	88.9	–	–	–
Conservation and sustainable use of biodiversity and genetic resources	129.0	129.6	–	–	–
Forests	56.7	48.8	–	–	–
Conservation and restoration of Brazilian biomes	96.8	89.4	–	–	–
Conservation, management and sustainable use of agro-biodiversity	23.6	29.4	–	–	–
Biodiversity	–	–	344.5	263.7	514.0
Forests, prevention and control of deforestation and fires	–	–	162.0	249.8	266.3
Total	406.0	386.1	506.4	513.6	780.3
Share of the federal budget outlays for environmental management	*8.9%*	*8.5%*	*8.0%*	*6.4%*	*8.9%*

Source: Senado Federal (2015), *Portal Orçamento* (database).

ICMBio administers most of the budget for biodiversity-related programmes, mainly for managing the federal official protected areas (Chapter 5), followed by the MMA. The real budget of ICMBio increased by 57% between 2008, when it started operating, and 2014, when it reached BRL 783 million (Chapter 2). In 2013, about half of ICMBio's budget was used for staff salaries; investment accounted for between 2% and 11% (Funbio, 2014).

6.2. *Biodiversity-specific funds and other sources of finance*

Several budget and extra-budgetary funds contribute to financing biodiversity-related expenditure. These include the National Fund for the Environment (Chapter 2); the Protected Areas Fund (Chapter 5); the Forest Development Fund, managed by the Brazilian Forest Service to promote sustainable forestry; and the Atlantic Forest Restoration Fund, managed by the MMA to finance environmental restoration and scientific research in the Atlantic Forest biome (Table 2.2).

One of the key funds is the innovative Amazon Fund, established in 2008 to invest in forest conservation and sustainable use and deforestation prevention and monitoring, thereby contributing to reducing GHG emissions resulting from deforestation and forest degradation. At least 80% of the fund's investments are earmarked for the Amazon region and up to 20% can be invested in deforestation monitoring and control in other Brazilian biomes or tropical countries. The fund is managed by the Brazilian Development Bank (BNDES) in co-ordination with the MMA. Most funds come from international donors, mainly Norway and, to a lesser extent, Germany, but also from companies such as Petrobras, the majority-government-owned oil company.[18] The total cumulated contributions received between 2009 and early 2015 amounted to over BRL 2 billion (or USD 970 million). By comparison, the federal budget allocation to ICMBio in 2009-14 was BRL 4 billion (at 2014 prices). The fund has supported an increasing number of projects (Figure 4.10). As of March 2015, the fund had supported 72 projects with USD 339 million, with most projects being in the states of Parà, Amazonas and Mato Grosso (Amazon Fund, 2015).

Figure 4.10. **The Amazon Fund has supported an increasing number of projects**

Projects financed by the Amazon Fund, 2011-15

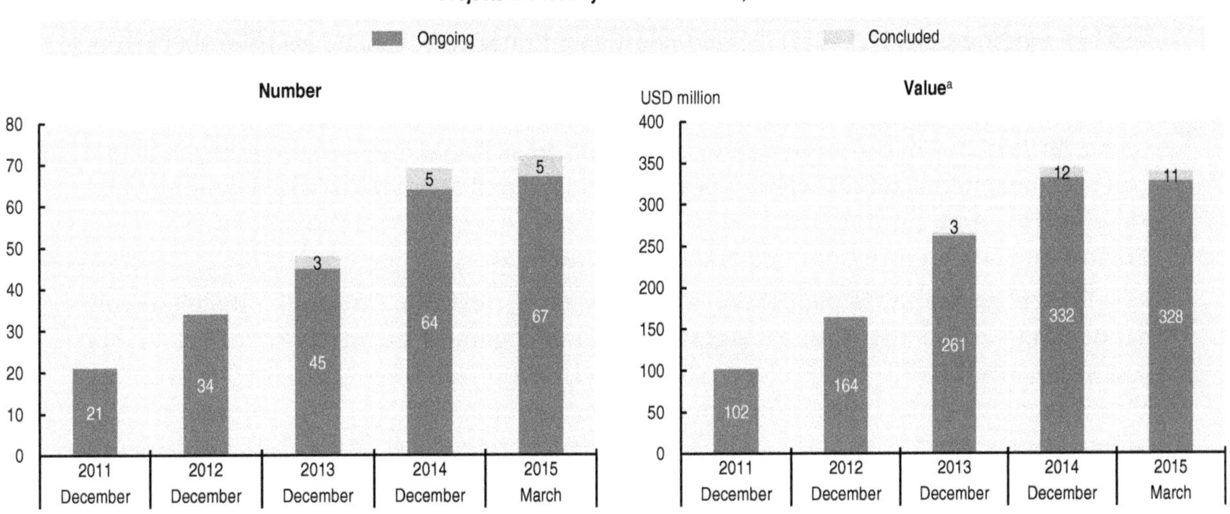

a) At 2015 prices and exchange rates.
Source: Based on Amazon Fund (2015), *Portfolio Report*, 31 March 2015.

StatLink http://dx.doi.org/10.1787/888933279748

Part of the Amazon Fund is channelled through the Brazilian Biodiversity Fund (Funbio), a private non-profit organisation that raises and invests financial resources for biodiversity conservation, mostly in protected areas, on behalf of the federal and state governments. In addition to the Amazon Fund, Funbio manages resources largely provided by partner countries and multilateral organisations such as the GEF (Chapter 5).

Brazil has received about half the total approved international finance from Reducing Emissions from Deforestation and Forest Degradation (REDD and REDD+) through the Amazon Fund (Norman et al., 2014). In June 2014, Brazil was the first country to submit its forest reference emission level for payments under REDD+ as required by the 2013 Warsaw Framework. A national REDD+ strategy has been under discussion since 2010, but has yet to be approved.

Overall, international multilateral and bilateral co-operation as well as private and corporate foundations play an important role in providing finance for biodiversity protection, especially in the Amazon. According to OECD statistics of official development assistance (ODA), in 2010-12 aid flows to Brazil targeting the objectives of the CBD increased four-fold to USD 675 million (at 2012 prices). They dropped to less than half this amount in 2013, however (Figure 3.10).

Estimates by Castro de La Mata and Riega-Campos (2014) indicate that from 2007 to mid-2013, the international funding for conservation of the whole Amazon forest (including that outside Brazil) amounted to USD 1.34 billion (or USD 206.2 million per year). The Brazilian Amazon received about 50% of these resources. Seven of the top ten donors were from international multilateral and bilateral co-operation, two were private foundations and one was an international NGO. National and subnational governments were the main recipients, followed by NGOs and the private sector.

7. Mainstreaming biodiversity into sectoral policies

7.1. Agriculture

Brazil is a major agricultural producer and exporter and agriculture accounts for about 15% of employment (Chapter 1; also see Basic Statistics). Since the mid-2000s, the government has placed a greater focus on encouraging the adoption of new technology and sustainable agricultural practices and discouraging conversion of forests in agricultural areas. As Section 4 notes, since 2008 access to subsidised rural credit in the Amazon biome has been conditional on the legitimacy of land claims and compliance with environmental regulations, and rural credit will be conditional on land registration in the Rural Environmental Cadastre from October 2017 (Section 5.2).

Special programmes support small family farms, organic farming and sustainable production such as the National Agroecology and Organic Production Plan 2012-15. For example, the Family Production Socio-environmental Development Programme (Proambiente) awards farmers and ranchers with up to one-third of the minimum wage when they use more environmentally sound production practices, such as no pesticides or sustainable agroforestry (OECD, 2013). In 2010, the government launched the Low-Carbon Agriculture programme to provide subsidised credits for implementing good environmental practices. While the focus of this programme is on reducing GHG emissions, it contributes to mitigating the impact on biodiversity (Box 4.10).

Demand for organic products has grown in recent years. This fact and higher product prices are making organic production a viable way for small-scale rural producers to increase their income. The Ministry of Agriculture, Livestock and Food Supply has developed an online system for registering organic producers. In 2014, there were more than 7 100 organic producers registered in the system (MMA, 2015). Yet organic farming accounts for a very small share of agricultural output and less than 1% of agricultural land area, and the area dedicated to organic practices has declined since 2010 (Figure 4.11).

Overall, the volume of the programmes to support sustainable agriculture is small compared to the total support provided to farmers. Most of the support and loans to agriculture are based on conventional agriculture practices (hybrid seeds, chemical fertilisers and pesticides), with potentially negative impacts on soil and water. The vast majority of support is tied to production, as it is based on commodity output and input use (Chapter 3). This is the most distorting and potentially environmentally harmful form of agricultural support.

Box 4.10. **The Low-Carbon Agriculture programme**

The Low-Carbon Agriculture (ABC) programme, launched in 2010 as part of the National Climate Change Policy (Chapter 2), consolidated a range of concessional credit lines that targeted good environmental practices and the reduction of GHG emissions with a view to facilitating investment. Unlike previous rural credit lines, the programme does not finance specific items (e.g. machinery, seeds, fertilisers), but may finance actions that jointly reduce environmental impacts. The programme took off slowly, due to various technical and capacity challenges, but disbursement picked up in 2012 as more financial intermediaries became involved, the interest rate was decreased, technical capacity strengthened and dissemination of information about the programme improved. The total contracted operations in 2013/14 amounted to BRL 3 billion, nearly double the amount of the 2011/12 growing season. By July 2014, total contracted operations had reached BRL 8.2 billion, 62% of the planned value (FEBRABAN, 2014).

Despite improvement, intermediary banks continue to show little interest in the programme: 91% of disbursements were executed by the public Banco do Brasil, while only 9% were transferred by private banks with funds from the BNDES. This is partly because an ABC credit with the BNDES entails high transaction costs (FEBRABAN, 2014). Information on the programme needs to be expanded and resources for training technical assistants and for financial officers increased. Prioritising areas for expansion (e.g. where GHG reduction potentials are greatest) would help increase the effectiveness of the programme while it is gradually scaled up. As the programme expands, efforts should be undertaken to monitor its effectiveness in reducing GHG emissions and pressures on biodiversity. Overall, the volume and scale of the ABC programme remain small when compared to conventional agricultural support.

Figure 4.11. **Agricultural organic area is small and has declined**

Agricultural organic area, 2005-12

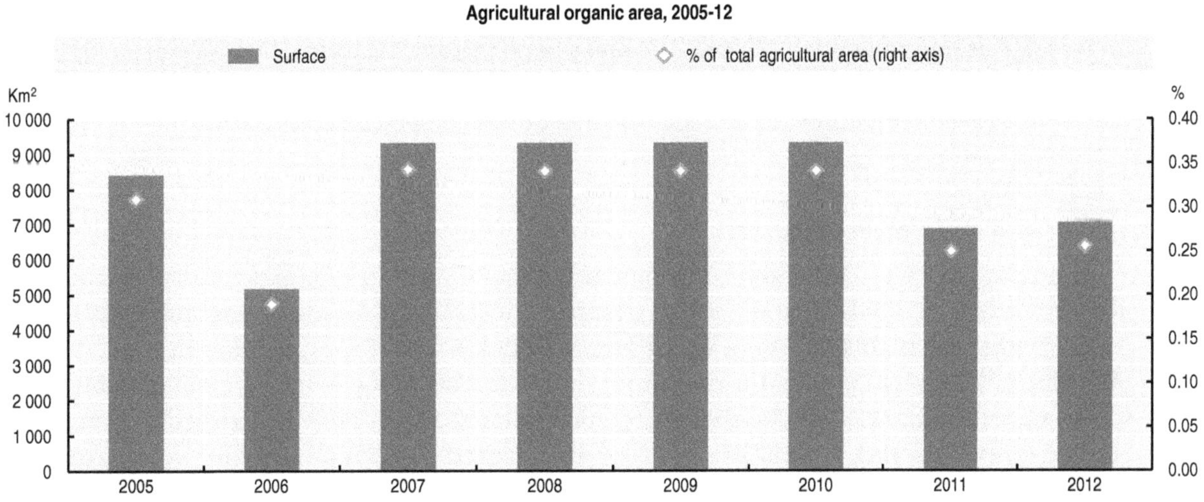

Source: FAO (2015), *FAOSTAT* (database).

StatLink http://dx.doi.org/10.1787/888933279755

By stimulating production and input use, and thereby agricultural intensification and expansion, these support and credit programmes risk increasing pressures on the natural resource base and encourage deforestation. These policies reduce incentives to use production factors more efficiently and tend to encourage agricultural production over other land uses, such as conservation, restoration and sustainable forestry. Agricultural support could be more strongly oriented to encouraging environmental improvement and efficient use of inputs, as well as to addressing infrastructure gaps. This could improve productivity of agriculture and cattle farming and reduce the impetus for converting land and clearing forests.

In addition, key agricultural inputs such as water, pesticides and fertilisers are implicitly subsidised. Water abstraction is not charged for in many regions (Section 5). Fertilisers and pesticides are exempt from some federal and state taxes, which has increased their use and related impact on human health, ecosystems and water and soil quality. Brazil is one of the world's largest consumers of fertilisers (after China, India and United States) and fertiliser use is particularly high for certain crops, such as soya, and in the South and South-east regions where large-scale farming prevails (Chapter 1). Several widely used pesticides are considered dangerous or highly dangerous for the environment and detrimental to pollinators (MMA, 2015); and the use of non-authorised pesticides is high (Jardim and Caldas, 2012).

The current regulation on pesticide approval should be revised to require periodic renewal of approvals, rather than these being granted permanently (MMA, 2015). When conducted, the review process often takes several years (Friedrich, 2013). In addition, tax exemptions for fertilisers and pesticides should be reconsidered with a view to encouraging more rational use of products that can harm human and animal health and ecosystems. The experience of other countries shows that this can lead to economic and environmental benefits. Indonesia, for example, gradually removed pesticide subsidies, while assisting farmers with the use of integrated pest management approaches. Three years later, this resulted in record levels of rice production and over USD 100 million in savings (OECD, 2013).

The Rural Land Tax (ITR), although not very significant, also incentivises agricultural production over conservation. The ITR is higher for "unproductive" land than for land under agricultural production. RL and APP areas benefit from ITR exemption, which partly compensates for the opportunity cost of not engaging in more intensive land use; however, the value of the exemption is so low that the incentive is negligible (MMA, 2015).

7.2. Forestry

Timber and non-timber resources

Brazil is a large producer and consumer of tropical timber. In 2007, the forestry sector accounted for 3.5% of GDP and 7.3% of exports, and employed about 7 million people (SFB, 2015b). Less than 1% of total forest area was designated for production in 2011/12 (SFB, 2013).[19] Legally extracted timber from native forests came from both sustainable forest management (49%) and authorised deforestation (51%) in 2007-10. Extraction from planted forests has almost doubled since 2000 and reached almost five times the volume of extracted timber from native forests in 2013. Planted forests can help reduce demand for timber products from native forests and generate employment and income. Most planted forests are located in southern Brazil, while timber from native forests primarily originates in the Amazon and, to a lesser extent, the Atlantic Forest (SFB, 2015b).

Non-timber forest products generated BRL 936 million in 2011, or 5.1% of total primary forest production (MMA, 2015). The extraction of non-timber forest products is a diffuse and informal economic activity, practiced mainly, though not exclusively, in remote regions by traditional and rural communities. Extractive activities often comprise an important (if not the only) source of their income. Products exploited for economic purposes include rubber, straws, reeds, leaves, fibres, seeds, resins and essential oils, but production scale varies significantly and species and/or environmental sustainability is not yet ensured for all products (MMA, 2015).

Production of such products has been encouraged through federal programmes such as the PNPSB (Section 5.7) and the creation of sustainable use protected areas (Chapter 5). In Manaus and Belém, productive chains are being developed to connect and co-ordinate extractive activities in forest communities with urban economic sectors, small and medium-size processing industries, local research and technological support institutions, and other relevant sectors (MMA, 2015). However, the production extracted from the forest in sustainable conditions amounts to less than 0.2% of the GDP of the Legal Amazon municipalities, mainly due to insufficient demand and a missing link between production and commercialisation (WWF, 2015).

Concessions for sustainable forest management

The government is committed to increasing the sustainable use of its forest resources, recognising that sustainable economic alternatives for local populations are needed to prevent deforestation and other environmentally harmful practises.

The 2006 Public Forests Management Law reinforced the right of local communities to manage their forests[20] and introduced concessions as an instrument to promote sustainable forest management for timber production. It established the SFB to manage concessions. The law allows federal, state and municipal governments to grant, through a bidding process, the legal right for private companies to harvest timber and non-timber forest products, provided that the forest is sustainably managed.[21] The selection of concessionaries is based on best price offers and on technical criteria such as lowest environment impact and highest social benefits. Forest concessions must be preceded by public hearings. Part of the concession area must be set aside and extractive activities need to respect local populations (SFB, 2013).

While the area of public forests is extensive, only a very small part of it is being used for sustainable forest management concessions. As of November 2012, Brazil had an area of 3.1 million km^2 registered as natural public forests in the National Public Forest Registry (CNPF),[22] representing 36% of the national territory (SFB, 2013). The first forest concessions were granted in 2008, but by 2013 only 0.2% of the public forest area available for concessions was under a federal or state concession regime.

Among the reasons for the slow take-off of concessions are insufficient expertise in technology for sustainable forest management in companies; the insufficient technical and economic capacity at government level to manage the concessions; lack of infrastructure in the concession areas; and unsolved land tenure conflicts. Forestry companies often complain about the high concession fees (for each cubic metre of wood harvested) and the technical specifications in contract terms. Rural communities have difficult access to concessions because they lack the ability to compete in a highly bureaucratic process (WWF, 2015). Systematic monitoring of areas under concessions is needed to ensure that forests are managed sustainably, according to the contract specifications, and that they achieve the expected environmental and social outcomes.

Timber certification

The forest management and chain of custody certification in Brazil is carried out by several companies through two certification systems: the Brazilian Programme for Forest Certification (Cerflor), bound to the Programme for the Endorsement of Forest Certification Schemes (PEFC), and the Forest Stewardship Council (FSC). Total area of certified forests has increased. By the end of 2012, more than 14 000 km^2 of forest was certified by Cerflor and another 72 000 km^2 by FSC (SFB, 2013).

Forest restoration

As Section 5.2 points out, a large share of rural holdings do not comply with forest conservation obligations set in the 2012 Forest Code and the tree cover will need to be restored on these lands, especially in the Amazon, Atlantic Forest and Cerrado biomes. As of April 2015, data registered in the CAR indicated the need to restore 80 000 km^2 of forest land (SFB, 2015a).

The National Plan for Native Vegetation Recovery (Planaveg), developed by the MMA and currently under public consultation, aims to promote large-scale forest restoration. The proposal projects recovery of at least 125 000 km^2 within 20 years,[23] primarily in APPs (46%) and RLs (37%), but also on degraded or low productivity areas where restoration is not required by law. The proposed plan includes several groups of actions aimed at raising awareness, making seedlings available and affordable, creating markets for products from restored forests and introducing new finance mechanisms (such as extending the existing tax-free infrastructure bonds to restoration investment), among other goals. It is expected to complement other initiatives, such as the ABC programme (Box 4.10) and ongoing land regularisation efforts. The MMA expects the plan to generate up to 191 000 direct jobs in rural areas.

Restoration costs are high, and can be prohibitive for small-scale land holders. Meeting Brazil's restoration targets is therefore challenging and will require significant resources, financial and human. The preliminary budget for implementation is BRL 181 million for the first five years,[24] but funding sources are yet to be defined. In addition to providing cost estimates, Brazil should prioritise the most important areas for restoration (e.g. using priority maps such as key areas for water production and biodiversity protection).

7.3. Fishery and aquaculture

The Brazilian government has committed to support growth of the fishery sector as an important tool for food security and regional socio-economic development. The capacity of fishing vessels and tools has increased, which is reflected in increased fishery production (Section 1.2). Most fisheries, however, are carried out by obsolete fleets very often directed at fish stocks that are already heavily exploited, resulting in negative outcomes with respect to both biodiversity and efficiency. Resource conflicts between artisanal and industrial fishing and among fishing communities tend to exacerbate pressures on fish stocks (OECD-FAO, 2015).

Aquaculture production has grown nearly five-fold since 2000 and it is expected to grow further, driven by increasing domestic demand and policy support to the sector (OECD-FAO, 2015).[25] Increasing aquaculture production may contribute to increase fish and seafood supply while reducing pressure on natural fishery resources, but policies aimed at expanding aquaculture needs to take into account potentially negative impacts on biodiversity and ecosystems, particularly when alien fish species (or Brazilian species outside of their original habitat) are being cultivated. Aquaculture activities are subject to environmental licencing.

Brazil has adopted a shared fishery management model based on permanent management committees involving government and civil society institutions. This model aims to address environmental sustainability and social inclusion concerns. No formal environmental licensing of fishing activities is required, but several measures apply to limit their environmental impact (e.g. on fishing periods and areas, and gear). However, an audit conducted by the Federal Court of Accounts (TCU) found that this structure was not fully implemented, with measures for the sustainable use of fishery resources still being carried out by the government alone. Limitations in data on aquatic habitats and fishery resources, insufficient mechanisms to monitor and control compliance, and difficult co-operation between the MMA and the Ministry of Fisheries and Aquaculture were found to pose further challenges to sustainable fishery management (MMA, 2015).

Additional measures, including fish catch quotas, effective management plans for overexploited species and the extension of marine protected areas, are needed, particularly in coastal and marine areas where fish stocks are at their limits. The Sectoral Plan for Sea Resources includes an initiative focusing on evaluation, monitoring and conservation of marine biodiversity (REVIMAR). For 2012-15, this initiative was to include establishing monitoring programmes for marine species, continuing the assessment and monitoring of mangrove areas and protected areas containing coral reefs, increasing the number of conservation plans for marine threatened species and expanding the total marine protected areas to 4% of Brazil's territorial waters and exclusive economic zone (Chapter 5).

7.4. Infrastructure development: the case of hydropower

Hydropower is, and will continue to be, a major energy source, but its expansion is constrained by location: most potential is located in the Amazon, which raises difficulties with environmental licensing and public acceptance (Box 2.8). Efforts are being made to develop new techniques to reduce the environmental impact of large hydropower plants, including platform hydropower, and, when suitable, new projects are designed as run-of-river (IEA, 2013). Yet hydropower plants can have a number of adverse impacts on biodiversity, disrupting river connectivity, changing habitats and interfering with the natural cycles of aquatic species. The development of dams for large hydro may also encourage road construction, migration and urbanisation, further increasing pressures on native vegetation. About 95% of deforestation in the Amazon occurs within 5 km of roads (or rivers) (Barber et al., 2014).

Like all infrastructure projects, hydropower plants are subject to environmental licensing and impact assessment (Chapter 2). However, the licensing process and allocation of water use permits has paid little attention to environmental flows, i.e. to how much water is needed to sustain freshwater ecosystems and ecosystem services to prevent negative (and often unexpected) impacts. Legislation in many countries requires environmental water needs to be considered as part of the licensing process (OECD, 2015).

The streamlining of biodiversity into large-scale infrastructure projects benefits from enhanced co-operation between the MMA and the Ministry of Mines and Energy. With a few exceptions, however, impacts are addressed through *ex post* mitigation measures, rather than being considered at the early planning stages. Better integration between the regulatory and institutional frameworks for the environmental and energy sectors would allow a shift from project-based planning to a more strategic integration of energy development and conservation objectives. Brazil could consider using strategic environmental assessment procedures for hydropower development (Chapter 2). This would make it possible, for example, to identify where energy capacity could be built with the least environmental impact and take account of cumulative impact (e.g. from a series of dams on the same river). This could help reduce the costs of mitigation the environmental and social impact of hydropower development projects, as identified by the environmental licence, which represent up to 12% of the total costs of these projects (World Bank, 2008).

8. Knowledge base and economic valuation for biodiversity policy making

8.1. *The knowledge base*

Brazil has made progress towards achieving national biodiversity target 19 on enhancing and systematising biodiversity-related knowledge (Annex 4.A). In 2014, the MMA released the updated lists of threatened flora and fauna species, based on extensive scientific assessment, and ICMBio has been monitoring the biodiversity conservation status in protected areas (Chapter 5). The SFB co-ordinates an annual national forest inventory. Many other initiatives are also being undertaken to monitor biodiversity in protected areas (Chapter 5).

Brazil is a world leader in monitoring deforestation via satellite imaging, which has been key in supporting government enforcement actions to fight deforestation in the Amazon biome (Section 4). Satellite deforestation monitoring has been implemented for the other biomes too, but it is less developed and the data are not fully compatible across systems. Reinforcing the satellite-based deforestation monitoring systems for all biomes and adapting them to detect forest degradation will be essential in order to enforce the new Forest Code and further reduce forest clearing (Section 5.2).

In 2010, the Ministry of Science, Technology and Innovation (MCTI) launched the online Information System on Brazilian Biodiversity (SiBBr), which aims to organise information on Brazilian biodiversity and ecosystems to support research and public policy. The first set of scientific data is being uploaded.[26] However, operational challenges remain with regards to regularly updating the databases and making them more user friendly (MMA, 2015). Brazil could benefit from the effective implementation of an umbrella system such as the SiBBr to compile, consolidate, systematise and regularly update existing and new biodiversity-related information and make it more accessible for research and policy design and evaluation.

8.2. *Economic valuation of biodiversity and ecosystems*

Despite the increasingly vast amount of information available, only modest progress has been achieved in terms of economic valuation of biodiversity and ecosystems. In 2012 the Institute for Applied Economics Research (IPEA) surveyed the existing biodiversity and ecosystem valuation studies in Brazil to identify knowledge gaps. After a review of 103 studies, IPEA concluded that the majority of the studies were thematic and site specific and therefore not conducive to estimating values on a larger scale (Roma et al., 2013). One notable exception is an assessment of the contribution of Brazil's protected areas to the national economy (Box 5.3).

However, valuation studies have rarely been used in decision-making processes. Progress has been made on including the value of water resources into national accounting and work is continuing on forest economic accounting. Brazil should build on these experiences to fully integrate the values of biodiversity and ecosystem services into the national accounts. Increased effort is needed to improve understanding of these values, and the risks associated with their loss, as a means of raising public awareness and providing support for policy making.

Progress has been made in this direction. As part of Brazil's international commitment under the CBD to implement a national TEEB (The Economics of Ecosystem and Biodiversity), in 2013 the MMA launched the Brazilian Natural Capital Initiative (EEB). The MMA and key partners are engaging in an national effort to: i) identify and highlight the benefits of conservation and sustainable use of national biodiversity and ecosystem services, as well as estimate the costs of their loss; ii) promote mainstreaming of the economics of ecosystems and biodiversity in decision-making processes at different levels, so that decisions may lead to the sustainable use of natural assets; and iii) influence the implementation of public policies and management instruments, as well as promote behavioural changes to ensure the long-term provision of natural assets. Box 4.11 describes the main activities and outcomes of EEB.

Box 4.11. **The Brazilian Natural Capital Initiative**

The Brazilian National Capital Initiative is conducted by a broad partnership, including the MMA and other federal ministries and agencies, industry organisations and international partners.* The EEB has three inter-related components: i) national policies (National TEEB); ii) internalisation of the value of ecosystem services in decision-making processes (Regional-Local TEEB); and iii) risks and costs of the loss of biodiversity to the business sector (Business Sector TEEB).

In November 2013, the EEB partnership identified the thematic priorities to be addressed in the first phase of the National TEEB: i) promotion of sustainable production chains through public procurement processes; ii) economics of ecological restoration; iii) impacts and dependence of the agriculture sector on ecosystem services; and iv) mapping of ecosystem services. The initiative has commissioned the work necessary to develop a work plan for these four priority themes. The next step will involve the engagement of strategic stakeholders, especially from sectors not yet sensitive to these themes.

The GIZ supports the development of a Regional-Local TEEB project on the basis of pilot projects to improve understanding about economic and financial instruments for biodiversity protection and approaches to incorporate biodiversity and ecosystem service values into policy making at regional and local levels. As part of the project, a manual for practitioners was released ("Integration of ecosystem services into development planning: A step-by-step guide for practitioners based on the TEEB Initiative") and two international events were held in 2014: i) the Brazil-India-Germany TEEB Dialogue; and ii) the International Workshop on Businesses and Natural Assets, which was an open event to strengthen co-operation among governments, the business sector, academia and civil society towards achieving the objectives of the CBD.

The Business Sector TEEB aims at highlighting the economic benefits of business initiatives that favour the conservation of biodiversity and maintenance of ecosystem services. In March 2014, a study comparing the environmental value of different agricultural practices for the production of palm oil (*dendê*) and soya in pilot projects of the Natura and Monsanto companies was published. In both cases, results suggest that conserving natural capital is good business.

* The EEB is a joint partnership of the MMA, the Ministry of Internal Revenue, the MCTI, the IPEA, the, Secretariat of Strategic Affairs of the President's Office, the IBGE, the United Nations Environment Programme, the National Industry Confederation, Conservation International Brazil and the German technical co-operation body, GIZ.

Source: MMA (2015), *Fifth National Report to the Convention on Biological Diversity.*

Recommendations on conservation and sustainable use of biodiversity

Knowledge base and evaluation

- Build on the Information System on Brazilian Biodiversity to compile, consolidate and systematise existing and new biodiversity-related information and make it more accessible for research and policy design and evaluation; ensure that the system is regularly and timely updated.
- Continue to develop satellite-based monitoring systems that detect forest deforestation and degradation and cover all biomes, especially the Cerrado, Caatinga and Pampa, where most vegetation clearing is expected; ensure that the systems generate up-to-date and compatible data series.
- Pursue the Brazilian Natural Capital Initiative; conduct a national ecosystem assessment at the earliest opportunity to improve knowledge of the values of biodiversity and ecosystem services and of the risks associated with their loss; ensure that the values of ecosystem services are integrated in national accounts and in policy design and evaluation.

Policy framework

- Maintain the policy focus on combatting deforestation and clarifying land tenure, and extend it to all the terrestrial biomes and to marine, coastal and inland water ecosystems.
- Streamline the multitude of biodiversity-related plans and programmes with a view to eliminating overlap and duplication of efforts and increasing cost-effectiveness; systematically evaluate the implementation of policies and measures in terms of results, costs and benefits, and revise policies and programmes accordingly.

Forest conservation, restoration and sustainable management

- Strengthen implementation of the Rural Environmental Cadastre (CAR) by providing economic incentives to encourage cadastre enrolment, promote compliance and support sustainable management and restoration of set-aside areas; build on the CAR information system to improve compliance monitoring, landscape planning and policy priority setting.
- Support the development of state-level environmental regularisation programmes and enhance implementation capacity of states and municipalities.
- Consider adjusting the Environmental Reserve Quota system to allow quota exchanges within the same priority areas, in terms of biodiversity value; systematically monitor the functioning of the system and allow for the adjustments necessary to achieve its forest preservation and restoration objectives.
- Scale up support for sustainable forestry and farming practices, including in protected areas, by providing training and technical assistance to rural and traditional communities and small farms and facilitating their access to credit and product markets.
- Speed up the use of concessions for sustainable forest management, including in eligible protected areas, by simplifying procedures and improving capacity of government officials to design and negotiate concession contracts; systematically monitor the areas under concession to ensure compliance with the contract specifications and delivery of the expected environmental and social outcomes.
- Accelerate the development of the proposed National Plan for Native Vegetation Recovery, estimate its costs and identify priority areas (with high biodiversity value) for restoration; identify funding sources and assess the feasibility of extending the existing tax-free infrastructure bonds to restoration investment.

Recommendations on conservation and sustainable use of biodiversity *(cont.)*

- Further encourage the private sector to implement sustainable and traceable value chains that would minimise their impact on biodiversity and ecosystems, including deforestation.
- Adopt a national REDD+ strategy at the earliest opportunity, indicating objectives, actions, institutional arrangements, monitoring mechanisms and the necessary resource allocation.

Payments for ecosystem services (PES)

- Continue discussing the current federal legislation proposal and adopt an overarching federal PES law to provide a framework for PES implementation and improve consistency across state regulations and programmes.
- Put in place a countrywide monitoring system for PES programmes, possibly within the framework of a federal PES law, with a view to verifying their effectiveness in maintaining the ecosystem services that are being paid for.
- Scale up and improve the management of Bolsa Verde and reinforce its link with the Rural Environmental Cadastre; ensure adequate training of beneficiaries to help them meet their conservation commitments.

Mainstreaming biodiversity in sectoral policies

- Re-orient agricultural support to encourage environmental improvement and efficient use of agricultural inputs.
- Reform land taxation to encourage land conservation and gradually remove the tax exemptions on fertilisers and pesticides; use the resulting tax revenue to improve farmers' knowledge of good agricultural practices such as alternative pest control methods; review the pesticide regulations to make licences subject to periodic renewal and intensify efforts to control unauthorised pesticide use.
- Introduce measures to improve sustainability of fishing in marine and inland waters, including fish catch quotas, management plans for overexploited species and the extension of marine protected areas, particularly in coastal and marine areas where fish stocks are at their limits.
- Introduce strategic planning, including environmental assessment procedures, for hydropower development so as to identify where energy capacity could be built with the least environmental impact, take account of cumulative effects and, ultimately, reduce the costs of mitigating the environmental and social impact.
- Clarify the rules for biodiversity and finance compensations in the framework of the licensing process; improve the quantification of the impact of infrastructure projects on biodiversity and ecosystems and the definition of the associated compensatory measures.

Notes

1. Together the 17 megadiverse countries in the world contain around 70% of the world's biodiversity.
2. A biome is a large naturally occurring community of flora and fauna occupying a geographic region.
3. The Amazônia Legal super-region corresponds to an area larger than the Amazon biome, encompassing both the Amazonian forest (about 4.1 million km^2) and transitional vegetation (1 million km^2); the Amazon biome covers only the forest area. Amazônia Legal takes in nearly nine states: Amazonas, Pará, Acre, Roraima, Rondônia, Amapá and Tocantins, and part of Mato Grosso and Maranhão.
4. The tracking of deforestation in Brazil's other five biomes began later than in the Amazon. Annual deforestation data started being produced in 2009.

5. These include 732 mammal, 1 980 bird and 4 507 marine and freshwater fish species.
6. These include cassava, pineapple, peanuts, cocoa, cashew, cupuassu, passion fruit, Brazil nut, guarana and jabuticaba.
7. The list of threatened flora species is based on the 2013 Red Book by the National Centre for Plant Conservation at the Rio de Janeiro Botanical Garden's Institute of Research.
8. For example, the North American Pinus pine replaced steppe habitat in the south of Brazil with simplified forest habitats (MMA, 2015),
9. These include the National Environment Council (CONAMA) (Chapter 2), the National Council for the Legal Amazon (CONAMAZ), the Council for the Management of the Genetic Patrimony, the Commission for the Management of Public Forests and the Commission for Sea Resources.
10. The consultation process, called "Dialogues on biodiversity: building the Brazilian strategy for 2020", involved participants from all sectors, including businesses, NGOs, academia, the federal and state governments, indigenous peoples and traditional communities, and the general public by means of an online public consultation process.
11. Some examples are the Vale Company, which invests through its Fundo Vale; Petrobras, which invests through Petrobras Ambiental; the cosmetic company Boticário, which invests through its Boticário Foundation; and the Natura cosmetic company (Box 3.8), which invests through Fundação Natura.
12. Life Certification was launched in 2009 under the aegis of the CBD. To obtain the certification, a company must implement a minimum set of biodiversity conservation and mitigation actions.
13. Some examples include pequi pulp, pine nuts, umbu and licuri, piassava palm babassu, buriti and carnauba palm, Brazil nut, andiroba and copaiba oils.
14. The National Supply Company (CONAB) implements the programme; it defines minimum prices and is responsible for operationalising the payment of benefits.
15. The operationalisation of subsidy payment is bureaucratic; the extractivists are required to possess personal documentation and a checking account.
16. In the case of babassu almond, the percentage of production subsidised by the PGPMBio was less than 2%. For rubber, a larger share of total production was subsidised, reaching almost 27% in 2012.
17. Obtaining a permit usually took about three years. Researchers have complained about the requirement of obtaining the consent of relevant communities for their research, arguing that they do not always know early on where a genetic resource is found (IEEP et al., 2012).
18. Payment into the Amazon Fund was based on reducing GHG emissions from historical average deforestation rates, using a formula that converted estimated CO_2 emission reductions from deforestation abatement against an average rate and applied a value of USD 5 per tonne of avoided GHG emissions. The pace of decline in deforestation rates, however, was actually higher than the rate at which funding from international donors, primarily Norway, was provided, so the funding mechanism followed a predetermined commitment and disbursement schedule instead (Birdsall et al., 2014).
19. Includes national forests, states forests and forest plantations.
20. Community forests are forests designated for the use by traditional people and communities, indigenous people, family farmers and settlers registered in the national land reform programme. The Brazilian Constitution safeguards the right of indigenous peoples and *quilombola* groups to their ancestral territories. Community forests amounted to 62% of the national registered public forests in 2012, most of which are indigenous lands or protected areas (extractive reserves and sustainable development reserves).
21. To qualify for sustainable forest management, producers may only explore forest or form secondary forest with prior approval of a sustainable forest management plan detailing technical guidelines and procedures by the competent forest agency. The forest management system used in the Amazon is polycyclic, based on a 35-year cutting cycle and on technical and environmental criteria to promote the regeneration of the managed forest species. In practice, only four to six trees per hectare are felled. Forest management in Caatinga is based on a monocyclic system, with a rotation period estimated at between 12 to 15 years. Trees are cut near the base to allow sprouting regeneration by regrowth (SFB, 2013).
22. The CNPF was established to produce and compile detailed information about the use, conservation and restoration of all forest resources, including those not designated for production. It gathers biophysical, socio-environmental and landscape data covering Brazil's entire territory.

23. The total area to be restored under Planaveg was defined based on Soares-Filho et al. (2014), who suggested that up to 92 000 km^2 (of the total compliance deficit of 210 000 km^2) could be offset through CRAs. Planaveg suggests that another 15 000 km^2 could be offset by buying "inholdings" in protected areas (Section 5.4). Planaveg's target thus exceeds by 22 000 km^2 the estimated restoration needed to achieve compliance with the new Forest Code.

24. The plan calls for the government to conduct a mid-term review after ten years of implementation as well as intermediate progress reviews after 5 years, with a view to refine strategies and actions based on the results achieved, lessons learned and advances in knowledge and experience, and to respond to potentially changing public and private demands.

25. The Harvest Plan for Fisheries and Aquaculture 2012-14 foresees investments of BRL 9.8 billion for expanding aquaculture and modernising and strengthening the fishing industry and fishery trade.

26. Other programmes are being implemented through the National Council for Scientific and Technological Development, including the National System of Research on Biodiversity (SISBIOTA), the Biodiversity Research Programme (PPBio) and the International Biodiversity Symposium System (SINBIO), with information on biological inventories compatible with SiBBr.

References

Amazon Fund (2015), "Portfolio Report, March 15", Amazon Fund, Brasília, *www.amazonfund.gov.br/FundoAmazonia/export/sites/default/site_en/Galerias/Arquivos/Informes/2015_03_informe_31mar15_engl.pdf.*

Assunção, J. et al. (2013), *Deforestation Slowdown in the Legal Amazon: Prices or Policies?*, Climate Policy Initiative, Rio de Janeiro.

Barber, C.P. et al. (2014), "Roads, deforestation, and the mitigating effect of protected areas in the Amazon", *Biological Conservation*, Vol. 177, pp. 203-209.

Bernasconi, P. (2013), *Custo-efetividade ecológica da compensação de reserva legal entre propriedades no estado de São Paulo [Ecological cost-effectiveness of the legal reserve compensation among properties in São Paulo state]*, project Policymix financed by the European Commission, Directorate General for Research, Brussels, *www.esaf.fazenda.gov.br/premios/premios-1/i-premio-florestal-brasileiro/3o-lugar-010p.pdf.*

Birdsall, N., W. Savedoff and F. Seymour (2014), *The Brazil-Norway Agreement for Performance-Based Payments for Forest Conservation: Successes, Challenges, Lessons*, CGD Climate and Forest Paper Series No. 4, Center for Global Development, Washington, DC, *www.cgdev.org/publication/ft/brazil-norway-agreement-performance-based-payments-forest-conservation-successes.*

Börner, J. et al. (2013), *Promoting Forest Stewardship in the Bolsa Floresta Programme: Local Livelihood Strategies and Preliminary Impacts*, Center for International Forestry Research, Rio de Janeiro, Fundação Amazonas Sustentável, Manaus, Zentrum für Entwicklungsforschung, Bonn, *http://fas-amazonas.org/versao/2012/wordpress/wp-content/uploads/2014/02/BF_report_ENG_web.pdf.*

Brito B. and P. Barreto (2009), "Os riscos e os princípios para a regularização fundiária na Amazônia" [The risks and principles for land regularisation in the Amazon], Imazon Belém, *http://imazon.org.br/PDFimazon/Portugues/estado_da_amazonia/os-riscos-e-os-principios-para-a-regularizacao.pdf.*

BV Rio (2014), *Operational Report 2011-13*, Rio de Janeiro Environmental Exchange, *www.bvrio.org/site/images/publicacoes/relatorio2013_ing_04.pdf.*

Cabrera, J. et al. (2014), *Overview of National and Regional Measures on Access and Benefit Sharing. Challenges and Opportunities in Implementing the Nagoya Protocol*, Centre for International Sustainable Development Law, Montreal, *www.cisdl.org/aichilex/files/Global%20Overview%20of%20ABS%20Measures_FINAL_SBSTTA18.pdf.*

Castro de La Mata, G. and S. Riega-Campos (2014), *An Analysis of International Funding in the Amazon*, Moore Foundation, Ecosystems Services, *www.vale.com/brasil/PT/aboutvale/news/Documents/Amazon-Conservation-Funding-Analysis-Publication-2014.pdf.*

CDB (n.d.), "Brazil – Country Profile", UN Convention on Biological Diversity, *www.cbd.int/countries/profile/default.shtml?country=br - facts* (accessed May 2015).

CEPAL, GIZ e IPEA (2011), *Avaliação do Plano de Prevenção e Controle do Desmatamento na Amazônia Legal: PPCDAm: 2007-2010 [Evaluation of the Action Plan for Prevention and Control of Deforestation in the Legal Amazon]*, United Nations Economic Commission for Latin America and the Caribbean, Brasília, Institute for Applied Economic Research, Brasília, and Deutche Gesellschaft fur International Zusammenarbeit (GIZ) GmbH, Bonn, *www. cepal.org/dmaah/publicaciones/sinsigla/xml/7/45887/IPEA_GIZ_Cepal_2011_Avaliacao_PPCDAm_2007-2011_web.pdf.*

CGU (2014), "Relatório de Acompanhamento n° 07/2014 Programa Bolsa Verde" [Follow-up Report No. 07/2014 of the Green Grant Programme], Comptroller General of the Union, Brasília.

Conservation International (2015), "Hotspots", Conservation International, *www.conservation.org/How/Pages/Hotspots.aspx* (accessed May 2015).

FAO (2015), *Global Forest Resource Assessment*, Food and Agriculture Organization of the United Nations, Rome.

FAO (2013), "Fishery and Aquaculture Country Profiles: Brazil", Food and Agriculture Organization of the United Nations, Rome, *www.fao.org/fishery/facp/BRA/en* (accessed December 2014).

FEBRABAN (2014), *The Brazilian Financial System and the Green Economy Alignment with Sustainable Development*, Brazilian Federation of Banks, São Paulo.

Financial Times (2015), "Brazil farmers eye gains on eco exchange" by J. Leahy, *Financial Times newspaper*, London, *www.ft.com/cms/s/0/60b19182-42ef-11e2-a3d2-00144feabdc0.html#ixzz3aUikxlS2* (accessed May 2015).

Friedrich, K. (2013), "Desafios para a avaliação toxicológica de agrotóxicos no Brasil: desregulação endócrina e imunotoxicidade" [Challenges for the evaluation pesticide and agro-chemical use in Brazil: endocrine disruption and immunotoxicity], *Vigilância Sanitária em Debate*, Vol. 1, No. 2, pp. 2-15, *http://dx.doi.org/10.3395/vd.v1i2.30*.

Funbio (2014), *O Futuro do Ambiente Financeiro das Áreas Protegidas [The Future of Finance for Protected Areas]*, Brazilian Biodiversity Fund, Rio de Janeiro, *www.funbio.org.br/o-funbio/tendencias-o-futuro-do-ambiente-financeiro-das-areas-protegidas*.

GEF (2012), *GEF Country Portfolio Evaluation. Brazil (1991-2011)*, Global Environment Facility, Washington, DC, *www.thegef. org/gef/sites/thegef.org/files/documents/CPE-Brazil-v1.pdf*.

Gibbs, H. et al. (2015), "Brazil's Soy Moratorium. Supply-chain governance is needed to avoid deforestation", *Science*, 23 January 2015, Vol. 347, Issue 6220, *www.sciencemag.org/content/347/6220/377.full.pdf*.

Guedes, F. and S. Seehusen (2011), *Pagamento por Serviços Ambientais na Mata Atlântica. Lições Aprendidas e Desafios [Payment for Ecosystems Services in the Atlantic Forests: Lessons learned and challenges]*, Ministry of the Environment, Brasília, *www.mma.gov.br/estruturas/202/_arquivos/psa_na_mata_atlantico_licoes_apredidas_e_desafios_202.pdf*.

IBAMA (2015), "Projeto de Monitoramento do Desmatamento dos Biomas Brasileiros por Satélite – PMDBBS" [Project for Satellite-based Deforestation Monitoring of Brazilian Biomes], Brazilian Institute of Environment and Renewable Natural Resources, Brasília, *http://siscom.ibama.gov.br/monitorabiomas/index.htm* (accessed February 2015).

IBGE (2013), *Indicadores de Desenvolvimento Sustentável [Sustainable Development Indicators]* (database), Brazilian Institute of Geography and Statistics, Rio de Janeiro (accessed March 2015).

ICMBio (2015), "Espécies Ameaçadas – Lista 2014" [Endangered Species List 2014], Chico Mendes Institute for Biodiversity Conservation, *www.icmbio.gov.br/portal/biodiversidade/fauna-brasileira/lista-de-especies.html* (accessed May 2015).

IEA (2013), *World Energy Outlook 2013*, International Energy Agency, IEA/OECD Publishing, Paris, *http://dx.doi.org/10.1787/weo-2013-en*.

IEEP, Ecologic and GHK (2012), "Study to analyse legal and economic aspects of implementing the Nagoya Protocol on ABS in the European Union", final report for the European Commission, DG Environment, Institute for European Environmental Policy, Brussels and London, April 2012, *http://ec.europa.eu/environment/nature/biodiversity/international/abs/pdf/ABS%20FINAL%20REPORT.pdf*.

INPA (2015), INPA website, National Institute for Amazon Reserach, *http://portal.inpa.gov.br/* (accessed May 2015).

INPE (2015), "Projeto PRODES: Monitoramento da floresta Amazônia Brasileira por satélite" [The PRODES Project: Monitoring the Brazilian Amazon forest by satellite], National Institute for Space Research, *www.obt.inpe.br/prodes/index.php* (accessed February 2015).

Instituto Life (2014), "Instituto Life", Instituto Life, Curitiba, *www.institutolife.org/* (accessed November 2014).

Jardim, A. and E. Caldas (2012), "Brazilian monitoring programs for pesticide residues in food – Results from 2001 to 2010", *Food Control*, Vol. 25, Issue 2, pp. 607-616, *http://dx.doi.org/10.1016/j.foodcont.2011.11.001*.

Leitão, S. (2014), "Isso é só o começo: sobre o Código Florestal" [This is just the beginning: on the Forest Code], in P. Little, *Os novos desafios da política ambiental brasileira [The new challenges of Brazilian environmental policy]*, IEB, Brasília.

MDA (2014), "Programa Terra Legal" [Terra Legal Programme], Ministry of Agrarian Development, Brasília, *www.mda.gov.br/sitemda/secretaria/serfal/apresenta%C3%A7%C3%A3o* (accessed November 2014).

MMA (2015), *Fifth National Report to the Convention on Biological Diversity*, Ministry of the Environment, Brasília, *www.cbd.int/doc/world/br/br-nr-05-en.pdf*.

MMA (2014), "Biomas" [Biomes], Ministry of the Environment, Brasília, *www.mma.gov.br/biomas* (accessed November 2014).

MMA (2010), *Fourth National Report to the Convention on Biological Diversity*, Ministry of the Environment, Brasília.

Nogueron R. and L. Cheung (2013), *Leveling the Playing Field for Legal Timber in Brazil*, World Resource Institute, Washington, DC, *www.wri.org/blog/2013/09/leveling-playing-field-legal-timber-brazil*.

Norman, M. et al. (2014), "Climate Finance Thematic Briefing: REDD+ Finance", *Climate Finance Fundamentals* 5, December 2014, Overseas Development Institute, London and Heinrich Böll Stiftung North America, Washington, DC, *www.odi.org/sites/odi.org.uk/files/odi-assets/publications-opinion-files/9330.pdf*.

OECD (2015), *Water Resources Governance in Brazil*, OECD Studies on Water, OECD Publishing, Paris, *http://dx.doi.org/10.1787/9789264238121-en*.

OECD (2013), *Scaling-up Finance Mechanisms for Biodiversity*, OECD Publishing, Paris, *http://dx.doi.org/10.1787/9789264193833-en*.

OECD (2012), *A Framework for Financing Water Resources Management*, *OECD Studies on Water*, OECD Publishing, Paris, *http://dx.doi.org/10.1787/9789264179820-en*.

OECD-ECLAC (2014), *OECD Environmental Performance Reviews: Colombia 2014*, OECD Publishing, Paris, *http://dx.doi.org/10.1787/9789264208292-en*.

OECD-FAO (2015), "Brazilian agriculture: Prospects and challenges", in OECD/FAO, *OECD-FAO Agricultural Outlook 2015*, OECD Publishing, Paris, *http://dx.doi.org/10.1787/agr_outlook-2015-5-en*.

Pinto, L.P. et al. (2012), "Mata Atlântica" [Atlantic Forest] in Scarano, F. et al. (eds), *Biomas do Brasil: retratos de um país plural [Brazilian Biomes: portraits from a diverse country]*, Casa da Palavra, Rio de Janeiro.

Pires, M.O. (2014), "A política de combate ao desmatamento na Amazônia e no Cerrado" [The policy to combat deforestation in the Amazon and Cerrado], in P. Little, *Os novos desafios da política ambiental brasileira [The new challenges of the Brazilian environmental policy]*, IEB, Brasília.

Prates, A. (2014), "Gestão da biodiversidade costeira e marinha: desafios da era do pré-sal", in P. Little, *Os novos desafios da política ambiental brasileira [The new challenges of the Brazilian environmental policy]*, IEB, Brasília.

Roma, J. et al. (2013), *A Economia dos Ecossistemas e da Biodiversidade (TEEB – Brasil): Análise de Lacunas [The Economics of Ecosystems and Biodiversity (TEEB - Brazil): Gap Analysis]*, Institute for Applied Economic Reserach, Brasília, *www.ipea.gov.br/portal/images/stories/PDFs/TDs/td_1912.pdf*.

Santos, P. et al. (2012), *Marco regulatório sobre pagamento por serviços ambientais no Brasil [Regulatory framework on payments for ecosystem services in Brazil]*, IMAZON, GVces, Belém.

Senado Federal (2015), "Portal Orçamento" *[Budget portal]*, *www12.senado.gov.br/orcamento/* (accessed May 2015).

Seroa da Motta, R. et al. (2011), *Climate change in Brazil: Economic, social and regulatory aspects*, Institute for Applied Economic Research, Brasília, *www.ipea.gov.br/agencia/images/stories/PDFs/livros/livros/livro_climatechange.pdf*.

SFB (2015a), "Cadastro Ambiental Rural: Boletim Informativo" [Rural Environmental Cadastre: Information Bulletin], 30 April 2015, Brazilian Forest Service, Brasília, *www.florestal.gov.br/noticias-do-sfb/balanco-do-cadastro-ambiental-rural-car*.

SFB (2015b), "Fundo Nacional do Desenvolvimento Florestal" [National Forestry Development Fund], Brazilian Forest Service, Brasília *www.florestal.gov.br/extensao-e-fomento-florestal/fundo-nacional-do-desenvolvimento-florestal/fundo-nacional-de-desenvolvimento-florestal* (accessed February 2015).

SFB (2014), "Os Biomas e Suas Florestas" [Brazilian biomes and its forests], Brazilian Forest Service, Brasília, *www.florestal.gov.br/snif/recursos-florestais/os-biomas-e-suas-florestas* (accessed February 2015).

SFB (2013), *Brazilian Forests at a Glance*, Brazilian Forest Service, Brasília, *www.forestcarbonpartnership.org/sites/fcp/files/2015/March/Brazilian_Forests_at_a_glance_2013%20(1).pdf*.

SMA (2013), *Action Plan of the State of São Paulo. Aichi targets 2020. Implementation in the State of São Paulo*, Government of the State of São Paulo, Secretary of the Environment, *www.ambiente.sp.gov.br/en/files/2015/04/Aichi_impressao_21_2_14_pdf_ENG_V.pdf*.

Soares-Filho, B. et al. (2014a), Supplementary material for "Cracking Brazil's Forest Code", *Science* 25 April, Vol. 344 no. 6182, *http://dx.doi.org/ 10.1126/science.1246663*.

Soares-Filho, B. et al. (2014b), "Cracking Brazil's Forest Code", *Science* 25 April, Vol. 344 no. 6182 pp. 363-364, *http://dx.doi.org/ 10.1126/science.1246663*.

Viana (2015), "Leveraging public programmes with socio-economic and development objectives to support conservation and restoration of ecosystems: the price-support policy for socio-biodiversity derived products and the Green Grant Programme of Brazil", Institute for Applied Economic Research, Brasília, *www.cbd.int/ecorestoration/doc/Brazil-case-study-Final-Version-20150114.pdf*.

World Bank (2008), "Summary report", *Environmental Licensing for Hydroelectric Projects in Brazil: A Contribution to the Debate*, Vol. 1 (of 3), World Bank, Washington, DC, *http://documents.worldbank.org/curated/en/2008/03/10155469/environmental-licensing-hydroelectric-projects-brazil-contribution-debate-vol-1-3-summary-report*.

WWF (2015), *The Brazilian Amazon: challenges facing an effective policy to curb deforestation*, World Wide Fund Brazil, Brasília, *http://wwf.panda.org/?240971/Brazilian-Amazon-challenges-to-an-effective-policy-to-curb-deforestation*.

ANNEX 4.A

Brazil's national biodiversity targets 2011-20

National biodiversity target	Mid-term assessment
Strategic Objective A: Address the underlying causes of biodiversity loss by mainstreaming biodiversity considerations across government and society.	
National Target 1: By 2020, at the latest, Brazilian people are aware of the values of biodiversity and the steps they can take to conserve and use it sustainably.	On the right track, but additional measures needed.
National Target 2: By 2020, at the latest, biodiversity values, geo-diversity values, and socio-diversity values are integrated into national and local development and poverty reduction and inequality reduction strategies, and are being incorporated into national accounting, as appropriate, and into planning procedures and reporting systems.	On the right track, but additional measures needed.
National Target 3: By 2020, at the latest, incentives harmful to biodiversity, including the so-called perverse subsidies, are eliminated, phased out or reformed in order to minimise negative impacts. Positive incentives for the conservation and sustainable use of biodiversity are developed and applied, consistent and in harmony with the CBD, taking into account national and regional socio economic conditions.	On the right track, but additional measures needed.
National Target 4: By 2020, at the latest, governments, private sector and stakeholders at all levels have taken steps to achieve or have implemented plans for sustainable production and consumption to mitigate or prevent negative impacts from the use of natural resources.	On the right track, but additional measures needed.
Strategic Objective B: Reduce the direct pressures on biodiversity and promote sustainable use.	
National Target 5: By 2020, the rate of loss of native habitats is reduced by at least 50% (in comparison with the 2009 rate) and, as much as possible, brought close to zero, and degradation and fragmentation is significantly reduced in all biomes.	The target can be exceeded in the Amazon, but additional measures are needed in the other biomes.
National Target 6: By 2020 all stocks of any aquatic organism are managed and harvested sustainably, legally and applying ecosystem based approaches, so that overharvesting is avoided; recovery plans and measures are in place for depleted species; fisheries have no significant adverse impacts on threatened species and vulnerable ecosystems; and the impacts of fisheries on stocks, species and ecosystems are within safe ecological limits, when scientifically established.	On the right track, but additional measures needed, especially for the recovery of depleted species and limiting the impact of fisheries on stocks, species and ecosystems.
National Target 7: By 2020 the incorporation of sustainable management practices is disseminated and promoted in agriculture, livestock production, aquaculture, silviculture, extractive activities, and forest and fauna management, ensuring conservation of biodiversity.	On track to achieve the target in silviculture, but additional measures needed in the other sectors.
National Target 8: By 2020, pollution, including from excess nutrients, has been brought to levels that are not detrimental to ecosystem function and biodiversity.	On the right track, but additional measures needed.
National Target 9: By 2020, the National Strategy on Invasive Alien Species is fully implemented, with the participation and commitment of states and the elaboration of a national policy, ensuring the continuous and updated diagnosis of species and the effectiveness of action plans for prevention, containment and control.	On the right track, but additional measures needed.
National Target 10: By 2015, the multiple anthropogenic pressures on coral reefs, and other marine and coastal ecosystems impacted by climate change or ocean acidification are minimised, so as to maintain their integrity and functioning.	On the right track, but additional measures needed.
Strategic Objective C: Improve the status of biodiversity by safeguarding ecosystems, species and genetic diversity.	
National Target 11: By 2020, at least 30% of the Amazon, 17% of each of the other terrestrial biomes and 10% of the marine and coastal areas, especially areas of particular importance for biodiversity and ecosystem services, are conserved through protected areas foreseen under the SNUC Law and other categories of officially protected areas such as Permanent Protection Areas, Legal Reserves and indigenous lands with native vegetation, ensuring and respecting the demarcation, regularisation and effective and equitable management, so as to ensure ecological interconnection, integration and representation in broader landscapes and seascapes.	On track to achieve the target in the Amazon, but additional measures needed in the other biomes (also see Chapter 5).

Brazil's national biodiversity targets 2011-20 *(cont.)*

National biodiversity target	Mid-term assessment
National Target 12: By 2020, the risk of extinction of threatened species has been significantly reduced, tending to zero, and their conservation status, particularly of those most in decline, has been improved.	On the right track, but additional measures needed.
National Target 13: By 2020, the genetic diversity of microorganisms, cultivated plants, farmed and domesticated animals and of wild relatives, including socio-economically as well as culturally valuable species, is maintained, and strategies have been developed and implemented for minimising the loss of genetic diversity.	On the right track, but additional measures needed.
Strategic Objective D: Enhance the benefits to all from biodiversity and ecosystem services.	
National Target 14: By 2020, ecosystems that provide essential services, including services related to water, and contribute to health, livelihoods and well-being, are restored and safeguarded, taking into account the needs of women, traditional peoples and communities, indigenous peoples and local communities, and the poor and vulnerable.	On the right track, but additional measures needed.
National Target 15: By 2020, ecosystem resilience and the contribution of biodiversity to carbon stocks has been enhanced through conservation and restoration actions, including restoration of at least 15% of degraded ecosystems, prioritising the most degraded biomes, hydrographic regions and ecoregions, thereby contributing to climate change mitigation and adaptation and to combatting desertification.	On track to achieve the target in the Amazon, but additional measures needed in the other biomes.
National Target 16: By 2015, the Nagoya Protocol on Access to Genetic Resources and the Fair and Equitable Sharing of Benefits Arising from their Utilisation is in force and operational, consistent with national legislation.	On the right track, but additional measures needed.
Strategic Objective E: Enhance the implementation through participatory planning, knowledge management and capacity building.	
National Target 17: By 2014, the national biodiversity strategy is updated and adopted as policy instrument, with effective, participatory and updated action plans, which foresee periodic monitoring and evaluation.	On the right track, but additional measures needed.
National Target 18: By 2020, the traditional knowledge, innovations and practices of indigenous peoples, family rural producers and traditional communities relevant for the conservation and sustainable use of biodiversity, and their customary use of biological resources, are respected, in accordance with their uses, customs and traditions, national legislation and relevant international commitments, and fully integrated and reflected in the implementation of the CBD, with the full and effective participation of indigenous peoples, family rural producers and traditional communities, at all relevant levels.	On the right track, but additional measures needed.
National Target 19: By 2020, the science base and technologies necessary for enhancing knowledge on biodiversity, its values, functioning and trends, and the consequences of its loss, are improved and shared, and the sustainable use of biodiversity, as well as the generation of biodiversity-based technology and innovation are supported, duly transferred and applied. By 2017, the complete compilation of existing records on aquatic and terrestrial fauna, flora and microbiota is finalised and made available through permanent and open access databases, with specificities safeguarded, with a view to identify knowledge gaps related to biomes and taxonomic groups.	Generally on track, but additional measures needed to the support and apply sustainable use of biodiversity and biodiversity-based technology and innovation.
National Target 20: Immediately following the approval of the Brazilian targets, resource needs assessments are carried out for the implementation of the national targets, followed by the mobilisation and allocation of financial resources to enable, from 2015 on, the implementation and monitoring of the Strategic Plan for Biodiversity 2011-20, as well as the achievement of its targets.	On the right track, but additional measures needed.

Source: MMA (2015), *Fifth National Report to the Convention on Biological Diversity.*

OECD Environmental Performance Reviews: Brazil 2015

PART II

Chapter 5

Protected areas

Brazil has massively expanded its network of protected areas. This chapter presents progress in extending the terrestrial and marine areas under environmental protection. It examines achievements and challenges related to the management of protected areas, including in terms of financial sustainability. The chapter describes the role of protected areas in improving the quality of life of traditional communities. Finally, it discusses the opportunities of opening protected areas to the public for tourism, recreation and environmental education, and for sustainable forest management.

1. Categories, extension and benefits of protected areas

1.1. The National System of Protected Areas

Protected areas have a long history in Brazil and are a cornerstone of its biodiversity policy. In 2000, in an effort to improve effectiveness of protected areas and to better preserve its tropical rainforests, Brazil established the National System of Protected Areas (SNUC), or conservation units, as such areas are known in the country.[1] SNUC integrated the heterogeneous landscape of protected areas, including those established by federal, state and municipal governments as well as those proposed by private actors (individuals, companies, non-government organisations), into one national system. It provided a common definition of protected areas and a framework for co-ordinated management and implementation at different levels of government. It also introduced the National Register of Protected Areas (CNUC) in 2006 as the official national database to consolidate information about protected areas at all levels of government.

SNUC defined 12 management categories (consolidating several existing categories and creating some new ones) in two broad groups: i) strict protection areas, with the primary objective of biodiversity conservation and forbidding direct use or consumption of natural resources; and ii) sustainable use areas, primarily aiming at conservation but permitting human settlements and various uses of natural resources in accordance with a sustainable management plan. Table 5.1 provides an overview of the objectives and activities allowed for each category. About two-thirds of the area under protection lies within sustainable use categories (Figure 5.1). This results from several factors, including the higher political and social acceptability of sustainable use areas, as they impose fewer restrictions on land and resource use; respect of traditional communities' rights and civil society movements in defence of these rights; and the government objective of stimulating sustainable timber logging in national forests (Veríssimo et al., 2011). The Brazilian example of extractive reserves has contributed to shaping the international classification of protected areas (Table 5.1).

The 2000 SNUC Law was the result of 12 years of parliamentary debate. It provided a sound legal basis for the establishment and management of protected areas and thus laid the groundwork for the remarkable expansion of the number and coverage of protected areas.[2]

1.2. Extension and coverage of protected areas

In the last decade, Brazil has become one of the world's top contributors to increasing the land area under environmental protection, as foreseen by the UN Convention on Biological Diversity (CDB) Strategic Plan 2002-10. Between 2003 and 2008, it accounted for more than 70% of the world's new terrestrial area placed under protection (Jenkins and Joppa, 2009). This period coincides with the first implementation stages of the Action Plan for Prevention and Control of Deforestation in Amazônia Legal, or PPCDAm (Chapter 4), and of the Amazon Region Protected Areas (ARPA) programme (Box 5.1).

Table 5.1. **Categories of protected areas under SNUC**

Brazilian management category	Land ownership	Main goal	Main features	International management category	Area (km²)
			Strict protection areas		
Ecological Station	Public	Nature preservation and scientific research	⊖ Scientific research ⊗ Public visitation ⊖ Education and environmental interpretation	Ia – Strict Nature Reserve	Federal: 74 691 State: 47 513 Municipal: 9
Biological Reserve	Public	Strict preservation of biota and other natural features	⊖ Scientific research ⊗ Public visitation ⊖ Education and environmental interpretation	Ia – Strict Nature Reserve	Federal: 39 034 State: 13 449 Municipal: 48
National/State/ Municipal Park	Public	Preservation of natural sites with ecological relevance or beautiful scenery	⊖ Public visitation ⊖ Scientific research ⊖ Education and environmental interpretation	II – National Park	Federal: 252 978 State: 94 889 Municipal: 221
Natural Monument	Public or private	Preservation of rare natural sites, with unique or beautiful scenery	⊖ Scientific research ⊖ Public visitation ⊖ Education and environmental interpretation	III – Natural Monument or Feature	Federal: 443 State: 892 Municipal: 73
Wildlife Refuge Area	Public or private	Protection of the natural environment to ensure conditions for the existence or breeding of local flora and fauna species	⊖ Scientific research ⊖ Public visitation ⊖ Education and environmental interpretation	III – Natural Monument or Feature	Federal: 2 017 State: 1 729 Municipal: 22
			Sustainable use areas		
Environmental Protection Area	Public or private	Protection of areas that are important to life quality and well-being of humans through biodiversity protection	(Vast areas; no buffer zone) ✓ Public visitation ✓ Scientific research	V – Protected Landscape/ Seascape	Federal: 100 101 State: 334 898 Municipal: 25 922
Area of Relevant Ecological Interest	Public or private	Maintenance of natural ecosystems with local or regional importance	(Small areas) ✓ Public visitation ✓ Scientific research	Mostly considered as IV – Habitat/Species Management Area	Federal: 447 State: 443 Municipal: 32
National/State/ Municipal Forest	Public or private	Multiple use of forest resources and scientific research, with emphasis on methods for sustainable use of native forests	✓ Permanence of traditional communities that already lived there when the protected area was created ✓ Public visitation ✓ Scientific research	VI – Protected Areas with Sustainable Use of Natural Resources (allowing local/ traditional communities in the Brazilian case)	Federal: 163 913 State: 136 053 Municipal: 0
Extractive Reserve	Public	Protection of areas inhabited by traditional populations living on extraction of natural resources, ensuring the sustainable use of the protected area	✓ Natural resource extraction by traditional populations living on the land ✓ Public visitation ✓ Scientific research ⊗ Exploitation of mineral resources ⊗ Hunting (neither amateur nor professional) ⊖ Commercial exploitation of timber	VI – Protected Areas with Sustainable Use of Natural Resources (with local/ traditional communities co-management in the Brazilian case)	Federal: 124 362 State: 20 208 Municipal: 0
Sustainable Development Reserve	Public	Protection of areas inhabited by traditional populations practising sustainable resources exploitation and use	✓ Public visitation ✓ Scientific research ✓ Sustainable natural resources exploitation ✓ Substitution of vegetation by cultivable species	VI – Protected Areas with Sustainable Use of Natural Resources (allowing local/ traditional communities co-management in the Brazilian case)	Federal: 1 026 State: 110 090 Municipal: 176
Fauna Reserve	Public	Technical and scientific research about sustainable economic management of wildlife resources	⊖ Public visitation ✓ Scientific research ⊗ Hunting (neither amateur nor professional)	IV – Habitat/Species Management Area	Federal: 0 State: 0 Municipal: 0
Private Natural Heritage Reserves	Private	Conservation of biodiversity	(no buffer zone) ✓ Public visitation ✓ Scientific research	IV – Habitat/Species Management Area	Federal: 4 832 State: 686 Municipal: 0

Notes:
✓ Activities allowed/encouraged as far as compatible with management plan
⊖ Activities allowed with restrictions established by management plans or in special circumstances
⊗ Prohibited activities
Public visitation includes tourism, recreation and environmental education.
Source: IUCN (2008), *Guidelines for Applying Protected Area Management Categories*; MMA (2015), "Areas protegidas", *www.mma.gov.br/areas-protegidas*; MMA (2015), "Cadastro Nacional de Unidades de Conservação" (accessed February 2015); WCMC-UNEP and IUCN (2015), "World Database on Protected Areas", *www.protectedplanet.net*.

Figure 5.1. **Strict protection categories cover about one-third of protected areas**

Official protected areas by category, 2015

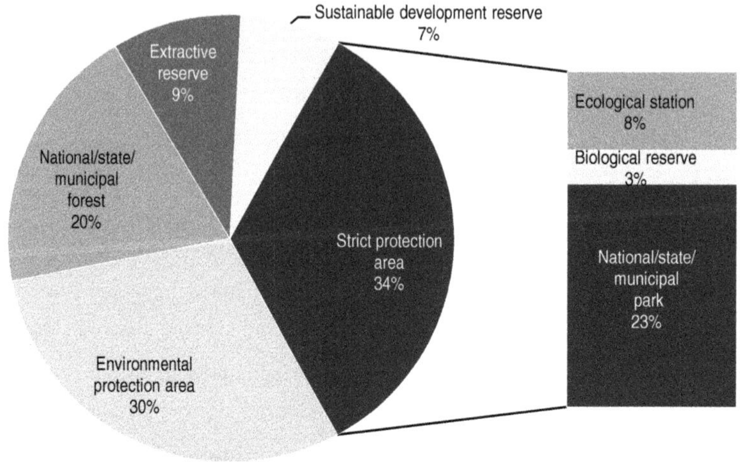

Note: Excluding natural monuments, wildlife refuge areas, areas of relevant ecological interest, fauna reserves and private natural heritage reserves, which together accounts for 0.7% of total officially protected area.
Source: MMA (2015), Cadastro Nacional de Unidades de Conservação.

StatLink http://dx.doi.org/10.1787/888933279763

Between 2000 and 2014, the number and extension of protected areas within SNUC more than doubled. As of early 2015, 1 940 protected areas covered a surface of more than 1.5 million km^2, almost three times the size of France, or 17.2% of Brazil's terrestrial and inland water areas and 1.5% of coastal and marine areas, including the exclusive economic zone (Figure 5.2). Therefore, Brazil achieved the 2020 Aichi target of protecting at least 17% of terrestrial and inland water areas well ahead of time.[3] The expansion of protected areas has levelled off since 2010, though their number has continued to increase. This reflects the recent focus on smaller-scale initiatives, as well as the partial elimination of some protected areas from SNUC (degazetting).

Figure 5.2. **The land area under nature protection has more than doubled**

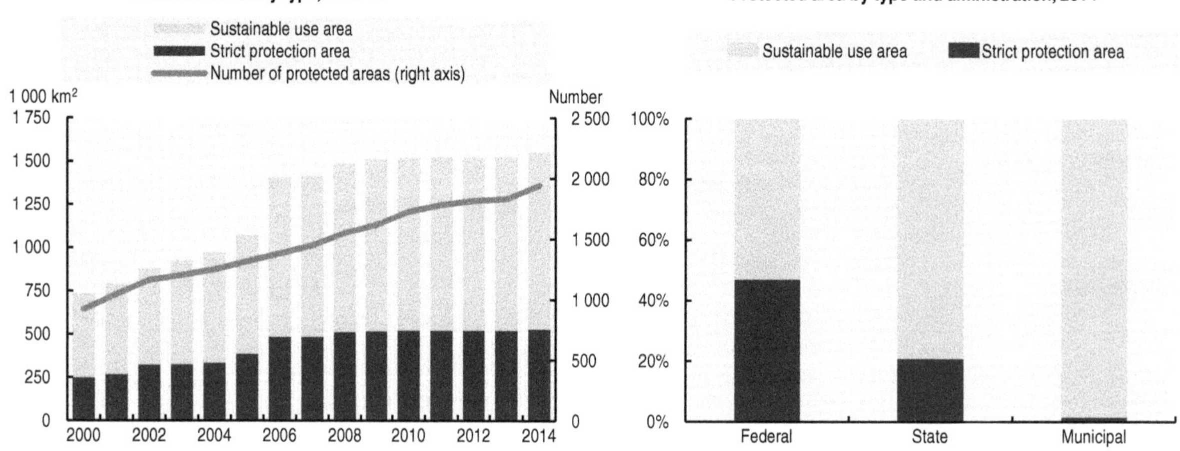

Source: MMA (2015), Cadastro Nacional de Unidades de Conservação.

StatLink http://dx.doi.org/10.1787/888933279776

Box 5.1. **The Amazon Region Protected Areas programme**

ARPA is one of the largest tropical forest conservation programmes in the world. ARPA was created with the goal of expanding and strengthening SNUC in the Amazon by establishing 600 000 km^2 of protected area. The programme is result-oriented and has four major components: establishment; management and consolidation; financial sustainability; and co-ordination, management and monitoring. It is co-ordinated by the Ministry of the Environment (MMA) and managed by the Brazilian Biodiversity Fund (Funbio; Box 5.7). It is funded by resources from the Global Environment Facility (GEF), the German Federal Ministry for Economic Co-operation and Development via the German Development Bank (KfW), WWF and the Brazilian Amazon Fund (Chapter 4).

ARPA was launched in 2002 and designed to be implemented in three phases. The first (2003-10) aimed to establish 180 000 km^2 of new protected area in the Amazon and to start the consolidation progress in 70 000 km^2. Both targets had been exceeded by 2010. The programme invested USD 83 million over the first phase, half of which was used for operating costs.

The second phase (2010-15) aimed at establishing additional 135 000 km^2 and consolidating 320 000 km^2 of protected areas. It also aimed at raising USD 70 million for the Protected Areas Fund (FAP, established under the first phase). Expenditure during the second phase (excluding disbursements under the FAP) reached USD 115 million.

The third phase focuses on ensuring the long-term financial sustainability of the programme. The ARPA for Life initiative was launched in May 2014 (in parallel with implementation of the second phase) to facilitate the transition from a donation-based system to a system financed by the federal and state budgets and environmental compensation (Section 4.4).[a] To achieve this, the share of government budget allocated to ARPA should gradually grow over a period of 25 years, while several partners would contribute USD 250 million to a transition fund (the ARPA for Life Fund).[b]

a) Funbio and the WWF estimated the financial need for the ARPA programme over 2011-20 at BRL 800 million, including both investment and operational costs. Revenue for the same period was estimated at BRL 530 million, for a financial gap of BRL 270 million (Funbio, 2012).

b) The German Ministry for Co-operation and Development, the Inter-American Development Bank, Funbio, the Gordon and Betty Moore Foundation, WWF-Brasil, WWF-US and the GEF.

Source: Funbio (2012), *Quanto custa o Programa Áreas Protegidas da Amazônia? Uma modelagem financeira para as Unidades de Conservação do Arpa*; MMA (2015), *Fifth National Report to the Convention on Biological Diversity*.

Federal and state protected areas account for 98% of total area under protection. About 40% of protected areas are Private Natural Heritage Reserves, which however cover less than 1% of the total area under SNUC. Municipal protected areas are often within cities and hence significantly smaller in size. Federal protected areas are roughly balanced with respect to strict protection and sustainable use areas, while subnational governments have primarily established sustainable use areas (Figure 5.2). Municipalities and many states use protected areas primarily as land management instruments.

The SNUC protected areas are complemented by several other land use or land management types that aim at, or contribute to, environmental conservation. These include indigenous lands (referred to as *latu sensu* protected areas) and *quilombola* lands (Box 5.2), as well as the so-called Areas of Permanent Preservation (APPs) and Legal Reserves (RLs) that landholders are required to preserve under the 2012 Forest Code (Law for the Protection of Native Vegetation). APPs and RLs are estimated to cover 12% and 30% of the national territory, respectively (MMA, 2010), corresponding to more than twice the

SNUC area. However, many private lands have not respected these quotas (Chapter 4). Brazil is also home to several World Heritage natural sites and 12 internationally recognised wetlands under the Ramsar Convention that are designated protected areas and cover over 65 000 km^2. The government aspires to obtain the designation of additional 10 Ramsar sites by 2017 (MMA, 2015a).

Brazil's terrestrial area is typically divided into six large ecosystems or biomes:[4] Amazon, Atlantic Forest, Caatinga, Cerrado, Pampa and Pantanal (Box 4.1). Sustainable use areas dominate in all biomes except the Pantanal (Figure 5.3). The coverage of protected areas across biomes varies widely. Over three-quarters of the SNUC area is in the Amazon biome, accounting for nearly 27% of this region's surface area, including its vast freshwater bodies (Figure 5.3 and Table 5.2). This reflects the use of protected areas as a primary policy tool to fight deforestation in the region. The SNUC coverage in the other biomes is smaller and more fragmented, ranging from 9% in the Atlantic Forest to about 3% in the Pampa biome (Table 5.2). Despite progress across biomes, Brazil did not meet its ambitious target of protecting 10% of land area within each biome, and 30% of the Amazon, by 2010.

Figure 5.3. **Most protected areas are in the Amazon**

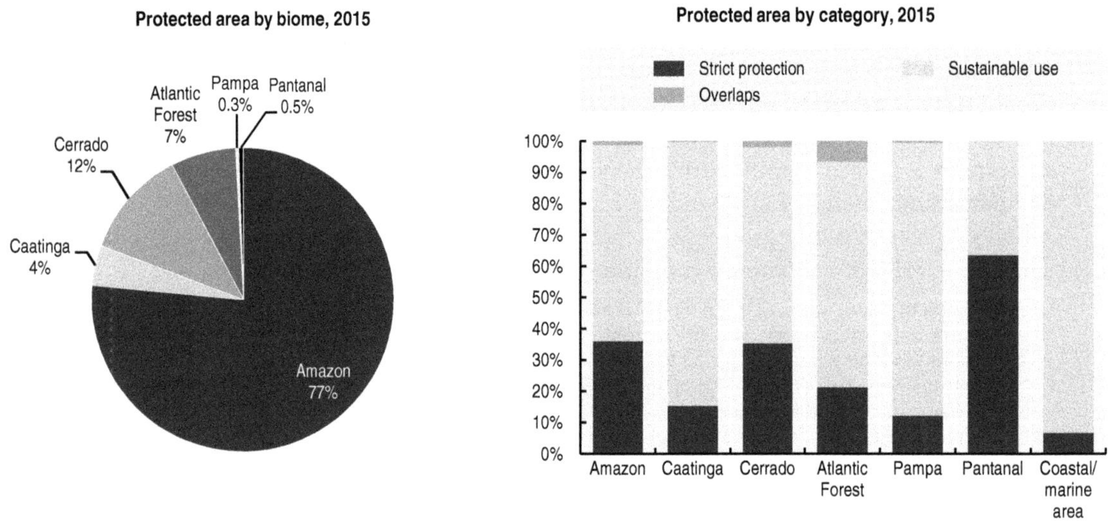

Source: MMA (2015), Cadastro Nacional de Unidades de Conservação (website).

StatLink http://dx.doi.org/10.1787/888933279783

In 2013, Brazil set a new national target of protecting 30% of the Amazon, 17% of other terrestrial biomes, and 10% of coastal and marine areas; these targets expanded the definition of protected areas, beyond areas covered under the SNUC Law, to also include indigenous lands, APPs and RLs so as to better account for the various conservation efforts in the country.[5] When indigenous lands are taken into account, half the Amazon territory is within protected areas, far above the target (Table 5.2).

Marine protected areas covered only 1.5% of Brazil's total coastal and marine area in 2015. Marine protected areas have long been used for conserving biodiversity and protecting essential marine habitats. About 70% of mangroves are within protected areas (MMA, 2015a). More recently, marine protected areas have been recognised as a fishery management tool and used to reduce conflicts between traditional fishing communities

Table 5.2. **Protected areas and indigenous lands by biome, 2015**

	% of total biome area						% of terrestrial and inland water area	% of coastal/ marine area
	Amazon	Caatinga	Cerrado	Atlantic Forest	Pampa	Pantanal		
2020 target[a]	**30**	**17**	**17**	**17**	**17**	**17**	**17**	**10**
2010 target[b]	**30**	**10**	**10**	**10**	**10**	**10**	**10**	**10**
SNUC protected areas[c]	26.6	7.6	8.2	9.0	2.7	4.6	17.2	1.5
Strict protection	9.6	1.2	2.9	1.9	0.3	2.9	5.8	0.1
Sustainable use	16.7	6.4	5.2	6.5	2.4	1.7	11.0	1.4
Indigenous lands	23.6	0.4	4.5	0.6	0.0	1.8	12.9	-
Total[d]	**50.2**	**8.0**	**12.7**	**9.6**	**2.7**	**6.4**	**30.1**	**1.5**

a) Includes protected areas under SNUC, indigenous land and protected area on private lands as required by the new Forest Code (APPs and RLs).
b) The 2010 targets include only protected areas that are part of SNUC.
c) The total SNUC area excludes overlaps between strict protection and sustainable use area, i.e. may be lower than the sum of the two groups of categories.
d) Total excludes RLs and APPs.
Source: Based on MMA (2015), *Cadastro Nacional de Unidades de Conservação* (accessed February 2015); MMA (2010), *Fourth National Report to the Convention on Biological Diversity.*

Box 5.2. **Indigenous lands**

About 13% of Brazil's territory is protected by designation of about 600 indigenous lands,[a] most of which are located in the Amazon. They are home to 230 indigenous peoples. Indigenous lands are not part of SNUC, as their primary objectives relate to cultural and social factors; however, they are recognised as effectively contributing to nature conservation and are therefore considered protected areas under the CBD and were included in Brazil's 2006 National Protected Areas Plan (Section 4.2). Indigenous lands tend to be well preserved, given indigenous communities' long-standing tradition of sustainable use of natural resources. For example, deforestation rates in these territories are among the lowest in the country: in 2014, only 1% of the total deforestation in the Amazon was within these areas. Indigenous lands are also integrated into "landscape mosaics" (Box 5.6). The Constitution also grants rights to *quilombola* people to collectively own the lands they have occupied since colonial times.[b]

Progress in the legislation on indigenous lands has helped address social issues associated with the management of protected areas (Irving, 2010). The 2007 National Policy for the Sustainable Development of Traditional Peoples and Communities and the 2012 National Policy on Territorial and Environmental Management of Indigenous Lands aim at promoting sustainable use of natural resources in indigenous lands, as well as defending the traditional knowledge of the communities involved. They have helped strengthen the relationships between environmental NGOs, the government and organisations working with indigenous peoples. Several other such initiatives are under way, some of which are supported by the National Environment Fund (Chapter 2) and international organisations. Co-ordination between programmes and involved institutions is weak, however (Irving, 2010). Conflicts about land use rights over indigenous lands can still arise, including with loggers, farmers and miners (Funai, 2015).

a) According to the Brazilian Constitution, the "lands traditionally occupied by indigenous peoples are those on which they live on a permanent basis, those used for their productive activities, those indispensable to the preservation of the environmental resources necessary for their well-being and for their physical and cultural reproduction, according to their uses, customs and traditions. The lands traditionally occupied by indigenous peoples are intended for their permanent possession and they shall have the exclusive usufruct of the riches of the soil, the rivers and the lakes existing therein".
b) *Quilombolas* are traditional groups or communities of African origin.

and fishing companies (OECD-FAO, 2015; also see Chapter 4). This is shown by the growth of marine sustainable use areas, where only traditional fishing activities are permitted. The Sectoral Plan for Sea Resources expects to increase the total marine protected areas to 4% of Brazil's territorial waters and exclusive economic zone by 2015. The government is sealing up efforts to bring this share to 5% by 2020. The Marine and Coastal Protected Areas project, supported by the Global Environment Facility, will contribute to this goal.

The WWF and ICMBio (2012) noted that federal protected areas do not adequately represent the totality of Brazilian ecosystems, nor do they sufficiently protect species against extreme population reduction or extinction, particularly in the Pampa biome (MMA, 2010). Federal protected areas cover nearly 60% of threatened flora and fauna species (Chapter 4). While Brazil needs to keep a tight focus on the Amazon biome, future efforts will need to concentrate on marine areas and the other terrestrial biomes, notably Cerrado and Caatinga, where protection through land-use zoning is low and the most future deforestation is expected (Soares-Filho et al., 2014; also see Chapter 4). The ecosystem representation of conservation may appear more balanced once the set-aside areas, as required under the Forest Code, are implemented and monitored.

1.3. *Environmental and economic benefits of protected areas*

The rapid expansion of protected area coverage in the Amazon biome has been primarily the result of an integrated and co-ordinated strategy to combat deforestation and illegal land grabbing, based upon the PPCDAm and the ARPA programme. It has also been driven by a desire to recognise traditional and local community rights. Since the mid-2000s, more than 500 000 km^2 of federal and state-level protected areas have been created in the Amazon, including along the so-called "deforestation arc" (comprising the eastern and southern edges of the forests in the states of Rondônia, Mato Grosso and Pará) and in areas expecting road infrastructure development. This was essential in slowing the advance of deforestation for land speculation purposes, which often occurs along new road as a consequence of easier access to the forest (CEPAL et al., 2011).

As Figure 5.4 shows, the establishment of protected areas greatly contributed to the decline of deforestation levels in the Amazon biome in the second half of the 2000s, together with the other measures discussed in Chapter 4. Between 2008 and 2012, nearly 95% of the deforestation in the region occurred outside protected areas. Deforestation is over four times less likely to occur in protected areas than outside these areas (TCU, 2013). This has also helped curb greenhouse gas (GHG) emissions; in 1996-2006, protected areas in the Amazon biome alone absorbed nearly 2 tonnes of CO_2 per hectare (TCU, 2013).

Protected areas contribute significantly to the provision and conservation of water resources and generate various economic benefits in terms of tourism, commercialisation of forest and biodiversity products and generation of tax revenue (Box 5.3). There is also evidence that marine protected areas have helped protect fish stocks (MMA, 2015a).

2. Institutional framework for protected areas

Government institutions

The national system of protected areas involves institutions at federal, state and municipal level. The MMA co-ordinates SNUC, while executing agencies at each level are responsible for implementation, including the proposal and establishment of new protected areas and their operation and management. The Chico Mendes Institute for

Figure 5.4. **Expanding protected areas has greatly helped reduce deforestation in the Amazon**

Protected areas and deforestation rates in the Amazon, 2000-14

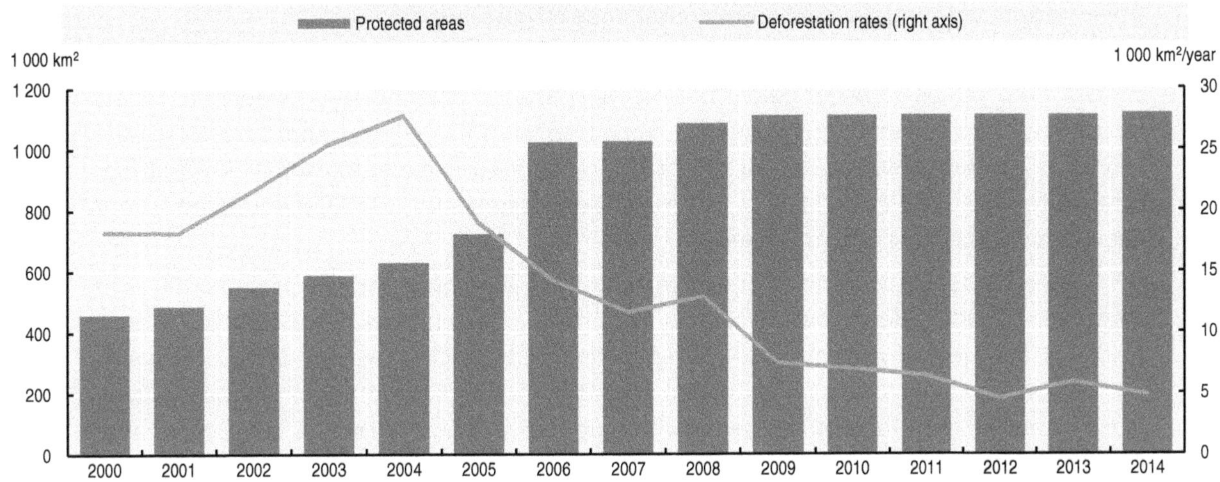

Note: Deforestation rates refer to the Amazônia Legal, which encompasses the Amazonian forest (about 4.1 million km²) and transitional vegetation (1 million km²).
Source: INPE (2015), "Projeto PRODES: Monitoramento da floresta Amazônia Brasileira por satélite"; MMA (2015), Cadastro Nacional de Unidades de Conservaçao.

StatLink http://dx.doi.org/10.1787/888933279797

Box 5.3. **The economic value of Brazilian protected areas**

Medeiros and Young (2011) estimated that sustainable timber logging in the Amazon protected areas generated value of between BRL 1.2 billion and BRL 2.2 billion annually. The extraction of non-timber forest products such as rubber and Brazil nuts (in extractive reserves) was estimated to generate between BRL 16 million and BRL 39 million annually. Investment to enhance productive capacity of workers in these reserves would significantly increase annual gains; certification could add value to the final products.

The economic gains from tourism in national parks estimated at some BRL 1.6 billion per year, and revenue from all federal and state protected areas may reach BRL 2.2 billion in 2016, when Brazil hosts the Olympic Games. However, many protected areas are not yet accessible enough to allow a significant flow of tourists; there is still significant room to enhance tourism potential (Section 5.1).

Brazil's protected areas system is estimated to have prevented the release of about 2.8 billion tonnes of carbon into the atmosphere, which in monetary terms would correspond to nearly BRL 96 billion. In addition, it greatly contributes to the provision and conservation of water resources. About 80% of hydropower comes from sources located within or downstream of federal protected areas; 9% of drinking water is directly captured in protected areas and 26% is collected in downstream sources; and 4% of the water used in agriculture and irrigation is taken from sources within or downstream of protected areas.

Source: Medeiros, R. and C. Young (2011), *Contribuição das unidades de conservação brasileiras para a economia nacional: Relatório Final.*

Biodiversity Conservation (ICMBio) is the executing agency for federal protected areas. It was established in 2007 as the result of the division of the Brazilian Institute of Environment and Renewable Natural Resources (IBAMA) into two agencies: one maintaining the IBAMA name and the principal functions of licensing, monitoring and enforcement; and ICMBio overseeing the establishment, management and monitoring of federal protected areas within SNUC.[6] The rationale for this change was to reinforce governance of the increasing number of federal protected areas and separate their preservation and management from compliance monitoring.

As federal protected areas are scattered through a vast territory, 11 ICMBio regional offices were set up to improve communication and co-ordination between the federal authority, the relevant subnational governments and local stakeholders. State and municipal protected areas are administered by the respective environment institutions, often with the support of ICMBio, non-government organisations (NGOs) and international development co-operation providers.

The establishment of an agency overseeing all aspects of federal protected areas is common to many federal countries, such as Canada and Colombia (OECD-ECLAC, 2014). In Brazil, it has helped improve the transparency and effectiveness of SNUC (Veríssimo et al., 2011). The large number of protected areas at all levels of government poses a challenge to effective co-ordination and co-operation among institutions. The Federal Court of Accounts (TCU) evaluated the governance and effectiveness of protected areas in the Amazon biome. It found that co-ordination was often insufficient, resulting in a duplication of efforts and reduced efficiency. The report found that about 70% of protected area managers believed co-operation among themselves, government bodies and NGOs was weak (TCU, 2013).

Non-government organisations

Many NGOs perform a complementary role in establishing and managing protected areas, and in supporting local communities living in and near them. In light of SNUC's constrained financial and human resources (Sections 4.3 and 4.4), NGOs can support activities such as developing technical studies and management plans, implementing management actions and promoting social participation.

NGOs are also involved in biodiversity and forest monitoring in protected areas. For example, SOS Mata Atlântica supported monitoring vegetation cover in the Atlantic Forest biome, Imazon runs a deforestation and forest degradation monitoring system in the Amazon, and the Instituto Socioambiental implemented a monitoring programme in Amazon protected areas and indigenous lands.

3. The establishment of protected areas

As in all countries, in Brazil the majority of lands that are or may be included in protected areas are inhabited. In addition, some areas may be important for potential infrastructure development (chiefly roads and hydropower plants) and other economic activities, such as agriculture and mining. Competition among environmental, social and economic interests is generally stronger in cities, as urban protected areas are likely to be on high-value land that can be used for urban expansion (Box 5.4). For protected areas to be established and managed effectively, consideration must be given to all these conflicting interests so as to avoid environmental, social and economic losses.

In acknowledging this need, the SNUC Law requires public consultation with local communities and stakeholders to be conducted prior to the establishment of protected areas at all levels of government (biological reserves and ecological stations are exempt). This is one of the main areas of progress represented by SNUC. In addition, the establishment of a federal protected area requires prior consultation of the ministries responsible for potentially affected sectors (e.g. mines, power plants, transport infrastructure, agriculture),

Box 5.4. **Urban protected areas in Brazil**

Protected areas in or at the edge of urban areas often provide high-value ecosystem services, such as drinking water, to nearby cities (e.g. São Paulo, Rio de Janeiro and Salvador) and opportunities for recreation and environmental education. They thus help improve the well-being of urban dwellers and build urban constituencies for nature conservation. Their establishment and operation entail specific complexities, however. Protecting urban areas involves several often conflicting interests; the areas are often potential sites for residential, commercial, industrial and government buildings and urban infrastructure such as roads and landfills.

In Brazil, urban protected areas are mostly managed by municipal governments, but there are examples of state-managed urban protected areas (e.g. in Belo Horizonte and São Paulo). Only a few urban protected areas are under federal jurisdiction, but they are among the largest (e.g. Tijuca National Park and Brasília National Park).

Tijuca National Park in Rio de Janeiro covers some 40 km^2 and is managed by ICMBio, in collaboration with the municipal and state governments. The collaboration was established in the late 1990s to meet urban interests related to transport and recreation and to respond to increasing pressures from urban expansion, especially from neighbouring *favelas*. In 2011, 28 national, state and municipal protected areas were consolidated to form the Carioca Protected Areas Mosaic. Tijuca National Park is an example of how strong inter-institutional co-operation can help regenerate large areas of degraded Atlantic forest.

Cantareira State Park, part of the São Paulo green belt, meets almost half the water demand of the urban area. In response to pressure from urban sprawl in the Cantareira mountains, in 2009 the state government launched a process aimed at nearly quadrupling the area under state protection. This required the purchase, transfer or expropriation of private land in seven municipalities. To this end, the state government co-operated closely with landowners and municipalities, surveying the perimeter of the proposed protected areas so as to tailor their boundaries to existing ecological, economic and political situations. Various kinds of protected area status were applied to allow compatible land uses to continue. This co-operation among different government levels, local communities and private landowners was a success. The protected areas were established in 2010.

Source: Trzyna (2014), *Urban Protected Areas: Profiles and best practice guidelines.*

as well as state governments. As in other countries, this process can take several years. While it is an important way to reduce the potential for conflict, bringing the various conflicting interests to consensus can be challenging and has sometimes prevented proposed protected areas from being established.

Some categories of SNUC protected areas, including national parks, are of exclusive public domain (Table 5.1). Establishing such a protected area requires private lands within its boundaries to be expropriated and the owners compensated. Traditional communities may reside in public sustainable development reserves and extractive reserves. While traditional communities do not own the land, which can only be bequeathed, they have the right to live on it and use its resources on the basis of management contracts and plans agreed with the responsible authorities (Section 5.3). In practice, activities and natural resource uses are allowed on 88% of the total SNUC area, including some strict protection areas; in the remaining areas the government seeks to enforce full restriction of the direct use of natural resources (Gurgel et al., 2009). Private ownership is permitted in some protected area categories if land use is compatible with the category's objectives (Table 5.1); there are also private natural heritage reserves, which are recognised as part of SNUC upon request of the landowner.

Some SNUC implementing regulations and actions were approved and undertaken with considerable delay, notably with respect to land expropriation and compensation, but also regarding permitted activities in sustainable use areas. Regulatory uncertainty has been reduced, but conflict over land ownership and use remains. The establishment of protected areas has sometimes been received with resentment, with some local authorities, landowners and communities fearing (sometimes rightly) to be dispossessed of their land or expectations of future ownership. For example, establishment of the Mata Escura Biological Reserve in 2003, as environmental compensation for a hydroelectric plant, sparked conflicts with the local *quilombola* community. The conflict was resolved only in 2012 with an agreement between the community and ICMBio that allowed the community to remain in the protected area under certain conditions (Vilela, 2013). Pontões Capixabas National Park, established in 2002, included nearly 400 farms within its boundaries; ultimately, in 2008, it had to be reclassified as a natural monument, where private property is allowed.

While redefining boundaries and reclassifying protected areas may in some cases allow for more effective and equitable management, the process also reveals how economic interests compete for land currently under environmental protection (Mascia et al., 2014.). In 2014, four protected areas were degazetted on grounds of national strategic interests such as the construction of hydroelectric plants. Some states have approved more flexible rules that make degazetting easier.

The establishment of sustainable use areas is generally less difficult because restrictions on resource use are less severe. Traditional communities have increasingly requested the establishment of this type of protected area, which can provide a means of improving living conditions and getting access to public services and social benefits (Section 5.3). In 2014, over 50 new extractive reserve proposals were filed by traditional fishermen alone (Prates, 2014).

The expropriation and compensation of private property for exclusively public protected areas are challenging, especially because of insufficient financial resources to compensate landowners and, to a lesser extent, unclear land tenure. In 2011, 20% of the Amazon area was supposedly public land, which facilitates the establishment of protected areas, while only 4% was covered by valid private property titles (Figure 4.4). About 70% of federal protected areas, or 7% of the surface area under federal protection, includes land on which there are private property claims, mostly in the Amazon, Cerrado and Atlantic Forest biomes (TCU, 2013; Veríssimo et al., 2011). TCU (2013) estimated that BRL 7.1 billion was needed to resolve this situation; the federal budget allocated about BRL 70 million per year in 2009-12 for this purpose. At that pace, it would take more than a century to complete the process. The resolution of problems related to territorial consolidation and land tenure sometimes exceeds the capacity and responsibility of environment authorities (TCU, 2013).

The Terra Legal Programme, launched in 2009 with the aim of regularising the occupation of federal public land in the Amazon (Box 4.3), is expected to lead to the establishment of new protected areas with clear land tenure. The programme helps clarify ownership and user rights of public lands among federal and state agencies. About 50 000 km^2 of federal public land was assigned to the MMA for the creation of protected areas. One protected area was created in 2014 (the Maues Ecological Station) and a group of new areas totalling more than 35 000 km^2 is being created along the Trans-Amazonia Highway in southern Amazonas state, a recent deforestation hotspot.

The new Forest Code introduced a land offset mechanism that could help consolidate public protected areas. It allows landholders that are not compliant with forest set-aside requirements to make up for this deficit by buying private property within official protected areas on behalf of the government. For this mechanism to operate, the Rural Environmental Cadastre will have to be fully implemented (Chapter 4).

In addition to these efforts, Brazil could consider alternative ways to increase the amount of land under environmental protection, including extending the network of private protected areas, which now account for a negligible share of the SNUC surface. Encouraging contractual agreements with landowners can be a cost-effective way of ensuring biodiversity conservation and sustainable use. In South Africa, for example, the Stewardship Programme between the government and landowners is estimated to cost only about one-tenth what it would cost to purchase land outright (OECD, 2013). Beyond cost savings, such approaches allow protected areas to be expanded in a way that considers the rights and interests of landowners.

4. The management of protected areas

4.1. *Management committees and plans*

The SNUC Law requires the creation of management committees, whose main function is to facilitate the active involvement of local communities and stakeholders in decisions concerning protected areas. These committees play decision or advisory roles, depending on the management category. They are composed of government officials and representatives of civil society and the private sector. As of 2013, out of the 320 federal protected areas (excluding private reserves), 253 had committees established and 25 were in the process of establishing them (ICMBio, 2014).

Some factors can limit effective social participation, including inadequate training for managers and committee members, insufficient involvement of potential stakeholders and lack of financial resources (Mendonça et al., 2014). In addition, most management committees have not yet defined their operating rules, so there is still a risk of exacerbating conflicts among committee members (Veríssimo et al., 2011).

The protected area management plan is the main planning and day-to-day management instrument. It should take account of the protected area's objectives and its physical and socio-economic features, as well as the zoning and regulations that guide natural resource use in the area. The existence of a management plan is a condition for public use activities (such as tourism and environmental education), as well as for sustainable logging and local community resource use. The SNUC Law requires the development of management plans within five years of the establishment of a protected area, and it mandates nature protection and basic management to guarantee the area's integrity until the plan is developed. Management plans may be complemented by other instruments: some sustainable use areas, for example, have a "plan of utilisation" as the first phase of the management plan, allowing signage and land regularisation to be carried out.

Due to limited resources and capacity, many protected areas still lack a management plan after the five-year deadline. In 2012, only 94 of the then 247 federal and state protected areas in the Amazon biome had an approved management plan; 40 federal protected areas had been managed without a management plan for more than 10 years (TCU, 2013). This pattern also holds in other biomes; only in the Atlantic Forest biome did more than half of federal protected areas have an approved management plan in 2013. The lack of a management plan implies that management is limited to monitoring and research, hence impeding socio-economic development, as the example described in Box 5.5 shows.

Box 5.5. **No management plan, no tourism: The case of Anavilhanas National Park**

Anavilhanas is one of the most extensive freshwater archipelagos in the world. It contains more than 400 islands, hundreds of rivers and lakes and, during the dry season, white sand beaches. In the early 1980s, an ecological station was established to strictly protect the area and allow access only for scientific purposes. In recognition of the area's tourism potential, the protected area was reclassified as a national park in 2008. The management plan, however, had been adopted to meet the objectives of an ecological station and has not yet been revised. In 2012, ICMBio issued temporary permission for tourism activities in the park under certain conditions. However, in 2014, expanding demand for tourism activities and constrained management capacity at the site led ICMBio to restrict the park management from allowing access to visitors, maintaining that, without a valid management plan, tourism could have an unacceptable impact on biodiversity.

Efforts to develop and approve management plans have intensified in recent years, but the gaps remain large (Veríssimo et al., 2011). Existing management plans are often based on sound scientific information and analysis, yet tend to lack management tools and practical applicability, resulting in a generally low level of implementation. In 2012, half the management plans of Amazonian federal and state protected areas were being applied very little, if at all, according to the TCU (2013). Other studies pointed to even lower levels of implementation (Semeia, 2012b). Developing a management plan tends to be costly and time-consuming. The lack of implementation highlights the need to develop management objectives and approaches that suit the specific protected area, so as to ensure that each plan is applicable in practice (Kinouchi, 2014). Management plans should include financial analysis and be periodically reviewed, and adjusted where they prove ineffective. There is also a need for better-trained protected area managers and for promotion of co-operation and exchange of experience and best practices among them.

4.2. Integrated management of multiple protected areas

The SNUC Law also introduced instruments for managing protected areas at landscape scale, allowing connections among and within ecosystems to be maintained or increased. It recognises ecological corridors as territorial management instruments to maintain ecological processes,[7] and introduces the possibility of integrating multiple protected areas into a "mosaic" if they occur in proximity or overlap.

Mosaics aim to facilitate co-ordination among mangers and local populations of the participating protected areas so as to find shared solutions to common issues such as land and resource use in border zones, access to the protected areas, enforcement, monitoring and evaluation of management plans, scientific research and allocation of resources

(MMA, 2010). As of 2014, the MMA had approved 14 mosaics; Box 5.6 describes an example. However, their implementation is challenging; many protected areas in Brazil are still managed as individual administrative units.

Box 5.6. **Managing protected areas at landscape scale: The Lower Rio Negro Mosaic**

The Lower Rio Negro Mosaic in Amazonas state covers more than 70 000 km^2 and encompasses 11 protected areas (three federal, seven state and one municipal) in five municipalities. The area includes dozens of riverine and indigenous villages that live off small-scale agriculture and extractive activities. Officially recognised in December 2010, the mosaic aims to improve the management of its participating protected areas by adopting a shared and participatory management model.

The mosaic has a common management committee, chaired by the manager of a participating national park, and a joint management plan in addition to the individual management plans of the areas involved. This structure allows park managers to share expertise, infrastructure and equipment and better engage with communities residing in border areas. For example, the personnel of a given protected area focus not only on issues related to that area, but also assume thematic responsibilities across the entire mosaic. The mosaic structure helps address environmental and socio-economic challenges, many of which are common to all protected areas, and facilitates the resolution of conflicts arising in border areas. Such conflicts are often linked to the monitoring and control of natural resource use.

In two of the mosaic's national parks (Anavilhanas and Jaú), for example, members of local communities residing nearby conduct traditional activities within the parks – such as turtle fishing, sand collection and logging – that are not permitted under national park regulations. While these are mostly carried out for community consumption as traditional activities, product sales to commercial companies are increasing; turtle trafficking, for example, has become a major challenge in the region. Enforcement of park regulations has caused many families to move to the neighbouring extractive reserve, where natural resource use is permitted.

The 2006 National Protected Areas Plan also attempted to integrate the various types of protected areas, those covered and not covered by SNUC (e.g. indigenous lands), into one holistic landscape planning process that would take account of the contribution of protected areas to poverty eradication and social inclusion. This plan probably has too many potentially conflicting objectives and has not been fully implemented. The heterogeneous characteristics and needs of the areas made it difficult for the responsible government agencies to reach consensus.

4.3. Human resources

Managing the vast territory covered by SNUC requires numerous well-trained staff. There is evidence that human resources are insufficient, however. According to ICMBio (2014), 1 079 civil servants were directly involved in the management of federal protected areas as of August 2014. This means, on average, one public servant per 700 km^2 of federal protected areas. In 2010, 305 people were employed in state-level protected areas in the Amazon region, but with large variations across states. In the state of Amazonas, for example, there was only one employee per 5 900 km^2 (Veríssimo et al., 2011). Medeiros and Young (2011) estimated that, in the late 2000s, staff density was among the lowest in the world. According to their analysis, an employee in a Brazilian protected area managed, on average, roughly 200 km^2, compared to less than 20 km^2 in South Africa (Figure 5.5).

Figure 5.5. **Each protected-area staff member in Brazil manages a much larger area than in other countries**

Protected area per staff unit, selected countries, late 2000s

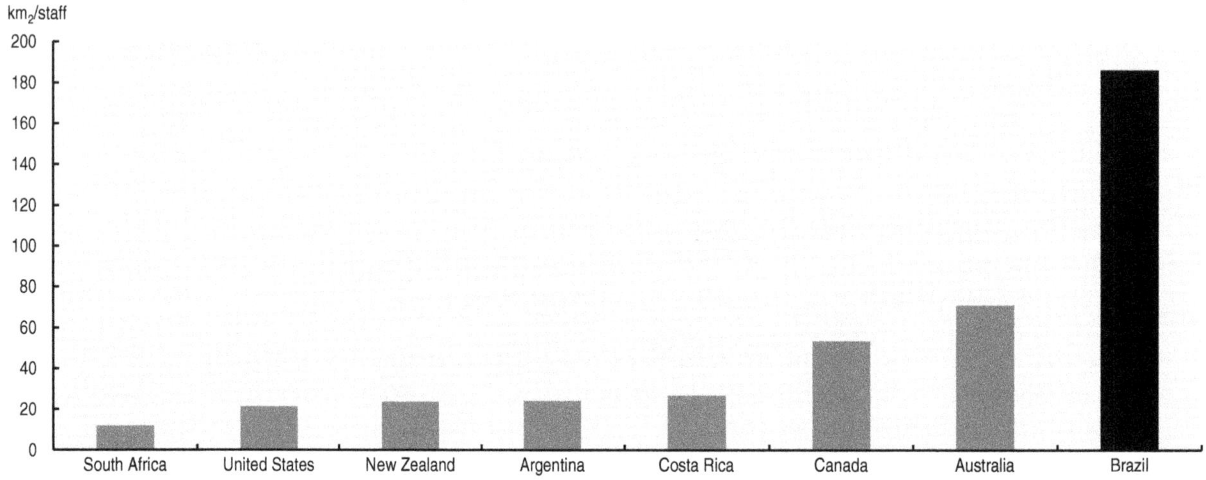

Source: Medeiros, R. and C. Young (2011), *Contribuição das unidades de conservação brasileiras para a economia nacional: Relatório final.*

StatLink http://dx.doi.org/10.1787/888933279807

Lack of human resources is a key reason for the insufficient implementation of many activities, especially those related to surveillance, conflict management, promotion and control of public use, and biodiversity monitoring. Estimates suggest that at least 19 000 additional workers are needed overall – 13 000 of them for field activities – in federal and state protected areas (MMA, 2009). At ICMBio alone there is a workforce deficit of 7 000 people, including employees, firefighters and volunteers, though new hiring processes have helped reduce the gap at the federal level in recent years. According to the TCU (2013), in 2012 one-quarter of federal and state protected areas in the Amazon region had no staff; only three protected areas reported that the number of staff was sufficient.

Staff turnover poses additional challenges to effective management. Attracting staff for the long term has proved difficult in some areas, notably remote parts of the Amazon, where working and living conditions (e.g. health, education, housing, transport) are demanding. Satisfactory working conditions are rare, given the generally weak infrastructure, resources and capacity. The lack of staff in protected areas has also been associated with Brazil's strict employment regulations and the red tape involved in hiring in the public sector.

While generally highly motivated and committed, many managers and staff are life scientists and are not trained for day-to-day management challenges, particularly those related to public use of protected areas (e.g. visitation for tourism, recreation and environmental education, and forest concessions), and the conflicts that arise among or with local stakeholders. This lack of capacity also results in poor quality projects, inability to attract financial resources and difficulty in efficiently spending what funds are allocated. Efforts are being made to reduce this knowledge deficit, including through the NGOs WWF and Institute for Ecological Research (IPE), which provide training to managers of ARPA-associated protected areas, and through ICMBio's internal capacity-building facility, ACADEBio.

4.4. Financial resources

The SNUC Law requires allocation of sufficient financial resources to protected areas to ensure that they are effectively managed and meet their goals. However, the expansion of protected areas has not been followed by a commensurate increase in resources. A 2012 survey among managers of protected areas revealed that 60% did not have sufficient resources to carry out their activities (Semeia, 2013).

While the exact amount of funding available for SNUC is not clear, several studies indicate a considerable financial gap for effective management of the huge area under protection – a situation common in much of Latin America (Bovarnick et al., 2010). The MMA (2009) calculated that maintaining federal protected areas in "satisfactory operational conditions" would require a budget increase of BRL 540 million; at the state level, the financial gap was BRL 360 million. In addition, an estimated BRL 610 million in investment would be needed to adequately consolidate federal protected areas (e.g. to put in place the necessary infrastructure), along with some BRL 1.2 billion for state protected areas (Funbio, 2009). Brazil invests much less in maintaining its protected areas than other countries, including Latin American countries and emerging economies (Figure 5.6). The lack of financial resources heavily constrains protected area managers from adequately meeting objectives and from hiring the staff necessary to manage the areas (Section 4.3).

Figure 5.6. **Investment in protected areas is lower than in other countries**

Investment per km² of protected areas, late 2000s

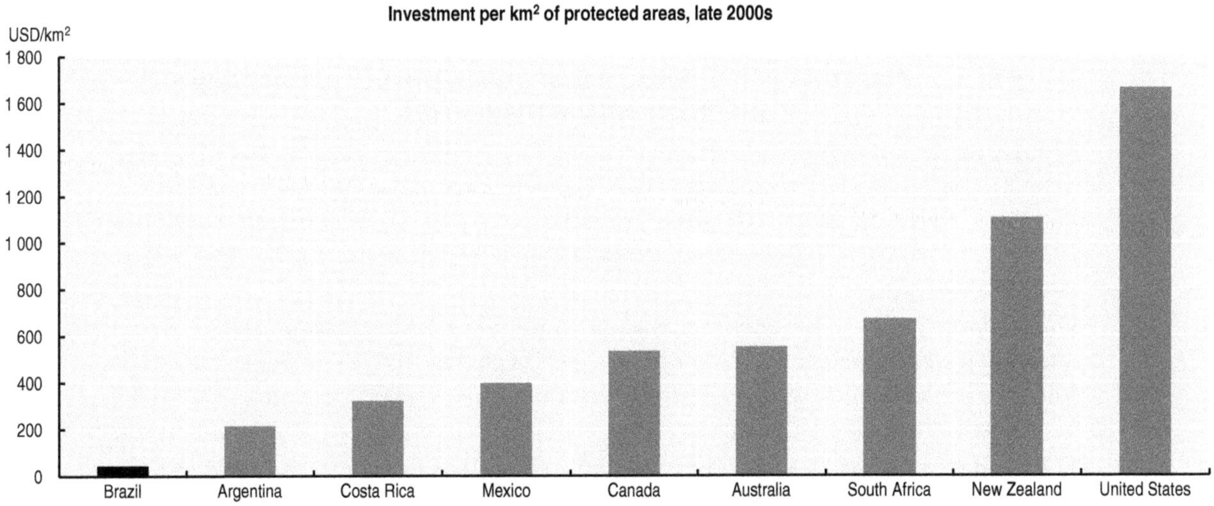

Source: Medeiros, R. and C. Young (2011), *Contribuição das unidades de conservação brasileiras para a economia nacional: Relatório final.*

StatLink http://dx.doi.org/10.1787/888933279819

Resources for protected area management originate from a variety of sources, the most significant one being the federal budget. The volume of public resources allocated to SNUC is not systematically tracked. The last assessment of financial resources available to federal protected areas was conducted in 2009 by the MMA and the Ministry of Planning and Budget.[8] It indicated that 85% of federal protected areas' resources came from budget allocations to ICMBio, 10% from budget allocations to other environmental institutions[9] and 5% from non-budgetary sources (MMA, 2009). Other sources include relatively limited amount of environmental compensation, national and international donations and revenue from tourism and sustainable forestry (Sections 5.1 and 5.2).

Overall, the operation of SNUC heavily relies on public budgets, mainly federal. This is true in many Latin American countries, although Brazil exhibits one of the highest levels of reliance on government budget outlays, which makes funding vulnerable to external factors and political negotiations (Bovarnick et al., 2010). Brazil should develop an integrated financial strategy to guarantee more efficient and effective use of resources for protected areas and for biodiversity policy more generally, and further explore alternative funding sources. These may include payments for ecosystem services (e.g. water supply and carbon sequestration); revenue from access fees to protected areas, branding and sale of merchandise; and part of the revenue from royalties, from financial compensation paid by hydropower plant and mine operators and from benefits generated from access to genetic resources (Chapter 4).

Brazil could helpfully extend the use of concessions for tourism services and sustainable forest management and, more generally, better engage the business sector in providing infrastructure and services in protected areas. It could also extend the use of public-private partnerships (PPPs) for partial or full management of protected areas, including environmental conservation. This would allow the public authorities to shift their attention from direct management to oversight of protected areas, which is less resource intensive, although it would require different staff capacities and skills. While a number of concessions for tourism activities are in place, the first example of a full management contract was concluded in 2015 (Box 5.7).

Box 5.7. **The Lund Route: Brazil's first public-private partnership for protected area management**

In 2012, the government of Minas Gerais state, in partnership with the NGO Semeia,[a] launched Brazil's first PPP for protected area management. It is for the Peter Lund Route, a hiking trail covering 24 km^2 in three protected areas north of the Belo Horizonte metropolitan area. The PPP is aimed at increasing tourism while improving the effectiveness of conservation.

The 30-year concession contract makes the concessionaire responsible for all conservation activities, including fire control, species control and scientific research. The government's role is limited to monitoring and supervising the concessionaire's performance, using defined indicators.

The proposed PPP model was open to public consultation for 60 days, and various workshops and discussions were held. The bidding process was submitted for public consultation in November 2013; by March 2015 the concession contract had been signed.

a) Semeia is a non-profit organisation that supports the development and implementation of new management models for Brazil's protected areas. It aims to encourage dialogue among government, private sector and civil society actors and to promote the creation of PPPs to manage protected areas.

Source: Semeia (2013), *Semeia Annual Report 2013*.

Budgetary allocations

The budget available to the federal SNUC system decreased by roughly 35% in real terms over 2000-08 (MMA, 2009) despite the significant expansion of the system (Section 1). In a welcomed development, the budget of ICMBio, the main source of SNUC finance, grew by 57% between 2008 and 2014, reaching BRL 783 million (Chapter 2). Resources are largely used to cover staff and running costs, with investment accounting for between 2% and 11% (Funbio, 2014a). There is no consolidated data about subnational budget and expenditure for protected areas.

Environmental compensation

Environmental compensation is the main private contribution to protected area finance. It involves obligatory payments by project developers in the framework of the environmental licensing of installations and infrastructure that could cause environmental degradation or pollution (Chapter 2). At the federal level the compensation can reach 0.5% of the total project costs, depending on the severity of project impact. The SNUC Law provides for resources from environmental compensation to be fully allocated to protected areas, with priority given to strict protection areas. IBAMA defines environmental compensation fees and decides which protected areas should benefit from collected resources. Payments can be made directly in the form of products or services benefitting the protected area or indirectly to a fund managed either by ICMBio or by third parties.[10] The level of execution is, however, very low. In 2008-14, only 8% of available compensation funds were actually spent. Legal uncertainty related to the compensation process is a major bottleneck for more efficient use of these resources; another is the lack of suitable projects in which the resources can be invested (Funbio, 2014a).

Ecological ICMS

Brazil pioneered the use of fiscal transfers as an incentive for biodiversity conservation in protected areas.[11] About half the states redistribute a share of the revenue from the state-level value added tax (ICMS) on the basis of environmental criteria under a mechanism called Ecological ICMS (or ICMS-E). By far the main parameter is the extension (and type) of protected areas and indigenous lands, followed by the presence of municipal waste collection services, public watersheds, and wastewater treatment (IBGE, 2014). Generally, more weight is given to strict protection areas. A similar mechanism, based on the redistribution of income-related federal taxes to the states based on protected areas, has been under discussion in Congress for years.

The ICMS-E was established to compensate municipalities for the opportunity cost of maintaining part of their territory under nature protection, as the use of protected areas for economic activities that can generate tax revenue is restricted. For some municipalities with high protected area coverage, the revenue from ICMS-E amounts to a significant share of the municipal budget.[12] It is possible, though not necessary, to use the ICMS-E revenue to finance expenditure in protected areas or for environmental purposes more generally.

The mechanism has helped increase the number and size of protected areas in Brazil, although its impact on biodiversity conservation is not very clear (May et al., 2012). Empirical studies show that there has been an increase in protected area coverage since the introduction of the ICMS-E in a number of states, although other factors may have contributed. Several municipalities have established large environmental protection areas

(APAs) with loose land-use restrictions (Table 5.1), the only goal being to increase their revenue (Ring et al., 2011). APAs cover 98% of municipal protected areas, with generally low effectiveness for biodiversity protection.

Only the state of Paraná, which introduced the system in the early 1990s, makes the revenue transfers conditional on quality indicators of the status of protected areas and buffer zones and on municipal resources dedicated to conservation actions. This approach is potentially more effective in encouraging good protected area management, but entails additional cost, including for periodic inspections. Overall, the degree of success in expanding protected area coverage appears correlated with technical and institutional capacity at the state and municipal levels (Peters, 2012).

International sources and fundraising partnerships

Brazil has managed to establish fundraising partnerships with bilateral and multilateral development co-operation organisations to finance activities related to protected areas. International finance contributes a minor share of the total budget available to SNUC (8% of the federal protected area budget in 2008), but has helped leverage domestic resources and improve resource use effectiveness by addressing some of the most pressing bottlenecks. However, funding from international partners is likely to gradually decline in the years to come.

The ARPA programme and its Protected Area Fund (Box 5.1) are the most important extra-budgetary source of finance for federal, state and municipal protected areas in the Amazon. Funbio was mandated by the MMA to carry out the financial management of the programme (Box 5.8), which receives large international donations (Germany is the largest donor). The Amazon Fund also helps finance the ARPA programme and other activities to control deforestation, including in protected areas (Chapter 4).

Box 5.8. **Brazilian Biodiversity Fund**

The Brazilian Biodiversity Fund (Funbio) was founded in 1996 as a private non-profit organisation to invest in biodiversity conservation in Brazil. It was created upon the initiative of the MMA and GEF to complement direct government efforts, the rationale being that a private institution would be less vulnerable to changes in government and able to attract more private finance. Funbio's main activity is the support of Brazilian protected areas. The volume and scope of support expanded massively in 2003 with the launch of the ARPA programme. By 2014, about one out of five public protected areas in Brazil received support from Funbio, either directly (e.g. management plans, infrastructure work, procurement of equipment, training of management councils, resolution of land tenure issues) or indirectly (research projects, species monitoring and management, capacity building for park managers, environmental education).

Since its creation, Funbio has mobilised about USD 500 million. Resources originate largely from bilateral and multilateral institutions (the GEF being a major supporter), the Amazon Fund and, to a lesser extent, private donations. Funbio has developed interesting financing schemes to increase private resources, such as the Adopt a Park programme, under which private companies can provide finance for infrastructure and facilities within a selected park. It has also launched mechanisms designed to receive resources from environmental fines and compensation, and manages Brazil's debt-for-swap agreements.

Source: Funbio (2014b), *Funbio and Protected Areas: 2014.*

Donations and private sector engagement

With the exception of some international donations, private voluntary donations to SNUC are limited. This situation has been attributed to the lack of tax incentives for donations and a limited culture of environmental philanthropy (Funbio, 2014b). Involving local businesses and entrepreneurs has generally proven challenging and possibilities for partnership schemes are limited. For example, there are few possibilities for donors to associate their brand with an area or service within protected areas. Nonetheless, specific donation initiatives have been successful in raising additional resources; in Funbio's Adopt a Park programme, for example, the energy companies OGX and MPX committed to support the national parks of Fernando de Noronha and Lençois Maranhenses with more than BRL 4 million each over 2012-18 (Funbio, 2014b).

There are a few examples of private companies financing infrastructure and other investment in protected areas, including companies that donated to the ARPA programme (including Natura, O Boticário and Anglo American). The majority-government-owned companies Petrobras (oil) and Vale (mining) have sponsored several biodiversity conservation initiatives, including in protected areas. For instance, Petrobras supports the Tamar project for the conservation of marine turtles, many nesting in marine protected areas such as Fernando de Noronha National Park. Vale finances the management of more than 12 000 km^2 of local protected areas in the Atlantic Forest, Amazon and Cerrado biomes (de Bulhões Mossri, 2012).

4.5. *Assessment of management and biodiversity conservation effectiveness*

Management effectiveness

Following the remarkable expansion of protected areas over the 2000s, Brazil now faces the challenge of effectively managing these areas. The management of many protected areas struggles to meet objectives, a problem that, as previous sections have shown, is linked to limited human and financial resources.

An assessment of federal protected areas by WWF and ICMBio (2012) found that about 30% of federal protected areas operated at low management effectiveness levels in 2010; this, however, was a significant improvement from the previous assessment in 2006, when the share was above 50% (Figure 5.7).[13] Improvements were made particularly with respect to planning, available human resources and infrastructure. Management effectiveness improved mainly in extractive reserves, ecological stations and national forests, as well as in protected areas in the Amazon and Cerrado biomes.

Areas supported by the ARPA programme (Box 5.1) showed a higher effectiveness level than the other federal protected areas (Figure 5.7). The better performance was directly linked to the result-based approach of the programme, the considerable financial resources invested in ARPA areas and the fact that both federal and state governments are required to contribute human resources for managing these areas (WWF and ICMBio, 2012). The need to be accountable to international donors may also have played a role.

Despite this improvement, the overall management performance is unsatisfactory. A more recent assessment of federal and state-level protected areas in the Amazon biome found that only 4% had a degree of implementation and management that was sufficient to fulfil the objectives set for these areas (TCU, 2013). While the available financial resources have increased in recent years, the capacity to spend these resources has worsened. This reflects inadequate management skills and substantial red tape. The low level of management effectiveness is of concern, notably in light of overall increasing pressures on

Figure 5.7. **Management effectiveness is low in many protected areas**

Index of management effectiveness of federal protected areas, 2005-06 and 2010

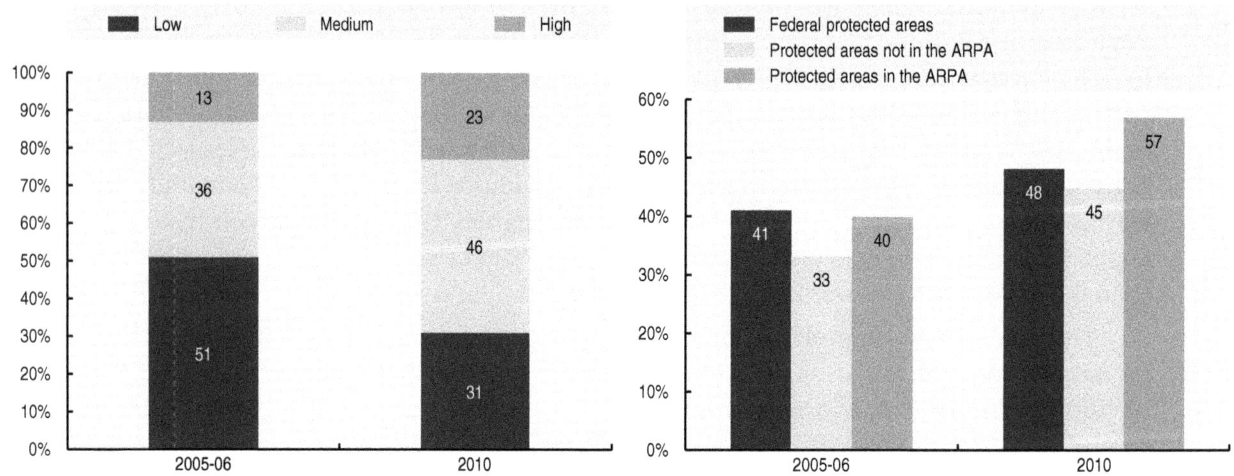

Notes: Index of management effectiveness of protected area according to the Rapid Assessment and Prioritization of Protected Area Management (RAPPAM) methodology. The overall effectiveness performance (based on context, planning, inputs, process and outcomes assessment) is expressed as a percentage of the maximum effectiveness that could be achieved. The intervals <40%; 40% -60%; and >60% define the respective classes of low, medium and high effectiveness of management.
Source: WWF and ICMBIO (2012), *Avaliação comparada das aplicações do método Rappam nas unidades de conservação federais, nos ciclos 2005-06 e 2010.*

StatLink http://dx.doi.org/10.1787/888933279827

protected areas from infrastructure development, hunting, resource extraction and invasive species (WWF and ICMBio, 2012). Overall, the weak management performance results in untapped economic, social and environmental potential of protected areas, especially in terms of public use (tourism, recreation and education), sustainable forest management and other income opportunities for traditional communities (Section 5).

While much progress has been made in registering the protected areas in the CNUC, notably with respect to federal and state protected areas, the information provided is usually limited to very basic data (mainly legal information and spatial data), with little on management and activities. As of early 2014, only 40% of the registered areas had provided statistics on the number of staff and visitors (Semeia, 2014). When fully implemented, the CNUC could be an important source of information for evaluating effectiveness of protected areas (Prates and Sousa, 2014).

Socio-environmental effectiveness

Monitoring and assessing management effectiveness require understanding of biodiversity trends in protected areas and of changes in the socio-economic conditions of the affected local communities. Most protected areas, however, do not systematically conduct such monitoring. Two-thirds of managers in federal and state protected areas in the Amazon biome have not monitored biodiversity for years, mainly due to insufficient infrastructure, equipment and access (TCU, 2013). More than half the managers of Amazonian extractive reserves and sustainable development reserves have reported that they lack the tools to monitor the results of social and environmental development activities.

ICMBio maintains an electronic system (SISBio) to provide researchers with permits to collect biological material in federal protected areas and to gather the information generated from research. It has monitored coral reefs in marine protected areas since 2002.

Monitoring results suggest that fish stocks and species diversity are higher in areas where fishing is not permitted than in marine sustainable use areas. Since 2010, ICMBio has conducted *in situ* monitoring programmes in several federal protected areas in the Amazon, Atlantic Forest, Caatinga and Cerrado biomes.

These programmes could be further extended with a view to generating information needed to assess the effectiveness of conservation initiatives. More generally, Brazil should invest in monitoring and assessing the effectiveness of protected areas in delivering their expected environmental, social and economic benefits as a way to build political and society support for protected areas and mobilise the necessary resources.

5. Sustainable use of protected areas

5.1. *Tourism and recreation*

According to the World Economic Forum, Brazil has the world's largest tourism potential with respect to natural resources but ranks only 53rd with respect to tourism competitiveness (TCU, 2013). There is, therefore, room to better exploit economic opportunities related to Brazil's natural wealth and protected areas. The economic benefits from public visitation of protected areas (including for tourism, recreation and environmental education) are estimated to be large. Brazil's national parks alone could generate between BRL 1.6 and 1.8 billion annually until 2016 (Medeiros and Young, 2011; also see Box 5.3). Semeia (2014) estimates that the potential income from tourism in protected areas could reach as much as BRL 53 billion over 10 years.

The number of people visiting federal protected areas more than tripled between 2006 and 2013, to 6.3 million (Figure 5.8). National parks attract by far the most visitors. Iguaçu and Tijuca national parks alone accounted for nearly 60% of visitors in 2013. Public investment in infrastructure and services, under programmes such as Parks of the World Cup and Tourism in the Parks, and concessions to private operators have helped increase tourist arrivals (ICMbio, 2012b). For example, concessions to private operators have been crucial for the tourism development of Foz do Iguaçu National Park. It has allowed the building of tourism infrastructure such as parking places, a visitor centre, inner-park transport and provision of food and beverage service and leisure and adventure activities. Concessions of this kind have also been used in other major parks, such as Tijuca and Fernando de Noronha, and new concessions are planned in coming years (ICMBio, 2012b).

While expanding, public visitation is still in its infancy. All protected area categories but two are open to visitors, but many areas receive none or very few (some areas receive visitors but do not register or track visitation). As of 2012, only 26 of the 68 national parks were officially open for tourism; the remaining received some visitors but with limited planning and control (ICMBio, 2012a). According to a survey conducted among protected area managers the same year, almost one-third of protected areas did not receive visitors at all and nearly 50% received fewer than 50 000 visitors a year. In addition, only 17% of protected areas that could receive visitors generated revenue from public visitation, with a slightly higher share for national parks (Semeia, 2012b).[14] This seems to be primarily related to the lack of adequate infrastructure and service provision for visitors (TCU, 2013; Semeia, 2012b), as the case of Chapada dos Veadeiros National Park shows (Box 5.9). In other cases, difficulty organising adequate fee collection systems is a major barrier.

Figure 5.8. **The number of visitors in national parks has increased**

Visitors to protected areas, 2006-13

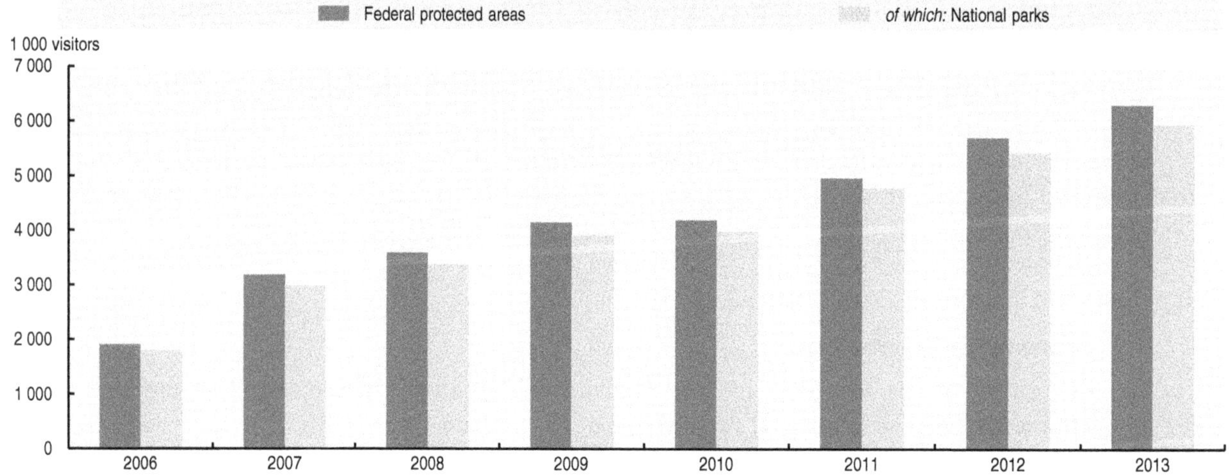

Source: ICMBio (2014), *Relatório de Gestão 2013.*

StatLink http://dx.doi.org/10.1787/888933279834

Box 5.9. **The untapped tourism potential of Chapada dos Veadeiros National Park**

Chapada dos Veadeiros National Park is a World Heritage site encompassing unique vegetation, hundreds of waterfalls and other water bodies, and walking trails across the Cerrado biome. The park is primarily a weekend and holiday destination for people from the Centre-West region, especially from Brasília. In 2009 a total of 22 950 tourists visited the park (Medeiros and Young, 2011). Only a very limited part of the protected area has infrastructure adequate for tourism and there is only one official park entrance, in São Jorge district of Alto Paraíso de Goiás. Cavalcante, a town in which tourism has been growing due to popular attractions such as waterfalls and trails on private land, does not have any access to the park.

While an entrance fee could be charged and there is demand for facilities to sell food, drinks and souvenirs, ICMBio has neither the personnel nor the infrastructure to develop such services. Red tape and administrative constraints, as well as capacity constraints at the park level, have so far blocked the proposed bidding process to award a concession for tourism-related services. Overall, the park remains little known and poorly visited by Brazilians and international tourists, resulting in missed opportunities to generate much needed revenue and build a constituency for nature conservation.

Expanding public visitation could help enhance the financial sustainability of SNUC and would help build public support for protected areas, as the example of Canada illustrates (Box 5.10). Tourism and other forms of public visitation in protected areas are a significant source of revenue in other countries. In South Africa, for example, the public agency managing national parks receives 75% of its budget from concession fees and private investment related to tourism (Semeia, 2012a). Resources can be raised from entrance fees and from tourism-related services such as transport, food and beverages, and leisure. In 2011, ICMBio received BRL 24 million from access fees and services in federal parks, with four parks accounting for most of the revenue (ICMBio, 2012a).

Box 5.10. The value of protected area visitation: The case of Parks Canada

Parks Canada, the agency in charge of protected areas, conducts periodic surveys of the Canadian population's attitudes towards natural parks. The 2012 National Survey of Canadians revealed that visitation was critical in helping the population connect with protected areas and the institutions that manage them.*

In 2012, more than three-quarters of people who had visited one of the country's national parks had a "sense of connection" to them. Only about 15% of people who had not visited a national park were able to say the same. Visiting is an important factor in helping give people a sense of stewardship towards their national parks. In 2012, more than nine in ten people who had visited national parks strongly felt that the parks were meant to be enjoyed by future generations as much as by people today, and nearly 80% would miss national parks if they were gone; among people who had not visited a park, both shares were lower.

Canadians who have visited a national park are more likely to be supportive of the activities Parks Canada undertakes to fulfil its mandate. In 2012, about half of the interviewed park visitors strongly supported the use of taxpayer money for the creation of new parks, compared to 40% of people who had never visited a park. About 80% of visitors were also in favour of using public funds to maintain existing national parks, compared to about half of non-visitors.

* The survey was conducted by telephone in February and March 2012. In total, 3 786 adults responded. Visitors: those who had visited a Parks Canada-administered national park in the last three years; non-visitors: those who had never visited a Parks Canada-administered national park.

Source: Parks Canada (2012), *The VALUE of Visiting...continues.*

Protected areas are not yet integrated into Brazil's national tourism strategy and most tourists are not aware that some of the country's main tourist attractions are located in protected areas (TCU, 2013). A survey conducted in 2012 revealed that 44% of Brazilians did not know what a protected area was; only 1% of those who had knowledge of protected areas believed that their purpose was recreation and tourism (MMA, 2012). Protected area laws and regulations seem to be relatively inadequate to promote tourism and visitation. This partly reflects the fact that the protected areas created over the 2000s had the primary objective of controlling deforestation, and that no major strategy to promote public use has been developed since. Only recently has the government stepped up efforts to promote public use (Burns and Moreira, 2013). There is room for better integrating protected areas into Brazil's wider tourism strategy and for building capacity of park managers to develop strategies and partnerships that would increase the attractiveness of tourism and environmental education services.

Partnerships with private businesses and non-profit organisations to manage visitation services are relatively rare. Semeia (2012b) found that only 13% of protected areas had PPPs or concessions in place, though most protected area managers would be interested in expanding such arrangements. The main stumbling blocks were regulatory constraints, a lack of adequate management plans and limited resources and capacity of the park management. At the same time, private businesses (notably small and medium-sized ones) often lack capacity to comply with the legal obligations required for business relations with the government. Designing and negotiating partnership agreements and contracts are time- and resource-intensive and often exceed the capacity of park managers. Some steps have been taken to facilitate the use of PPPs and concessions, including dedicated training programmes. In 2011, the MMA and the Ministry of Planning, Budget and Management agreed to launch pilot PPP agreements in ten national parks with high tourism potential. Brazil would benefit from expanding the use of PPPs and concessions, as they open possibilities to improve infrastructure and services for public visitation when public resources and capacities are limited.

5.2. *Sustainable forest use and forest concessions*

The government began granting forest concessions to promote sustainable timber logging in 2008, but a very little of the area eligible has been affected (Chapter 4). The MMA estimated income from forest concessions at about BRL 190 million annually over 2010-20 (MMA, 2010). The majority of such forests are located outside protected areas, but some categories of protected areas, such as national forests, are eligible for concessions. While the granting of forest concessions for large-scale forestry can be burdensome, small-scale extraction by traditional communities residing in public forests can also generate significant resources. In Tapajos National Forest in Pará state, for example, small-scale timber logging generated more than BRL 3 million in 2012 (TCU, 2013).

Despite the interest of national forest managers, the use of forest concessions in protected areas has been limited. In the early 2000s, only 3 of the 65 national forests had granted concessions, with part of the revenue channelled back to the protected areas (Funbio, 2014a). This situation is partly linked to the fact that most protected areas have not yet approved their management plan, which is necessary for such activities, or set the required zoning provisions (TCU, 2013). These problems add to the challenges that are common to sustainable forest concessions outside protected areas, including insufficient technical capacity, lack of infrastructure and unresolved land tenure conflicts (Chapter 4).

5.3. *Sustainable use of natural resources by local communities*

Many protected areas in Brazil are inhabited by small traditional communities, which depend on natural resources (e.g. fish, wood, nuts, oils, rubber) for their livelihoods. Effective management of such areas requires offering the communities meaningful economic opportunities to sustainably use natural resources. Although traditional communities generally have good knowledge about the use of natural resources, they often lack sufficient expertise for sustainable farming, forestry and fishing that meet market demand levels, and generally have limited access to markets (Prates and Sousa, 2014). This lack, in turn, may translate into a risk of increasing the pressure on the natural asset base.

For example, in the 2000s, Chico Mendes Extractive Reserve in Acre state experienced increased deforestation levels, partly due to declining demand for and prices of rubber and Brazil nuts, as well as poorly controlled local beef markets; this combination of factors had made forest conversion to cattle ranching more attractive (TCU, 2013). Similarly, low return on crabs harvested in Soure Marine Extractive Reserve in Pará state, and difficulties in transporting the animals to city markets, could result in increased harvest efforts and pressures on the mangrove ecosystem.[15]

Implementation problems persist in extractive reserves, including the lack of management plans and management agreements with local communities to regulate their use of natural resources. In addition, poor land delimitation and signposting in some areas create uncertainty about the protected area boundaries and associated restrictions on activities. Only 25% of protected areas in the Amazon biome are delimited and signposted (TCU, 2013). Staff is largely insufficient to manage extractive reserves. For example, in the early

2010s, Tapajós-Arapuins Extractive Reserve in the Amazon had only three staff members to manage an area of more than 6.7 million km^2 with about 18 000 inhabitants (TCU, 2013).

In addition to viable forms of livelihood, much of the population within extractive reserves needs better access to social services, such as education, health, housing and sanitation. Overall, this mix of issues goes beyond the responsibilities of the MMA and other environment authorities and necessitates stronger intersectoral co-ordination.

Multiple policy instruments have helped address these issues. They include the conditional cash-transfer programmes Bolsa Floresta and Bolsa Verde and the National Plan to Promote the Production Chain of Socio-Biodiversity Products (PNPSB). As Chapter 4 noted, Bolsa Floresta and Bolsa Verde aim at rewarding and improving the quality of life of traditional and poor communities that live from the use of natural resources and are committed to reducing deforestation and using resources sustainably. As many beneficiary families live in protected areas, these programmes contribute to the economic viability of living in such locations. The PNPSB includes a minimum price policy for socio-biodiversity products. As benefiting from such programmes tends to be easier in sustainable use protected areas, some producers have requested protected area status, in particular that of extractive reserve, for the areas they live and work in.

Recommendations on protected areas

Expansion and consolidation of the national system of protected areas

- Strengthen inter-institutional co-operation to ease the resolution of land tenure issues within existing or proposed new protected areas and improve social service provision to communities living in sustainable use reserves.
- Further expand the area under environmental protection to fully achieve the national 2020 targets and international commitments (including through official protected areas, indigenous lands and set-aside areas required by the Forest Code); prioritise areas with high biodiversity values and where pressures from infrastructure development, urbanisation and agriculture are the highest; expand the coverage of protected areas in marine and coastal zones to achieve the Aichi target.
- Develop a strategy for the territorial consolidation of protected areas; encourage the use of financial and land offset mechanisms provided in the protected area legislation and in the Forest Code once the Rural Environmental Cadastre is fully operational; and explore the use of transitional contractual agreements with landowners within protected areas to ensure compatible land use until property rights are clarified.

Management of protected areas

- Develop a comprehensive financial strategy for the National System of Protected Areas (SNUC), with a view to reducing dependency on the public budget and on international finance; explore alternative funding sources, including payments for ecosystem services, access fees, branding and sale of merchandise, and benefits generated from genetic resources.
- Strengthen efforts to develop the management plans of protected areas and review their implementation; ensure that the plans set clear priorities, targets and progress indicators.
- Develop targeted capacity building and skill development programmes for protected area managers and staff, with a view to enhancing management effectiveness; promote networks of protected area managers and exchange of experiences and best practices.

Recommendations on protected areas *(cont.)*

- Continue to periodically assess protected area management effectiveness and efficiency; further encourage protected area managers to provide accurate and timely information to the National Register of Protected Areas (CNUC), and systematically review this information to derive system-level recommendations.
- Develop standard biodiversity monitoring methods with a view to generating the information needed to assess the environmental effectiveness of protected areas; further expand federal monitoring programmes.

Scaling up public visitation

- Integrate protected areas into national and state tourism strategies and identify areas with high tourism potential; develop tourism products linked to protected areas.
- Extend the use of concessions and other public-private partnerships for public visitation and tourism in protected areas; simplify procedures and improve capacity of government officials and protected area managers to design and negotiate contracts; implement pilot programmes to test and develop new management models.
- Consider including regular visits to protected areas in educational programmes of schoolchildren.

Notes

1. The SNUC was established by Law 9985/2000 and is regulated by Decree 4340/2002.
2. This chapter uses the term "protected area" to refer to *stricto sensu* protected areas as defined and governed by the SNUC Law.
3. In 2010, the parties of the Convention on Biological Diversity adopted the Strategic Plan for Biodiversity 2011-20 with the mission of halting biodiversity loss and enhance the benefits biodiversity provides to people. The Strategic Plan includes 20 targets (the Aichi Targets), organised under five strategic goals.
4. A biome is a large naturally occurring community of flora and fauna occupying a geographic region.
5. The MMA is developing methodology to assess the ecological status of indigenous lands, as well as their management, demarcation and land regularisation, to verify their contribution to the national protected area targets (MMA, 2015a). The contribution of APPs and RLs will be known only after the full registration of these lands in the Rural Environmental Cadastre (Chapter 4).
6. In May 2015, ICMBio was responsible for the management of 320 protected areas (all federal protected areas except private natural heritage reserves).
7. Ecological corridors are areas of habitat connecting wildlife populations separated by human activities or structures such as roads development or logging.
8. The budget available to state and municipal protected areas was not studied.
9. The MMA, for example, channelled 20% of its 2008 budget to SNUC, and the Brazilian Forest Service allocated 30% to the SNUC national forests. IBAMA contributed to the SNUC budget through its fire prevention and control activities (MMA, 2009).
10. Resources from environmental compensation can be used for activities such as land tenure and demarcation, management plans, procurement of goods and services, technical studies and environmental education programmes.
11. As of 2011, only Portugal had followed, though similar systems had been proposed in India and Indonesia.
12. In 2009, the 11 states that had the ICMS-E in place received between USD 312 million and USD 1.5 billion to be distributed among municipalities (MMA, 2010).
13. The evaluation was based on the Rapid Assessment and Prioritization of Protected Area Management (RAPPAM) tool, a methodology adopted by the WWF that is internationally recognised for assessing

management effectiveness of protected areas. Effectiveness is understood as the capacity for achieving the objectives of the protected area.

14. National parks generate between BRL 50 000 and BRL 1 million per year (Semeia, 2012b).

15. About 10 000 people live in the reserve, where crab harvesting is the main economic activity. The inefficient transport of crabs results in the deaths of many crabs, which ordinarily are sold alive.

References

Bovarnick, A. et al. (2010), *Financial Sustainability of Protected Areas in Latin America and the Caribbean: Investment Policy Guidance*, United Nations Development Programme and The Nature Conservancy, *www.undp.org/content/dam/aplaws/publication/en/publications/environment-energy/www-ee-library/biodiversity/financial-sustainability-of-protected-areas-in-latin-america-and-the-caribbean/financial_sus_pa_lac.pdf.*

Burns, R. and J. Moreira (2013), "Visitor Management in Brazil's Protected Areas: Benchmarking for Best Practices in Resource Management", *The George Wright Forum*, Vol. 30, No. 2, pp. 163-170.

CEPAL, GIZ e IPEA (2011), *Avaliação do Plano de Ação para a Prevenção e Controle do Desmatamento na Amazônia Legal: PPCDAm: 2007-2010 [Evaluation of the Action Plan for Prevention and Control of Deforestation in the Legal Amazon]*, United Nations Economic Commission for Latin America and the Caribbean, Brasília, Institute for Applied Economic Research, Brasília, and Deutche Gesellschaft fur International Zusammenarbeit (GIZ) GMbH, Bonn, *www. cepal.org/dmaah/publicaciones/sinsigla/xml/7/45887/IPEA_GIZ_Cepal_2011_Avaliacao_PPCDAm_2007-2011_web.pdf.*

De Bulhões Mossri, B. (2012), *Biodiversidade e Indústria: Informações para uma Gestão Responsável [Biodiversity and Industry: Information for Responsible Management]*, National Confederation of Industries, Brasília.

Funai (2015), "Terras Indigenas" [Indigenous Lands], National Indian Foundation, *www.funai.gov.br/index.php/indios-no-brasil/terras-indigenas* (accessed May 2015).

Funbio (2014a), *O futuro do ambiente financeiro das áreas protegidas [The future of finance for protected areas]*, Brazilian Biodiversity Fund, Rio de Janeiro, *www.funbio.org.br/o-funbio/tendencias-o-futuro-do-ambiente-financeiro-das-areas-protegidas.*

Funbio (2014b), *Funbio and Protected Areas. 2014*, Brazilian Biodiversity Fund, Rio de Janeiro, *www.funbio.org.br/wp-content/uploads/2014/11/Livro_Funbio_Areas_Protegidas_Web_Ing.pdf.*

Funbio (2012), *Quanto custa o Programa Áreas Protegidas da Amazônia? Uma modelagem financeira para as Unidades de Conservação do Arpa [How much does the Amazon Protected Areas Programme cost? Financial modelling for the ARPA protected areas]*, Brazilian Biodiversity Fund, Rio de Janeiro.

Funbio (2009), *Quanto custa uma unidade de conservação federal? Uma visão estratégica para o financiamento do Sistema Nacional de Unidades de Conservação (Snuc) [How much does a federal protected area cost? A strategic vision for the financing of the National Protected Areas System]*, Brazilian Biodiversity Fund, Rio de Janeiro.

Gurgel, H. et al. (2009), "Unidades de conservação e o falso dilema entre conservação e desenvolvimento" [Protected areas and the false dilemma between conservation and development], *Boletim Regional, Urbano e Ambiental*, No. 3, pp. 109-120.

IBGE (2014a), *Perfil dos Estados Brasileiros 2013 [Profile of Brazilian States 2013]*, Brazilian Institute of Geography and Statistics, Rio de Janeiro.

ICMBio (2014), *Relatório de Gestão 2013 [Management Report 2013]*, Chico Mendes Institute for Biodiversity Conservation, Brasília, *www.icmbio.gov.br/portal/images/stories/o-que-somos/relatorio gestaoicmbio 2013_.pdf.*

ICMBio (2012a), "Dos 68 parques nacionais, 26 estão oficialmente abertos ao tourismo"[26 of the 68 national parks are officially open to tourism], Chico Mendes Institute for Biodiversity Conservation, Brasília, *www.icmbio.gov.br/portal/comunicacao/noticias/4-geral/3280-dos-69-parques-nacionais-26-estao-oficialmente-abertos-aos-turistas.html* (accessed May 2015).

ICMBio (2012b), "Com o ICMBio, parques receberam mais investimentos e visitação triplicou" [With ICMBio, parks received more investment and visitation tripled], Chico Mendes Institute for Biodiversity Conservation, Brasília, *www.icmbio.gov.br/portal/comunicacao/noticias/icmbio-5-anos/3295-com-o-icmbio-parques-receberam-mais-investimentos-e-visitacao-triplicou.html* (accessed May 2015).

Irving, M.A. (2010), "Áreas protegidas e inclusão social – uma equação possível em políticas públicas de proteção da natureza no Brasil?" [Protected areas and social inclusion – a possible equation in policies for nature conservation in Brazil], *Sinais Sociais*, Vol. 4, No. 12, pp. 122-147.

IUCN (2008), *Guidelines for Applying Protected Area Management Categories*, International Union for Conservation of Nature and Natural Resources, Gland.

Jenkins, C.N. and L. Joppa (2009), "Expansion of the Global Terrestrial Protected Area System", *Biological Conservation*, Vol. 142, No. 10, pp. 2166-2174.

Kinouchi, M. (2014), "Plano de manejo: fundamentos para a mudança" [Management plans: foundations for change], in Bensusan and Prates (2014), *A diversidade cabe da unidade? Áreas protegidas no Brasil [Diversity fits the unit? Protected areas in Brazil]*, pp. 220-248, Mil Folhas IEB, Brasília.

Mascia, M.B. et al. (2014), "Protected area downgrading, downsizing, and degazettement (PADDD) in Africa, Asia, and Latin America and the Caribbean, 1900-2010", *Biological Conservation* 169, pp. 355-361.

May, P. et al. (2012), "The 'Ecological' Value Added Tax (ICMS-Ecológico) in Brazil and its effectiveness in State biodiversity conservation: a comparative analysis", paper presented at 12th Biennial Conference of the International Society for Ecological Economics, Rio de Janeiro.

Medeiros, R. and C. Young (2011), *Contribuição das unidades de conservação brasileiras para a economia nacional: Relatório final [Contribution of Brazilian protected areas to the national economy: Final report]*, UNEP-WCMC, Brasília.

Mendonça, F.C., V. Talbot and H.S. Macedo (2014), "Reflexões sobre participação social em unidades de conservação e a contribuição do Instituto Chico Mendes de Conservação da Biodiversidade" *[Reflections on social participation in protected areas and the contribution of the Chico Mendes Institute for Biodiversity Conservation], in Bensusan and Prates (2014) A diversidade cabe da unidade ? Áreas protegidas no Brasil* [Diversity fits the unit? Protected areas in Brazil], pp. 268-306, Mil Folhas IEB, Brasília.

MMA (2015a), *Fifth National Report to the Convention on Biological Diversity*, Ministry of the Environment, Brasília.

MMA (2015b), "Areas protegidas" [Protected areas], Ministry of the Environment, Brasília, *www.mma.gov.br/areas-protegidas* (accessed May 2015).

MMA (2015c), "Cadastro Nacional de Unidades de Conservação" [National Protected Areas Register], Ministry of the Environment, Brasília, *www.mma.gov.br/areas-protegidas/cadastro-nacional-de-ucs* (accessed February 2015).

MMA (2012), *O que o Brasileiro Pensa do Meio Ambiente e do Consumo Sustentável: Pesquisa Nacional de Opnião: Principais Resultados [What Brazilians think of the Environment and Sustainable Consumption: National Opinion Reseach: key findings]*, Ministry of the Environment, Brasília.

MMA (2010), *Fourth National Report to the Convention on Biological Diversity*, Ministry of the Environment, Brasília.

MMA (2009), *Pilares para a Sustentabilidade Financeira do SNUC [Pillars for the Financial Sustainability of the SNUC]*, second edition, Ministry of the Environment, Brasília.

OECD (2013), *OECD Environmental Performance Reviews: South Africa 2013*, OECD Publishing, Paris, *http://dx.doi.org/10.1787/9789264202887-en*.

OECD-ECLAC (2014), OECD Environmental Performance Reviews: Colombia 2014, OECD Publishing, Paris, *http://dx.doi.org/10.1787/9789264208292-en*.

OECD-FAO (2015), "Brazilian agriculture: Prospects and challenges", in OECD/FAO, *OECD-FAO Agricultural Outlook 2015*, OECD Publishing, Paris, *http://dx.doi.org/10.1787/agr_outlook-2015-5-en*.

Parks Canada (2012), *The VALUE of Visiting...continues*, Parks Canada, Gatineau.

Peters, S. (2012), "The Role of Green Fiscal Mechanisms in Developing Countries: Lessons Learned – Case Study", Inter-American Development Bank, Technical Notes IDB-TN-364, March.

Prates, A.P. (2014), "Oceanos, a nova fronteira de conservação no Brasil: desafios para o cumprimento da meta 11 de Aichi" [Oceans, the new conservation frontier in Brazil: challenges for achieving the Aichi target 11], in Bensusan and Prates (2014), *A diversidade cabe da unidade? Áreas protegidas no Brasil [Diversity fits the unit? Protected areas in Brazil]*, pp. 82-118.

Prates, A.P and N. Sousa (2014), "Panorama geral das áreas protegidas no Brasil: desafios para o cumprimento da meta 11 de Aichi" [Overview of protected areas in Brazil: challenges for achieving the Aichi target 11], in Bensusan and Prates (2014) *A diversidade cabe da unidade? Áreas protegidas no Brasil [Diversity fits the unit? Protected areas in Brazil]*.

Ring, I. et al. (2011), "Assessing Fiscal Transfers for Conservation Policies and Their Role in a Policy Mix", paper presented at the 9th International Conference of the European Society for Ecological Economics, Istanbul, *www.esee2011.org/registration/fullpapers/esee2011_761c79_1_1304087168_4605_2321.pdf.*

Semeia (2014), *Unidades de conservação no Brasil: a contribuição do uso público para o desenvolvimento socioeconômico [Protected areas in Brazil: the contribution of public use for socio-economic development]*, Instituto Semeia, São Paulo.

Semeia (2013), *Semeia Annual Report 2013*, Instituto Semeia, São Paulo.

Semeia (2012a), "Braços adicionais para conservação: o papel estratégico das parcerias com o setor privado" [Additional arms for conservation: the strategic role of partnerships with the private sector], in NEXUCS, *Unidades de Conservação no Brasil – o Caminho da Gestão para Resultados [Protected Areas in Brazil – the Management Path to Results]*, Instituto Semeia, São Paulo.

Semeia (2012b), *Análise 2012: Uso Público e Parcerias para Conservação e Desenvolvimento [Analysis 2012: Public Use and Partnerships for Conservation and Development]*, Instituto Semeia, São Paulo.

Soares-Filho, B. et al. (2014), "Cracking Brazil's Forest Code", *Science*, Vol. 344, No. 6182, pp. 363-364.

TCU (2013), *Relatório de Auditoria Operacional: Governança das Unidades de Conservação do Bioma Amazônia [Operational Audit Report: Governance of the Amazon Biome Protected Areas]*, Federal Court of Accounts, Brasília.

Trzyna, T. (2014), *Urban Protected Areas: Profiles and Best Practice Guidelines*, Best Practice Protected Area Guidelines Series No. 22, International Union for Conservation of Nature, Gland.

Vilela, R.O. (2013), "Quilombos contemporâneos e a proteção da Biodiversidade: o caso da Reserva Biológica da Mata Escura e da Communidade Mumbuca" [Contemporary Quilombos and biodiversity protection: The case of the Mata Escura Biological Reserve and the Mumbuca Community], Vale do Jequitinhonha/MG, 2013, Dissertation, Brasília University, Brasília.

Veríssimo, A. et al. (eds) (2011), *Protected Areas in the Brazilian Amazon: Challenges and Opportunities*, Imazon, Belém; Socioenvironmental Institute, São Paulo, *www.socioambiental.org/banco_imagens/pdfs/10381.pdf.*

WCMC-UNEP and IUCN (2015), "World Database on Protected Areas", World Conservation Monitoring Centre of the United Nations Environment Programme and International Union for Conservation of Nature, *www.protectedplanet.net.*

WWF and ICMBIO (2012), *Avaliação comparada das aplicações do método Rappam nas unidades de conservação federais, nos ciclos 2005-06 e 2010 [Comparative assessment based on the Rappam method in federal conservation units in cycles 2005-06 and 2010]*, World Wide Fund Brazil and Chico Mendes Institute for Biodiversity Conservation, Brasília, *www.icmbio.gov.br/portal/images/stories/comunicacao/downloads/relatrio%20rappam%202005%20x%202010%20-%20verso%20integral.pdf.*

ORGANISATION FOR ECONOMIC CO-OPERATION AND DEVELOPMENT

The OECD is a unique forum where governments work together to address the economic, social and environmental challenges of globalisation. The OECD is also at the forefront of efforts to understand and to help governments respond to new developments and concerns, such as corporate governance, the information economy and the challenges of an ageing population. The Organisation provides a setting where governments can compare policy experiences, seek answers to common problems, identify good practice and work to co-ordinate domestic and international policies.

The OECD member countries are: Australia, Austria, Belgium, Canada, Chile, the Czech Republic, Denmark, Estonia, Finland, France, Germany, Greece, Hungary, Iceland, Ireland, Israel, Italy, Japan, Korea, Luxembourg, Mexico, the Netherlands, New Zealand, Norway, Poland, Portugal, the Slovak Republic, Slovenia, Spain, Sweden, Switzerland, Turkey, the United Kingdom and the United States. The European Union takes part in the work of the OECD.

OECD Publishing disseminates widely the results of the Organisation's statistics gathering and research on economic, social and environmental issues, as well as the conventions, guidelines and standards agreed by its members.

OECD PUBLISHING, 2, rue André-Pascal, 75775 PARIS CEDEX 16
(97 2015 15 1 P) ISBN 978-92-64-24006-3 – 2015

www.ingramcontent.com/pod-product-compliance
Ingram Content Group UK Ltd.
Pitfield, Milton Keynes, MK11 3LW, UK
UKHW051459290926
15471UKWH00008B/1296

9 789264 240063